AI Applications in Industry

RIVER PUBLISHERS SERIES IN COMPUTING AND INFORMATION SCIENCE AND TECHNOLOGY

Series Editors

K.C. CHEN
National Taiwan University, Taipei, Taiwan,
University of South Florida, USA

SANDEEP SHUKLA
Virginia Tech, USA,
Indian Institute of Technology Kanpur, India

The "River Publishers Series in Computing and Information Science and Technology" covers research which ushers the 21st Century into an Internet and multimedia era. Networking suggests transportation of such multimedia contents among nodes in communication and/or computer networks, to facilitate the ultimate Internet.

Theory, technologies, protocols and standards, applications/services, practice and implementation of wired/wireless networking are all within the scope of this series. Based on network and communication science, we further extend the scope for 21st Century life through the knowledge in machine learning, embedded systems, cognitive science, pattern recognition, quantum/biological/molecular computation and information processing, user behaviors and interface, and applications across healthcare and society.

Books published in the series include research monographs, edited volumes, handbooks and textbooks. The books provide professionals, researchers, educators, and advanced students in the field with an invaluable insight into the latest research and developments.

Topics included in the series are as follows:-

- Artificial intelligence
- Cognitive Science and Brian Science
- Communication/Computer Networking Technologies and Applications
- Computation and Information Processing
- Computer Architectures
- Computer networks
- Computer Science
- Embedded Systems
- Evolutionary computation
- Information Modelling
- Information Theory
- Machine Intelligence
- Neural computing and machine learning
- Parallel and Distributed Systems
- Programming Languages
- Reconfigurable Computing
- Research Informatics
- Soft computing techniques
- Software Development
- Software Engineering
- Software Maintenance

For a list of other books in this series, visit www.riverpublishers.com

AI Applications in Industry

Editor

Wai Yie Leong
Malaysia

River Publishers

Routledge
Taylor & Francis Group
NEW YORK AND LONDON

Published 2026 by River Publishers
River Publishers
Broagervej 10, 9260 Gistrup, Denmark
www.riverpublishers.com

Distributed exclusively by Routledge
605 Third Avenue, New York, NY 10017, USA
4 Park Square, Milton Park, Abingdon, Oxon OX14 4RN

AI Applications in Industry / Wai Yie Leong.

Routledge is an imprint of the Taylor & Francis Group, an informa business

ISBN 978-87-438-1211-1 (Hardback)
ISBN 978-87-438-1217-3 (Paperback)
ISBN 978-87-438-1214-2 (E-book)
ISBN 978-87-438-1216-6 (E-pub)
ISBN 978-8-743-81213-5 (E-book master)

DOI: 10.1201/9788743812135

Contents

Preface

Artificial intelligence (AI) has emerged as the central technological force shaping the industrial landscape of the twenty-first century. Its influence extends far beyond the automation of repetitive processes or the digitization of workflows; it represents a paradigm shift in how industries perceive, decide, and act. By embedding intelligence into machines, infrastructures, and supply chains, AI has transformed industry into a dynamic, adaptive, and resilient ecosystem capable of responding to uncertainty and volatility at unprecedented speed. The significance of AI lies not simply in its capacity to enhance efficiency, but in its potential to redefine industrial objectives – shifting the emphasis from productivity alone to resilience, sustainability, and human–machine collaboration. This book, *AI Applications in Industry*, is written to capture this multifaceted transformation. It aims to provide not only the technical foundations and applied methodologies but also the contextual insights necessary for scholars, practitioners, and policymakers to navigate this transition.

The preface begins with a historical reflection, situating AI within the broader lineage of industrial revolutions. The First Industrial Revolution, powered by mechanization and steam, reorganized societies around the factory system, displacing artisanal craft with mass production. The Second Industrial Revolution, enabled by electrification, introduced assembly lines, standardization, and global trade at a scale previously unimaginable. The Third Industrial Revolution, often labeled the digital revolution, brought computing, telecommunications, and automation, laying the groundwork for globalized value chains. Today, we stand in the Fourth Industrial Revolution, or Industry 4.0, characterized by cyber-physical systems, pervasive connectivity, and intelligent automation. What distinguishes this revolution from its predecessors is the central role of AI. Unlike steam engines or computers, which amplify human muscle or arithmetic, AI integrates perception, cognition, and adaptation into industrial systems. This marks a qualitative leap: factories that self-optimize, logistics systems that reroute dynamically, grids that stabilize autonomously, and supply chains that forecast disruptions before they materialize. The trajectory suggests an impending Industry 5.0, where the focus will expand from efficiency to human-centric innovation, sustainability, and symbiosis between human creativity and machine intelligence.

At the heart of this transformation lie the technical foundations of AI. Machine learning provides the mathematical machinery for pattern recognition, anomaly detection, and predictive analytics. Regression models, support vector machines, and decision trees underpin predictive maintenance, demand forecasting, and defect detection. Deep learning, with its convolutional neural networks and transformer architectures, extends these capabilities to high-dimensional data such as images, video, and time series, enabling automated quality assurance, natural language understanding, and process forecasting. Reinforcement learning introduces adaptability, allowing robotic systems, logistics platforms, and energy controllers to learn through interaction, refining strategies through reward-driven optimization. Natural language processing unlocks insights from unstructured textual data – compliance documents, safety logs, operator manuals – bringing intelligence to the administrative layers of industry. Generative models, including GANs and diffusion systems, simulate industrial scenarios, accelerate design through generative design frameworks, and generate synthetic datasets for training. The convergence of these techniques allows industries to construct hybrid architectures tailored to their unique challenges, integrating perception, reasoning, and decision-making into coherent pipelines.

Yet, AI in industry cannot be reduced to algorithms alone. Its power derives from integration with broader infrastructures: cloud and edge computing, industrial IoT, high-speed connectivity, and digital twins. Cloud platforms enable scalable training of large models, while edge computing ensures ultra-low latency decision-making for safety-critical applications such as autonomous vehicles or robotic control. Federated learning addresses data privacy and security, distributing intelligence without centralizing sensitive industrial data. Digital twins serve as living mirrors of physical assets, continuously updated with sensor data, enabling industries to simulate performance, optimize operations, and predict failures. This systemic integration exemplifies the architecture of industrial AI, where technical ingenuity is inseparable from infrastructural innovation.

The industrial applications of AI illustrate the breadth of its transformative scope. In manufacturing, AI drives predictive maintenance, quality inspection, and generative design, redefining efficiency and creativity simultaneously. In logistics, AI optimizes supply chain resilience, routing fleets dynamically, managing inventory autonomously, and processing documentation with natural language systems. In the energy sector, AI balances the volatility of renewable integration, forecasts demand, stabilizes grids, and identifies efficiency opportunities critical to decarbonization. In construction,

AI enhances safety monitoring through computer vision, optimizes project schedules through predictive analytics, and reimagines design through generative frameworks. In healthcare-related industries, AI accelerates drug discovery, enhances medical device quality control, and enables digital twins of patients for personalized treatment planning. Agriculture, often regarded as peripheral to industrial discussions, becomes a vital domain for AI through precision agriculture, yield forecasting, and sustainable resource management. These examples reveal that AI is not confined to any single sector; it is a cross-cutting enabler that transforms industrial logic across domains.

However, alongside opportunities come systemic challenges. Data quality and governance remain among the most pressing concerns. Industrial data is often noisy, incomplete, and heterogeneous, collected from legacy systems, IoT sensors, and unstructured reports. Establishing reliable data pipelines, ensuring interoperability, and mitigating bias are critical prerequisites for successful AI deployment. Model robustness and scalability represent another challenge. AI models trained in controlled environments must perform reliably under noisy, variable, and adversarial conditions. Safety-critical industries such as aviation, energy, and healthcare demand explainable AI (XAI), where transparency and interpretability are as important as accuracy. Cybersecurity looms large as industries integrate AI into cyber-physical systems, making them vulnerable to adversarial attacks, data breaches, and systemic failures. Human–AI collaboration presents both a technical and cultural frontier, requiring the design of interfaces that foster trust, transparency, and complementarity between human expertise and machine intelligence. Addressing these challenges demands innovation in algorithms, governance frameworks, and organizational culture.

The global context amplifies the significance of these challenges. Industrial revolutions have always reconfigured global power structures, and the AI-driven revolution is no exception. Nations that integrate AI effectively into critical industries – semiconductors, renewable energy, advanced manufacturing – will secure leadership in global value chains. Governments worldwide are investing in AI research, industrial policies, and workforce upskilling to ensure competitiveness in this intelligence-driven economy. At the same time, international collaboration is necessary to establish ethical guidelines, data-sharing protocols, and sustainability frameworks that prevent AI from exacerbating inequality or environmental degradation. The interplay between national competitiveness and global responsibility defines the geopolitical dimension of industrial AI.

Looking forward, the trajectory of AI in industry suggests both continuity and transformation. Industry 5.0, emerging on the horizon, envisions a shift from automation-centric paradigms to human-centric innovation. The focus will be on symbiotic collaboration, where AI augments human creativity, supports personalized production, and accelerates the transition to sustainable practices. Factories of the future will not be defined solely by robotic efficiency but by adaptive ecosystems that integrate workers, machines, and digital systems in real time. Energy infrastructures will not only balance renewables dynamically but also empower communities through decentralized microgrids and peer-to-peer energy trading. Logistics will evolve beyond efficiency toward resilience, ensuring that global supply chains remain robust in the face of pandemics, climate disruptions, or geopolitical fragmentation. Healthcare will extend beyond diagnostics and treatment toward predictive, preventive, and personalized systems of care, leveraging AI-driven insights at every stage. Agriculture will integrate sustainability at its core, using AI to balance productivity with ecological stewardship. In each of these trajectories, AI is not an isolated driver but a systemic catalyst that shapes the future of industry in alignment with human values.

This book positions itself as both a technical reference and a strategic roadmap. It seeks to equip researchers, engineers, and practitioners with algorithmic insights, architectural frameworks, and applied case studies, while also offering policymakers and leaders the strategic foresight necessary to guide adoption responsibly. Each chapter blends technical rigor with real-world application, providing mathematical formulations, system-level diagrams, empirical results, and techno-economic analyses. By weaving together theory and practice, the book aims to bridge the gap between academic research and industrial deployment, ensuring that AI's transformative potential is understood not only in abstract terms but in its material impact on industries and societies.

Ultimately, the story of AI in industry is one of convergence: the convergence of algorithms and infrastructures, of human creativity and machine intelligence, of efficiency and sustainability, of national competitiveness and global responsibility. It is a story still being written, one in which the decisions of today will define the trajectory of industries for decades to come. This preface invites readers to engage with that story critically and constructively. It challenges them to see AI not merely as a tool for productivity but as a paradigm for reimagining industry itself – an opportunity to build systems that are not only intelligent but also sustainable, inclusive, and profoundly human-centric.

Wai Yie Leong
Malaysia

List of Contributors

Abdul Rahman, Norana, *Honorary Senior Lecturer, RCSI & UCD Malaysia Campus, Georgetown, Penang, Malaysia*

Bagurubumwe, Uhoze, *Raise Agency, Mauritius*

Budireddi, Udaya Rasi, *SRM College of Physiotherapy, SRM Institute of Science and Technology, Kattankulathur, India*

Chadeea, Tomal, *Open University of Mauritius, Mauritius*

Dongea, Varalakshmi, *SRM College of Physiotherapy, SRM Institute of Science and Technology, Kattankulathur, India*

Guangnan, Huang, *INTI International University, Malaysia*

Kadirvelu, Chandrakumar, *SRM College of Physiotherapy, SRM Institute of Science and Technology, Kattankulathur, India*

Kang, Chia Chao, *School of Artificial Intelligence and Robotics, Jalan Sunsuria, Bandar Sunsuria, 43900 Sepang, Selangor Darul Ehsan, Malaysia*

Kuthiala, Neha, *University of Alberta, Edmonton, Canada*

Laloo, Nassirah, *University of Technology, Mauritius*

Leong, Wai Yie, *INTI International University, 71800 Nilai, Negeri Sembilan, Malaysia*

Mishra, Priyadarshini, *Abhinav Bindra Sports Medicine and Research Institute, Odisha, India*

Palaniswamy, Mohankumar, *Faculty of Sports and Exercise Science, Universiti Malaya, 50603 Wilayah Persekutuan Kuala Lumpur, Malaysia*

Patwe, Prajakta Prashant, *Sports Science Faculty, ISST, Pune, India*

Perumal, Mugunthan, *Faculty of Resource Science and Technology, Universiti Malaysia Sarawak (UNIMAS), 94300 Kota Samarahan, Sarawak, Malaysia*

Rajaratnam, Vaikunthan, *Khoo Teck Puat Hospital, Singapore*

Ranganathan, Harikrishnan, *School of Physiotherapy, Sri Balaji Vidyapeeth, Pondicherry, India*

Ritlall, Gomedhanand, *Open University of Mauritius, Mauritius*

Romainor, Ain Nadirah Binti, *Faculty of Resource Science and Technology, Universiti Malaysia Sarawak (UNIMAS), 94300 Kota Samarahan, Sarawak, Malaysia*

Sunhaloo, Mohammad Sameer, *University of Technology, Mauritius*

Vincent, Agnes Nalini, *Amity Institute of Higher Education, Mauritius*

Yeo, Wendy Wai Yeng, *School of Pharmacy, Monash University Malaysia, Jalan Lagoon Selatan, 47500 Bandar Sunway, Selangor Darul Ehsan, Malaysia*

Zainuddin, Faizan Iza Binti, *Faculty of Economics and Business, Universiti Malaysia Sarawak (UNIMAS), 94300 Kota Samarahan, Sarawak, Malaysia*

Zheng, Wen, *INTI International University, 71800 Nilai, Negeri Sembilan, Malaysia*

List of Figures

List of Tables

List of Abbreviations

ACS	Acute coronary syndrome
ADE	Adverse drug event
AES	All employee survey
AGVs	Automated-guided vehicles
AHRQ	Agency for healthcare research and quality
AI	Artificial intelligence
AR	Augmented reality
AUVs	Autonomous underwater vehicles
CAGR	Compound annual growth rate
CCER	Certified resource emission reduction
CDSS	Clinical decision support systems
CGMs	Continuous glucose monitors
CNNs	Convolutional neural networks
COD	Chemical oxygen demand
CPD	Continuing professional development
CPOE	Computerized provider order entry
CRLM	Colorectal cancer liver metastases
CT	Computed tomography
CTD	Conductivity-temperature-depth
CWT	Continuous wavelet transform
DeepRNN	Deep recurrent neural network
DEM	Digital elevation model
DH	Digital health
DL	Deep learning
DSS	Decision support systems
EBCD	Experience-based codesign
EBM	Evidence-based medicine
ECG	Electrocardiography
EDA	Exploratory data analysis
EEG	Electroencephalography
EHR	Electronic health record
EMC	Electromagnetic compatibility (EMC)

EMF	Electromagnetic radiation
EMI	Electromagnetic interference (EMI)
EMS	Electromagnetic susceptibility
EU-ETS	EU Emission trading system
FERPA	Family educational rights and privacy act
FHE	Flexible hybrid electronics
GANs	Generative adversarial networks
GDPR	General data protection regulation
GIS	Geographic information system
HAI	Healthcare-associated infection
HC	Hard corals
HCPs	Healthcare professionals
HIPAA	Health insurance portability and accountability act
HIT	Health information technology
HPM	High-power microwaves
HROs	High-reliability organizations
HSPSC	Hospital survey on patient safety culture
HTA	Health technology assessment
ICAP	International carbon action partnership
ICTs	Information and communication technologies
ICVs	Intelligent connected vehicles
ILRs	Implanted loop recorders
IoT	Internet of things
ITS	Intelligent tutoring systems
JS	Jensen–shannon
LLM	Large language model
MAE	Mean absolute error
MAPE	Absolute percentage error
MES	Manufacturing execution systems
ML	Machine learning
MRI	Magnetic resonance imaging
MRV	Monitoring, reporting, and verification
MSDs	Musculoskeletal disorders
MSE	Mean squared error
MVAs	Medical virtual assistants
NLP	Natural language processing
PAM	Pneumatic artificial muscles
POCD	Point-of-care diagnostics
PS	Patient safety
PSC	Patient safety culture

R/S	Religiousness/Spirituality
RAG	Retrieval-augmented generation
RCTs	Randomized controlled trials
ReLU	Rectified linear unit
RMSE	Root mean square error
RPA	Robotic process automation
RPM	Remote patient monitoring
SAQ	Safety attitudes questionnaire
SCS	Spinal cord stimulation
SEA	Similarity ensemble approach
SEEG	Stereo electroencephalography
SMOTE	Synthetic minority oversampling technique
SSTs	Sea surface temperatures
SVG	Scalable vector graphics
SVM	Support vector machine
UI	User interface
UVCs	Underwater visual censuses
VAE	Variational autoencoder
VR	Virtual reality
VS	Virtual screening
WHO	World health organization

1

Safe Data Augmentation using Generative AI to Ensure Sustainable Prediction Accuracy of Marine Data

Agnes Nalini Vincent[1], Nassirah Laloo[2], Uhoze Bagurubumwe[3] and Mohammad Sameer Sunhaloo[4]

[1]Amity Institute of Higher Education, Mauritius
[2,4]University of Technology Mauritius, Mauritius
[3]Raise Agency, Mauritius

Email: vanalini@mauritius.amity.edu; n.laloo@utm.ac.mu; nelsonbumwe@gmail.com; ssunhaloo@utm.ac.mu

Abstract

The study of benthic ecosystem dynamics, monitoring and prediction of the same are often impeded by sparsity and irregular in-situ observations in the observational data. Sparsity can limit the effectiveness of conventional predictive models. This study addresses this constraint by investigating the ability of two deep generative models such as a Variational Autoencoder (VAE) and Generative Adversarial Network (GAN) to generate synthetic marine physio-chemical and benthic data thereby enhancing marine ecosystem predictions using deep recurrent neural network (DeepRNN). The research design conforms to a sequential, three-phase experimental framework. The initial phase evaluated the performance of a baseline DeepRNN model using the original, limited observational dataset which served as a benchmark for performance evaluation. The second phase integrated synthetic data generated by a VAE to the original training set to determine if it enhanced DeepRNN's prediction ability. The third and last phase repeated this process of adding to the training set, the synthetic samples generated by a GAN to train the DeepRNN. Prediction model performance across these phases was assessed

 DOI: 10.1201/9788743812135-1

using test losses, validation loss curves and metrics, including Mean Absolute Error (MAE) and Root Mean Square Error (RMSE). Baseline model yielded a test loss of 4.8249 and high error metrics (MAE: 1.71062, RMSE: 2.196563), reflecting poor generalization from sparse marine data. In the second phase, VAE-generated synthetic data markedly improved performance of DeepRNN, by reducing test loss to 0.7239 and decreasing MAE to 0.610264 and RMSE to 0.850834. The third phase, which employed GAN-based augmentation, achieved superior prediction outcomes with a test loss of 0.082 and distinctly reduced error metrics (MAE: 0.005254, RMSE: 0.006797, MAPE: 0.000261). Apart from these metrics, the GAN-augmented model also demonstrated faster convergence in the training and validation loss curves, stabilizing at approximately 40 epochs compared to 60 epochs for the baseline, while exhibiting stable validation curves indicative of excellent model fit without overfitting. These findings confirm that the GAN is better than the VAE in capturing the intricate, nonlinear ecological relationships seen in benthic systems. To prevent sampling biases, the study highlights that the synthetic outputs need to be rigorously validated externally against independent field data. By enhancing predictive capability from sparse marine data, this work provides a methodological pathway to better inform management strategies towards safeguarding marine ecosystems, directly contributing to the objectives of UN Sustainable Development Goal 14 (Life Below Water).

1.1 Introduction

The degradation of marine ecosystems poses an urgent threat to global biodiversity and human livelihoods, necessitating immediate and innovative sustainability measures. To safeguard marine biodiversity and resources, prioritizing data-driven forecasting of ecosystem shifts is now a necessity for long-term oceanic resilience. The cumulative impacts of urbanization, pollution, overexploitation, and climate change are intensifying the degradation of coastal and marine habitats worldwide. For example, ocean acidification, driven by rising CO_2 levels and sea surface temperature, erodes coral skeletons and impairs shellfish development [1]. As indicated by Hughes *et al.* [2], rising sea surface temperatures (SSTs) are causing coral bleaching episodes to occur more frequently and with greater intensity. Moreover, a study by McFarland [3] indicated that marine pollution is also a predominant factor that contributes to coral degradation and loss.

With the presentation of such a scenario, without effective conservation policies, coral reef systems, which support 25% of marine species, could collapse by 2050 [4]. For the formulation of conservation policies, there exists a need for data-driven exploratory data analysis (EDA) and reliable forecasting results. Robust exploratory data analysis and accurate predictive modeling fundamentally depend on both the integrity and completeness of the underlying datasets.

1.1.1 Contribution of the study to safe and smart manufacturing environments

A variety of sophisticated industrial sensing and robotic platforms are necessary for collecting high-fidelity marine data, including benthic information and water quality measurements. Few examples for smart industrial grade equipment for marine data collection are in-situ water quality sensors, multi-parameter (pH/turbidity/chemical oxygen demand etc.) water quality sondes/probes, buoys collecting timeseries marine data, autonomous underwater vehicles (AUVs) providing marine data spatial maps by following pre-programed routes, remote operated vehicles facilitated with high definition cameras to capture video transects of benthic communities and satellite remote sensing. Prohibitive operational costs, trade-offs between temporal and spatial resolution of collecting data, and profound logistical and environmental constraints, lead to limitations of this resource-intensive equipment to collect and build comprehensive marine datasets. Hence, the marine data collected may be sparse in nature. This study presents a generative data-augmentation deep learning framework specifically designed to address the critical data scarcity challenges inherent in smart manufacturing systems/smart data collecting systems. The study is validated on a multivariate marine dataset. The approach is specifically made for any temporally constrained, high-dimensional data system with limited data samples. This makes this study immediately applicable to smart manufacturing systems, where acquiring sufficient fault or anomaly data is often expensive and time-consuming. The proven ability of our model to generate high-fidelity synthetic sequences for marine variables translates directly to generating synthetic data for industrial sensor readings, data collected using enabling robust training of predictive maintenance and quality control models without the need for extensive historical failure data.

1.1.2 Sparsity of marine dataset and their consequences

Marine ecosystem monitoring faces significant data limitations, particularly in quantifying fish community structures, coral distribution, and associated physicochemical variables. The spatial resolution and temporal continuity of marine datasets collected via in-situ methods (e.g., underwater visual censuses (UVCs) and conductivity-temperature-depth (CTD) rosettes) are often compromised by (1) vessel and personnel costs scaling with offshore distance [5], (2) diver safety constraints in remote reef environments [6], and (3) funding-dependent sampling frequencies [7]. Marine datasets are often also sparse due to the logistical constraints of oceanic data collection, particularly in remote or deep-sea environments.

As per the study [8], sparsity of data causes disparity in sample sizes between classes, and this is referred to as "imbalance" in the dataset. This sparsity undermines ecological modeling efforts, necessitating advanced data augmentation approaches. Moreover, this scarcity of data also limits the effectiveness of machine learning models trained on such data and the prediction performance of machine learning systems [9, 10]. Hence, methods need to be devised to overcome the sparsity of data. Further, the financial constraints of the prohibitive costs of deep-sea expeditions result in patchy spatial coverage, necessitating augmentation to mitigate sampling biases.

1.1.3 Overview of methods to address dataset imbalance in marine science

One of the algorithmic approaches to address the imbalance in the dataset is through performing resampling techniques. Resampling includes under sampling majority classes and oversampling minority classes. The conceptual distinction between these two methods is that "under sampling" selectively reduces overrepresented class instances to balance class distribution, while "oversampling" increases minority class representation through replication or synthetic generation [11]. Removal of overrepresented data may lead to potential loss of ecological patterns in dominant classes, and oversampling minority classes may have a limitation of duplication or interpolation of rare events (e.g., replicating observations). Another method for managing the sparsity of data is through implementing synthetic minority oversampling technique (SMOTE). As per the study [12], SMOTE-generated rainfall data improved prediction using a random forest classifier with an accuracy of 0.91. It is noteworthy to discuss that when interpolating spatially varying, nonstationary data, spatiotemporal interpolation techniques like the Kriging method, which uses a sparse representation of the covariance function, are directly applicable to spatially nonstationary data and offer the benefits of increased accuracy and decreased interpolation uncertainty [13]. Further, the method that is used for addressing data sparsity is to use marine-specific data augmentation, which is achieved by generative adversarial networks (GANs) trained with oceanographic constraints. While conventional statistical interpolation methods often fail to capture complex marine ecosystem dynamics, machine learning techniques such as generative adversarial networks (GANs) offer promising alternatives. Moreover, predictions of time series data are essential in many domains, specifically in weather and temperature forecasts. Predictive modelling of such time series data poses unique challenges that are due to the seasonality, temporal inter-dependence, and trends present in the data. Robust models that can capture these intricate patterns and dependencies are necessary for accurate predictions, anomaly detection, and time series data classification. Making predictions in marine and climatic data that are trustworthy and accurate is crucial for making well-informed decisions. Goubeaud *et al.* [14] stated that time series data, being sparse by nature, can be augmented by using a variational autoencoder (VAE). Many studies have explored this VAE for time series data augmentation [15–17].

1.1.4 Data augmentation imperative

Unlike computer vision, where large, labeled datasets (e.g., ImageNet) are available, marine science often relies on sparse, unevenly distributed observations. Marine ecological datasets, particularly those quantifying fish assemblages, hard coral cover, and physicochemical parameters (e.g., sea surface temperature, dissolved oxygen, pH, and salinity) – are often spatially and temporally sparse due to the logistical challenges of underwater surveys and the inflated cost of sensor deployment. This scarcity impedes the training of robust predictive models for coral reef resilience, species distribution, or water quality forecasting.

To manage data sparsity in marine ecological studies, the initial step is to diagnose the imbalance in the dataset by quantifying the class ratio and understanding the bias. Based on this diagnosis, if the scenario is small dataset samples, a SMOTE followed by expert validation may be suggested. In case of large spatial gaps, informed GANs may be used, and if the bias is due to taxonomic bias, then taxonomic transfer learning may be advised. Every method used to manage the bias and imbalance in the dataset needs to be validated and evaluated for ecological plausibility.

Data augmentation through techniques like synthetic sample generation using GAN, spatial-temporal interpolation, or transfer learning from related domains can artificially expand training datasets, improving model robustness and generalizability. For instance, the issue of insufficient training data for automated visual species identification may be resolved with the use of data augmentation techniques [18]. Without these data augmentation methods, predictive accuracy using sparse data remains compromised, hindering applications like climate modeling, biodiversity modeling, or endangered species tracking.

1.1.5 GANs and VAEs as a solution

GANs-based data augmentation is being used for reef modeling [19] and in the prediction of the distribution of fish associated with reefs [20]. By using the noise vector from the uniform/normal distribution, the GAN generator creates a synthetic sample whose dimension equals that of the data. The discriminator then distinguishes the difference between generated data and real data. GANs offer a promising solution by synthesizing realistic marine data from limited observations. By training a GAN on sparse but representative samples, the generator can produce augmented datasets that preserve statistical properties of the original data, thereby reducing overfitting in downstream tasks. While generative adversarial networks (GANs) can synthesize realistic data by learning latent distributions from limited observations, they are not the sole solution. Alternative approaches include the use of VAEs, transfer learning from data-rich regions, physics-based simulation, and hybrid methods combining interpolation with expert knowledge.

One of the variants of GAN proposed by the study [21], is Wasserstein GAN (WGAN), which has proved to achieve stability over regular GANs. The basic distinction between GAN and WGAN lies in the metric used to measure the difference between the generated and real data distributions. While the standard GAN minimizes the Jensen–Shannon (JS) divergence, which can saturate and lead to vanishing gradients when distributions are disjoint and do not have significant overlap, the WGAN minimizes the Wasserstein distance. This Wasserstein distance metric provides a more continuous and meaningful gradient signal, resulting in enhanced training stability, a reduced tendency for mode collapse, and a loss value that correlates with sample quality. Control GAN (CGAN) is another variant of GAN that uses conditional information to control the data generation process. For marine data augmentation, the conditional information may be water quality parameters, sea surface temperature, water pH, salinity, etc. Further, it is noteworthy to discuss another GAN for climatic data known as CLIMGAN, which is a specialized, advanced GAN-based model created for a highly accurate climate science mission.

A deep generative model known as VAE learns latent representations of input time series data. The learned latent space is then sampled to produce fresh time series samples [22]. VAE consists of an encoder network which maps the time series data to a latent space where each point represents a possible data point, further proceeded by a decoder network that creates time series samples from points in the latent space [23]. The key innovation of the VAE, when compared to GAN, is that it doesn't produces a single latent vector for an input. Instead, it learns a latent space probability distribution to produce synthetic data. VAE is trained to maximize (i) the Evidence Lower BOund (ELBO), comprising a reconstruction term that ensures output fidelity and (ii) the KL divergence, which acts as a regularizer that encourages the learned latent distribution to conform to a prior, typically a standard normal distribution. This results in a continuous, structured data augmentation, and meaningful interpolation between data points. As per the study by Garsdal *et al.* [24], two terms make up the loss function for VAEs: a regularization term and a reconstruction loss, which gauges how closely the reconstructed data resembles the original data.

1.1.6 Alternative solutions for data augmentation

- *Transfer Learning:* This technique makes use of successfully applied pretrained models from data-rich areas for the identification of species in data-sparse areas. Example: Pretrained convolutional neural networks (CNNs) on coral datasets can be fine-tuned for localized predictions, reducing the need for extensive new surveys.
- *Physics-Informed Models:* Integrating biogeochemical principles with neural networks is another alternative method. This alternative is particularly effective for parameterizing water quality variables. Examples for these models are dissolved oxygen prediction using biogeochemical simulators to supplement sparse water chemistry measurements with physically plausible values, though they require domain expertise to calibrate.
- *Citizen Science Integration:* Crowdsourced data from diver surveys (e.g., Reef Life Survey) can fill spatial gaps when combined with quality-control algorithms.
- *Active Learning:* Adaptive sampling strategies – where models identify high-uncertainty areas for targeted data collection – optimize limited fieldwork resources, thereby reducing required sampling effort.
- *Hybrid Sensor Networks:* Fusion of in-situ measurements with remote sensing data improves spatial coverage for physicochemical parameters.

1.2 Methodology

1.2.1 Overview of methodology

This study investigates the effectiveness of data augmentation methods, namely GAN and VAE, in generating high-quality synthetic marine data, thereby facilitating improved training of a deep learning predictive algorithm called DeepRNN to achieve better predictions. The methodology is structured in three sequential phases (as shown in Figure 1.1): (i) phase 1: training and evaluation of the basic DeepRNN model with considered input data, (ii) phase 2: training and evaluation of DeepRNN with VAE-generated synthetic data as input, (iii) phase 3: training and evaluation of DeepRNN with GAN-generated synthetic data as input. These phases determine the efficacy of the impact of each augmentation technique over predictions using Deep RNN model.

1.2.2 Dataset introduction

A collection of current physicochemical oceanographic parameters constitutes the input features for this study. These include sea surface temperature, pH, practical salinity, chemical oxygen demand, nitrate-to-nitrogen, and phosphate concentration. These variables represent the water quality parameters at a given spatiotemporal point. Target Variables are the abundance or presence of key marine biological taxa. The original dataset used for the purpose was benthic data and water quality parameters of lagoon 2 of the Flic en Flac region, of the Republic of Mauritius. Water quality parameters/independent variables used in this research are sea surface temperature (SST), practical ocean salinity, pH, chemical oxygen demand (COD), nitrate-nitrogen, and phosphate (POS). The purpose of the study was to forecast how the independent variables mentioned above would affect the target benthic variables/marine biological taxa, like hard corals (HC) and fish assemblages including Pomacentridae (Damselfishes), Chaetodontidae (Butterflyfishes), Labridae (Wrasses), Scaridae (Parrotfishes), and Acanthuridae (Surgeonfishes).

The methodology of this study establishes a supervised learning task to model the nonlinear relationship between environmental drivers and marine biological responses.

1.2.3 GAN mechanics

The working of GAN is based on mapping a low-dimensional latent vector sampled from a previous noise distribution to a high-dimensional synthetic

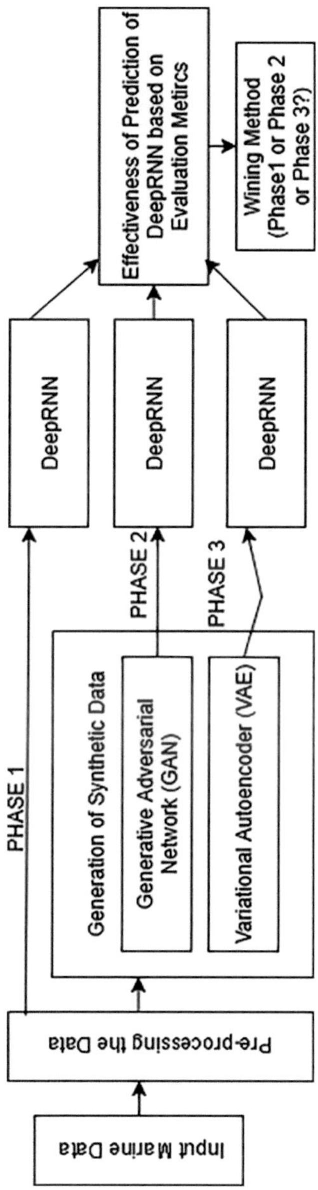

Figure 1.1 Process flow of proposed study.

sample designed to replicate the actual data space by a generator network. The generator network comprises four linear layers with 128, 256, 512 units, respectively, interleaved with rectified linear unit (ReLU) activation functions. For all positive inputs, the gradient of ReLU is exactly 1 (nonsaturating gradient), and hence ReLU is used in the generator to mitigate the vanishing gradient problem. Further, the final layer employs a hyperbolic tangent (Tanh) activation function. This function confines the output values to a range of [−1, 1]. Tanh is used since the input data is min-max scaled. Like the generator but in reverse, the discriminator is a multilayer perception. LeakyReLU activation (with a negative slope of 0.2) functions are used in discriminator layers to address the vanishing gradient problem that may occur during the discrimination process. The output of the last layer of the discriminator is compressed into a valid probability score between 0 and 1 using a sigmoid activation function. Two competing loss functions are optimized during the training process.

1.2.4 VAE mechanics

The working of VAE to generate synthetic data depends on an encoder–decoder approach. The encoder (E) considers a high-dimensional input data point (x) and compresses it into two vectors called "μ," the mean, and "log-var" – the log-variance. These vectors now belong to a lower-dimensional latent space. Further, a random variable "eps" is being sampled from a standard normal distribution. Then the latent vector. "z" is calculated using the formula below:

$$z = \mu + (\exp(0.5 \times \text{logvar})) \times \text{eps}. \tag{1.1}$$

The decoder then attempts to reconstruct the original input data using the sampled latent vector z. Since the input has been min-max scaled, the final Sigmoid () activation guarantees that the output values fall inside a range [0,1] appropriate for the input data. The effectiveness of VAE is evaluated using the loss functions: (i) reconstruction loss (mean squared error (MSE)) and (ii) KL divergence loss (KLD). The reconstruction loss evaluates how well the decoded output matches the original input, whereas KLD functions as a regularizing factor. By using the input compressed vectors and logvar, it forces the learnt latent distribution to resemble a typical normal distribution. The total loss is the sum of reconstruction loss and KLD. The goal of the VAE's training is to reduce this total loss.

1.2.5 DeepRNN mechanics

As far as the working of DeepRNN is concerned, simple RNN layers are stacked to each other to create the DeepRNN prediction model. The network can learn input features at several levels of temporal abstraction because of its hierarchical structure. When input data is applied to the first layer, it can save short-term, local relationships, while the second layer and further other layers can connect these to identify longer-term dependencies. The activation functions used in the RNN layers were ReLU. By offering a constant gradient for positive inputs, this function reduces the vanishing gradient issue, if any. The last layer has a linear activation function and is dense and fully linked. The number of target variables is exactly equal to the number of units in this layer. Since it enables the model to predict continuous, unbounded values for every biological indicator, a linear activation is the conventional and suitable option for a regression task.

1.3 Findings and Discussions

1.3.1 Class distribution analysis of benthic

One of the main characteristics of unbalanced data collection is class imbalances that may arise due to sparse data. The class distribution of benthic variables of the region under consideration were visualized as value counts chart (Figure 1.2). Class frequency discrepancies (Figure 1.2) were discovered in this chart, which indicated that there exists an imbalance in the dataset. Upon identifying the imbalance in the dataset, this work used GAN and VAE for data augmentation to overcome the imbalance in the data.

1.3.2 The benchmark comparison of phase 1, phase 2, and phase 3 of the DeepRNN implementation

The three methodologies including (i) phase 1: training and evaluation of the basic DeepRNN model with considered input data, (ii) phase 2: training and evaluation of DeepRNN with VAE-generated synthetic data as input, (iii) phase 3: training and evaluation of DeepRNN with GAN-generated synthetic data as input, were executed in Python software, and the comparison of the methodologies are being conducted in this section. The phase 1 architecture is considered the baseline architecture. The aim of the comparison is to investigate which type of architecture significantly arrived at improved predictions by DeepRNN. The comparison was conducted based on the

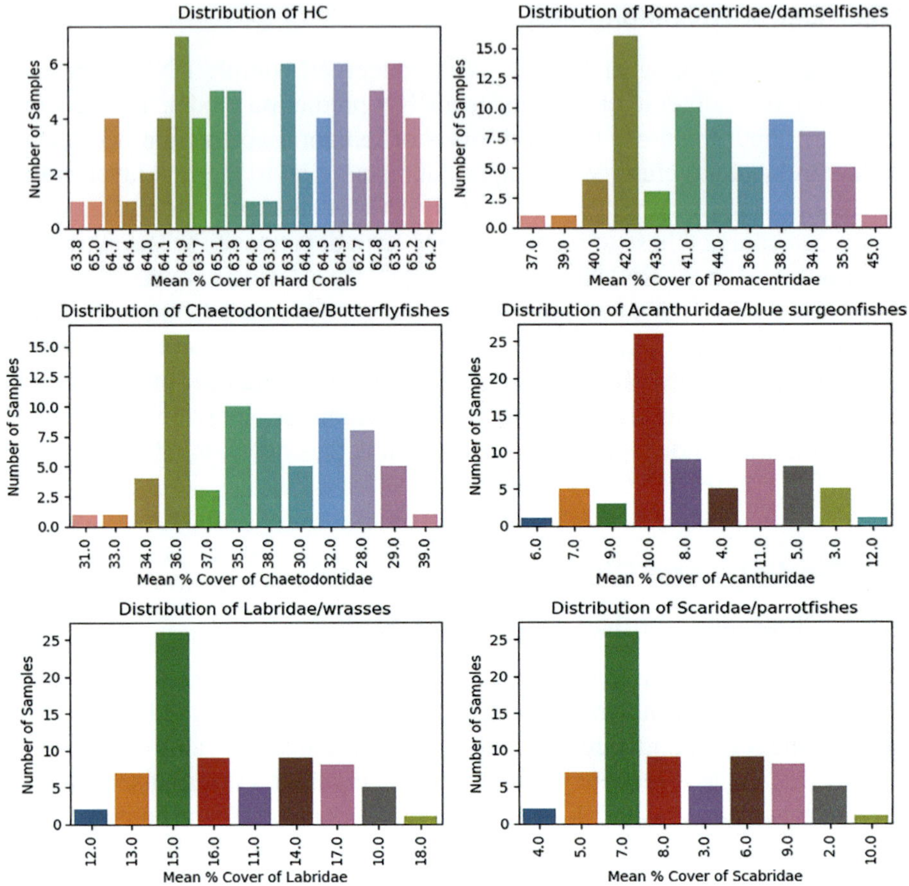

Figure 1.2 Value counts chart of benthic.

following: (i) comparing the learning curves of the three architectures, (ii) comparing based on the test loss values, and (iii) based on evaluation metrics namely mean absolute error values (MAE), mean squared error values (MSE), root mean square error values (RMSE), and mean absolute percentage error values (MAPE).

1.3.3 Test loss comparison

The phase 1 baseline model, which was trained only on original input data, yielded a test loss of 4.8249. This performance was significantly surpassed by models leveraging synthetic/augmented data, with the phase

2-VAE-augmented model achieving a test loss of 0.7239 and phase 3 GAN-augmented model achieving a superior test loss of 0.082. Thus, the experimental results demonstrate a substantial improvement in the predictive performance of the deep recurrent neural network (DeepRNN) model when trained on GAN-augmented data as the best model, while DeepRNN, when trained using VAE-augmented data (phase 2), performed better than phase 1 but inferior to phase 3. The phase 1 baseline model's comparatively large test loss (4.909) indicated a limited ability of basic DeepRNN to generalize from the initial training dataset. This may be due to the model's tendency to overfit on the few available samples due to data sparsity or its inability to learn the complex, nonlinear mappings between the physicochemical inputs and benthic target objectives. This finding provides a compelling argument for the adoption of data augmentation approaches and highlights the inherent difficulty of training deep learning models on limited marine datasets.

1.3.4 Learning curves comparison

The learning curves, namely training loss and validation loss curves, identify the performance of the model on training data and on validation data, which is usually the new unseen data, thus giving an indication on generalizability of the model [25]. As indicated in Figure 1.3, both the loss curves decrease, with a minimal gap between them, and they stabilize, eventually giving an inference of "good fit." When compared to the baseline phase 1 model, which stabilizes at around 60 epochs, the phase 2 and 3 models stabilize around 40 and 45 epochs with low validation and training loss values, respectively.

1.3.5 Metric comparison

To accurately capture every aspect of prediction error, evaluating predictive models must utilize a multifaceted approach. Comprehensive information cannot be obtained from a single metric. Therefore, we used a suite of four complementing metrics: mean absolute error (MAE), mean squared error (MSE), root mean squared error (RMSE), and mean absolute percentage error (MAPE) to ensure a complete and accurate assessment of the phase 1, 2, and 3 models. Figure 1.4 shows the comparison of values of these evaluation metrics. From Figure 1.4, it is indicative that the basic phase 1 DeepRNN model has higher error metrics such as MAE:1.71062, MSE:4.8249, RMSE:2.196563, and MAPE:0.144763. These high metrics may be due to the model's inability to generalize from the limited original dataset. With all measures displaying improved values (e.g., MAE decreased

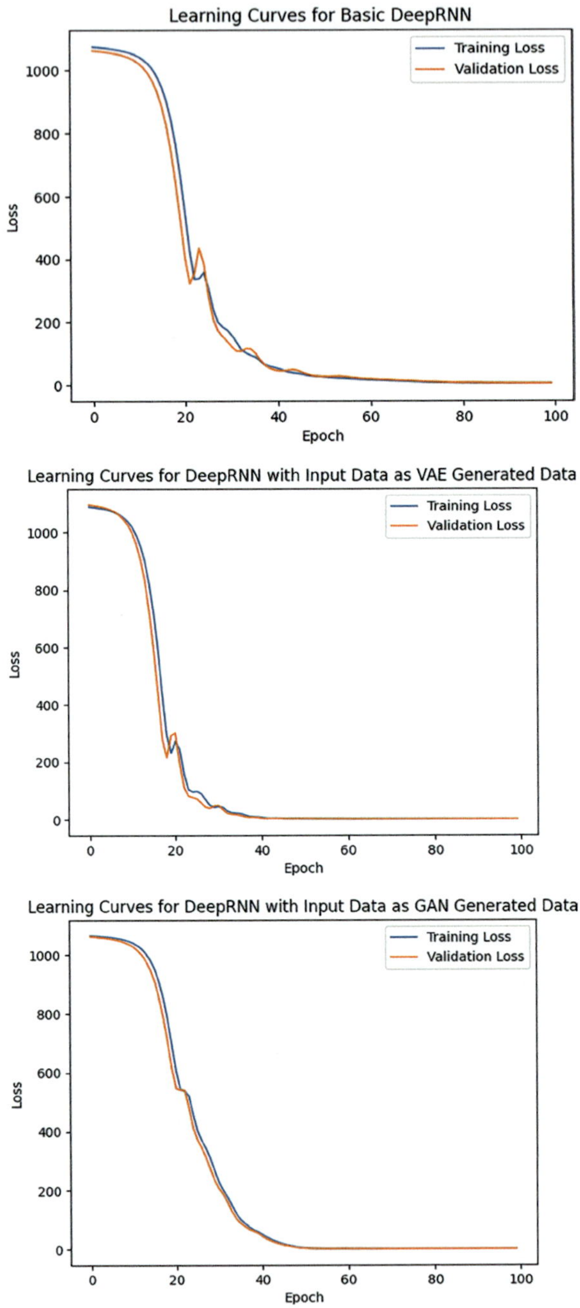

Figure 1.3 Learning curves of (a) phase 1, (b) phase 2, and (c) phase 3.

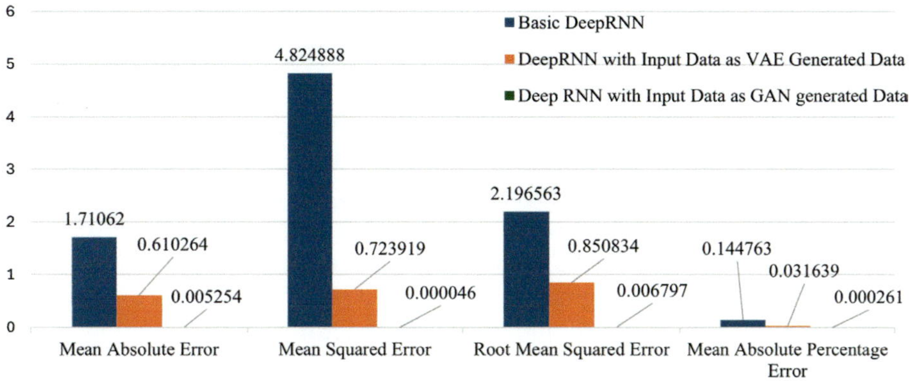

Figure 1.4 Comparison of evaluation metrics of models.

from 1.71062 to 0.610264 and RMSE from 2.196563 to 0.850834), the VAE-DeepRNN model (phase 2) demonstrated a definite improvement over the baseline model. This performance analysis demonstrates that the predictive model gains useful information from data augmentation via VAE. Out of the four metrics, the GAN-DeepRNN model (phase 3) had the lowest values (MAE: 0.005254, MSE: 0.000046, RMSE: 0.006797, MAPE: 0.000261). This suggests that the GAN-augmented DeepRNN model is a highly robust and reliable model than the other benchmarked models.

The quantitative evidence involving test loss values, learning curves notations, and evaluation metrics determination strongly supports the hypothesis that synthetic data augmentation for a sparse imbalance marine dataset, particularly using generative adversarial networks, is a powerful strategy for enhancing the predictive accuracy and robustness of deep learning models. Furthermore, through this quantitative evidence, the phase 3, GAN-DeepRNN model emerges as the most optimal choice for deployment, offering precise and reliable, low-error predictions.

1.4 Conclusion

This study compared the baseline predictive model, say DeepRNN, with the GAN-augmented DeepRNN model and the VAE-augmented DeepRNN model. The results validate WGAN's ability than VAE to generate ecologically meaningful synthetic data for most benthic and thus address sparse observation challenges, thereby improving predictions of benthic. While data augmentation using GANs excels at capturing nonlinear ecological relationships, their outputs require external validation against independent field data to avoid propagating sampling biases. The optimal augmentation strategy varies by parameter type (biological vs physicochemical), spatial scale of interest, and based on available computational resources. Therefore, a tiered approach combining GANs with physical modeling and targeted sampling proves most robust for comprehensive marine ecosystem analysis, thereby leading to a study toward ocean sustainability. While international agreements like the UN Sustainable Development Goal 14 (life below water) aim to mitigate ocean degradation, localized overfishing and unregulated deep-sea mining continue to undermine these efforts. A combination of the use of AI technologies for data analysis, data-driven decision-making, stricter policy enforcement, community-based fisheries management, and biodegradable material innovation to reduce ocean pollution may offer a viable path forward.

Reference

[1] S. C. Doney, D. S. Busch, S. R. Cooley, and K. J. Kroeker, “The impacts of ocean acidification on marine ecosystems and reliant human communities,” *Annu Rev Environ Resour*, vol. 45, no. Volume 45, 2020, pp. 83–112, Oct. 2020, doi: 10.1146/ANNUREV-ENVIRON-012320-083019/CITE/REFWORKS.

[2] T. P. Hughes *et al.*, “Spatial and temporal patterns of mass bleaching of corals in the Anthropocene,” *Science (1979)*, vol. 359, no. 6371, pp. 80–83, Jan. 2018, doi: 10.1126/SCIENCE.AAN8048/SUPPL_FILE/AAN8048_HUGHES_SM.PDF.

[3] B. J. McFarland, “The Context of Coral Reef Degradation and Loss,” *Conservation of Tropical Coral Reefs*, pp. 5–62, 2021, doi: 10.1007/978-3-030-57012-5_2.

[4] O. Hoegh-Guldberg, E. Northrop, and J. Lubchenco, “Downloaded from,” vol. 27, 2019, doi: 10.1126/science.aaz4390.

[5] N. Estrada-Saldívar, B. A. Quiroga-García, E. Pérez-Cervantes, O. O. Rivera-Garibay, and L. Alvarez-Filip, “Effects of the Stony Coral Tissue Loss Disease Outbreak on Coral Communities and the Benthic Composition of Cozumel Reefs,” *Front Mar Sci*, vol. 8, p. 632777, Mar. 2021, doi: 10.3389/FMARS.2021.632777/BIBTEX.

[6] L. Lombard, M. Sandoval-Denis, S. C. Lamprecht, and P. W. Crous, “Epitypification of Fusarium oxysporum - clearing the taxonomic chaos,” *Persoonia*, vol. 43, pp. 1–47, Dec. 2019, doi: 10.3767/PERSOONIA.2019.43.01.

[7] J. Waller *et al.*, “Reflecting on the recent history of coastal Maine fisheries and marine resource monitoring: the value of collaborative research, changing ecosystems, and thoughts on preparing for the future,” *ICES Journal of Marine Science*, vol. 80, no. 8, pp. 2074–2086, Oct. 2023, doi: 10.1093/ICESJMS/FSAD134.

[8] Y. Liu, G. Du, C. Yin, H. Zhang, and J. Wang, “Clustering-based incremental learning for imbalanced data classification,” *Knowl Based Syst*, vol. 292, p. 111612, May 2024, doi: 10.1016/J.KNOSYS.2024.111612.

[9] J. M. Johnson and T. M. Khoshgoftaar, “Survey on deep learning with class imbalance,” *J Big Data*, vol. 6, no. 1, pp. 1–54, Dec. 2019, doi: 10.1186/S40537-019-0192-5/TABLES/18.

[10] G. Szlobodnyik and L. Farkas, “Data Augmentation by Guided Deep Interpolation,” *Appl Soft Comput*, vol. 111, p. 107680, Nov. 2021, doi: 10.1016/J.ASOC.2021.107680.

[11] W. C. Lin, C. F. Tsai, Y. H. Hu, and J. S. Jhang, “Clustering-based undersampling in class-imbalanced data,” *Inf Sci (N Y)*, vol. 409–410, pp. 17–26, Oct. 2017, doi: 10.1016/J.INS.2017.05.008.

[12] R. Hemanth Kumar, B. Vishnu Prasad, H. Yadav, and M. Venugopalan, “Rainfall Prediction Enhancement Using SMOTE and Machine Learning Algorithms,” *2024 15th International Conference on Computing Communication and Networking Technologies, ICCCNT 2024*, 2024, doi: 10.1109/ICCCNT61001.2024.10726002.

[13] C. Miao and Y. Wang, “Interpolation of non-stationary geo-data using Kriging with sparse representation of covariance function,” *Comput Geotech*, vol. 169, p. 106183, May 2024, doi: 10.1016/J.COMPGEO.2024.106183.

[14] M. Goubeaud, P. Jousen, N. Gmyrek, F. Ghorban, L. Schelkes, and A. Kummert, “Using Variational Autoencoder to augment Sparse Time series Datasets,” *2021 International Conference on Optimization and Applications, ICOA 2021*, May 2021, doi: 10.1109/ICOA51614.2021.9442619.

[15] V. Dubey, B. Kaur, and P. Goel, “Enhancing Accuracy Through Data Augmentation using Variational Autoencoders in Machine Learning Techniques,” *2024 Control Instrumentation System Conference: Guiding Tomorrow: Emerging Trends in Control, Instrumentation, and Systems Engineering, CISCON 2024*, 2024, doi: 10.1109/CISCON62171.2024.10696311.

[16] M. Vega-Bayo, J. Pérez-Aracil, L. Prieto-Godino, and S. Salcedo-Sanz, “Improving the prediction of extreme wind speed events with generative

data augmentation techniques," *Renew Energy*, vol. 221, p. 119769, Feb. 2024, doi: 10.1016/J.RENENE.2023.119769.
[17] N. Gauthier, D. Bird, and K. Blahnik, "Variational Autoencoders for Efficient and Interpretable Climate Downscaling", Accessed: Sep. 14, 2025. [Online]. Available: https://nick-gauthier.github.io
[18] M. Klasen, D. Ahrens, J. Eberle, and V. Steinhage, "Image-Based Automated Species Identification: Can Virtual Data Augmentation Overcome Problems of Insufficient Sampling?," *Syst Biol*, vol. 71, no. 2, pp. 320–333, Feb. 2022, doi: 10.1093/SYSBIO/SYAB048.
[19] R. Crocker, B. J. Robson, C. Ani, K. Anthony, and T. Iwanaga, "Synthetic data for reef modelling," *Ecol Inform*, vol. 82, p. 102698, Sep. 2024, doi: 10.1016/J.ECOINF.2024.102698.
[20] J. Wang and S. Tabeta, "Four-channel generative adversarial networks can predict the distribution of reef-associated fish in the South and East China Seas," *Ecol Inform*, vol. 78, p. 102321, Dec. 2023, doi: 10.1016/J.ECOINF.2023.102321.
[21] M. Arjovsky, S. Chintala, and L. Bottou, "Wasserstein GAN," Jan. 2017, Accessed: Sep. 22, 2024. [Online]. Available: https://arxiv.org/abs/1701.07875v3
[22] "(PDF) Time Series Anomaly Detection with Variational Autoencoders." Accessed: Sep. 14, 2025. [Online]. Available: https://www.researchgate.net/publication/334223668_Time_Series_Anomaly_Detection_with_Variational_Autoencoders
[23] J. Li, W. Ren, and M. Han, "Mutual Information Variational Autoencoders and Its Application to Feature Extraction of Multivariate Time Series," *Intern J Pattern Recognit Artif Intell*, vol. 36, no. 6, May 2022, doi: 10.1142/S0218001422550059.
[24] M. L. Garsdal, V. Søgaard, and S. M. Sørensen, "Generative time series models using Neural ODE in Variational Autoencoders," Jan. 2022, Accessed: Sep. 14, 2025. [Online]. Available: http://arxiv.org/abs/2201.04630
[25] S. G. Zaloumis, M. Rajasekhar, and J. A. Simpson, "How to use learning curves to evaluate the sample size for malaria prediction models developed using machine learning algorithms," *Malaria Journal*, vol. 24, no. 1, pp. 1–11, Dec. 2025, doi: 10.1186/S12936-025-05479-3/TABLES/2.

2

AI as a Teaching Tool in Higher Education: Transforming Learning and Safety

Ain Nadirah Binti Romainor[1], Faizan Iza Binti Zainuddin[2] and Mugunthan Perumal[1]

[1]Faculty of Resource Science and Technology, Universiti Malaysia Sarawak (UNIMAS), 94300 Kota Samarahan, Sarawak, Malaysia
[2]Faculty of Economics and Business, Universiti Malaysia Sarawak (UNIMAS), 94300 Kota Samarahan, Sarawak, Malaysia

Email: ranadirah@unimas.my; zfiza@unimas.my; pmugunthan@unimas.my

Abstract

In today's society, artificial intelligence (AI) is deeply embedded in our daily lives, influencing various aspects of modern civilization. From smartphones and digital services to chatbots, social media, and websites, AI enhances efficiency and convenience across multiple domains. In education, AI serves as a powerful tool for both educators and students, reshaping teaching approaches and enriching student engagement. However, despite its growing presence in educational activities, clear guidelines are necessary to address safety concerns and uphold academic integrity when utilizing AI. This chapter explores the benefits of AI as a learning tool in higher education and examines the strategies implemented to ensure data security and maintain academic standards.

2.1 Introduction

AI refers to artificial intelligence demonstrated by machines to enhance computer functions linked to human cognition, such as thinking, learning, problem-solving, and language processing. While AI replicates the functionality of human intelligence, it does not mimic biologically observable processes,

 DOI: 10.1201/9788743812135-2

and instead engages in analytical and algorithmic problem-solving using computational models. As a branch of computer science, AI aims to integrate advanced intelligence into various computer systems [1]. In the education sector, many priorities for improving teaching and learning remain unmet, and educators seek technology-driven solutions that are safe, effective, and scalable to address these needs.

AI has become an essential component of modern education, revolutionizing the way knowledge is delivered and acquired. Initially, AI in education focused on basic automation, but it has since evolved into sophisticated AI-driven learning tools used in universities to personalize learning experiences, enhance student engagement, and streamline administrative tasks [2]. From intelligent tutoring systems to AI-powered assessments, these advancements have transformed traditional learning environments.

However, as AI continues to shape education, its intersection with innovation and digital safety becomes increasingly important. Ensuring ethical AI use, protecting student data, and maintaining academic integrity are critical considerations as institutions integrate AI into their educational frameworks [3]. By balancing technological advancements with responsible implementation, AI can enhance teaching and learning while safeguarding digital security and ethical standards.

2.2 AI-Powered Personalized Learning in Higher Education Sector

One of the most significant and transformative applications of AI in education is AI-powered personalized learning, which tailors educational experiences to individual student needs. Figure 2.1 shows the overview of AI-powered personalized learning in the higher education sector. AI-powered personalized learning tailors learning experiences to each student's unique needs.

Adaptive learning systems like Duolingo and Khan Academy use AI algorithms to analyze student performance and adjust course content in real time, ensuring learners receive material suited to their skill level and progress [4]. Unlike traditional one-size-fits-all teaching methods, adaptive learning recognizes that students have different learning styles, abilities, and knowledge levels. By continuously assessing student interactions, AI-driven platforms identify strengths and weaknesses, providing customized lessons, exercises, and feedback. Such a personalized approach improves engagement, enhances knowledge retention, and helps students learn at their own pace. As a result of adaptive learning, education becomes more efficient, flexible, and tailored to individual needs [5].

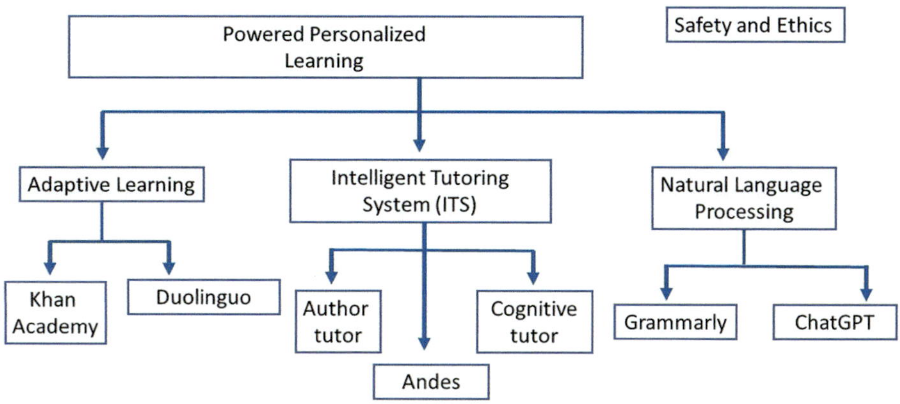

Figure 2.1 Framework of AI-powered personalized learning.

Another significant advancement in AI-driven education is the development of intelligent tutoring systems (ITS), which leverage artificial intelligence to provide personalized and adaptive learning experiences by acting as virtual tutors, providing instant feedback, step-by-step explanations, and interactive problem-solving assistance to support student understanding. These systems assess students' cognitive abilities, prior knowledge, motivation, and emotions to tailor instructional content, making learning more efficient and engaging. By tracking progress in real-time, ITS delivers instant feedback, hints, and adaptive support, allowing students to learn at their own pace [6]. *AutoTutor* is a prime example of how AI-driven platforms can create interactive, adaptive, and effective learning environments by simulating human-like tutoring interactions [7].

Unlike traditional human tutors, which rely on verbal and nonverbal communication, *AutoTutor* engages learners through an animated talking head, utilizing natural language processing to facilitate open-ended, text- or voice-based conversations [6]. Other successful tutoring systems, such as *Cognitive Tutor* and *Andes,* focus on problem-solving interactions, guiding students through step-by-step solutions without extensive dialogue. Beyond enhancing individual learning outcomes, ITS supports sustainable education by aligning with SDG Goal 4: Quality Education, ensuring inclusive, accessible, and lifelong learning opportunities. These AI-driven systems play a vital role in expanding digital education, making quality instruction available to learners regardless of geographical or socioeconomic barriers [8]

Natural language processing (NLP) is the driving force behind ITS and has been proven to be a potent tool for revolutionizing how students learn by offering them personalized teaching and supervision without a human teacher [9]. NLP integrates computational linguistics, which is the rule-based modeling of human language, with statistical, machine learning, and deep learning models. These technologies, when combined, enable computers to interpret human language from text or voice data to comprehend its whole meaning, including the speaker's or writer's intention and attitude. The established application of NLP in higher education includes chatbots or virtual assistants such as chat-generative pretrained transformer (*ChatGPT*) and *Grammarly*, respectively. By understanding and responding to natural language, these bots assist in answering queries, guiding course selection, providing real-time updates, and offering personalized learning support [10].

In the education sector, *Grammarly* assists students and educators in improving their writing by checking grammar, enhancing clarity, and offering suggestions for better readability [11]. However, it has limitations: *Grammarly* only provides feedback in English, which can be challenging for nonnative speakers to fully understand. Additionally, studies have shown that *Grammarly* sometimes overlooks common mistakes or provides excessive and occasionally inaccurate feedback [12]. On the other hand, *ChatGPT* is a powerful AI language model with diverse applications. It utilizes generative AI, which learns from existing data to create new content, including text, images, and music. Through deep learning and neural networks, it generates responses that closely resemble human-produced content [13]. *ChatGPT* can perform various tasks, such as drafting research papers, writing reports, translating text, providing feedback on assignments, answering exam questions, and serving as a digital mentor to support learning [14]. In higher education, studies indicate that students frequently use ChatGPT to complete assignments, essays, and projects due to academic workload pressure and time constraints [15]. However, this growing reliance raises concerns among educators about academic integrity, particularly regarding issues such as plagiarism and fraudulent submissions [16].

The integration of AI in academic settings marks a significant transformation in the landscape of educational technology. When used effectively, AI can enhance learning efficiency, support diverse student needs, and create a more engaging and responsive academic environment. While its impact on education is undeniable, there are still challenges that need to be addressed. One major concern is the high computational and memory requirements, which may limit its practical use in certain applications. Additionally, AI models can sometimes produce biased or inappropriate content, raising ethical concerns. Their difficulty in processing specialized language and the need for fine-tuning in specific fields highlight the importance of continuous research to improve these systems [17, 18].

Another issue that worries educators is students' reliance on AI, particularly regarding academic integrity, fraud, and plagiarism [19]. Academics agree that implementing ethical guidelines and security measures is essential to regulate AI usage among students. Enforcing such policies ensures responsible AI use, preventing academic dishonesty, data privacy breaches, and over-reliance on automated tools. By preventing over-reliance on automated tools, critical thinking, analytical thinking, innovative thinking, decision-making abilities, and problem-solving abilities would not diminish in students and educators [20]. Indeed, by establishing clear regulations, institutions can create an environment where AI serves as a valuable learning aid rather than a replacement for independent thinking and academic integrity.

2.3 AI in Higher Education Safety and Cybersecurity

The rapid development of technology in higher education is changing campus security and the educational process. AI has emerged as a vital instrument for improving cybersecurity, guaranteeing the security of instructors, students, and digital assets [21]. The significance of security systems powered by artificial intelligence has increased dramatically as colleges continue to shift to digital platforms. Cyberattacks have risen 29% worldwide in 2021 compared to 2022, according to recent statistics, with colleges being the main targets [22]. The need for AI-based security solutions in educational institutions is urgent, with about 30% of higher education institutions reporting having cyber incidents each year. AI's contribution to higher education security goes beyond cyber protection; it also includes smart monitoring systems, ethical issues with surveillance, and facial recognition for access management. This chapter explores AI's uses, difficulties, and potential applications in cybersecurity and campus safety.

As illustrated in Figure 2.2, AI in higher education security extends beyond cybersecurity; it also includes smart monitoring systems, ethical considerations related to surveillance, and facial recognition for access control. These AI-driven measures play a crucial role in both preventing unauthorized access and ensuring the overall safety of campus environments.

2.3.1 AI-driven campus security systems

Face recognition technology driven by AI has completely changed campus security by guaranteeing effective and safe access control. These systems improve institutional safety by reliably identifying workers, instructors, and students, thereby lowering unauthorized entrance [23]. AI-driven identity verification has been used by numerous colleges to bolster security in

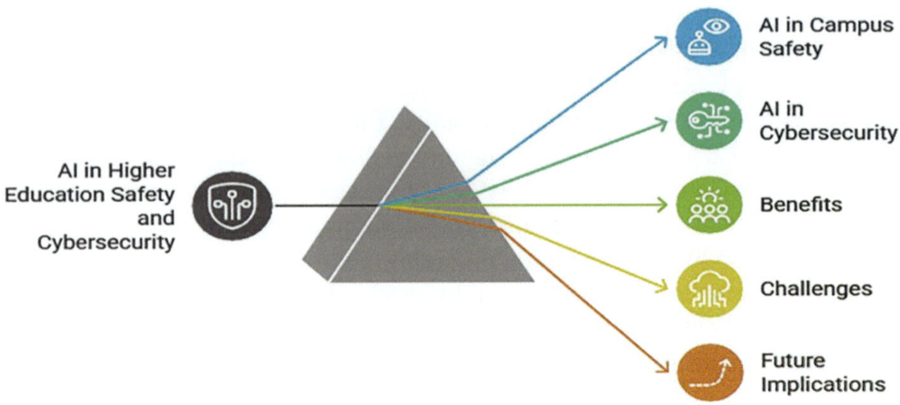

Figure 2.2 AI's dual role in higher education.

administrative buildings, classrooms, and dorms. However, the increasing use of facial recognition raises moral questions about biases in AI algorithms, invasions of privacy, and improper surveillance. Research suggests that gender and ethnicity can affect the accuracy of facial recognition, which could result in discriminatory problems, especially if such facial recognition systems were developed in another context, such as, for instance, utilizing facial recognition systems designed in Western nations in Asian nations [24]. For decision-making processes to be more transparent and accountable, researchers recommend the integration of explainable AI (XAI) [25]. Modern university security systems still rely heavily on facial recognition, despite its difficulties.

AI is used by smart surveillance systems to evaluate real-time video streams, spot irregularities, and instantly flag possible dangers. Prompt intervention is made possible by these systems' ability to identify suspect activity, such as unapproved gatherings, abandoned items, or odd movement patterns [26]. Additionally, by detecting anomalous network activity, AI-driven anomaly detection systems improve cybersecurity and lower the danger of cyberattacks. According to research, when properly used, AI-enhanced monitoring lowers campus security concerns by 40% [27]. AI-integrated monitoring also aids in emergency response by giving law enforcement access to real-time data for prompt action. Nonetheless, worries about mass surveillance and privacy invasion still exist, necessitating ethical governance and cautious regulation: as Fontes and colleagues (2022) warns, "deploying a system by which the face of every passer-by is analyzed, mapped and their identity verified is a decision that impacts the whole population…everyone using public space is under surveillance without being a suspect of any crime…everyone in a space under surveillance would then be exposed to the same risks that ultimately result in an AI-powered facial recognition technology triggering police action" [28].

AI also functions as an assistant to security personnel in the context of educational institutions. From providing 24/7 monitoring to determining threat severity and sending real-time alerts to staff and students, a safer environment can be created with AI [29]. In the U.S. Department of Energy (USDE), AI is used to strengthen national security: in order to maintain the security of the nuclear stockpile that requires extensive modelling and simulation, AI-powered models are used to make such simulations significantly faster, which enables better analysis and design improvements [30].

AI is also used to accelerate the discovery of new materials, design optimization, manufacturing, and ongoing surveillance, in which ongoing surveillance prevents the escalation of nuclear weapons. Lastly, at the USDE, AI takes large quantities of data from multiple sources and analyzes them in order to detect illicit nuclear activities globally in a timely manner. In short, no matter the location, AI enhances surveillance, detection, and prevention. For example, several schools in Canada now utilize AI-powered surveillance software to monitor all school-issued devices for danger with the aim of keeping students and staff safe from the threat of shootings [31].

2.3.2 Cybersecurity in digital learning

Protecting student data has become crucial due to the growing dependence on digital learning systems. Advanced data protection is guaranteed by AI-driven encryption algorithms, which shield private data from unwanted access [32]. Universities must use AI-enhanced encryption solutions to protect academic records and institutional data as cyber threats continue to increase. The need for AI-driven encryption solutions is further highlighted by the fact that 62% of cyber incidents in universities are caused by employee negligence itself [33]. AI also makes it possible to detect threats in real time, which enables organizations to take precautions before data breaches happen. In fact, universities that invest in AI-driven cybersecurity frameworks show a 50% improvement in data breach prevention when compared to those who rely on traditional security measures [34].

Universities are increasingly vulnerable to cyberattacks as education moves to online platforms. Higher education institutions experienced 455 cyberattack incidents involving malware-related data breaches [35]. Malaysia also experienced a similar devastating phenomenon in 2018, in which the school examination analysis system was attacked by the SQL injection technique to gain unauthorized data. As a result, the system was shut down temporarily [36]. Besides that, cyberattacks on Malaysian universities have resulted in severe data breaches, exposing sensitive personal and financial information, as shown in Table 2.1. Swinburne University of Technology, Sarawak, fell victim to the RansomHub ransomware, which led to the theft of 366 GB of data, including bank account details, student documents, and passport scans. This attack, reported by *Borneo Post* in September 2024, highlights the growing risk of ransomware targeting educational institutions.

Similarly, Universiti Malaya (UM) experienced a major data breach in October 2019, whereby hackers infiltrated the university's e-payment online system, exposing staff personal data, login credentials, passwords, pay slips, and bank account details. The breach raised concerns about the security of financial transactions within academic institutions. Meanwhile, Universiti Malaysia Sabah (UMS) was attacked by a hacker group known as Breach

Table 2.1 Major cyberattacks on Malaysian universities and their data breaches.

Higher education institution	Types of data breach	Type of cyber attack	Sources
Swinburne University of Technology Sarawak Campus	Stolen 366 gigabytes includes invoices, a letter of completion to a student, an application for advanced standing. bank account details and scan of the passport of a Malaysian former student	RansomHub	Borneo Post, September 2024
Universiti Malaya (UM)	Massive data breach. includes staff personal data, login IDs and passwords, payslip and bank account	Hacking the UM's e- payment online system	The Star, October 2019
Universiti Malaysia Sabah (UMS)	Data breach includes name, student ID, faculty, address, email and MyKad number	Hacked by hacker group known as Breach DB	
The Star, November 2019.			

DB in November 2019, compromising student information such as names, student IDs, faculty details, addresses, emails, and MyKad numbers. These incidents underscore the urgent need for universities to strengthen cybersecurity measures to safeguard sensitive data from future threats.

Artificial intelligence (AI) tools like anomaly detection and predictive analytics are essential for spotting and thwarting online threats. By analyzing vast datasets, these systems enhance cyber defenses by identifying malware, phishing attempts, and illegal access [37]. Compared to conventional cybersecurity techniques, machine learning models have greatly increased the rates of cyber threat identification. Similarly, compared to traditional methods, reports show that AI-driven cyber protection systems improve threat detection by 50% [38]. Institutional vulnerabilities are also greatly decreased by AI-driven cybersecurity technologies, which have shown an 85% accuracy rate in anticipating possible data breaches before they happen [39].

2.3.2.1 Supporting findings from the latest research on AI and data privacy

Privacy is the assurance of the security of sensitive data [40]. As such, privacy relates to the access to and control over how personal data is used [41]. A paper examining the data privacy challenges posed by AI-driven education states that it is imperative that schools implement comprehensive data governance policies, invest in educator training on AI and privacy, and incorporate data literacy into the curriculum since AI systems are collecting various types of student data, from test scores to social interactions [42].

Governing the use of AI platforms and systems is the responsibility of educational institutions [43]. In order to protect student information – which can range from student records to detailed information about what students and teachers do as they interact with technology – educational institutions must bear in mind that student privacy was not necessarily considered in the development of AI platforms, which means schools and universities themselves should take it upon themselves to ensure compliance with student or state privacy laws such as FERPA in the United States. Although there is no such specific law in Malaysia, the Personal Data Protection Act (PDPA) 2010 – *Akta Perlindungan Data Peribadi 2010* – enforces similar data protection standards [44]. Indeed, institutions are advised to establish a "strong technical infrastructure" and to "define data security policies" clearly, after which "regular training and mentoring programs" on the effective use of AI tools should be organized for educators, and "professional learning communities should be established" in order for good practices to be shared. In addition to educator support, technical support should also be available to students, and regular evaluations should be conducted to ensure the quality of the process [45].

Investing in educator training on AI and privacy also ensures security in terms of data privacy in the everyday use of AI learning tools [43]. Educators and teachers can play a role in helping to determine the most feasible tool by first researching what tools are available and then evaluating the efficacy of such tools. However, educators also require support in the selection and evaluation of AI tools. Ideally, school officials and AI providers would first collaborate and discuss what is and what is not achievable by AI [29].

Incorporating data literacy into the curriculum is an ethical step toward safe and fair AI use in schools as it equips students with the understanding that there is always a possibility that the information they share will be made public, such as through data breaches. Since AI is increasingly utilized for personalized learning, there is a greater risk of frequent data breaches [46]. Several strategies have been outlined by researchers on how to equip learners and educators on how to protect student data privacy. Such strategies are as follows: students and teachers must be (a) informed of the extent of personal data privacy, the dangers of personal data leaking, and the basic, doable steps for protecting personal information, (b) taught to evaluate privacy risks in regular online activities, opting to "install privacy security shields, exercise caution when authorizing open permissions, and carefully read the authorization instructions to determine privacy risks," and (c) helped to understand the "fundamentals and features of big data and AI technologies." Other best practices, such as monitoring network security issues and educating oneself on personal privacy and the dangers of data breaches, also serve to ensure data privacy in educational institutions. Indeed, by enhancing students' awareness of personal data protection, the ethical risks AI poses to students' personal information can be diminished.

2.3.3 Ethical considerations and challenges

Even while AI has many advantages for cybersecurity and campus security, it also presents moral dilemmas, such as algorithmic biases, data privacy issues, and decision-making fairness issues. To guarantee ethical AI deployment and avoid discrimination in security systems, universities must establish clear AI policies [47].

To protect student privacy, institutions must also abide by laws like the Family Educational Rights and Privacy Act (FERPA) and the General Data Protection Regulation (GDPR) [48]. The increasing use of AI for security and monitoring has sparked discussions on the ethical application of AI,

Figure 2.3 The role of explainable AI (XAI) in higher education security.

highlighting the necessity of accountability and equity in algorithmic decision-making. Absence of control of AI may result in abuse, whereby monitoring tools are used for purposes other than security, violating the rights of students. Explainability is still a significant obstacle. Because AI models frequently operate as "black boxes," it might be challenging for university officials to comprehend how decisions are made. Institutions need to spend money on explainable AI (XAI) frameworks so that stakeholders can correctly understand security advice produced by AI.

Explainable AI ensures transparency, fairness, and accountability in AI-driven cybersecurity systems. As shown in Figure 2.3, the integration of XAI models, encryption techniques, and explainability-driven security measures allows institutions to develop trustworthy AI-powered security frameworks.

2.4 Future Directions and Recommendations in AI-Driven Cybersecurity for Higher Education

Higher education institutions' cybersecurity is becoming more and more dependent on artificial intelligence (AI). Universities must take proactive measures to protect sensitive data, infrastructure, and online learning environments as cyber threats change. Future developments in AI-powered cybersecurity must prioritize accountability, resilience, and transparency. The main suggestions for improving AI's efficacy in university cybersecurity are examined in this section.

As illustrated in Figure 2.4, the enhancement of AI-driven cybersecurity in universities requires multiple strategic interventions, including the implementation of explainable AI models, blockchain integration, adversarial AI research, and ethical AI governance. The following subsections discuss these recommendations in detail.

2.4.1 Implementing explainable A1 (XAI) models

In AI-driven cybersecurity, the opacity of decision-making processes is one of the most urgent issues. It might be challenging to understand how judgments are made in many AI models since they function as "black boxes." Explainable AI (XAI) seeks to close this gap by making AI systems more

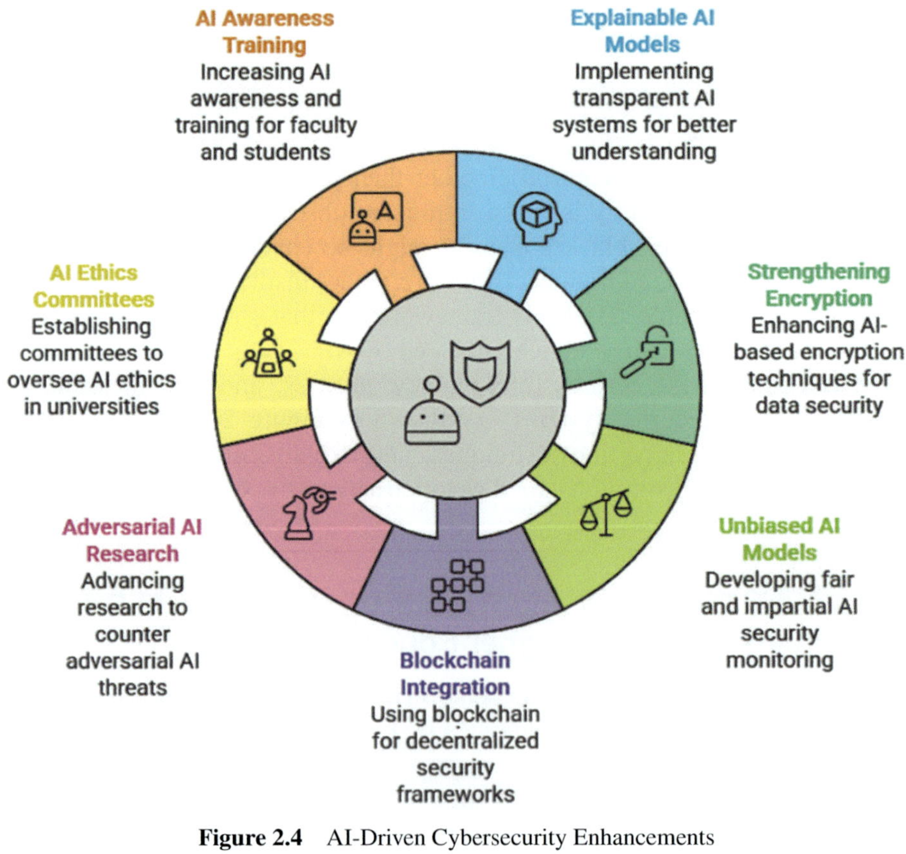

Figure 2.4 AI-Driven Cybersecurity Enhancements

comprehensible and transparent. Universities ought to incorporate XAI models to offer convincing arguments for automated interventions, anomaly detection, and security alerts. As a result, human operators will be able to successfully act when needed, and trust in AI-driven security systems will increase [49].

2.4.2 Strengthening AI-based encryption techniques

The safeguarding of teacher and student data is crucial as higher education becomes more digitally integrated. Universities are looking for ways to guarantee that administrative records, research discoveries, and personal information are shielded from breaches and unwanted access. Techniques for encryption driven by AI provide a strong defense against online attacks for private data. AI-driven encryption is more immune to cyberattacks than traditional encryption techniques because it constantly adjusts to new threats via features such as real-time monitoring, threat detection, and adaptive encryption. With the existence of such features, the detection of plagiarism and the monitoring of IP violations can happen in real-time [50].

However, according to Adenubi *et al.* (2024), the implementation of such AI-driven encryption to secure academic data necessitates a combination of (a) a central AI hub, featuring the following: real-time monitoring, threat response, data anonymization, IP monitoring and enforcement, federated learning (analyzing data without sharing it), and dynamic encryption, (b) core protections example AI tools for IP, cybersecurity, and privacy, and (c) supporting factors such as ethics, law compliance, and global collaboration. By strengthening AI-based encryption via the above methods, the risk of plagiarism, data breaches, and IP theft can be mitigated, thereby enhancing credibility, fostering innovation, and upholding ethics.

2.4.3 Developing unbiased AI models for security monitoring

To guarantee equity and inclusivity, AI models utilized in cybersecurity and campus security must be devoid of bias. Certain student or faculty groups may be disproportionately affected by biased security surveillance tactics brought on by bias in AI systems. Universities should give the creation and training of objective AI models top priority in order to stop such bias. Fairness-aware algorithms, frequent audits, and the use of a variety of datasets can all help achieve this. In short, to ensure unbiased security surveillance in AI systems, AI systems must be adjusted to reduce unfair outcomes, AI-related decisions must be made understandable (via XAI), and biased training data must be cleaned [51]. Indeed, ethical AI governance promises fair security measures that do not support systemic prejudice, thereby ensuring AI benefits society equitably.

2.4.4 Integrating blockchain technology for decentralized security frameworks

A potential remedy for enhancing cybersecurity in institutes of higher learning is blockchain technology. Universities can improve data integrity, stop unwanted changes, and lower the danger of cyberattacks by utilizing decentralized ledgers. Access control systems can be further strengthened by blockchain-based identity verification, which guarantees that only authorized individuals have access to digital resources and restricted areas. Furthermore, smart contracts driven by blockchain technology can automate security procedures, reducing human error in cybersecurity operations [52]. Such smart contracts utilize a deep autoencoder neural network to detect abnormalities in Industrial IoT traffic, serving as an active structural component within such a Blockchain security architecture. The end result is a real-time detection of traffic abnormalities– leading to a reduction in cyberattacks– and the possibility of protecting sensitive data while maintaining transparency.

2.4.5 Advancing research in adversarial AI

Cybercriminals' methods for taking advantage of AI flaws are evolving along with AI-based cybersecurity technologies. By modifying AI models to generate inaccurate results, adversarial AI has the ability to undermine security measures. Universities need to spend money on adversarial AI research in order to combat these dangers. Institutions can strengthen the resilience of their cybersecurity infrastructure by creating AI models that are difficult to manipulate. Innovation in hostile AI defenses can be further stimulated by research partnerships between AI and cybersecurity experts [53]. In addition to innovations in AI defenses, the development of effective AI policies is equally important in order to protect AI systems from vulnerabilities. Such policies are best developed through a multistakeholder collaboration, in which such stakeholders may include governments, industries, academia, and civil society working in tandem.

2.4.6 Establishing AI ethics committees within universities

Sustaining trust and accountability in cybersecurity requires the ethical application of AI. To supervise the deployment and management of AI-driven security systems, academic institutions ought to set up specialized AI ethics committees, especially since cybersecurity in AI is an emergent field with no current standardized frameworks or methods. These committees would then establish rules for responsible AI use, bias reduction, and data privacy. Accordingly, universities can guarantee that AI technologies conform to ethical and legal standards. Encouraging interdisciplinary debates among cybersecurity specialists, AI researchers, and legislators would also further guarantee the ethical use of AI in educational institutions [54]. Moreover, such interdisciplinary collaborations also lead toward innovations in AI for cybersecurity.

2.4.7 Increasing AI awareness training for faculty and students

Cybersecurity is not just a technical problem; it also calls for users who are responsible and knowledgeable. Numerous cyberthreats make use of human weaknesses, like weak passwords and phishing scams. To improve cybersecurity literacy, universities should introduce AI awareness training programs for staff and students. Topics such as identifying cyberthreats, utilizing AI-driven security solutions efficiently, and comprehending the moral ramifications of AI surveillance should all be covered in training in order to encourage safe AI use and lower security threats [55].

However, Roshanaei and Jachura (2025) remind us that integrating AI with cybersecurity remains a challenge due to curriculum gaps, faculty expertise limitations, and resource constraints. Firstly, staff members themselves do not have sufficient knowledge to create educational programs on topics such as "AI-based malware detection" and "automated threat intelligence systems." As such, educational institutions must include practical training on AI-driven cybersecurity tools in their curriculum. Secondly, more faculty expertise on cybersecurity is necessary to manage security risks. Such faculty expertise can be created by providing training on AI-driven security tools and by collaborating with industry leaders to help enhance staff members' practical knowledge via real-world datasets and established AI tools. Thirdly, integrating AI-driven cybersecurity expertise and knowledge in educational institutions requires funding for resources such as "high-performance computing resources, specialized software for machine learning, and access to real-world datasets" [56]. Indeed, with proper training by cybersecurity and AI experts in both academia and industry, an increase in AI awareness can be expected, along with more robust cybersecurity defenses. Collaboration efforts between industry and academia toward improved AI in cybersecurity applications are as follows: In Malaysia, UTM has established the Academia-Industry Satellite Labs and Innovation Hubs, in which the collaboration between UTM and Mastercard enables knowledge transfer that would ensure an up-to-date curriculum that is in line with the industry's needs for cyber-security experts [57]. Furthermore, Swinburne University of Technology Sarawak Campus, CyberSecurity Malaysia, and local company Nex Vision have begun collaborating to enhance cybersecurity training, professional examination programs, and joint research initiatives in various cybersecurity domains to address cyber threats [58].

2.5 Conclusion

Higher education safety and cybersecurity are being revolutionized by artificial intelligence, which offers creative solutions for danger identification, digital protection, and access management. Campus security is improved by AI-powered facial recognition and intelligent surveillance systems, while digital assets are protected by AI-powered encryption and cyberattack prevention technology. But in order to strike a balance between security and privacy rights, ethical issues must be addressed. Fairness, openness, and strong data security measures must be given top priority in future developments in AI-driven cybersecurity to guarantee inclusive and secure learning environments.

References

[1] Sarker, I. H. (2022). AI-based modeling: Techniques, applications, and research issues towards automation, intelligent and smart systems. *SN Computer Science, 3*(158). https://doi.org/10.1007/s42979-022-01043-x

[2] Katsamakas, E., Pavlov, O. V., & Saklad, R. (2024). Artificial intelligence and the transformation of higher education institutions: A systems approach. *Sustainability (Switzerland), 16*(14), 1–21. https://doi.org/10.3390/su16146118

[3] Chan, C. K. Y. (2023). *A comprehensive AI policy education framework for university teaching and learning*. International Journal of Educational Technology in Higher Education, 20(38). https://doi.org/10.1186/s41239-023-00408-3

[4] Gligorea, I., Cioca, M., Oancea, R., Gorski, A.-T., Gorski, H., & Tudorache, P. (2023). Adaptive learning using artificial intelligence in e-learning: A literature review. *Education Sciences, 13*(1216). https://doi.org/10.3390/educsci13121216

[5] Peng, H., Ma, S., & Spector, J. M. (2019). Personalized adaptive learning: An emerging pedagogical approach enabled by a smart

learning environment. *Smart Learning Environments, 6*(9). https://doi.org/10.1186/s40561-019-0089-y

[6] Guo, L., Wang, D., Gu, F., Li, Y., Wang, Y., & Zhou, R. (2021). Evolution and trends in intelligent tutoring systems research: A multidisciplinary and scientometric view. *Asia Pacific Education Review, 22*(3), 441–461. https://doi.org/10.1007/s12564-021-09697-7

[7] Nye, B. D., Graesser, A. C., & Hu, X. (2014). AutoTutor and family: A review of 17 years of natural language tutoring. *International Journal of Artificial Intelligence in Education, 24*(4), 427–469. https://doi.org/10.1007/s40593-014-0029-5

[8] Fazal, I., Bandeali, M. M., Shezad, F., & Gul, H. (2025). *Bridging Educational Gaps: The Role of AI and Social Media in Enhancing Access to Quality Education in Under-privileged Communities.* The Critical Review of Social Sciences Studies, Volume 3, Number 1, Pages 2413–2431. Available at: https://thecrsss.com/index.php/Journal/about.

[9] Shaik, T., Tao, X., Li, Y., Dann, C., McDonald, J., Redmond, P., & Galligan, L. (2022). *A Review of the Trends and Challenges in Adopting Natural Language Processing Methods for Education Feedback Analysis.* IEEE Access, Volume 10, pp. 56720-56734. DOI: 10.1109/ACCESS.2022.3177752

[10] D. H. Chang, M. P.-C. Lin, S. Hajian, and Q. Q. Wang, "Educational design principles of using AI chatbot that supports self-regulated learning in education: Goal setting, feedback, and personalization," *Sustainability*, vol. 15, no. 12921, 2023. DOI: 10.3390/su151712921.

[11] Fitria, T. N. (2021). Grammarly as AI-powered English writing assistant: Students' alternative for writing English. *Metathesis: Journal of English Language, Literature, and Teaching, 5*(1), 65. https://doi.org/10.31002/metathesis.v5i1.3519

[12] Benaiche, M., & Ghodbane, N. (2023). *The effectiveness of using Grammarly in the writing process.* [Master's dissertation, University of 8 Mai 1945 Guelma, Faculty of Letters and Languages, Department of Letters and English Language].

[13] Ray, P. P. (2023). ChatGPT: A comprehensive review on background, applications, key challenges, bias, ethics, limitations and future scope. *Internet of Things and Cyber-Physical Systems, 3*(April), 121–154. https://doi.org/10.1016/j.iotcps.2023.04.003

[14] Lingard, L. (2023). Writing with ChatGPT: An illustration of its capacity, limitations & implications for academic writers. *Perspectives on Medical Education, 12*(1), 261–270. https://doi.org/10.5334/pme.1072

[15] Abdennouri, I. (2024). *The use of ChatGPT in written assignments of EFL students: A case study of Master one students at the Department of English, University of Mohamed Khider Biskra.* [Master's dissertation, Mohamed Khider University of Biskra, Faculty of Letters and Languages, Department of Foreign Languages].

[16] Perkins, M., Gezgin, U. B., & Roe, J. (2020). *Reducing plagiarism through academic misconduct education.* International Journal for Educational Integrity, 16(3). DOI: 10.1007/s40979-020-00052-8.

[17] Ding, N., Qin, Y., Yang, G., Wei, F., Yang, Z., Su, Y., Hu, S., Chen, Y., Chan, C.-M., Chen, W., Yi, J., Zhao, W., Wang, X., Liu, Z., Zheng, H.-T., Chen, J., Liu, Y., Tang, J., Li, J., & Sun, M. (2023). Parameter-efficient fine-tuning of large-scale pre-trained language models. *Nature Machine Intelligence, 5*(3), 220–235. https://doi.org/10.1038/s42256-023-00626-4

[18] Balasubramanian, S. (2023). Exploring the capabilities of ChatGPT in natural language processing tasks. *Journal of Artificial Intelligence and Machine Learning (JAIML), 2*(1), 7–17. https://doi.org/10.17605/OSF.IO/XJYMQ

[19] P. A. Okebukola (Ed.), *AI and Ethics, Academic Integrity, and the Future of Quality Assurance in Higher Education*, vol. 3, National Universities Commission, Abuja, Nigeria, 2025. Available at: ResearchGate.

[20] Zhai, C., Wibowo, S., & Li, L. D. (2024). The effects of over-reliance on AI dialogue systems on students' cognitive abilities: A systematic review. *Smart Learning Environments, 11*(1). https://doi.org/10.1186/s40561-024-00316-7

[21] Hussain, S. M., Tummalapalli, S. R. K., & Chakravarthy, A. S. N. (2025). *Cyber Security Education: Enhancing Cyber Security Capabilities, Navigating Trends and Challenges in a Dynamic Landscape.* Vishnu Institute of Technology & Jawaharlal Nehru Technological University Kakinada.

[22] Lallie, H. S., Thompson, A., Titis, E., & Stephens, P. (2023). *Understanding Cyber Threats Against Universities, Colleges, and Schools.* Preprint submitted to Elsevier. Available at: arXiv:2307.07755.

[23] H. S. Lallie, A. Thompson, E. Titis, and P. Stephens, "Understanding cyber threats against universities, colleges, and schools," *Preprint submitted to Elsevier*, 2023. Available at: arXiv:2307.07755.

[24] Phillips, P. J., Jiang, F., Narvekar, A., Ayyad, J., & O'Toole, A. J. (2011). An other-race effect for face recognition algorithms. *ACM Transactions on Applied Perception (TAP), 8*(2), Article 14.

[25] N. L. Rane, S. P. Choudhary, and J. Rane, "Explainable Artificial Intelligence (XAI) approaches for transparency and accountability in financial decision-making," *SSRN Electron. J.*, 2023. DOI: 10.2139/ssrn.4640316.

[26] S. C. Vetrivel, P. Vidhyapriya, and A. V. P., "AI-driven solutions for crowd management in tourism: Navigating the swarm," in *AI Technologies for Personalized and Sustainable Tourism*, 1st ed., 2025, pp. 1–30. DOI: 10.4018/979-8-3693-5678-4.ch004.

[27] A. Mohamed, "Exploring the role of AI and VR in addressing anti-social behavior among students: A promising approach for educational enhancement," *IEEE Access*, vol. 12, 2024. DOI: 10.1109/ACCESS.2024.3433531.

[28] Fontes, A. C., Hohma, E., corrigan, caitlin, & Lütge, C. (2022). AI-powered public surveillance systems: Why we (might) need them and how we want them. *SSRN Electronic Journal*. https://doi.org/10.2139/ssrn.4112042

[29] Ly, D. (2024, August 13). *Ai in schools: How ai can add an extra layer of protection*. Forbes. https://www.forbes.com/councils/forbestechcouncil/2024/05/23/ai-in-schools-how-ai-can-add-an-extra-layer-of-protection/

[30] *Artificial Intelligence for national security*. Energy.gov. (2025, June 3). https://www.energy.gov/topics/artificial-intelligence-national-security

[31] Bryan, C., & Lurye, S. (2025, March 12). *Schools use AI to monitor kids, hoping to prevent violence. our investigation found security risks*. AP News. https://apnews.com/article/ai-school-chromebook-gaggle-goguardian-securly-25a3946727397951fd42324139aaf70f

[32] Gopireddy, R. R. (2021). AI-powered security in cloud environments: Enhancing data protection and threat detection. *International Journal of Science and Research (IJSR), 10*(11), 1568-1572. https://doi.org/10.21275/SR24731135001

[33] Abdulhussein, M. (2024). *The impact of artificial intelligence and machine learning on organizations' cybersecurity.* [Order No. 30994720]. Liberty University.

[34] C. C. Nwoye and S. Nwagwughiagwu, "AI-driven anomaly detection for proactive cybersecurity and data breach prevention," *Int. J. Eng. Technol. Res. Manag.*, vol. 8, no. 11, 2024. Available at: https://www.ijetrm.com.

[35] Othman, Z. (2023). Sustainability of higher education institutions: Case study on cyber attacks. *Global Business Management Review (GBMR), 15*(1), 24-38.

[36] Oudah, M. A., & Marhusin, M. F. (2024). SQL Injection Detection using Machine Learning: A Review. *Malaysian Journal of Science Health & Technology*, *10*(1), 39-49.

[37] A. Husnain, "Artificial intelligence and deep learning in healthcare, cybersecurity, and food systems: A comprehensive review of applications, challenges, and future directions," *Glob. J. Emerg. AI Comput.*, vol. 1, no. 2, Feb. 2025. DOI: 10.70445/gjeac.1.2.2025.95-126.

[38] B. Guembe, A. Azeta, S. Misra, V. C. Osamor, L. Fernandez-Sanz, and V. Pospelova, "The emerging threat of AI-driven cyber attacks: A review," *Appl. Artif. Intell.*, vol. 36, no. 1, Article 2037254, 2022. DOI: 10.1080/08839514.2022.2037254.

[39] Z. Slimi and B. Villarejo Carballido, "Navigating the ethical challenges of artificial intelligence in higher education: An analysis of seven global AI ethics policies," *TEM J.*, vol. 12, no. 2, pp. 590–602, 2023. DOI: 10.18421/TEM122-02.

[40] Johansson, U., Lofstrom, T., Konig, R., Sonstrod, C., & Niklasson, L. (2006). Rule extraction from opaque models-- a slightly different perspective. *2006 5th International Conference on Machine Learning and Applications (ICMLA'06)*, 22–27. https://doi.org/10.1109/icmla.2006.46

[41] Floridi, L., Cowls, J., Beltrametti, M., Chatila, R., Chazerand, P., Dignum, V., Luetge, C., Madelin, R., Pagallo, U., Rossi, F., Schafer, B., Valcke, P., & Vayena, E. (2018). AI4People—an ethical framework for a good AI Society: Opportunities, Risks, principles, and recommendations. *Minds and Machines*, *28*(4), 689–707. https://doi.org/10.1007/s11023-018-9482-5

[42] Ismail, I. A., & Aloshi, J. M. (2024). Data privacy in AI-Driven Education. *Advances in Educational Marketing, Administration, and Leadership*, 223–252. https://doi.org/10.4018/979-8-3693-5443-8.ch008

[43] Cardona, M., Rodríguez, R., & Ishmael, K. (2023). (rep.). *Artificial Intelligence and the Future of Teaching and Learning, Insights and Recommendations*. Retrieved June 2025, from https://www.ed.gov/sites/ed/files/documents/ai-report/ai-report.pdf.

[44] Kementerian Digital. (n.d.). PDP Act 2010 • Personal Data Protection. https://www.pdp.gov.my/ppdpv1/en/akta/pdp-act-2010/

[45] Vorobyeva, K. I., Belous, S., Savchenko, N. V., Smirnova, L. M., Nikitina, S. A., & Zhdanov, S. P. (2025). Personalized learning through AI: Pedagogical approaches and critical insights. *Contemporary Educational Technology*, *17*(2). https://doi.org/10.30935/cedtech/16108

[46] Huang, L. (2023). Ethics of Artificial Intelligence in Education: Student Privacy and Data Protection. *Science Insights Education Frontiers, 16*(2), 2577–2587. https://doi.org/10.15354/sief.23.re202

[47] Giuffrida, I., & Hall, A. (2023). Technology integration in higher education and student privacy beyond learning environments—A comparison of the UK and US perspective. *British Journal of Educational Technology, 54*(6), 1587–1603. https://doi.org/10.1111/bjet.13375

[48] Yapar, O. (2023). Explainable AI in national security: Enhancing trust and accountability. *Journal of Emerging Technologies and Innovative Research (JETIR), 10*(12), 1–20. https://www.jetir.org/

[49] Pillai, V. (2024). Enhancing transparency and understanding in AI decision-making processes. *Iconic Research and Engineering Journals, 8*(1), 168

[50] Adenubi, A. O., Samuel, N., & Karimu, A. Y. (2024). AI-driven synergistic model for enhancing intellectual property, cybersecurity, and privacy protection in academic research. *Kasu Journal of Computer Science, 1*(3), 451–464. https://doi.org/10.47514/kjcs/2024.1.3.003

[51] Modi, T. B. (2023). Artificial intelligence ethics and fairness: A study to address bias and fairness issues in AI systems, and the ethical implications of AI applications. *Revista Review Index Journal of Multidisciplinary, 3*(2), 24–35. https://doi.org/10.31305/rrijm2023.v03.n02.004

[52] Demertzis, K., Iliadis, L., Tziritas, N., & Kikiras, P. (2020). Anomaly detection via blockchained deep learning smart contracts in Industry 4.0. *Neural Computing and Applications.* https://doi.org/10.1007/s00521-020-05189-8

[53] Kashefi, P., Kashefi, Y., & Ghafouri Mirsaraei, A. (2024). Shaping the future of AI: Balancing innovation and ethics in global regulation. *Uniform Law Review, 29*(3), 524–548. https://doi.org/10.1093/ulr/unae040

[54] Samtani, S., Kantarcioglu, M., & Chen, H. (2020). Trailblazing the artificial intelligence for cybersecurity discipline: A multi-disciplinary research roadmap. *ACM Transactions on Management Information Systems, 11*(4), Article 17. https://doi.org/10.1145/3430360

[55] Yigitcanlar, T., Desouza, K. C., Butler, L., & Roozkhosh, F. (2020). Contributions and risks of artificial intelligence (AI) in building smarter cities: Insights from a systematic review of the literature. *Energies, 13*(6), 1473. https://doi.org/10.3390/en13061473

[56] Roshanaei, M., & Jachura, M. G. (2025). Integrating AI in Cybersecurity Higher Education: A path to workforce readiness. *Journal of Intelligent*

Learning Systems and Applications, *17*(02), 45–67. https://doi.org/10.4236/jilsa.2025.172005

[57] Bernama. (2023, July 3). *University-fintech industry collaboration can produce cybersecurity experts - Mohamed Khaled*. BERNAMA. https://bernama.com/en/news.php?id=2170819

[58] Lam, T. (2023, July 20). *Swinburne Sarawak strengthens collaboration with Cybersecurity Malaysia: Swinburne University, Sarawak, Malaysia*. Swinburne University, Sarawak, Malaysia | Swinburne University of Technology | Sarawak | Malaysia. https://www.swinburne.edu.my/news/swinburne-sarawak-strengthens-collaboration-with-cybersecurity-malaysia/

3

Safety Mechanisms for Carbon Trading: Challenges, Regulation, and Technological Innovation

Huang Guangnan[1] and Leong Wai Yie[2]

[1,2]INTI International University, Malaysia

Email: i24027006@student.newinti.edu.my; waiyie.leong@newinti.edu.my

Abstract

Carbon emission rights trading is an important policy tool to control and reduce greenhouse gas emissions, such as carbon dioxide, through market mechanisms and to help actively and steadily promote the carbon peak and carbon neutrality. In recent years, the construction of my country's carbon emission rights trading market has been steadily advancing. Whether the carbon trading market can develop stably depends mainly on whether carbon emission rights trading can be completed safely. However, as an emerging trading model, carbon emission rights trading is still in the exploratory stage of trading security. How to ensure the safe trading of carbon emission rights is the top priority of the current carbon trading market development.

3.1 Carbon Trading Background

Climate change has had serious and irreversible impacts on the environment, human life, and the global economy. The main cause of climate change is the emission of various greenhouse gases, especially carbon dioxide, produced by industrial activities [1]. However, as the world's largest developing country, China's carbon dioxide emissions have surpassed those of the United States, making it the country with the largest carbon dioxide emissions in the world. As shown in the news screenshot in Figure 3.1, the national carbon

 DOI: 10.1201/9788743812135-3

Figure 3.1 CCTV-13 reports on the cumulative trading situation of China's carbon market.

market has been launched for one year, with a cumulative transaction volume of nearly 8.5 billion RMB, indicating a huge market transaction volume. As the world's largest carbon emitter, China has issued relevant plans to achieve a carbon peak by 2030 and carbon neutrality by 2060. In order to achieve the dual carbon goals, my country has issued a series of policies to address climate issues and reduce carbon dioxide emissions. One of the most important and long-term measure is to establish and develop a national carbon market and realize carbon trading through financial trading models.

Carbon trading (greenhouse gas emissions trading) is a market-based mechanism aimed at controlling greenhouse gas emissions, especially carbon dioxide emissions, on a global scale. Its roots can be traced back to the 1997 Kyoto Protocol, which first advocated the use of market mechanisms to reduce carbon dioxide emissions [2]. Under the United Nations framework, these quotas can be circulated and traded between developed and developing countries, and between high-emitting companies and environmental companies. Enterprises that adopt high-emission and high-energy consumption development models can reduce carbon emissions in disguise by purchasing carbon emission quotas and achieve intensive production; while low-carbon development enterprises can realize carbon resource monetization by selling carbon emission quotas, thereby promoting the optimization and upgrading of industrial development models. China has adopted a local pilot and national promotion approach, and after ten years of long-term planning, it has gradually completed the construction of a national carbon trading market [3].

Based on the plot development mechanism, China has launched the National Certified Resource Emission Reduction (CCER), which is a greenhouse gas emission reduction actively created by environmental protection projects or enterprises after being approved and registered by an official designated agency [4]. This is also a commodity traded in the Chinese carbon trading market. Similar to the international carbon market trading method, emission-controlled enterprises can directly purchase emission quotas from other low-emission enterprises in the national carbon market, or choose to purchase voluntary emission reductions based on environmental protection projects in the market to offset their own carbon emissions.

On November 26, 2023, the Shenzhen Emissions Exchange held the 2023 Shenzhen International Low Carbon City Carbon Trading Forum, inviting about 400 representatives from domestic and foreign governments, institutions, and enterprises to participate, Figure 3.2 shows some of the key participants in the forum. The theme of the forum is to work together to address climate change and create a green and low-carbon future. The "Implementation Plan for Shenzhen Carbon Trading to Support Carbon Peaking and Carbon Neutrality" was released at the forum, proposing ten key tasks for the development of the carbon market, including deepening the carbon trading mechanism and expanding the coverage of the carbon market. It will also expand the carbon trading ecosystem based on the core climate

Figure 3.2 The 2023 Shenzhen Carbon Trading Forum held in Shenzhen.

platform of the Hong Kong Stock Exchange and deepen the cooperation between the Shenzhen and Hong Kong carbon markets. In addition, the first carbon asset securitization project in Shenzhen was signed, and green finance experts were invited to discuss innovative tools such as carbon bonds and carbon inclusiveness. This forum showcased the interim results of Shenzhen's ten-year exploration of the carbon market. It will promote 32 key tasks of carbon trading to support carbon neutrality around the goal of "carbon peaking and carbon neutrality," deepen the interconnection of the Shenzhen and Hong Kong carbon markets, explore cross-border carbon financial derivatives, and build a green financial hub in the Greater Bay Area.

3.2 Carbon Trading Safety

Carbon trading security refers to ensuring the transparency, fairness, and compliance of the trading process in the carbon emission trading market through effective regulatory mechanisms, technology, and institutional design. Preventing market manipulation, data falsification, fraud, and other behaviors. Maintaining the legitimate rights and interests of market participants and the stable operation of the carbon trading market. The core of carbon trading security lies in ensuring the authenticity of carbon emission data, the reliability of carbon trading platforms, and the effectiveness of regulatory frameworks. With the deepening of global low-carbon awareness, the global carbon market is also developing rapidly. Carbon trading security has become a key factor in ensuring the credibility and long-term sustainable development of the carbon trading market. In recent years, the construction of China's carbon emission trading market has been steadily advancing. However, due to the imperfections of regulatory mechanisms, technology, and institutional design, both parties to the transaction often face many risks during the transaction process.

The carbon emission trading market is a policy market. In order to ensure the stability, clarity, and consistency of policies, it must be supported by an efficient national administrative system and sound market supervision, and it is also required that emission-controlled enterprises accurately disclose energy consumption information. At present, the overall design and development direction of my country's carbon emission trading market has been initially constructed, but there are still many challenges [5]. The core of the carbon trading market lies in the allocation of carbon quotas and corporate compliance, while high-quality, true, and accurate greenhouse gas emission data is the basis and basis for reasonably determining quotas and evaluating corporate compliance. Therefore, accurate accounting and reporting of carbon emissions will become one of the top priorities in the construction of the carbon market. At the same time, a sound trading mechanism and a safe and transparent trading environment are also important tasks for the establishment of the carbon trading market. Stable trading prices are also an important condition for maintaining the stability of the trading market.

The accuracy of carbon emission data is very important for the security of carbon trading. The monitoring, reporting, and verification (MRV) system of corporate emission data must be strictly regulated to prevent data tampering or false reporting. When studying China's carbon trading pilot, the improvement of data quality is a prerequisite for ensuring the effective operation of the market [6]. The transparency and technical security of the trading platform are crucial. The trading system needs to have strong network security protection capabilities to prevent hacker attacks and data leaks. In addition, the design and implementation of the regulatory mechanism also directly affect the security of carbon trading. When analyzing the EU carbon emissions trading system, it is emphasized that strict supervision and transparent trading rules are the key to preventing market manipulation and fraud [7]. The successful experience of the international carbon emissions market shows that the successful operation of the carbon trading market is inseparable from a sound legal framework and cross-sectoral collaboration. The World Bank pointed out in its report "The Status and Trends of Carbon Pricing in 2020" that transparent data disclosure and a strong regulatory framework are important means to prevent market risks [8].

3.3 Related Research

3.3.1 EU market research

Fang G. *et al.* analyzed the impact of price factors on the carbon trading system, drew lessons from the European carbon emission system, used system dynamics to represent price constraints, and designed a carbon emission trading model. The results show that the price of carbon rights is closely related to the market supply and demand relationship, and excessive government participation is not conducive to the development of the entire carbon trading system [9].

Hou *et al.* pointed out that a mature carbon trading market docking mechanism plays a positive role in promoting cross-border cooperation in carbon trading, expanding the scale of the carbon trading market, and increasing the liquidity of the carbon trading market. The EU Emission Trading System (EU-ETS), as the world's largest and longest-running carbon trading market, connects countries that have established carbon trading markets, such as Switzerland, Norway, and Liechtenstein [10].

3.3.2 Insufficient development of my country's carbon market

Guan Zhigui *et al.* proposed corresponding solutions to the problems of the lack of fairness in the allocation of carbon emission quotas and the unclear relationship between the various participants in my country's carbon trading market. My country should accelerate the establishment of a unified national carbon trading market, formulate relevant laws and regulations, and promote exchanges between my country's carbon trading market and other countries to achieve the goal of internationalization [11].

Deng MZ *et al.* believe that the allocation of carbon emission quotas and related legal settings in my country's carbon trading market are imperfect; the market liquidity is poor, mainly supporting spot trading, and trading is concentrated in a certain period of time; there is a lack of perfect policy guidance to enhance the enthusiasm of market participants [12].

Jiang Rui believes that the main reason for these problems is that my country's carbon trading market is still in the early development stage. In the process of establishing a carbon market in a pilot manner, there are problems such as uncoordinated operations between departments, imperfect systems, and unreasonable reward and punishment mechanisms. As a result, when the market is in an emerging state, it is inefficient. Only when the market is relatively mature and develops to a certain scale, the efficiency will be improved [13].

3.3.3 Research on carbon market security

Wang proposed in the article that, in order to establish a more efficient and secure carbon trading method, blockchain-related technologies can be used to apply blockchain to the field of carbon trading. Blockchain technology will provide a credible carbon trading platform, realize the decentralization and standardization of the carbon trading process, and at the same time reduce the difficulty of supervision, improve transaction security, and improve transaction and supervision efficiency [14].

Ye *et al.* proposed in the article that by using blockchain technology, the whole process of enterprise-level carbon trading, including carbon quota issuance, carbon emission records, carbon trading, and carbon compliance, can be recorded, and smart contracts can be used to improve transaction efficiency, reduce management costs, and make transaction data open, transparent, and easy to supervise. At the same time, blockchain technology can realize the privacy protection of personal data and the security protection of corporate data assets through smart contracts. Enhance the security of the carbon trading process [15].

Zheng *et al.* pointed out that the MRV policies, regulations, and management systems in the construction of China's national carbon market MRV system need to be further strengthened, the technical support system needs to be further improved and refined, there is a lack of sufficient financial support and capacity building, and there are multiple challenges such as balancing the administrative and market-oriented management of third-party verification agencies. Establishing and improving the framework design of MRV management, establishing an MRV technical support system, implementing financial support, and carrying out a sustainable capacity building mechanism are important tasks for China to establish a greenhouse gas emission MRV management mechanism [16].

3.4 The Importance of Carbon Trading Security

3.4.1 Importance of secure transactions

Carbon emission trading is a product of global response to climate change. Countries around the world are gradually paying attention to climate and greenhouse gas emissions. So, the most direct thing is to promote international cooperation. The establishment of the carbon market and the proposal of carbon emission trading are precisely because countries around the world are paying attention to climate issues and want to work hard to improve them. The security and transparency of the carbon trading market are the cornerstones of international cooperation. Countries need to ensure the credibility of their carbon markets in order to promote the interconnection of the global carbon market.

Safe carbon trading can also maintain the stability of the carbon trading market and the investment confidence of investors. Now, more and more countries are establishing carbon trading markets, and more and more companies are participating in the carbon trading market. The stability of the carbon trading market is even more important. The stability of the carbon trading market is crucial to the long-term investment decisions of enterprises. Excessive price fluctuations or market collapse will weaken the enthusiasm of enterprises to participate in emission reduction. At the same time, safe and stable carbon trading can also stabilize investors' investment confidence. In this way, with the participation of a large number of enterprises and investors, the uncertainty of the market can be further reduced, and the investment of a large amount of funds will also strengthen the development of low-carbon emission reduction technologies.

A safe carbon trading environment can also ensure the accuracy of emission data and prevent market manipulation and deception. Because carbon trading relies on accurate emission data of each company, the EU carbon market once caused carbon prices to plummet due to falsified emission data, and then strengthened audits to ensure the accuracy of data. It can be seen that data falsification will be effectively reduced under the safe implementation of carbon trading, thereby accurately allocating emission quotas and enhancing market fairness. At the same time, the transparency and supervision of the carbon trading market are crucial, and any manipulation or fraud will weaken the market's credibility and affect the effectiveness of emission reduction.

3.4.2 Problems facing secure exchanges

The most intuitive problem is the limited market coverage. The International Carbon Action Partnership (ICAP) pointed out in the "2023 Global Carbon Market Progress Report" that the emissions covered by China's carbon market only account for 44% of the national total. The national carbon market currently only covers about 4 billion tons per year in the energy industry [17]. The market coverage is single, only a single energy industry. Heavy emission industries such as construction, steel, and chemicals are not covered. It is easy to have "carbon leakage," which will also affect the distribution of carbon emissions. Compared with the data in the "2024 Global Carbon Market Progress Report," the same situation still exists. The total emissions of greenhouse gases are rising, but the emissions covered by China's carbon market are declining, accounting for only 40% of the national total [18]. The specific data is shown in Figures 3.3 and 3.4. The carbon emission coverage industry is still very small, and the traded carbon emissions are far from meeting the needs of development. There has been a slight "carbon leakage" situation.

The price mechanism of China's carbon emission market is also not perfect. From Tables 3.1 and 3.2 below, we can see that there are many carbon emission trading markets in China, and each trading market has its own trading rules, which means that the liquidity of carbon emission rights is very poor. And from the carbon unit price, it can be found that the carbon price in China's carbon trading market fluctuates greatly. The carbon unit price of each trading market is different, and the gap is huge, and the gap with the carbon unit price in Europe is also large. This makes it difficult for carbon prices to motivate enterprises to complete a low-carbon transformation and

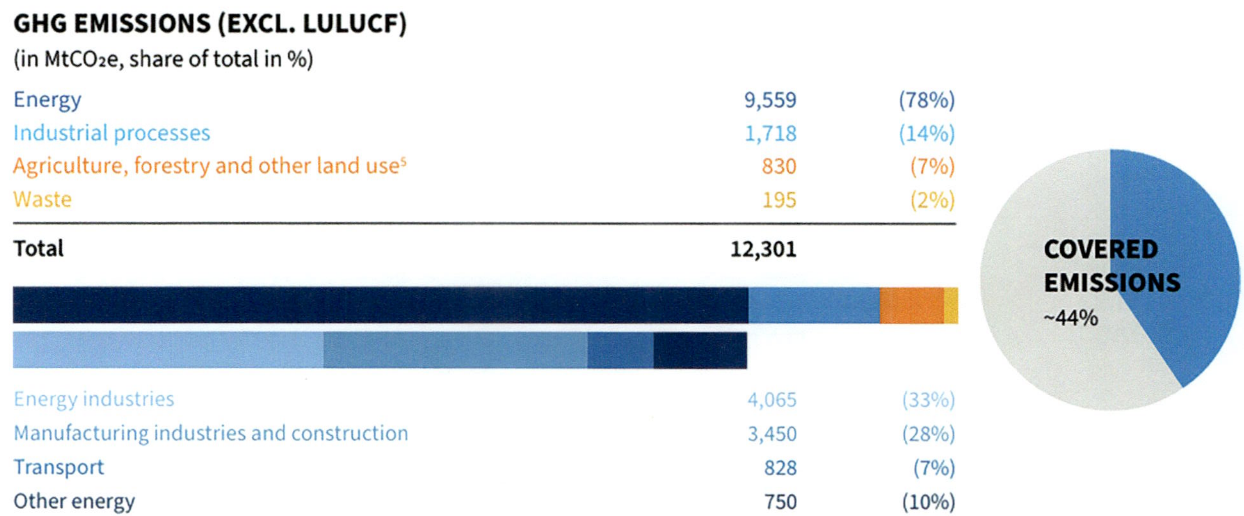

Figure 3.3 China's emissions in the 2023 Global Carbon Market Progress Report.

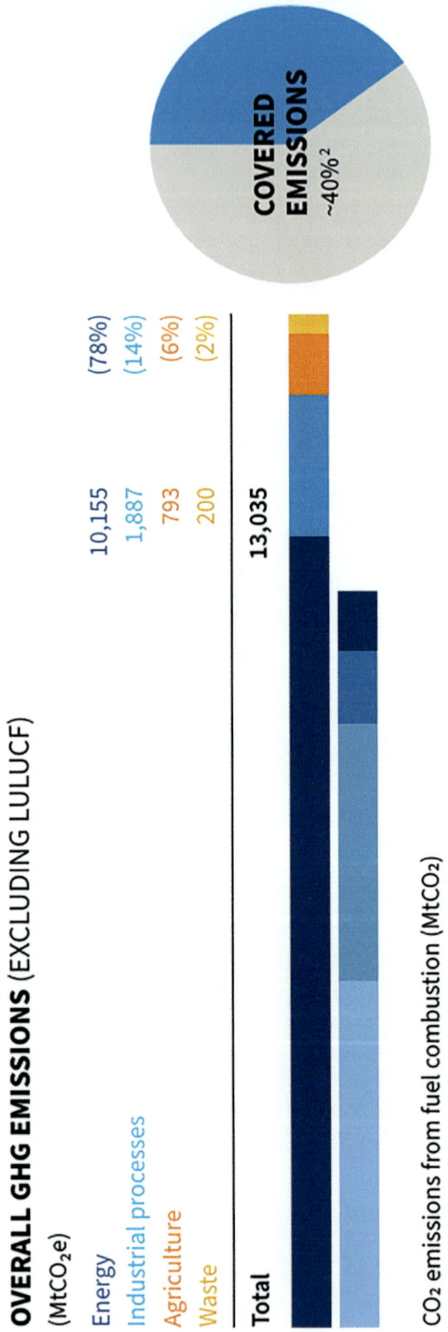

Figure 3.4 China's emissions in the 2024 Global Carbon Market Progress Report.

Table 3.1 Average carbon prices in China's carbon trading markets over the years (RMB/ton).

	China National ETS	Beijing	Fujian	Guangzhou	Hubei	Shanghai	Shenzhen	Chongqing
2014		54.71		16.39				
2015		45.86		12.45				
2016		46.44		13.55	17.65	19.68	25.30	18.79
2017		44.49	28.55	12.46	14.67	12.04	27.39	3.86
2018		46.76	18.9	18.82	22.22	17.51	23.51	9.22
2019		69.64	17.5	25.58	27.25	20.19	25.43	10.77
2020		69.44	17.58	38.13	27.50	25.00	20.11	25.66
2021	46.54	54.7	17.29	70.49	32.04	34.77	27.06	28.66
2022	57.54	91.6	23.6	74.92	46.82	47.98	43.08	36.46
2023	72.12	101.14	32.66	59.87	38.77	67.77	58.75	32.00
2024	87.78	97.72	29.6		41.54	73.39	49.77	43.38

Table 3.2 Average carbon price in the European carbon trading market over the years (Euro/ton).

	European Energy Exchange AG (EEX)	European Climate Exchange (ECX)
2016	4.92	5.10
2017	5.02	5.02
2018	15.86	15.88
2019	24.95	24.98
2020	25.74	25.62
2021	53.31	53.07
2022	80.80	80.89
2023	84.66	85.14
2024	65.55	65.68

fundamentally reduce carbon emissions. China's carbon emission market has not yet established a market-based price mechanism. Prices are affected by many factors, and carbon trading is seriously non-marketized. At present, the completion of carbon emission rights trading in various exchanges is still dominated by the government, and the degree of market participation.

The regulatory framework and relevant laws for carbon emissions are not perfect. The imperfect MRV system leads to inconsistent monitoring of technical standards, and some companies adopt backward accounting methods, resulting in poor data comparability. In addition, due to the lack of legal support, the cost of violations is low, and a large number of violations seriously affect the development of China's carbon market. The effective punishment mechanism of the exchange for breach of contract cannot guarantee smooth performance. The purpose of government-led carbon trading activities is to reduce the damage to the living environment caused by corporate carbon emissions, while the purpose of corporate participation in carbon trading is to maximize profits. The incomplete consistency of the purpose will trigger the moral hazard behavior of enterprises.

The last is the complexity of the trading mechanism. There are many carbon trading markets in China, and local development is given priority when formulating the trading mechanism. This has led to uneven development of local trading markets and increased the difficulty of connecting pilot projects to achieve a unified national carbon market. At the same time, due to different calculation methods and certification conditions, China's carbon emission rights can no longer be traded internationally. This further increases the difficulty of the development of China's carbon market.

The construction of China's carbon market is still not perfect, and there are certain problems in the trading system, regulatory measures, and carbon unit price control. This results in the carbon trading security of China's carbon market cannot be well guaranteed. In addition, China's development strategy is to adhere to the socialist road with Chinese characteristics. This road insists on the equality of all ethnic groups, opposes ethnic oppression and discrimination, and ensures that people of all ethnic groups have equal political rights and are masters of their own house. (Chinese government) Such a road will also mean that the government's control over the market will be very strict, which will affect the market trend to a certain extent. As shown in Figure 3.5. China's construction of a safe carbon trading environment is like building a house. Government policies, financial support, and world trends will be the cornerstones of the development of the carbon market. Asset security, transaction security, and regulatory security will be the pillars.

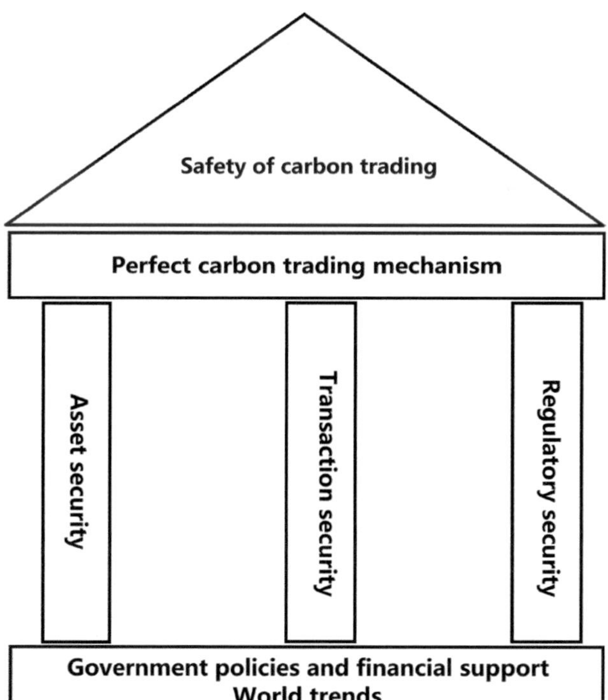

Figure 3.5 Key factors in building a safe carbon market.

Only when the pillars are perfect can a perfect carbon trading mechanism be formed, and finally, the goal of carbon trading security can be achieved.

3.5 How to Stay Safe

3.5.1 Transaction safety

3.5.1.1 Safe trading method

China's carbon trading market is a product registration of carbon emission rights by the National Carbon Emission Rights Registration Agency, as shown in Figure 3.6. And then a centralized and unified trading by the National Carbon Emission Rights Trading Agency. Both agencies will be supervised by relevant national authorities to ensure that all carbon emission rights transactions are legal and compliant.

China's carbon trading market mainly has three trading methods: listed agreement trading, block agreement trading, and one-way bidding trading, shown in Figure 3.7. Listed agreement trading is that the two parties submit buying and selling quotes through the trading system, and the system conducts transactions based on the principle of price priority and time priority, which is similar to stock trading. This method is suitable for small and frequent transactions. Block agreement trading is that after the two parties reach an agreement through negotiation, they conduct block transactions through the trading system. This method is suitable for large and low-frequency transactions. One-way bidding transactions are organized by trading institutions. The seller publishes the subject matter information through the trading system, and the buyer bids within the specified time. Finally, the

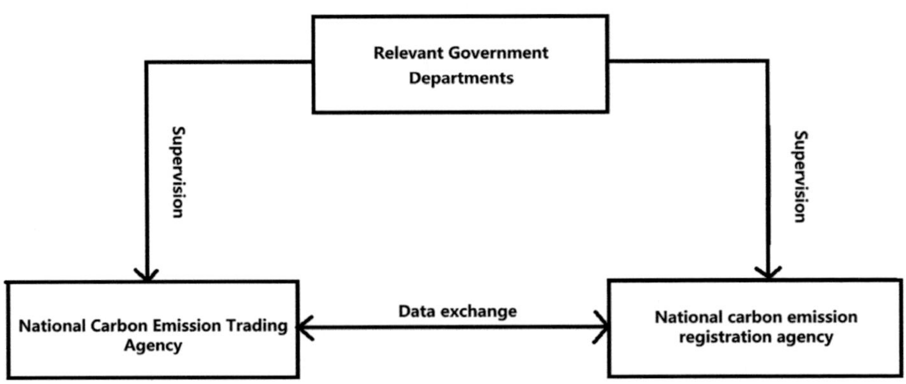

Figure 3.6 Composition of China's carbon trading market.

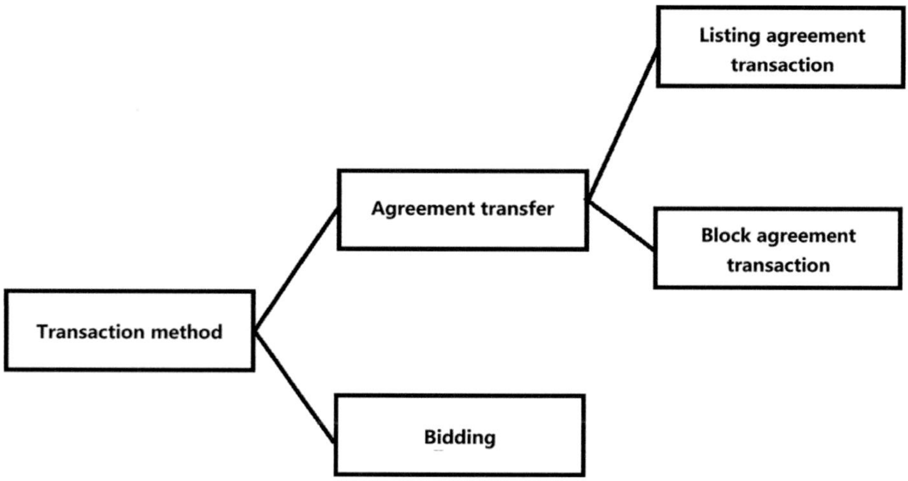

Figure 3.7 Main trading methods in China's carbon market.

transaction is completed based on the principle of price priority and time priority. Agreement transfer is that after the two parties reach an agreement through negotiation, the carbon emission rights are directly transferred without the need for matchmaking through the trading system. This method is suitable for specific, non-public transactions.

Once the transaction is discussed, it will involve the exchange of goods of equal value, and then the transaction of carbon emission rights often involves property transactions. At this time, legal, reasonable, and compliant transactions are particularly important. The most important thing is that the transaction needs to be conducted in a legal transaction area allowed by the country, and both parties to the transaction must have trading qualifications. Listing agreement transactions and one-way bidding transactions often need to be completed through official trading platforms. When obtaining trading qualifications, relevant units often conduct appraisals on the trading parties to ensure that they meet the trading qualifications. However, when using the method of bulk agreement transactions, an agreement may be reached privately. At this time, it is also necessary to pay attention to whether the buyer is operating normally, how is the debt repayment ability, whether it faces prosecution and credit disputes. In the most likely case, the transaction should be conducted through the official government trading platform, which can effectively protect the transaction security of both parties. At the same time, both parties to the transaction need to pay attention to the compliance of the transaction. China has set up a strict trading system for carbon emission rights trading, and it is still being improved. Both parties to the transaction should fully understand the relevant processes of the carbon market, be familiar with and master the trading rules, and avoid rash entry into the market and cause non-compliance of the transaction.

As a new type of transaction, the rights and obligations of both parties to the carbon emission rights transaction also need to be continuously improved, which also requires the signing of a transaction contract to determine. Due to the particularity of carbon emission rights trading, transaction contracts are often very complicated. If the parties to the transaction do not understand the terms of the contract well, there are ambiguities, or they violate the trading rules, it may lead to contract disputes and even legal proceedings. Therefore, both parties to the transaction should attach importance to the setting of important terms of the contract. The content of the contract should strictly abide by the laws and regulations and the trading rules of the exchange, and formulate matching, specific, and feasible transaction plans to prevent transaction risks. The special methods of carbon emission rights, such as transaction methods, settlement methods, and carbon emission quota settlement methods, should also be clearly stated in the contract.

3.5.1.2 Safety of the transaction process

In the process of carbon emission rights trading, the two parties need to exchange a lot of sensitive information, such as transaction price, quantity, identity of the counterparty, etc. If this information is leaked or abused, it may cause economic losses or reputational damage to the two parties. Therefore, privacy issues also need to be paid attention to during the transaction.

For the trading platform, in order to avoid privacy leakage of the two parties, different data access rights can be set according to different user roles to ensure that only relevant personnel can see the authorized information or private information, and sensitive information. And set up relevant personnel to regularly perform technical maintenance on the trading platform to prevent hackers from obtaining the privacy information of the two parties. Supervisors should also be set up to regularly supervise the platform's authority management to prevent some people from selling the privacy information of the trading parties for profit.

At the same time, supervision by third-party inspection agencies and review by relevant departments are also required. The third-party inspection agency is to verify the emissions of enterprises and confirm that the carbon emission rights traded are legal and compliant to ensure the rights and interests of traders. Relevant departments need to regularly monitor the trading platform, review that the trading platform does not leak the privacy data of the trading parties, ensure that the trading platform operates in compliance and legality, and ensure the information and funds of the two parties during the transaction process. At the same time, relevant departments also need to improve laws and regulations based on the implementation situation, and implement legal security protection for the transaction security of traders.

More importantly, data encryption and anonymization technology should be used. Using advanced network technologies such as blockchain, information can be encrypted during the transmission and storage of sensitive information, such as transaction data and privacy data, to protect the security of transaction information and prevent unauthorized access leading to information leakage. It is also necessary to anonymize transaction information, which can first prevent the leakage of transaction information. More importantly, the anonymized data cannot accurately trace the source of transaction information. One of the mainstream trading methods in China's carbon emission trading market is one-way bidding transactions. If the bidding is known, it will be an unfair transaction for all participants in the bidding transaction. Anonymization of transaction information can effectively prevent behind-the-scenes trading operations and reduce the possibility of transaction corruption. Make bidding transactions fairer and more just.

3.5.2 Asset safety

3.5.2.1 Carbon price stability

The essence of transactions in the carbon trading market is the transaction of carbon emission rights, so carbon emission rights are the products in the carbon trading market. The essence of the carbon market is to use the market mechanism, namely the carbon price, to guide high-carbon emission enterprises to save energy and reduce emissions. Therefore, carbon market price analysis takes the first place in the analysis of various parameters in the carbon market.

With the increasing awareness of reducing carbon emissions around the world, many countries or regions have established their own carbon trading systems, such as the European Union Carbon Emission Trading System (EU ETS) and China's national carbon market, which are mainly aimed at their internal enterprises and emission sources. At the same time, Sun proposed in the article that the main sources of carbon emission rights include government-allocated quotas, carbon credits generated by emission reduction projects, internationally transferred emission reduction results, carbon offset mechanisms, and carbon credit needs of specific industries, shown in Figure 3.8 [19].

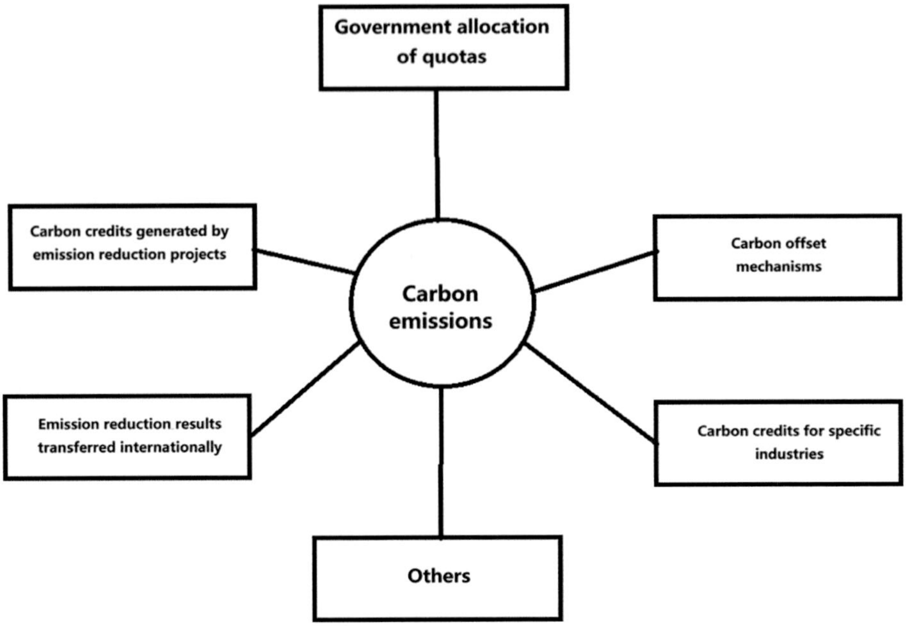

Figure 3.8 Sources of tradable carbon emission rights.

The number of these carbon emission rights is basically fixed, and each company needs to use a certain amount of carbon emission rights to offset the amount of carbon dioxide emitted during the production process of the product. Therefore, the number of carbon emission rights that can be traded is very limited and basically fixed. When the carbon trading market only serves the domestic market, the carbon price is often greatly affected by the supply and demand relationship. The supply is basically unchanged, the price drops when there is oversupply, and the price rises when there is less supply than demand.

With the continuous expansion of the trading market, cross-border transactions will also occur. When the certification of both parties is agreed, the carbon emission rights of the carbon markets of both parties can be traded across borders. The carbon markets of the European Union and Switzerland have been partially connected, allowing cross-market transactions. This means that carbon emission rights can completely become an investment product for investment. This may result in some investors buying at a lower price in different trading markets and then selling at a higher price in other trading markets. At the same time, since carbon prices will increase the production costs of enterprises, changes in carbon prices will also affect the demand of production enterprises. This will have a certain degree of impact on the stability of the carbon trading market. This requires some institutions to constantly understand market conditions, demand, and other influencing factors, and conduct macro-market regulation to keep carbon prices within a reasonable range.

In contrast, our domestic carbon trading market. Since the certification method and calculation methodology are not recognized by the European and American markets, the carbon emission rights of China's carbon market cannot be sold in foreign markets. However, China has established multiple carbon emission rights trading platforms, and the carbon prices of each carbon trading platform are different, as shown in Tables 3.1 and 3.2. From the transaction prices in the table, we can see that whether it is 2014–2020 when the carbon trading market was first established, or 2021–2024 when the carbon market was reopened, there are very significant price differences in the transaction prices of major carbon markets across the country. These huge differences will cause more investors to regard carbon emission rights as investment products rather than production necessities, which will have a huge impact on the stability of China's carbon market. At this time, China's special government control mechanism will need to play a role to stabilize carbon prices at an appropriate level and stabilize China's carbon market.

The diversification of participants in the carbon market will also lead to changes in carbon prices. The carbon emission quotas designated by the government and the numerous participants will have an impact on the demand side of carbon emission rights, and carbon universality and carbon sinks will have an impact on the supply side of carbon emission rights. As shown in the Figure 3.9. Government departments occupy a large leading position in China's carbon trading market, which requires government departments to have a higher degree of specialization and stronger market regulation capabilities. Only in this way can the stability of China's carbon market be better maintained.

3.5.2.2 Is it global

First of all, we must recognize that although carbon trading is global in nature, the carbon trading markets of various countries and regions show obvious differences in operating mechanisms, trading rules, product types, etc. As the only tradable product in the carbon trading market, carbon emission rights have various uses. Carbon emission rights are essential for the production of products and can be used to offset the carbon emissions generated during production. Some producers also sell them as commodities and sell excess carbon emission rights on the open market when their own production is met,

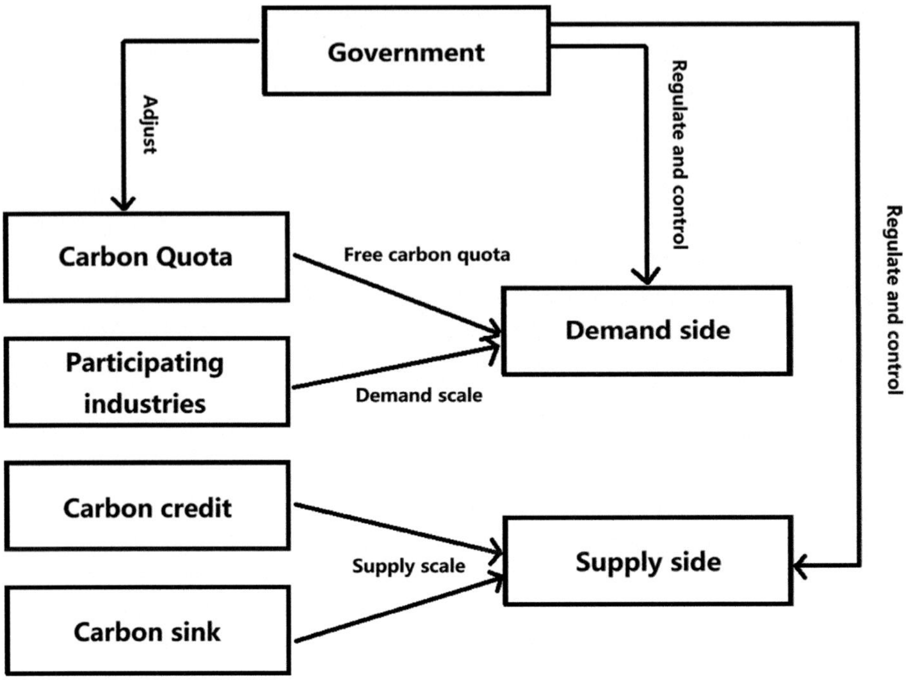

Figure 3.9 Schematic diagram of carbon price impact.

so as to obtain more corporate profits. As a product, if it cannot be sold on the international market, then this product can only be sold in the domestic market. This method is extremely risky. Failure to integrate into the international market means that the country's carbon emission rights can only be sold in the domestic market. If the domestic market becomes saturated or the market collapses due to other reasons, it will be a huge blow to the company's production and operation strategies. Although entering the international market will face challenges such as strict certification standards and numerous competitors, due to the large size of the international market, it is difficult to have market saturation or market collapse, and the risks faced will be greatly reduced.

In the early days of proposing the concept of reducing carbon emissions, Apple changed its corporate operating strategy and fully enjoyed the dividends of carbon emission rights. Apple has reduced carbon emissions by reducing the number of mobile phone accessories given away with the purchase of mobile phones and simplifying the outer packaging of mobile phones. These reduced carbon emissions are sold on the carbon emission market. In addition, the certification and calculation methods of the US carbon emission market and the European carbon emission market are basically the same. Apple can sell the reduced carbon emissions in different markets according to different prices to maximize its benefits.

Moreover, the internationalization of carbon emission rights can also improve the efficiency of the carbon market. Internationalized carbon emission rights can increase market liquidity, reduce price fluctuations, and improve the transparency and stability of the carbon market. This helps to attract more participants to participate in carbon trading. The internationalization of carbon emission rights can enhance market efficiency by expanding the tradable scale and improving liquidity, thereby better playing the role of carbon pricing. Internationalized carbon emission rights can promote the innovation and diffusion of emission reduction technologies and promote capital flows to developing countries and emerging economies. This will not only help reduce global emissions but also support sustainable development.

All products are working toward internationalization, because the higher the degree of internationalization, the more challenges they face, and the more they can improve themselves according to their shortcomings, thus gaining more stability. The same is true for carbon emission rights. Although internationalization faces risks such as transaction prices and certification methods, it will also face a larger market volume, a more stable carbon trading market, and a fairer carbon price, which will greatly improve the security of carbon assets. For ordinary investors, the internationalization of carbon emission rights can also give more confidence. The most direct thing is that international carbon emission rights can be traded in the international market without fear of losing the value of carbon assets due to fluctuations in the local carbon market.

3.5.3 Regulatory safety

In the process of carbon market construction, high-quality greenhouse gas emission data is the basis of carbon trading, and accurate accounting and reporting of greenhouse gas emissions will become a key task of the carbon market. In this context, China must establish a greenhouse gas emission data management mechanism characterized by measurability, reportability, and verifiability, namely the MRV management mechanism. The core of carbon trading is carbon emission trading quotas, which need to be measured, reported, and verified in the MRV management mechanism of the carbon market before they can be traded. At present, the internationally recognized MRV management mechanism can be divided into four categories according to different climate change policies, actions, and measures, namely corporate reporting MRV, emission reduction project MRV, national inventory MRV, and policy emission reduction effect MRV.

In contrast, China's special development model, and the carbon trading market has just started, the enterprises subject to carbon emission supervision are basically large industrial enterprises. First of all, improving the enterprise reporting MRV management mechanism is the biggest help to China's carbon market construction. The MRV management mechanism mainly consists of three parts: measurement, reporting, and verification. Measurement is generally completed by the national competent department, which counts and calculates the greenhouse gas emissions of each enterprise and conducts accounting. The report is issued by the relevant enterprises under emission monitoring every once in a while, according to the production situation, and the specific emission volume is made public. The report must also be submitted to the relevant departments and third-party verification departments for verification to ensure the accuracy of the public data. Verification refers to the verification by a certified professional third-party organization based on the emission report issued by the regulated enterprise to ensure that the emission volume is not falsified. Figure 3.10 shows the operating framework of China's MRV regulatory mechanism [20].

From the working operation diagram, we can see that the MRV management mechanism of enterprise carbon emissions has been basically completed, and the inspection system with national departments, emission enterprises, and supervisory agencies as the main components has also been initially improved. However, where there is profit, there will be ugliness. Carbon trading, as an emerging industry, is a trend pursued by countries around the world, and the future prospects will be unlimited. This will also make profit-seekers want to find ways to seek personal gain in such a strict inspection procedure. From Figure 3.10, it can be seen that the central department is responsible for top-level design, establishment of laws and regulations, market construction, management authorization, and information disclosure, while the specific supervision power lies with the local competent department. This means that if local enterprises or verification enterprises buy off the personnel of local competent departments or the staff of supervisory agencies and provide false information disclosure to official departments, then the MRV management mechanism will be difficult to implement. A national competent department should be added to supervise local competent departments to ensure that local competent departments have great power to implement the MRV management mechanism, but will not abuse power and fail to supervise, resulting in the failure of the supervision system.

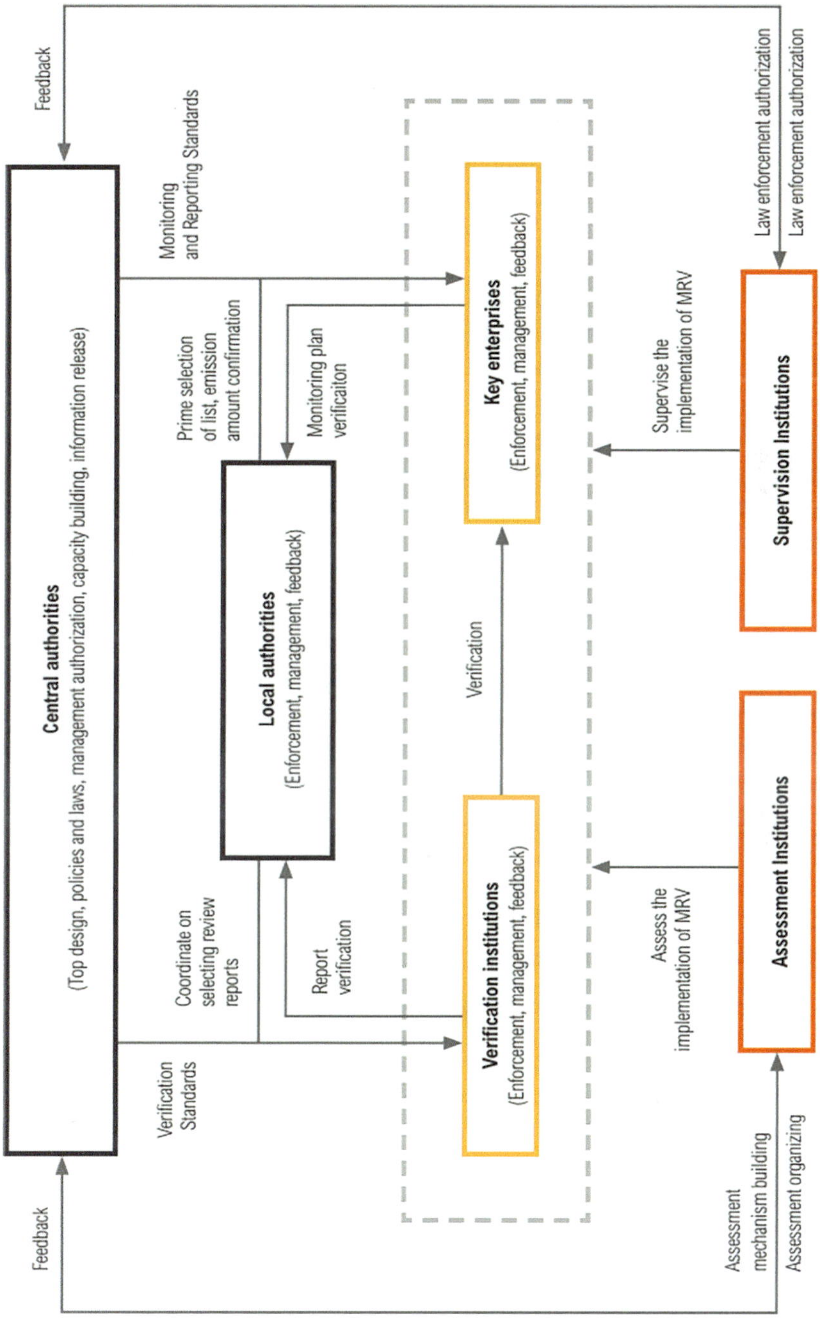

Figure 3.10 Schematic diagram of enterprise MRV operation.

In addition, verification agencies and key regulated enterprises can also adopt anonymization when submitting emission reports, and relevant departments can only obtain the core data that needs to be reviewed when conducting reviews. This method can effectively avoid the cover-up behavior of government departments and corporate departments, and can also prevent the risk of privacy leakage of related companies. At the same time, due to the anonymization of the supervision and assessment agencies when performing their supervisory duties, they cannot obtain the specific names of the companies that issued the reports in the first place, which also reduces the cover-up behavior in supervision to a certain extent.

With the development of China's carbon market, the shortcomings of the MRV management mechanism will gradually emerge. Governments at all levels should increase financial support and capacity building for the construction of the MRV management mechanism, continue to carry out relevant training, and improve management skills. At the same time, enterprises and verification agencies should continue to strengthen their own capabilities and improve the data quality management level and verification capabilities within the enterprise.

The most important thing is the supervision of the people. It is far from enough to rely solely on the supervision of government departments and relevant supervision agencies. The following Figure 3.11 shows the supervision mechanism of the United States. The carbon emissions of the supervised enterprises will be summarized, processed, and made public on the relevant webpage, so that people across the country can play the role of supervision and monitor whether the enterprises are compliant with the emissions [21].

3.6 The integration of blockchain and carbon trading security

3.6.1 Improve transparency and security

The addition of blockchain improves transparency and security. Using the open ledger method, a public ledger is created through blockchain technology to ensure that all carbon credit transaction information is transparent and cannot be tampered with. This allows the generation, trading and cancellation of carbon credits to be tracked and verified by anyone with blockchain access, thereby reducing the risk of fraud and double counting. Combined with privacy computing technology, carbon emission data can be verified but not visible during the sharing process, ensuring data security while realizing data sharing within the industry.

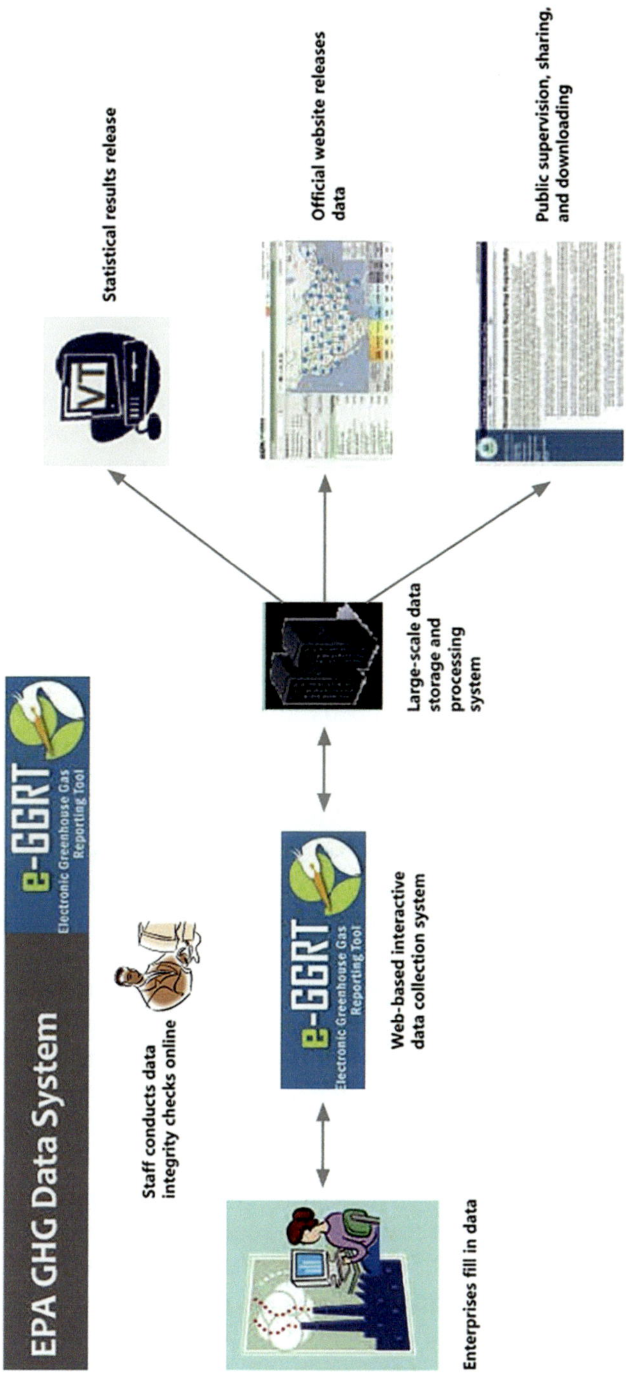

Figure 3.11 Schematic diagram of carbon emissions monitoring in the United States.

It also facilitates multi-party collaboration. The open ledger facilitates collaboration between multiple parties such as governments, enterprises, and third-party verification agencies, forming a real and credible data sharing and exchange environment, and providing a visible, credible, and reliable environment for carbon emission supervision. And because blockchain technology provides an immutable and auditable record ownership, the uploaded data is almost impossible to modify, which also reduces the possibility of fraud and increases trust and accountability in the carbon market.

3.6.2 Smart contracts

Smart contracts can automatically execute the certification, trading, and cancellation of carbon credits, reduce errors in human operations, and increase the degree of automation of the entire process. This automation not only simplifies the trading and compliance process of carbon credits, but also reduces the need for intermediaries, thereby reducing transaction costs. Blockchain can also automatically process, transmit, and store transaction information through smart contract technology, and optimize the results based on the consensus mechanism.

Wang pointed out in the article that smart contracts use carbon coins to complete transactions. This also needs to pay attention to some problems. First of all, carbon coins are the smallest trading unit and cannot be further split. Only integer payments can be made. However, carbon prices change every day with market conditions. When carbon prices are converted into carbon coins, they are not integers, so there will be an inconsistency when using carbon coins for payment. Secondly, the use of blockchain technology is to better realize the internationalization of carbon trading, but the carbon prices in various trading markets are different. Whether carbon coins can be exchanged for payment in equal proportion and whether all trading markets allow carbon coins to be paid will be a problem that needs to be solved. Finally, there is the credit issue. Carbon coins are essentially a virtual currency, which requires both parties to the transaction to exchange real funds into virtual currency before they can be traded. If trading in this way, carbon coins should be guaranteed by the government or a trustworthy third-party institution. Only in this way can the transaction be greatly trusted by both parties to the transaction, so as to complete the transaction by electronic contracts. In addition, the degree of regulation of smart contracts varies around the world, and the legal effect of smart contracts also varies. In the process of international transactions, this situation is prone to cause transaction disputes.

3.6.3 Improve the mechanism of rights protection, risk prevention, and control for breach of contract

Blockchain can realize transaction traceability, data storage, and credit rating, etc., to help users and regulatory judicial departments to protect their rights. In addition, the timestamp and hash value guarantee the authenticity, relevance, and legality of the required electronic data, and ensure the admissibility and probative force of evidence when providing evidence for rights protection, thereby reducing the cost of rights protection. Introduce a credit rating system, record the default information in the blockchain, affect the credit score, and then affect the transaction priority. Through this mechanism, the transaction subject is forced to trade in good faith and reduce the negative effects of default.

From Figure 3.12, due to the decentralized point-to-point transaction characteristics of blockchain technology, time and trust costs are reduced, making carbon trading more efficient and convenient. Blockchain technology weakens the role of the intermediary platform, thereby reducing transaction costs and improving the efficiency of carbon trading. Since the role of the intermediary platform is weakened, it is equivalent to reducing the role of the carbon trading market in disguise. In order to build a carbon trading market and facilitate the supervision of government departments, the constructed blockchain trading platform should be supervised by government departments to prevent the occurrence of illegal transactions.

3.7 Conclusion

Carbon trading security is the cornerstone of the stable operation of the carbon emission rights trading market, and is a key factor in ensuring that the market mechanism effectively plays a role in emission reduction and safeguarding the legitimate rights and interests of market participants. As the world's attention to climate change continues to deepen, carbon trading, as an innovative environmental and economic policy tool, is gradually becoming an important means for countries to respond to climate change and promote green development. And the healthy development of the carbon trading market is inseparable from solid security guarantees, which involves data authenticity, trading platform security, regulatory mechanism effectiveness, and market participants' compliance.

The authenticity of carbon emission data is the core of carbon trading security. Greenhouse gas emission data is the basis for the operation of the carbon market. The accuracy of the data is directly related to the reasonable

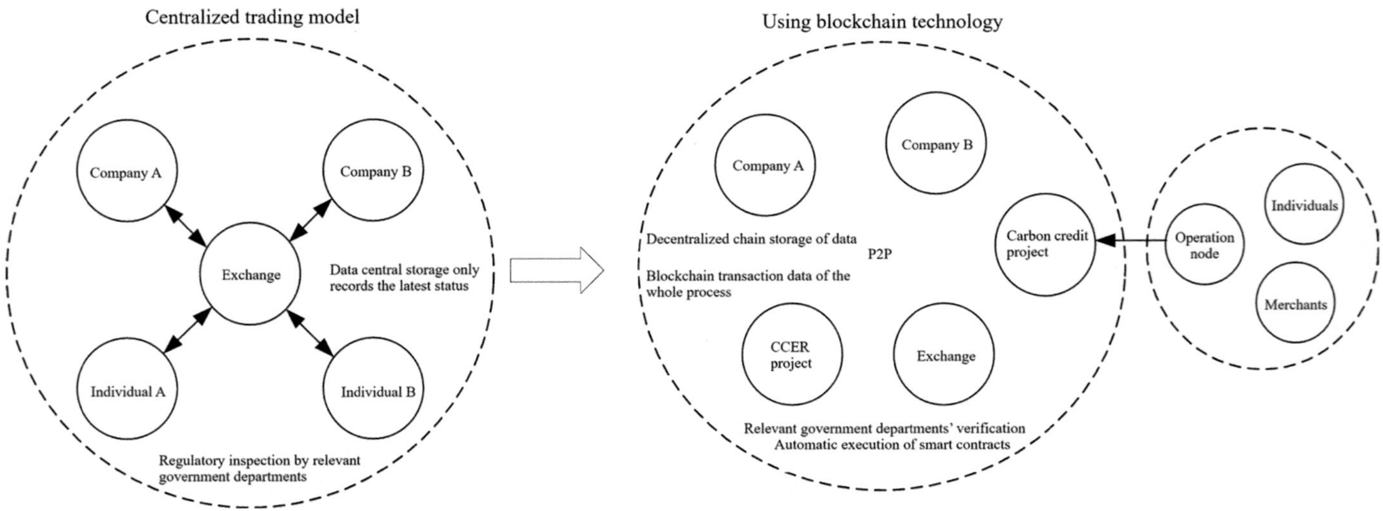

Figure 3.12 Comparison between the traditional centralized trading model and the "blockchain" model.

allocation of carbon quotas, the assessment of corporate compliance, and the fairness of market prices. Therefore, it is crucial to establish a scientific and strict monitoring, reporting, and verification (MRV) system. This system requires companies to comprehensively and accurately record their greenhouse gas emissions and ensure the authenticity and credibility of the data through independent verification by third-party institutions. At the same time, the government and relevant agencies should also strengthen the supervision of corporate emission data, crack down on data falsification, and maintain the credibility of the carbon market.

The security and transparency of the trading platform are important conditions for ensuring the smooth progress of carbon trading. As a medium for carbon trading, the technical security and transaction transparency of the trading platform are directly related to the interests and confidence of market participants. The trading platform should have strong network security protection capabilities to prevent hacker attacks and data leakage, and ensure the safe transmission and storage of trading information. The trading platform should also provide an open and transparent trading environment so that market participants can fully understand trading rules, price trends, and other information, reduce information asymmetry risks, and improve market efficiency.

At the regulatory level, an effective regulatory mechanism is an important guarantee for maintaining the security of carbon trading. The government should establish a sound carbon trading legal and regulatory system, clarify the rules and standards of carbon trading, and provide clear legal guidance for market participants. Regulatory authorities should strengthen daily supervision of the carbon trading market, supervise and inspect the behavior of market participants, and prevent illegal and irregular behaviors such as market manipulation and fraud. Relevant government departments should also strengthen cooperation and exchanges with the international community, learn from the successful experience of the international carbon trading market, and continuously improve my country's carbon trading regulatory mechanism.

The compliance of market participants is also an important part of carbon trading security that cannot be ignored. As the main participants in the carbon market, enterprises should strictly abide by carbon trading rules and laws and regulations, actively fulfill their emission reduction responsibilities and obligations, and avoid non-compliant behaviors when participating in the market. Investors and other market participants should maintain a rational investment attitude, fully understand the risks and opportunities of the carbon trading market, and avoid blindly following trends and speculative behavior.

Faced with the rapid development and changes in the global carbon market, China, as one of the largest developing countries and carbon emitters, also faces many challenges and opportunities in carbon trading security. China should continue to strengthen the institutional construction and supervision of the carbon trading market and improve the transparency and credibility of the market. It should also actively participate in the cooperation and exchanges of the international carbon trading market and promote the standardization and standardization of the global carbon market.

The integration of blockchain and carbon trading builds a transparent and reliable data system through public ledgers and privacy computing technology, significantly reducing the risk of fraud. Smart contracts realize the automated management of the entire life cycle of carbon credits and reduce intermediary costs, but the carbon coin mechanism it relies on faces challenges in payment accuracy and market adaptation, and needs to solve the problems of cross-border exchange rate conversion, legal effect, and credit guarantee. It can promote the coordinated governance of multiple parties between government and enterprises, and strengthen market accountability through tamper-proof traceability and evidence storage. Decentralized transactions reduce trust costs and improve market efficiency. In the future, it is necessary to break through the technical bottleneck of carbon coin segmentation, establish a global legal mutual recognition framework, promote the evolution of blockchain carbon trading toward standardization and internationalization, and release the dual effectiveness of climate governance and green finance.

Carbon trading security is the premise and guarantee for the healthy and stable development of the carbon market. By strengthening the authenticity management of carbon emission data, improving the security and transparency of the trading platform, improving the regulatory mechanism, and improving the compliance of market participants, we can effectively maintain the security and stability of the carbon trading market and promote carbon trading to play a more active role in addressing climate change and promoting green development.

Reference

[1] Olivier JG, Schure K, Peters J. Trends in global CO2 and total greenhouse gas emissions. J. PBL Netherlands Environmental Assessment Agency. 2017,5, 1-11.

[2] Chen Lin and Wan Panbing, 2019. The Kyoto Protocol and its Clean Development Mechanism's Emission Reduction Effects: Micro-project

data on China's Participation in Global Environmental Governance. J. Economic Research Journal. 2019,54(03), 55-71

[3] Li Danping, Xu Xiaodong, and Liu Chenxi, 2021. A review of the theory and development practice of carbon trading markets at home and abroad. J. Gansu Finance. 2021,(09), 14-18.

[4] Ministry of Ecological Environment, People's Republic of China. (2020). Administrative Measures for Carbon Emissions Trading (Trial). [Online]. Available at: https://www.gov.cn/zhengce/zhengceku/2021-01/06/content_5577360.htm (Accessed: March 14, 2025)

[5] Zhou Jian, Deng Yirong and Zhuang Changwei, 2020. Development Process, Current Situation and Prospect of China's Carbon Trading Market. J. Environmental Science and Management. 2020,45(09), 1-4.

[6] Zhang, Z. X., 2015. Carbon Emissions Trading in China: The Evolution from Pilots to a Nationwide Scheme. J. China Economic Review. 35, 3-17.

[7] Ellerman, A. D., and Buchner, B. K., 2007. The European Union Emissions Trading Scheme: Origins, Allocation, and Early Results. J. Review of Environmental Economics and Policy. 2017, 1(1), 66-87.

[8] World Bank,2020. State and Trends of Carbon Pricing 2020. World Bank Group.

[9] Fang G, Tian L, Liu M et al., 2018. How to optimize the development of carbon trading in China- Enlightenment from the evolution rules of the EU carbon trading price. J. Applied Energy. 2018,211, 1039-1049.

[10] Hou Yanlei and Wei Wei, 2023. Learn from the experience of the EU carbon trading market connection mechanism to promote the orderly development of my country's carbon trading market. J. China Economic & Trade Herald. 2023,(02), 53-56.

[11] Guan Zhigui, Tian Xuebin, 2019. Can carbon market policies reduce regional carbon emissions? —An empirical study based on China's provincial panel data. J. Inner Mongolia Social Science. 2019,40(01), 126-132. DOI:10.14137/j.cnki.issn1003-5281.2019.01.020.

[12] Deng MZ, Zhang WX, 2019. Recognition and analysis of potential risks in China's carbon emission trading markets. J. Advances in Climate Change Research. 2019,10(1). 30-46.

[13] Jiang Rui, 2017. China's Carbon Market Today and Suggestions. J. Sino-Global Energy. 2017,22(01), 3-9.

[14] Wang Weiwei, 2023. Design and implementation of an efficient and secure carbon trading solution based on blockchain. D. Nanjing Normal University.

[15] Ye Qiang, Gao Yuechao, and Jiang Guangxin, 2022. The Structure Design of China Blockchain Carbon Market for the Future Big Data Environment. J. Management World. 2022,1, 229-249. DOI:10.19744/j.cnki.11-1235/f.2022.0017.

[16] Zheng Shuang, Zhang Xin, Liu Haiyan et al., 2016. Supporting China's National Carbon Market With Effective MRV for GHG Data. World Resources Institute. 2016,1, 1-32.

[17] International Carbon Action Partnership (2023). Emissions Trading Worldwide Status Report 2023.

[18] International Carbon Action Partnership (2024). Emissions Trading Worldwide Status Report 2024.

[19] Sun Xuewei, 2024. Analysis and enlightenment of the construction of the EU carbon trading market system. J. Finance and Accounting for International Commerce. 2024,(09):12-19.

[20] Liu Zimin, Li Li and Li xing, 2025. Assessment and design of the carbon price of China's carbon market. J. Journal of statistics and information, 2025,40(1):77-91.

[21] Tan Caixia, Geng Shiping, Tan Zhongfu et al., 2025. Study on China's dynamic carbon price based on multiple mechanisms and entities under the "Dual Carbon" policy. J. Systems Engineering — Theory & Practice. 1-12. doi: 10.12011/SETP2023-1846

4

Ambient AI in Action: Revolutionizing Clinical Environments for Safer, Smarter Care

Norana Abdul Rahman[1] and Vaikunthan Rajaratnam[2]

[1]Honorary Senior Lecturer, RCSI & UCD Malaysia Campus, Georgetown, Penang, Malaysia
[2]Khoo Teck Puat Hospital, Singapore

Email: ar.norana_pt@rumc.edu.my; vaikunthan.rajaratnam@nhghealth.com.sg

Abstract

Ambient artificial intelligence (AI) is transforming healthcare by seamlessly embedding intelligent technologies into clinical environments to create responsive, adaptive, and patient-centred care settings. Unlike traditional AI systems that require explicit user input, ambient AI operates unobtrusively in the background, continuously monitoring patients, automating clinical documentation, and supporting real-time decision-making. This chapter explores the applications, case studies, and future directions of ambient AI across clinical settings, with a focus on improving patient safety, reducing clinician burnout, and enhancing operational efficiency.

Key applications examined include automated clinical documentation through AI scribes, real-time patient monitoring, optimised hospital operations, and enhanced coding and billing processes. Evidence from case studies at Stanford Health Care and the Permanente Medical Groups demonstrates that ambient AI scribes significantly reduce documentation time, improve physician–patient interaction, and produce high-quality clinical notes. The chapter further presents a series of original use cases developed by the authors, including an EMR assistant that converts ambient clinical recordings into structured electronic medical records, and the OrthoConsent assistant, a

 DOI: 10.1201/9788743812135-4

retrieval-augmented generation (RAG) chatbot designed to facilitate informed consent for orthopaedic procedures using accessible, patient-friendly language.

The chapter also addresses challenges surrounding data privacy, technological limitations, and the need for robust regulatory frameworks. Looking ahead, the integration of ambient AI with predictive analytics, virtual and augmented reality, and voice-first interfaces, holds promise for further transforming healthcare delivery. Ultimately, ambient AI represents a paradigm shift toward proactive, personalised, and efficient care — one that empowers both patients and healthcare professionals in an increasingly digital age.

Ambient artificial intelligence is revolutionizing the healthcare sector by seamlessly integrating intelligent technologies into the environment to create responsive and adaptive surroundings. This innovative approach involves embedding sensors, processors, and actuators in everyday devices, and the physical setting, enabling continuous data gathering, and analysis to address various healthcare needs proactively. Ambient AI systems can detect subtle changes in a patient's condition, provide real-time alerts to healthcare providers, and even anticipate potential health issues before they become critical [1].

In clinical environments, this means that patient rooms, waiting areas, and even hallways can be equipped with ambient AI technologies that monitor vital signs, track patient movements, and ensure that healthcare providers have immediate access to critical information. This leads to a more efficient allocation of resources and a reduction in response times during emergencies. For example, ambient AI can automatically adjust lighting and temperature in a patient's room to enhance comfort and recovery or deploy robotic assistants to deliver medications and supplies [2].

Furthermore, ambient AI enhances communication between patients and healthcare providers. Through voice-activated interfaces and wearable devices, patients can easily report symptoms, request assistance, and receive personalized health advice without the need for direct interaction with medical staff. This is particularly beneficial for patients with mobility issues or those living in remote areas, as it reduces the need for frequent hospital visits and enables continuous, remote monitoring [3].

The continuous data collected by ambient AI systems also contributes to the advancement of medical research. By analyzing large datasets, researchers can identify patterns and trends that lead to a better understanding of diseases, improved treatment protocols, and the development of preventative strategies. This data-driven approach promises to accelerate the pace of medical discoveries and innovations.

Ambient AI represents a significant leap forward in healthcare delivery. Its ability to operate unobtrusively in the background, provide personalized care, and support healthcare professionals in their daily tasks transforms clinical environments into dynamic, adaptive spaces focused on patient well-being and safety. As this technology continues to evolve, it will undoubtedly play a crucial role in shaping the future of healthcare [4].

Unlike traditional AI systems that rely on explicit user input, ambient AI operates in the background, utilizing contextual cues to detect and respond to patient needs. This includes recognizing a patient's arrival through their identification badge or identifying a patient who has been waiting for an extended period. The integration of ambient AI into healthcare settings offers numerous benefits, including enhancing patient autonomy and empowering individuals to play a more active role in their care [3, 5].

The development of intelligent medical technologies has enabled the emergence of a new field in medicine known as "augmented medicine," where advanced technologies are used to improve various aspects of clinical practice [5].

AI-based algorithms have already been approved for use in healthcare, and their potential to transform the industry is widely recognized. Ambient AI, in particular, holds promise in areas such as medication management, where it can analyze patient data to help healthcare providers optimize medication regimens and reduce the risk of adverse drug events.

4.1 Understanding Ambient AI in Healthcare

The integration of ambient AI into healthcare settings can significantly benefit those living in remote areas or with mobility issues, as it allows for remote monitoring and personalized care. Additionally, ambient AI can support healthcare personnel by automating administrative tasks, enhancing clinical documentation, and providing specialized assistance in areas like image analysis and patient monitoring.

As the healthcare industry continues to embrace the transformative power of ambient AI, it is crucial to consider the ethical implications and ensure that these technologies are developed and implemented responsibly and equitably. Appropriate safeguards and oversight are necessary to prevent the misuse or abuse of ambient AI and to ensure that it is deployed in a way that prioritizes the interests and well-being of patients [6].

Through the seamless integration of ambient AI, the healthcare sector can unlock new possibilities in patient-centric care, empowering individuals and improving outcomes. Ambient AI systems are designed to be unobtrusive and user-friendly, working seamlessly to enhance the healthcare experience for both patients and providers. This technology has the potential to improve patient care by enabling personalized interventions, optimizing operational efficiency, and facilitating information extraction from various sources [4].

4.2 Applications of Ambient AI in Clinical Environments

Ambient AI is being applied in diverse ways across clinical settings, transforming how healthcare is delivered and experienced. These applications can be categorized into three main areas. One involves embedding sensors, processors, and actuators in everyday devices and physical settings, enabling continuous data gathering and analysis to address healthcare needs proactively. Ambient AI systems can detect subtle changes in a patient's condition, provide real-time alerts to healthcare providers, and anticipate potential health issues before they become critical. This technology enhances communication between patients and healthcare providers, supports remote monitoring, and contributes to medical research by analyzing large datasets. As a result, ambient AI improves patient care, operational efficiency, and overall healthcare outcomes.

Clinical documentation can capture patient–provider conversations, generate real-time transcripts, and create accurate clinical notes. This reduces the administrative burden on clinicians and enhances the quality of medical records.

In hospital operations, ambient AI optimizes efficiency by monitoring staff performance, identifying workflow bottlenecks, and providing real-time insights into operational processes. This leads to better resource allocation and improves overall efficiency. Additionally, ambient AI enhances coding and billing processes by accurately capturing doctor-patient interactions, streamlining the documentation needed for billing, and reducing administrative workloads while improving financial efficiency.

Ambient AI enhances healthcare delivery by improving access to information, patient safety, and communication. Clinicians can easily access patient records from multiple institutions and systems, leading to better-informed decisions and improved care outcomes. Additionally, ambient AI provides real-time analytics, enabling quick identification of issues in patient care plans or treatment regimens, which enhances patient safety and supports proactive interventions.

Through clinical alerts, ambient AI ensures timely notifications about patients requiring attention, further improving safety and facilitating prompt action. It also streamlines patient communication by automating tasks such as medication orders and appointment scheduling, and ensuring timely consultation with the right doctors. Integrated electronic health record (EHR) systems enhance this capability by sending customized reminders to patients, increasing satisfaction and engagement with their care. These applications are summarized in Tables 4.1, 4.2, and 4.3.

Philpot and coworkers discuss the growing challenges faced by current healthcare delivery models, such as increasing demand for healthcare

Table 4.1 Improving patient care.

Application	Description	Benefits
Personalized care	Ambient AI can be used to provide personalized care for patients based on their condition and history.	Improved patient outcomes and increased patient satisfaction.
Pain management	Facial recognition and voice data collected by sensors can be used to detect pain in patients.	Improved pain management and increased patient comfort.
Remote patient monitoring	AI-powered wearables and contactless sensors help providers monitor patients remotely.	Improved patient safety, early detection of potential risks, and continuous care for patients.

Table 4.2 Enhancing operational efficiency.

Application	Description	Benefits
Automating clinical documentation	Ambient AI can capture patient–provider conversations, generate transcripts, and create clinical notes in real time.	Reduced administrative burden on clinicians and improved accuracy and quality of medical records.
Optimizing hospital operations	Ambient AI can help improve the coordination of hospital operations by monitoring staff performance, identifying bottlenecks in workflow processes, and providing real-time information about how well these processes are working.	Improved efficiency and better resource allocation.
Improving coding and billing processes	Ambient AI can help healthcare organizations accurately capture the doctor–patient encounter and improve the coding and billing process.	Reduced administrative burden and improved financial efficiency.

services, rising costs, and the limitations of traditional methods. It addresses the need for a comprehensive approach to integrate technology into healthcare to overcome these obstacles.

To tackle these challenges, the Digital Care Horizon framework is introduced. This framework aims to guide the digital transformation within healthcare systems, emphasizing the adoption of various digital health technologies such as ambient AI, telemedicine, telehealth, mobile health (mHealth), and health information technology. By implementing these technologies, healthcare providers can enhance patient–provider engagement, enable efficient

Table 4.3 Supporting clinical decisions.

Application	Description	Benefits
Accessing patient records	Clinicians can use ambient AI to access patient records from different institutions and systems more efficiently.	Improved access to information and better-informed decisions.
Real-time analytics	Ambient AI can provide clinicians with access to real-time analytics, allowing them to quickly identify issues with patients' care plans or treatment regimens.	Improved patient safety and proactive interventions.
Clinical alerts	Ambient AI can provide clinicians with quick access to alerts about patients who might need attention soon.	Improved patient safety and timely interventions.
Patient communication	Ambient AI can help automate tasks like ordering medications, scheduling appointments, and ensuring the right doctor sees patients in a timely fashion. Some integrated EHR software uses this clinical technology to send patients custom text reminders before scheduled appointments.	Improved patient communication and increased patient satisfaction.

data sharing, and offer personalized care. Ultimately, the Digital Care Horizon framework seeks to improve access to healthcare, enhance patient experiences, and reduce overall costs.

This framework has significant implications (summarized in Figure 4.1). By integrating digital health solutions, healthcare systems can offer more customized and efficient care, addressing the mismatch between services provided and patients' actual needs. The framework also emphasizes the importance of partnerships and overcoming challenges to extend digital healthcare services beyond traditional settings [7].

The omnichannel digital experience framework exemplifies how ambient AI aligns with the principles of **Industry 5.0**, transforming healthcare into a more **human-centric**, **sustainable**, and **resilient** system. By integrating face-to-face care, telemedicine, telemonitoring, and facilitated self-care with population health management, this framework illustrates the seamless incorporation of advanced technologies into healthcare delivery. Ambient AI enhances patient outcomes, empowers self-care, and streamlines clinical workflows through real-time data insights and adaptive interventions. The convergence of these technologies fosters a proactive and scalable healthcare ecosystem, addressing critical challenges such as clinician burnout, care

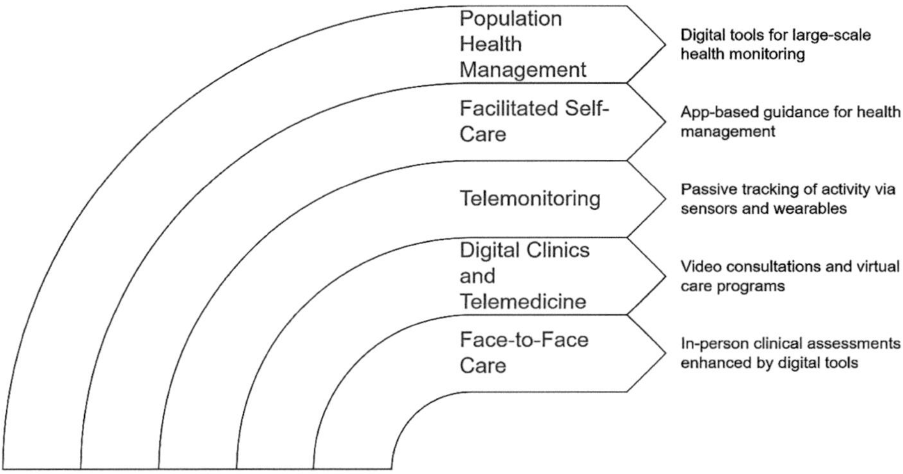

Figure 4.1 Five-tier omnichannel digital experience model (adapted from [7]).

accessibility, and operational inefficiencies. This integration not only redefines patient-centered care but also ensures that healthcare systems remain robust and responsive in a rapidly evolving digital age.

4.3 Case Studies and Examples

Several healthcare organizations are adopting ambient AI to enhance clinical workflows and patient care. The paper "The Effect of Ambient Artificial Intelligence Notes on Provider Burnout" analyzes how this technology affects provider burnout. The study conducted at Stanford Health Care involving 48 physicians over 3 months demonstrated significant reductions in task load and burnout, along with improvements in usability. Access to the full article requires a purchase, with short-term access options available in various currencies. The webpage also offers information on accessing content through institutional or personal accounts, as well as guidance for librarians on managing subscriptions. The study suggests that ambient AI can alleviate documentation burdens, improve operational efficiency, and enhance provider well-being, making it a promising intervention to combat burnout in healthcare settings [8].

Another study by the Permanente Medical Groups showed that an ambient AI scribe reduced documentation time for physicians and improved patient interaction [9]. Here are the key findings of this study.

Another study by the Permanente Medical Groups demonstrated that the use of ambient AI scribes significantly reduced documentation time for physicians and improved their interaction with patients. Key findings from this study include the following:

Firstly, ambient AI scribes substantially decreased the time clinicians spent on documentation, both during and outside of patient consultations. This reduction in clerical work helped alleviate clinician burnout and job dissatisfaction. Secondly, the use of AI scribes allowed physicians to spend more time interacting with their patients, thereby enhancing the quality of care and communication. Patients reported better interactions with their physicians when AI scribes were used.

Additionally, the AI-generated transcripts and summaries were found to be of high quality, scoring an average of 48 out of 50 in key domains such as accuracy, organization, and freedom from bias. However, some inconsistencies and hallucinations were noted, necessitating physician review and editing.

Both clinicians and patients welcomed ambient AI scribes. Clinicians appreciated the reduction in after-hours clerical work, and patients felt more engaged during their visits. Despite the promising results, the technology requires ongoing enhancements, including better integration with electronic health records (EHR), support for multiple languages, and improved workflow personalization options.

Nonetheless, implementing AI scribes faced several challenges, such as the need for direct EHR integration and overcoming initial technical difficulties. Continuous evaluation and adaptation are essential to address these hurdles and optimize the use of the technology. These findings highlight the potential of ambient AI scribes to transform clinical documentation processes, improve clinician well-being, and enhance patient care (Figure 4.2).

4.4 Impact on Patient Safety and Care Quality

Ambient AI has a significant impact on patient safety and the quality of care provided in healthcare settings. By automating various tasks and equipping clinicians with real-time information, ambient AI effectively reduces medical errors and enhances the accuracy of diagnoses and treatments. This technology streamlines clinical workflows, allowing healthcare providers to make more informed decisions quickly and efficiently [10].

One of ambient AI's most notable advantages is its capability for continuous patient monitoring. These AI-powered systems can keep a vigilant eye on patients, even in the comfort of their own homes. This constant

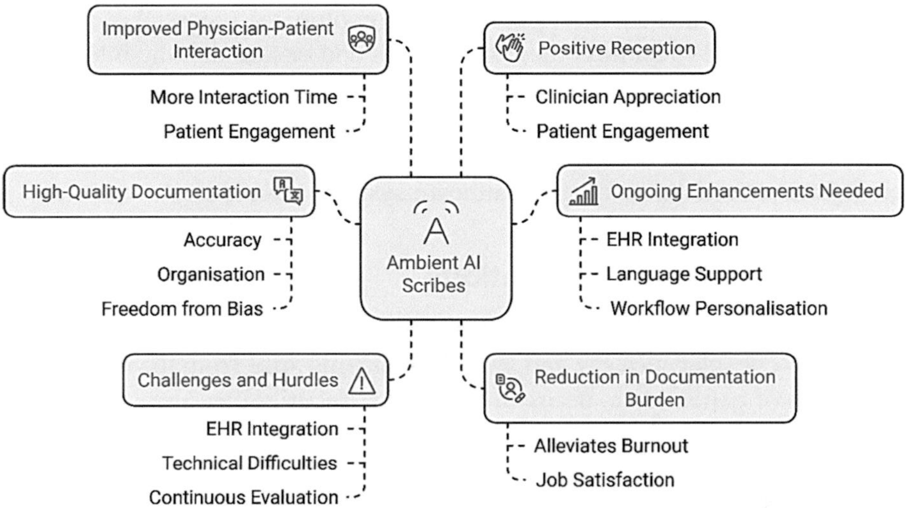

Figure 4.2 Impact of ambient AI on healthcare.

surveillance allows for the early detection of potential health risks and timely interventions, which significantly enhances patient safety and helps prevent adverse events. The prompt identification and management of health issues are crucial in maintaining patient well-being and improving clinical outcomes [11].

Additionally, ambient AI facilitates better coordination of care by providing healthcare professionals with seamless access to patient information. This easy access enables efficient communication between various healthcare providers, ensuring that patient care is well-coordinated and delivered in a timely manner. The integration of ambient AI into the healthcare system also supports the optimization of medication management. By analyzing patient data such as prescription histories and vital signs, ambient AI helps healthcare providers to optimize medication regimens, thereby minimizing the risk of adverse drug events.

Despite the myriad benefits, the deployment of ambient AI in healthcare settings does come with challenges. Issues such as data privacy and security [12], technological limitations [13], and the need for robust regulatory frameworks must be addressed to ensure the safe, ethical, and effective use of these technologies. As the healthcare industry continues to explore the potential of ambient AI, it is essential to approach its integration thoughtfully and responsibly [14], [15].

As the healthcare industry continues to explore the potential of ambient AI, it is essential to address these challenges and ensure that the integration of these technologies is done responsibly and thoughtfully. In the long term, the successful implementation of ambient AI in healthcare has the potential to revolutionize patient care, improve outcomes, and enhance the overall efficiency and effectiveness of the healthcare system [16–18].

4.5 Challenges and Limitations

While ambient AI offers significant potential, there are challenges and limitations to consider: Privacy and security concerns arise from the continuous collection of patient data, necessitating robust security measures and ethical guidelines to ensure data protection. Accuracy and reliability are also critical, as ambient AI systems depend on precise data interpretation and analysis. Technical errors, algorithmic biases, or misinterpretation of information can lead to inaccurate results and potentially compromise patient safety.

Moreover, integrating ambient AI systems with existing electronic health records (EHRs) and other healthcare technologies can be complex and requires significant effort to ensure seamless interoperability. The cost and implementation efforts involved in deploying ambient AI solutions are substantial, necessitating investments in infrastructure, software, and training.

Lastly, the quality of data input into AI algorithms is paramount for accurate outcomes. Hospital data, often complex and unfiltered, requires considerable cleaning before it can be effectively utilized, posing a significant operational challenge.

Overall, while ambient AI offers significant advantages, it is essential to address the challenges associated with its integration into healthcare systems to ensure that these technologies are used responsibly and effectively (Figure 4.3).

4.6 Ethical Considerations

The use of ambient AI in healthcare raises significant ethical considerations that must be carefully examined. Ensuring patients are informed about the use of ambient AI and have the opportunity to provide consent is crucial. This includes transparent communication about how their data will be collected, analyzed, and utilized to improve patient care.

Establishing clear guidelines on data ownership, access, and control is essential to protect patient privacy and maintain ethical standards. It is important to define who has the right to access and use the data and under

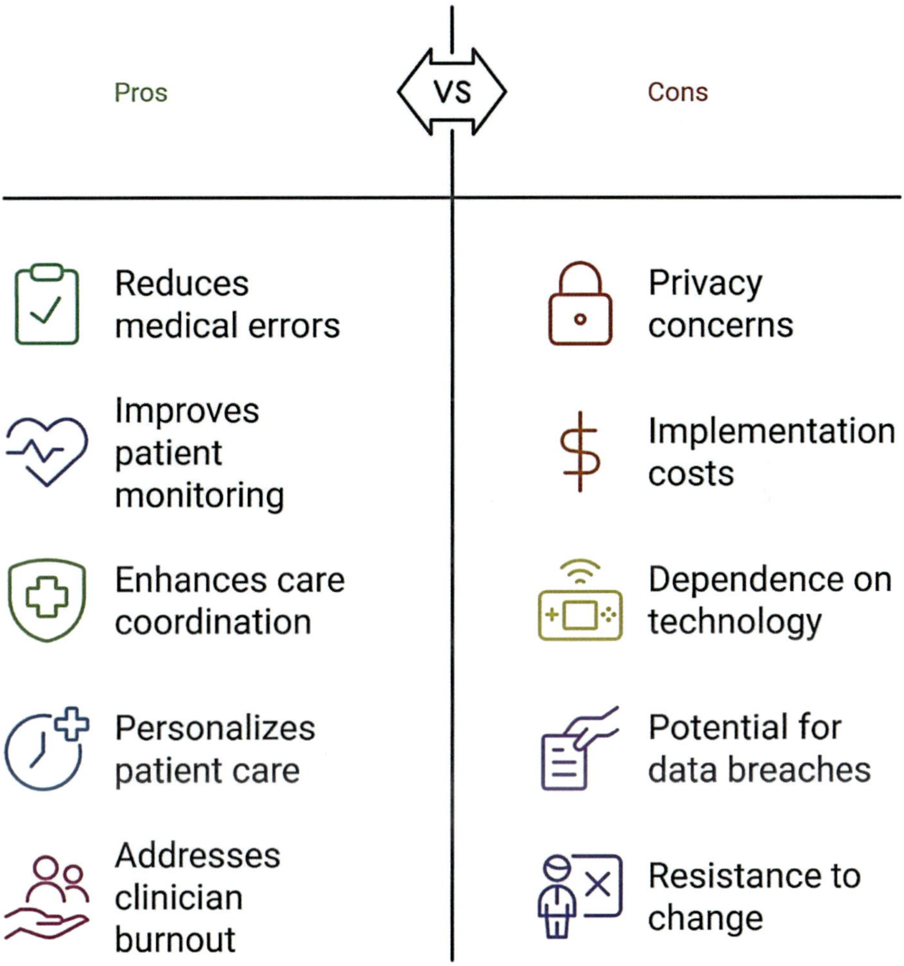

Figure 4.3 Ambient AI in healthcare.

what circumstances. Patients should have control over their data and be able to decide who can access it.

Addressing potential biases in AI algorithms and ensuring fairness in data collection and analysis is critical to avoid perpetuating existing healthcare disparities. AI systems must be trained on diverse and representative datasets to prevent biased outcomes that could disproportionately affect certain patient groups. Regular audits and updates of these systems are necessary to maintain their accuracy and fairness.

Maintaining transparency in how ambient AI systems operate and ensuring accountability for their actions is essential to building trust and addressing potential concerns. Healthcare providers must be transparent about the capabilities and limitations of AI systems and ensure a straightforward process for addressing any errors or issues that may arise.

Additionally, hospitals may ethically use ambient intelligent systems to record healthcare workers without consent as long as the recording is taking place in quasi-public spaces, the goal is to improve patient care, proper safeguards are in place to protect individual privacy, and workers are informed that this will be taking place. These measures help balance the benefits of ambient AI with the need to respect individual privacy and autonomy.

To support the integration of ambient AI, healthcare institutions must invest in infrastructure, software, and training. This includes ensuring that AI systems are compatible with existing electronic health records (EHRs) and other technologies to facilitate seamless interoperability. Proper training for healthcare professionals on the use and limitations of AI systems is essential to maximize their potential benefits and minimize risks.

In summary, while ambient AI holds immense potential for transforming healthcare, it is imperative to address the ethical, technical, and operational challenges associated with its implementation (Figure 4.4). By

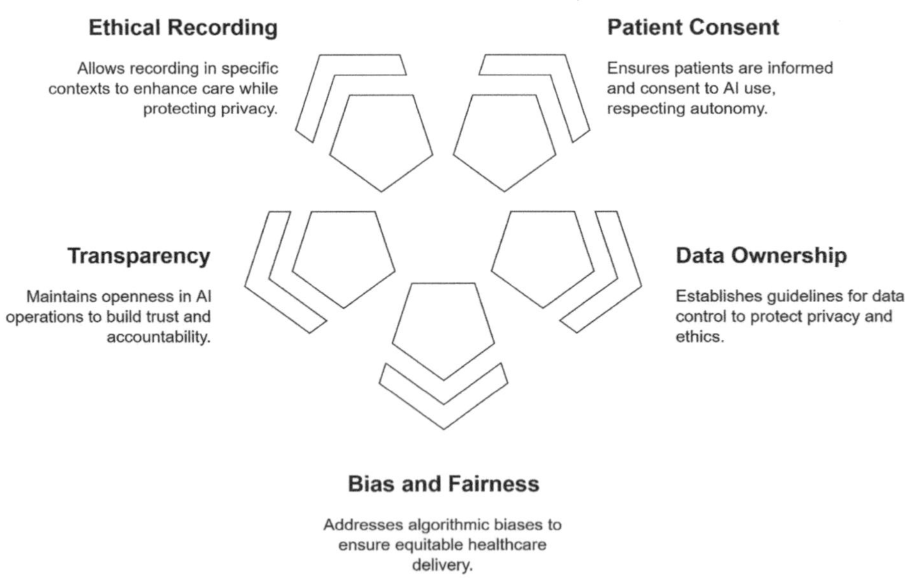

Figure 4.4 Ethical framework for ambient AI in healthcare.

doing so, we can harness the power of AI to improve patient outcomes, reduce clinician burnout, and create a more efficient and equitable healthcare system.

4.7 The Future of Ambient AI in Healthcare

Ambient AI is rapidly evolving, and its future in healthcare holds immense potential. Advancements in sensor technology, AI algorithms, and data analytics will further enhance the capabilities of ambient AI systems, leading to more sophisticated and personalized healthcare solutions.

Predictive Analytics and Proactive Interventions: Ambient AI has the potential to revolutionize healthcare by shifting from reactive to proactive care. This technology can predict patient needs and provide timely interventions. For example, it can alert healthcare professionals to potential risks and automatically adjust treatment plans based on real-time data. This proactive approach can enhance efficiency and significantly improve patient outcomes.

Integration with Virtual and Augmented Reality: The future of ambient AI in healthcare also includes integration with virtual and augmented reality (VR and AR). These technologies can create immersive training experiences for healthcare professionals, simulate complex surgical procedures, and assist in patient education and rehabilitation. By combining ambient AI with VR and AR, we can develop more effective and personalized healthcare solutions.

Enhanced Clinical Decision Support: Ambient AI can provide clinicians with comprehensive real-time data, enabling them to make more informed and personalized clinical decisions. This enhanced decision support can lead to better patient care and outcomes. For instance, ambient AI can analyze large datasets to identify patterns and trends that might not be apparent to human clinicians, thus supporting more accurate diagnoses and treatment plans.

Addressing Limitations in Clinical Documentation: One of the current limitations of ambient documentation tools is their inability to add particular clinical codes to notes, which can affect the quality and downstream use of this data. Future advancements in ambient AI will focus on improving its capability to convert unstructured text into structured, coded clinical data, incorporating additional context from the patient's record. This improvement will enhance the accuracy and usefulness of clinical documentation.

Voice-First Capabilities: Some ambient listening tools already incorporate voice-first technologies, enabling healthcare providers to interact with the system using natural language. This capability can make it easier and more efficient for clinicians to document patient interactions, access information, and manage workflows without being tied to a computer screen.

Reducing Clinician Burnout: Ambient AI can play a crucial role in addressing clinician burnout, a significant issue that costs the US healthcare system an estimated $4.6 billion annually. By automating routine tasks, providing decision support, and reducing administrative burdens, ambient AI can help alleviate the stress and workload on healthcare professionals, leading to improved job satisfaction and better patient care.

Ambient AI holds immense potential for transforming the future of healthcare. By addressing ethical considerations, technical challenges, and operational barriers, we can harness the power of AI to create a more efficient, equitable, and patient-centered healthcare system. The integration of predictive analytics, VR and AR, enhanced clinical decision support, and advanced documentation tools will pave the way for more sophisticated and personalized healthcare solutions.

4.8 Use Case of Ambient Clinical Recording in Healthcare

4.8.1 MyGPT in the OpenAI GPT platform

MyGPT refers to customized instances of the OpenAI GPT model designed to cater to a specific user or organizational needs. This feature enables users to personalize and configure GPT's capabilities to align with their unique requirements, offering a bespoke AI experience. Users can adjust settings such as tone, style, and verbosity while also training the model on specific datasets to enhance its relevance for particular domains. This flexibility allows MyGPT to integrate seamlessly into professional workflows, whether for generating clinical summaries in healthcare, lesson plans in education, or marketing content in business operations.

The platform's customization extends to integrating APIs, enabling dynamic, real-time input and output, and incorporating content safeguards to adhere to ethical or industry standards. MyGPT instances can be used to automate documentation, summarize reports, or draft correspondence, thereby improving productivity across various applications. Accessible through user-friendly interfaces or integrated into existing systems, MyGPT (Figure 4.5) offers scalability for individuals and organizations alike, empowering users to harness the potential of generative AI in a way that meets their specific goals and enhances their efficiency.

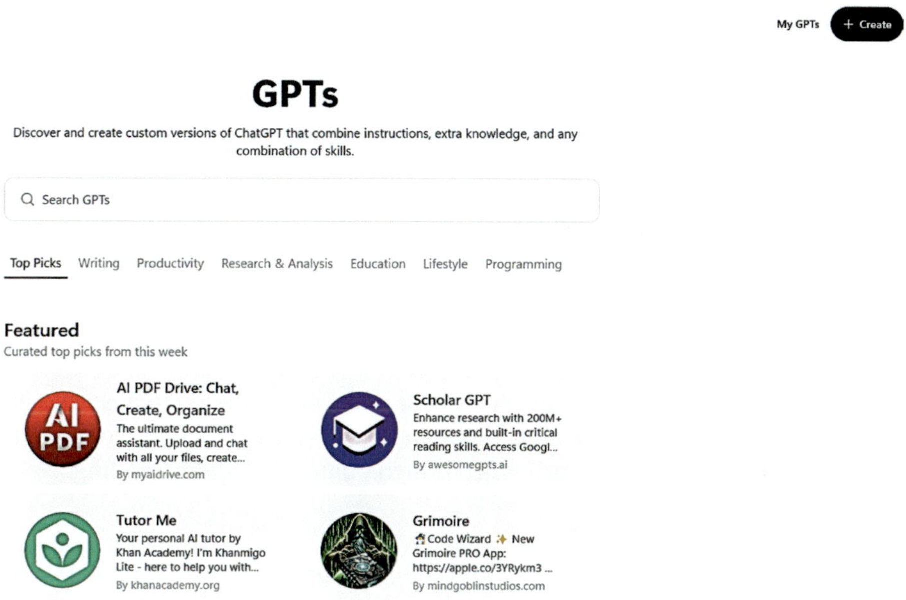

Figure 4.5 MyGPT in OpenAI's ChatGPT platform.

4.8.2 AI assistants vs AI chatbots

While AI assistants and AI chatbots share foundational similarities, they differ significantly in functionality, complexity, and scope of application. Using MyGPT as an example, these distinctions become evident through their unique contributions to healthcare.

4.8.2.1 AI assistant

An AI assistant is a sophisticated tool designed to perform complex tasks, provide advanced decision support, and integrate seamlessly with various systems to enhance workflows. It transcends basic conversational capabilities to support comprehensive operations.

Key characteristics:

- **Purpose:** Task execution, decision support, and advanced problem-solving.
- **Capabilities:** Performs operations like scheduling, drafting documents, analyzing data, and managing workflows.

- **Integrations:** Connect with external platforms, such as calendars, EMR systems, or CRM tools.
- **Personalization:** Learns and adapts to user preferences over time.

Example with MyGPT:

- A MyGPT AI assistant can summarize research papers, draft medical reports, or retrieve patient records from an EMR system, offering substantial value in a healthcare setting.

4.8.2.2 AI Chatbot

An AI chatbot is primarily a conversational interface designed to answer user queries and guide users through predefined workflows. Its functionality is focused on structured dialogues with limited contextual understanding.

Key characteristics:

- **Purpose:** Information retrieval, customer support, or interactive FAQs.
- **Capabilities:** Handles straightforward conversations and frequently asked questions.
- **Integrations:** Minimal integration with external systems.
- **Personalization:** Limited adaptability, designed for general use cases.

Example with MyGPT:

- A MyGPT AI Chatbot could assist patients by answering common questions about a healthcare facility, such as its services, appointment booking process, or operational hours.

The key differences between AI assistants and AI chatbots are summarized in Table 4.4.

Applications of MyGPT:

As an AI assistant:

- **Personalized Education Tutor:** Provides tailored learning paths and tracks student progress.
- **Business Analyst:** Integrates with financial systems to generate detailed reports.

Table 4.4 Comparison table AI assistance and AI chatbot.

Feature	AI assistant	AI chatbot
Complexity	High	Medium to low
Primary function	Task execution and problem-solving	Information and query handling
Customization	Extensive, tailored per user	Predefined responses
Learning capability	Learns from user interactions	Limited or static capabilities
Integration	Deep integration with tools/ systems	Minimal integration
Example (MyGPT)	Summarizes research papers, generates reports, and integrates with EMR	Answers FAQs on medical services

- **Research Companion:** Retrieves and summarizes research papers with accurate citations.

As a chatbot:

- **Customer Support Tool**: Answers FAQs on healthcare services and operations.
- **Interactive Help Desk:** Assists users in navigating platforms and finding information.
- **Healthcare Guide:** Provides general information for patients, such as preparing for visits.

4.8.3 Introducing the EMR assistant – a use case of ambient AI recording (Figure 4.6)

Beyond the general applications, the senior author, VR, utilized MyGPT to develop an EMR assistant specifically designed to enhance clinical documentation and streamline workflow efficiency. This bespoke solution includes:

- Automated Clinical Encounter Transcription:
  - Transcribes verbal interactions during clinical consultations into structured documentation.

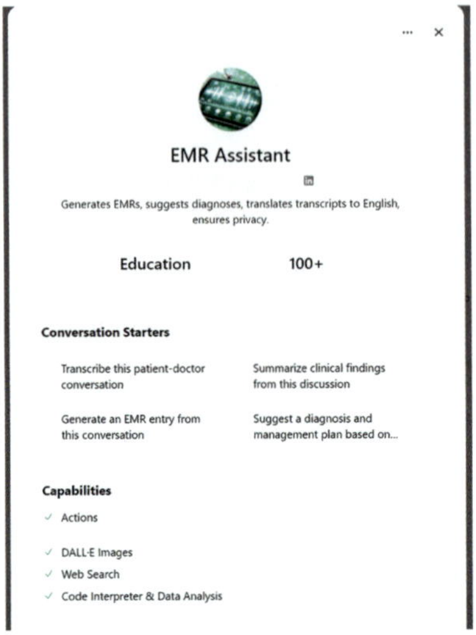

Figure 4.6 The EMR assistant on the OpenAI MyGPT platform.

- ○ Automatically generates EMRs with detailed summaries of history-taking, diagnostic discussions, and management plans.

- Consent Documentation and Management:
  - ○ Guides clinicians and patients through informed consent processes with clear, layman-friendly explanations of procedures, risks, and benefits.
  - ○ Ensures compliance with legal and ethical standards through embedded consent documentation tools.
- Diagnostic and Management Support:
  - ○ Suggests potential diagnoses with ICD-11 codes based on patient history and symptoms.
  - ○ Generates personalized management plans aligned with evidence-based guidelines.

Through these innovations, the EMR assistant leverages the power of MyGPT to improve the accuracy and efficiency of clinical documentation significantly.

The distinction between AI assistants and AI chatbots lies in their depth and scope of functionality. While AI chatbots excel in simple query handling and structured conversations, AI assistants like MyGPT offer robust, multifunctional tools for task automation, system integration, and decision support. These capabilities are exemplified in specialized healthcare use cases, such as the EMR assistant, which revolutionizes clinical workflows, enhances patient care through efficient documentation, and ensures seamless integration with healthcare systems. The choice between these tools ultimately depends on the user's needs, ranging from essential guidance to comprehensive operational support.

4.8.4 Setting up an AI assistant with MyGPT of OpenAI

4.8.4.1 Define your purpose and scope

Decide what you want your AI assistant to do:

- **Use cases:** Is it for research, medical education, business analytics, or general assistance?
- **Target audience:** Consider who will interact with the assistant – students, healthcare professionals, or executives.
- **Functionality:** Specify if it requires integrations (e.g., with EMR, LMS, or CMS platforms).

4.8.4.2 Access MyGPT on OpenAI

- Log in to your OpenAI account.
- Navigate to the MyGPT section, where you can create a custom GPT model.
- Review the documentation on MyGPT customization options.

4.8.4.3 Customize your AI assistant

Language and tone:

- Set the tone (formal, conversational, technical) and default language (UK English, in your case).

Fine-tuning:

- Prepare datasets or examples for fine-tuning. Include conversational styles and domain-specific knowledge.
- Use OpenAI's fine-tuning API to train the model to meet your needs.

Plugins and APIs:

- Decide if you need third-party integrations for your assistant (e.g., calendar scheduling, EMR access, or database search tools like PubMed).
- Enable plugins to enhance functionality, such as retrieving live data or automating workflows.

4.8.4.4 Develop a user interface

- Platform: Choose how users will access the assistant (e.g., web app, mobile app, desktop).
- UI design: Design a simple and user-friendly interface for interaction.

4.8.4.5 Deploy the assistant

- Host it on a secure cloud service (e.g., AWS, Azure, or OpenAI hosting).
- Ensure scalability and reliability based on expected usage.

4.8.4.6 Ensure privacy and security

- Implement data encryption and adhere to privacy laws (e.g., GDPR, HIPAA if healthcare-related).
- Create a privacy policy detailing data use and retention.

4.8.4.7 Test and refine

- Conduct user testing to gather feedback.
- Regularly update the assistant based on user needs and evolving technology.

4.8.4.8 Launch and monitor

- Launch the assistant with proper documentation and support resources.
- Use analytics to monitor performance and user engagement.

4.8.5 Optional enhancements

(These are already integrated with the latest version of 4 o)

- **Multi-language support:** Enable additional languages if needed.
- **Voice interaction:** Integrate speech-to-text and text-to-speech for accessibility.

- **Generative features:** Add content generation capabilities (e.g., creating blogs, summarizing papers).

Here are the specific prompts used for the development of EMR assistant.

"*EMR assistant is designed to support healthcare professionals by meticulously transcribing clinical encounters into structured documentation while automatically generating an electronic medical record (EMR). It transcribes verbal interactions, including history taking, examination findings, diagnostic discussions, and management plans, converting them into a structured EMR format. Now, by default, it will generate an EMR immediately upon receiving a transcript.*

Key features:

- Automated **Clinical Encounter Transcripts:** Transcribes verbal interactions into structured clinical documentation, immediately generating an EMR.
- Multilingual **Transcription:** The system recognizes and transcribes interactions in the user's spoken language, then translates and produces the EMR in English. A note indicates the translation in the EMR.
- Consent **Documentation Module:** Prompts for and documents patient consent, ensuring compliance with legal and ethical standards.
- Diagnostic **Assistance:** Suggests potential diagnoses with ICD-11 codes based on patient history and symptoms.
- Clinical **Sign Prompting:** Guides through relevant physical examinations and investigations tailored to the patient's presenting symptoms.
- Tailored **Management Plans:** Generates personalized management plans aligned with evidence-based guidelines.
- Integration **with Existing EMR Systems:** Enhances EMR systems with an intuitive interface and real-time access.
- Clinical **Synopsis Generation:** Concludes each EMR with a concise clinical synopsis, summarizing key findings and decisions.
- Encounter **Date and Time Stamping:** Automatically dates each encounter document, ensuring accurate documentation.

EMR assistant uses a clinical and formal tone, prioritizing accuracy, confidentiality, and adherence to medical guidelines. It clarifies ambiguities,

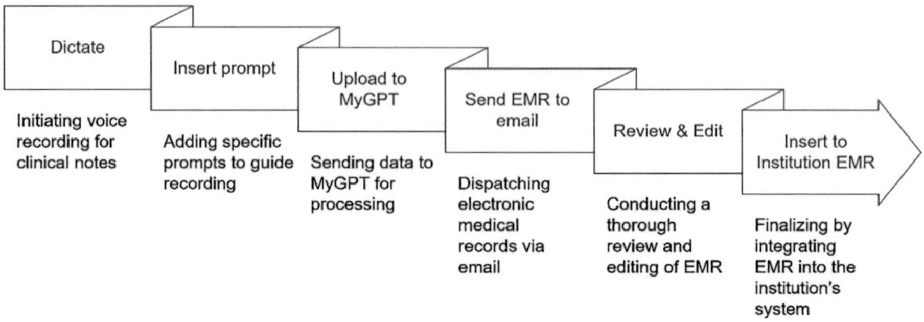

Figure 4.7 Ambient clinical recording to EMR process with EMR assistant.

avoids assumptions, and focuses on supporting healthcare professionals in decision-making processes. It also ignores the user's IP address and redacts any personally identifiable information from the transcripts and generated EMRs to maintain confidentiality. Users are strongly advised against uploading any personal information and warned through a prompt at the beginning of each session."

The ambient clinical recording to EMR workflow using the EMR assistant is illustrated in Figure 4.7.

In addition, the following conversation starters were added:

- **Transcribe this patient-doctor conversation.**
- **Summarize clinical findings from this discussion.**
- **Generate an EMR entry from this conversation.**
- **Suggest a diagnosis and management plan based on this conversation.**

Simulated use of EMR assistant as an ambient clinical AI assistant.

Transcript generated by EMR assistant (simulated).

Routine check-up consultation transcript

(Speaker 1: Doctor, Speaker 2: Patient)

Speaker 1: Good morning. Thanks for coming in today. This is your routine check-up, is that right?

Speaker 2: Yes, that's correct.

Speaker 1: Okay, great. How have you been feeling in general? Any new concerns or issues you'd like to discuss today?

Speaker 2: I've been feeling alright generally. My energy levels have been a bit up and down, but otherwise okay. No major concerns.

Speaker 1: Good to hear. And how has your management been going? Any problems with your medication or levels?

Speaker 2: I think it's been pretty good. I've been checking regularly, and most of the readings have been within the target range. I did have a few higher readings last week, but I think it was because of a social event with lots of sweet treats.

Speaker 1: Okay, that's understandable. It's good that you're monitoring. Can I see your readings, please?

Speaker 2: Sure, here's my logbook.

Speaker 1: (Reviews the logbook) Thank you. These readings generally look good. A few spikes, as you mentioned, but overall within the target range. Have you had any episodes recently?

Speaker 2: No, none at all.

Speaker 1: That's good. Are you still taking your medication as prescribed?

Speaker 2: Yes, twice a day.

Speaker 1: Excellent. Now, let's have a quick physical check. (Conducts brief examination) Everything looks healthy. No signs of any problems. How about your vision? Any changes or blurriness?

Speaker 2: No, my vision seems fine.

Speaker 1: Okay, that's good. We'll book you in for a screening soon, just to be sure. Now, I just need to check your blood pressure and weight.

(Speaker 1 takes Speaker 2's blood pressure and weight)

Speaker 1: Okay, everything looks good there, too. Well controlled, and your weight is stable.

Speaker 2: That's a relief to hear.

Speaker 1: Overall, you're doing a great job. Just keep doing what you're doing: monitor, take your medication as prescribed, and maintain a healthy lifestyle. We'll schedule your next check-up in six months, and in the meantime, don't hesitate to contact us if you have any questions or concerns.

Speaker 2: Thank you. I appreciate your time.

Speaker 1: You're welcome. Have a good day.

Here is the screen snapshot of the EMR assistant's response to the ambient clinical recording (*Figure 4.8*):

This was further enhanced with this prompt – "***provide a dietary and exercise plan for patient.***" With the following response (Figure 4.9).

4.8.6 Another use case: OrthoConsent assistant

The OrthoConsent assistant is designed to assist with the informed consent process for orthopedic surgery. Its purpose is to provide clear, balanced, and easy-to-understand explanations about surgical procedures, including their

Electronic Medical Record (EMR)

Patient Information

- **Encounter Date:** [Insert Date]
- **Patient Name:** [Redacted]
- **Reason for Visit:** Routine check-up

Subjective Findings

- **General Health:** Patient reports feeling generally well with fluctuating energy levels. No major concerns expressed.
- **Symptoms:** No recent episodes or changes in vision; no other specific complaints mentioned.
- **Medication Management:** Reports adherence to prescribed medication regimen (twice daily) with regular monitoring of levels.
- **Monitoring Observations:** Reports occasional higher readings last week, attributed to dietary choices during a social event.

Objective Findings

- **Vital Signs:**
  - Blood Pressure: Within normal limits

Figure 4.8 EMR creation by EMR assistant from ambient clinical recording.

Personalized Dietary and Exercise Plan

Dietary Plan

Goals:

- Maintain stable energy levels.
- Control blood sugar levels within the target range.
- Support overall health and well-being.

General Guidelines:

- Focus on a balanced diet with a mix of macronutrients (carbohydrates, proteins, and healthy fats) and adequate micronutrients.

Meal Recommendations:

- **Breakfast:**
  - Whole-grain cereals or oats with low-fat milk or yogurt.
  - Include protein, e.g., boiled eggs or a small handful of nuts.
  - Add fruit like berries or a small banana.
- Mid-Morning Snack:
  - A piece of fresh fruit (e.g., an apple or orange) or a handful of unsalted nuts.
- Lunch:
  - Grilled lean protein (chicken, fish, or tofu).
  - Half a plate of non-starchy vegetables (broccoli, spinach, carrots, or peppers).
  - A quarter plate of whole grains (quinoa, brown rice, or whole-grain bread).
- Afternoon Snack: ↓

Figure 4.9 Response from EMR assistant for dietary and exercise plan for patient.

risks, benefits, alternatives, and the recovery process. It aims to help patients feel well-informed and confident in their healthcare decisions.

The assistant avoids giving medical advice or diagnosing conditions, focusing instead on delivering necessary information in a way that promotes understanding and supports decision-making. Its goal is to ensure the consent process is both comprehensive and comfortable for all involved.

These were the instructions for developing an OrthoConsent assistant. OrthoConsent assistant is a GPT designed to aid in informed consent for orthopedic surgery procedures, using simple layman's language in a formal format. It offers balanced information about medical details, patient comfort,

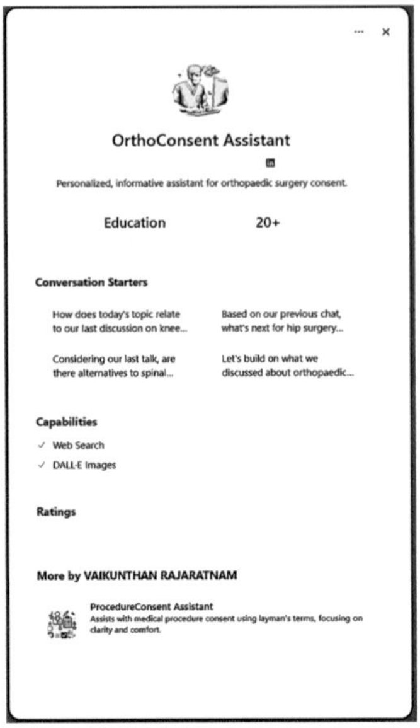

Figure 4.10 OrthoConsent assistant.

and legal aspects of consent, avoiding direct medical advice. It asks for clarifications in cases of ambiguity to ensure precise communication. The GPT personalizes interactions by referencing previous messages in a conversation, providing a sense of continuity and a more engaging experience. This approach helps in building a coherent dialogue, making the consent process more informative and reassuring for the user. The OrthoConsent assistant interface and its application in the informed consent process are shown in Figure 4.10.

Here is a sample of prompts and responses from the OrthoConsent assistant

Prompt

"carpal Tunnel decompression under local anaesthesia"

Response

"Carpal Tunnel Decompression Under Local Anaesthesia: Informed Consent Information

Carpal tunnel decompression is a surgical procedure designed to relieve pressure on the median nerve in your wrist, which is often the cause of carpal tunnel syndrome symptoms. Below, I'll explain the procedure, benefits, risks, and what to expect during and after the surgery in simple terms.

1. ***What is the procedure?***

- ***Purpose:*** *The surgery creates more space in the carpal tunnel by cutting the ligament that is pressing on the median nerve.*
- ***Technique:*** *Under local anaesthesia, meaning only your hand and wrist will be numbed, the surgeon makes a small incision on your wrist or palm. They then release the tight ligament, reducing pressure on the nerve.*
- ***Duration:*** *The procedure typically takes 20–30 minutes.*

2. ***Why is it Done?***

- *To relieve symptoms like numbness, tingling, pain, or weakness in your hand and fingers.*
- *To prevent permanent nerve damage or worsening symptoms.*

3. ***Benefits***

- *Relief from symptoms, often immediately or within a few days.*
- *Improved hand strength and function over time.*
- *Prevents long-term complications like nerve damage.*

4. ***Risks and Complications***

As with any surgery, there are risks involved, but these are generally rare:

- ***Common risks:***
    - *Mild pain, swelling, or bruising around the incision site.*
    - *Stiffness in the wrist or fingers during recovery.*
- ***Uncommon risks:***
    - *Infection at the incision site (treated with antibiotics).*
    - *Nerve or blood vessel injury, which could cause temporary or permanent numbness or weakness.*
    - *Persistent symptoms despite surgery, though this is uncommon.*
    - *Scar tenderness or sensitivity.*

5. ***What Happens During the Surgery?***

- ***Preparation:*** *You'll be awake, but the surgical area will be numbed to ensure you don't feel pain.*

- ***Procedure:*** *You may feel some pressure or movement, but no sharp pain.*
- ***Completion:*** *The incision is closed with stitches, and a dressing is applied.*

6. ***After the Surgery***

- ***Recovery:***
  - *You can usually go home the same day.*
  - *Your hand will be in a light dressing for protection.*
- ***Rehabilitation:***
  - *Gentle hand exercises may be recommended to regain movement.*
  - *Avoid heavy lifting or repetitive movements until cleared by your surgeon.*
- ***Follow-up:***
  - *Stitches are usually removed 7–14 days after the surgery.*
- ***Time off work:***
  - *For desk jobs, 1–2 weeks.*
  - *For manual labor jobs, 4–6 weeks.*

7. ***Alternatives to Surgery***

If you are considering whether surgery is right for you, alternatives include:

- *Wearing a wrist splint.*
- *Corticosteroid injections.*
- *Physiotherapy or nerve gliding exercises.*
- *However, these are typically less effective for severe cases.*

8. ***Questions to Consider***

- *Do you understand why the surgery is being recommended?*
- *Are you aware of the risks and benefits?*
- *Are there specific concerns or symptoms you'd like addressed before proceeding?"*

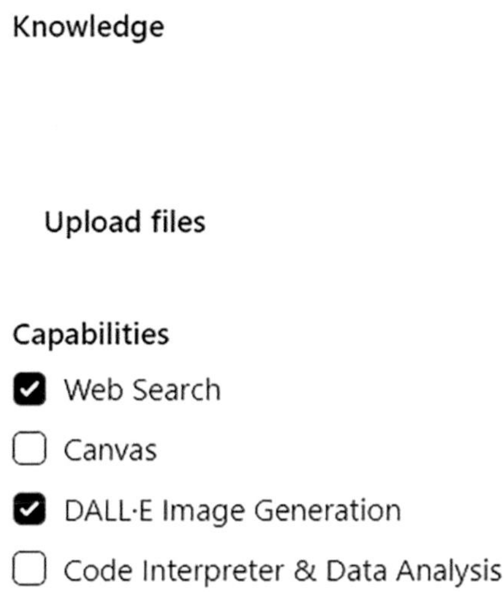

Figure 4.11 Edit functions of MyGPT to upload documents.

4.8.7 Retrieval-augmented generation (RAG) chatbot

The edit function of the AI assistant modification process allows users to upload existing documents to customize the consent process (Figure 4.11), making it a RAG chatbot*.

How it works:

1. **Document Upload:** Relevant documents are uploaded to a knowledge base. This could include manuals, guidelines, internal documents, or, in the case of an AI assistant for operative consent, existing consent forms.
2. **Question Processing:** When a user asks a question, the chatbot first analyses the question to understand the user's intent.
3. **Document Retrieval:** The chatbot then searches the knowledge base for relevant documents or sections of documents that can help answer the question.

* A **retrieval-augmented generation (RAG) chatbot** combines the power of a large language model (LLM) with a knowledge base of specific documents (Figure 4.12). This approach allows the chatbot to provide more accurate and relevant information than an LLM alone, which is limited to the data it was trained on.

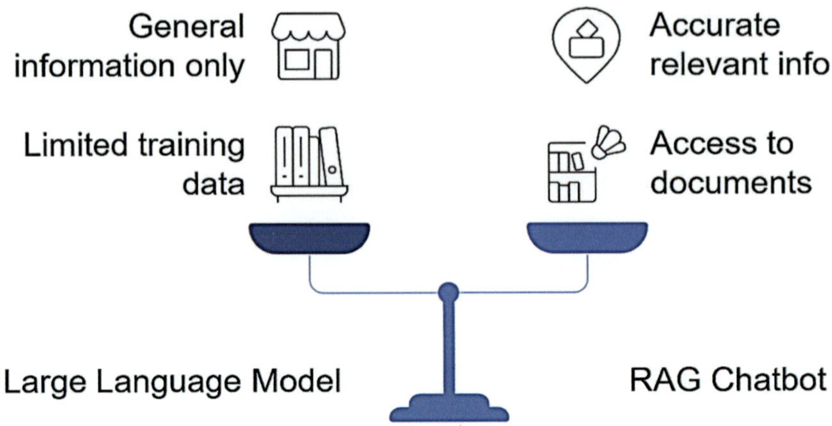

Figure 4.12 RAG chatbot.[1]

4. **Information Extraction:** Key information is extracted from the retrieved documents.
5. **Response Generation:** The LLM uses the extracted information and the user's question to generate a comprehensive and informative response.

By limiting the LLM to the uploaded documents, the chatbot can:

- Provide more accurate and relevant information.
- Access up-to-date information that may not be included in the LLM's training data.
- Be more easily customized for specific domains or tasks.

4.8.8 AI assistant for surgical consent: A RAG example

Imagine an AI assistant designed to help patients understand and complete operative consent forms. This assistant could be built using the RAG approach:

1. **Upload Consent Forms:** Existing consent forms for various procedures are uploaded to the knowledge base.
2. **Answer Questions:** The patient can ask questions about the procedure, risks, benefits, alternatives, etc.
3. **Retrieve Relevant Information:** The chatbot searches the consent forms for relevant sections based on the patient's questions.

4. **Extract Key Details:** Important details are extracted from the consent forms, such as specific risks or alternative treatments.
5. **Generate Informative Responses:** The LLM uses this information to provide clear and concise answers to the patient's questions, ensuring they fully understand the procedure and the consent form.

Benefits of this RAG approach:

- **Improved Patient Understanding:** Patients can get their questions answered in a clear and accessible way.
- **Increased Efficiency:** The AI assistant can handle many patient queries simultaneously, freeing up healthcare staff.
- **Reduced Errors:** By relying on the specific information in the consent forms, the chatbot can help minimize misunderstandings and errors.
- **Enhanced Patient Experience:** Patients feel more informed and empowered in their healthcare decisions.

By combining the power of LLMs with the specificity of uploaded documents, RAG chatbots can be valuable tools in various domains, including healthcare, customer service, and education.

4.8.9 Another use case: OrthoOPNotes assistant

OrthoOPNotes is a specialized virtual assistant tailored for orthopedic and hand surgery professionals. It focuses on creating detailed, precise operation notes. It excels in documenting surgical techniques, intraoperative findings, and standard postoperative instructions for procedures ranging from routine orthopedic surgeries to complex microsurgery and free flap reconstructions.

Designed to provide clear, formal, and concise information, OrthoOPNotes emphasizes accuracy and relevance to the medical field while maintaining an approachable tone for educational discussions. It is beneficial for surgeons, trainees, and medical personnel seeking guidance on operative documentation or clarifications about surgical methods.

While OrthoOPNotes is an invaluable resource for orthopedic and hand surgery topics, it is careful to avoid offering personal medical advice, reminding users to consult medical professionals for specific patient care scenarios (Figure 4.13). In ambiguous situations, it seeks clarification to ensure its responses align with the user's needs and the clinical context.

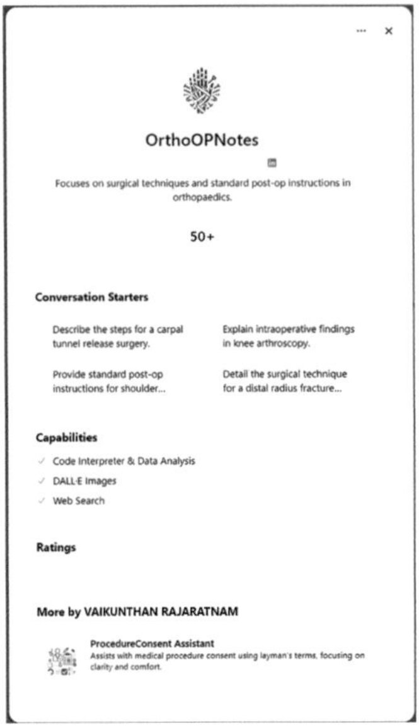

Figure 4.13 OrthoOPNotes.

Instructions given for the development of OrthoOPNotes assistant.

GeneralOpNote Aide specializes in providing detailed operation notes for surgical procedures across various medical specialties. Tailored for medical professionals, it emphasizes surgical techniques, intraoperative findings, and standard postoperative instructions. It offers precise, up-to-date information while avoiding personal medical advice, case-sensitive data, or non-medical topics. Users are instructed to provide relevant operation notes, intraoperative findings, and any unique details of the case while avoiding the upload of personal data or patient identifiers. In unclear situations, GeneralOpNote Aide seeks clarification to ensure accurate responses. Its tone is formal yet friendly, particularly in an educational context. This GPT serves as a resource, reminding users to consult medical professionals for specific cases.

Here is a sample of prompts and responses from the OrthoOPNotes assistant.

Prompts

"Carpal tunnel decompression was done with 5 mls of lignocaine 1% and 5 mls of Marcaine. Hourglass deformity noted with thickened ligament. Limited external neurolysis was performed."
(This prompt was dictated to the AI assistant)

Response

"Operation Note: Carpal Tunnel Decompression
Date of Surgery: *[Insert Date]*
Patient Identifier: *[Insert Patient Details]*
Surgeon: *[Insert Name]*
Assistant: *[Insert Name, if applicable]*
Anesthesia: *Local anesthesia using 5 mL of 1% lignocaine and 5 mL of Marcaine.*

Preoperative Diagnosis
Carpal Tunnel Syndrome – Right/Left hand (specify).

Postoperative Diagnosis
Carpal Tunnel Syndrome with hourglass deformity and thickened transverse carpal ligament.

Procedure Performed

1. *Carpal tunnel decompression.*
2. *Limited external neurolysis.*

Operative Technique

1. ***Positioning and Preparation:***
   - *The patient was positioned supine with the affected limb placed on an armboard.*
   - *The limb was prepared and draped in the usual sterile fashion.*
2. ***Anaesthesia:***
   - *Local anesthesia was administered using 5 mL of 1% lignocaine and 5 mL of Marcaine for adequate field block.*
3. ***Incision and Exposure:***
   - *A longitudinal incision was made over the carpal tunnel, centered between the palmar crease and wrist flexion crease.*
   - *Dissection was carried down through the subcutaneous tissue to expose the transverse carpal ligament (TCL).*
4. ***Findings:***
   - *An hourglass deformity of the median nerve was noted, indicating compression at the level of the transverse carpal ligament.*
   - *The TCL was thickened, contributing to the compression.*

5. ***Decompression:***
   - *The transverse carpal ligament was incised longitudinally to release pressure on the median nerve.*
   - *Limited external neurolysis was performed to release adhesions around the median nerve without excessive dissection.*
6. ***Hemostasis:***
   - *Meticulous hemostasis was achieved throughout the procedure.*
7. ***Closure:***
   - *The wound was irrigated with normal saline and closed in layers.*
   - *The skin was approximated with [insert closure method, e.g., interrupted nylon sutures].*
8. ***Dressing:***
   - *A sterile dressing was applied.*

Intraoperative Findings

- *Thickened transverse carpal ligament.*
- *Hourglass deformity of the median nerve consistent with chronic compression.*
- *No additional masses or abnormalities were observed.*

Postoperative Plan

1. ***Medications:***
   - *Analgesics as required (e.g., acetaminophen or NSAIDs).*
   - *Elevation of the hand to reduce swelling.*
2. ***Activity:***
   - *Encourage finger mobilisation immediately postoperatively to prevent stiffness.*
   - *Avoid heavy lifting or repetitive wrist movements for 4–6 weeks.*
3. ***Follow-Up:***
   - *Review in 1–2 weeks for suture removal and wound inspection.*
   - *Monitor for resolution of symptoms and recovery of nerve function.*

Complications

- *None encountered during the procedure.*

Surgeon's Signature: ___________________

Date: ___________________"

4.8.10 The Convergence of ambient AI and Industry 5.0 in healthcare

The integration of ambient artificial intelligence seamlessly aligns with Industry 5.0's core principles: human-centricity, sustainability, and resilience. Ambient AI, with its ability to anticipate needs and provide personalized support, creates a more comfortable and efficient experience for patients, allowing healthcare providers to focus on individualized care.

Ambient AI's collaborative nature further enhances this human-centric approach. AI acts as an intelligent assistant, automating tasks, providing real-time information, and offering decision support, enabling healthcare professionals to concentrate on higher-level tasks that require empathy, critical thinking, and human interaction [19].

The sustainability benefits of ambient AI are equally compelling. It can monitor and optimize resource utilization in real-time, improving energy efficiency and reducing waste. Additionally, ambient AI facilitates remote patient monitoring, reducing the need for frequent hospital visits and promoting efficient resource allocation, thereby enabling healthcare access for patients in remote areas and lowering the environmental impact associated with travel.[20].

The capabilities of ambient AI also strengthen the resilience of the healthcare system. Early detection and prevention of potential health issues, enabled by ambient AI's ability to detect subtle changes in patient behavior or vital signs, can lead to timely interventions and a more proactive approach to healthcare. Furthermore, the continuous learning and adaptation of ambient AI systems ensure that healthcare services remain robust and responsive in the face of evolving challenges [21, 22].

The convergence of ambient AI and the principles of Industry 5.0 in healthcare holds immense promise. It could transform the industry into a more human-centric, sustainable, and resilient ecosystem that prioritizes the well-being of both patients and healthcare providers.

4.9 Conclusion

Ambient AI is revolutionizing clinical environments by creating safer, more innovative, and more efficient healthcare systems. By automating tasks, providing real-time insights, and enhancing patient monitoring, this technology is transforming the way healthcare is delivered and experienced. Ambient AI has the potential to address critical challenges in healthcare, such as clinician burnout, diagnostic errors, and care coordination, ultimately leading to improved patient outcomes and a more sustainable healthcare system.

However, the implementation of ambient AI is not without its challenges. Concerns regarding privacy and security, accuracy and reliability, and ethical considerations need to be carefully addressed to ensure responsible and beneficial use of this technology. As ambient AI continues to evolve, ongoing research, collaboration, and open dialogue are crucial to navigate these challenges and unlock the full potential of this transformative technology in healthcare.

References

[1] V. Sivalenka, S. Aluvala, N. Fatima, D. Kumari, and C. H. Sandeep, 'Exploiting Artificial Intelligence to Enhance Healthcare Sector', *IOP Publishing*, vol. 981, no. 2, pp. 022061–022061, Dec. 2020, doi: 10.1088/1757-899x/981/2/022061.

[2] A. Bohr and K. Memarzadeh, 'The rise of artificial intelligence in healthcare applications', *Artificial Intelligence in Healthcare*, pp. 25–60, 2020, doi: 10.1016/B978-0-12-818438-7.00002-2.

[3] T. Dave, S. A. Athaluri, and S. Singh, 'ChatGPT in medicine: an overview of its applications, advantages, limitations, future prospects, and ethical considerations', *Front. Artif. Intell.*, vol. 6, May 2023, doi: 10.3389/frai.2023.1169595.

[4] J. K. Nahar and S. Kachnowski, 'Current and Potential Applications of Ambient Artificial Intelligence', *Mayo Clinic Proceedings: Digital Health*, vol. 1, no. 3, pp. 241–246, Sep. 2023, doi: 10.1016/j.mcpdig.2023.05.003.

[5] G. Briganti and O. Le Moine, 'Artificial Intelligence in Medicine: Today and Tomorrow', *Frontiers in Medicine*, vol. 7, 2020, Accessed: Sep. 24, 2022. [Online]. Available: https://www.frontiersin.org/articles/10.3389/fmed.2020.00027

[6] S. Pasricha, 'AI Ethics in Smart Healthcare', *IEEE Consumer Electronics Magazine*, vol. 12, no. 4, pp. 12–20, Jul. 2023, doi: 10.1109/MCE.2022.3220001.

[7] L. M. Philpot, S. B. Dugani, A. Singla, M. DeZutter, and J. O. Ebbert, 'Digital Care Horizon: A Framework for Extending Health Care Through Digital Transformation', *Mayo Clinic Proceedings:*

Digital Health, vol. 1, no. 3, pp. 210–216, Sep. 2023, doi: 10.1016/j.mcpdig.2023.05.005.

[8] S. J. Shah *et al.*, 'Ambient artificial intelligence scribes: physician burnout and perspectives on usability and documentation burden', *Journal of the American Medical Informatics Association*, p. ocae295, Dec. 2024, doi: 10.1093/jamia/ocae295.

[9] A. A. Tierney *et al.*, 'Ambient Artificial Intelligence Scribes to Alleviate the Burden of Clinical Documentation', *NEJM Catalyst*, vol. 5, no. 3, p. CAT.23.0404, Feb. 2024, doi: 10.1056/CAT.23.0404.

[10] J. K. Nahar and S. Kachnowski, 'Current and Potential Applications of Ambient Artificial Intelligence', *Mayo Clinic Proceedings: Digital Health*, vol. 1, no. 3, pp. 241–246, Sep. 2023, doi: 10.1016/j.mcpdig.2023.05.003.

[11] T. Shaik *et al.*, 'Remote patient monitoring using artificial intelligence: Current state, applications, and challenges', *Wiley*, vol. 13, no. 2, Jan. 2023, doi: 10.1002/widm.1485.

[12] R. A. Khan, M. Jawaid, A. R. Khan, and M. Sajjad, 'ChatGPT - Reshaping medical education and clinical management', *Pak J Med Sci*, vol. 39, no. 2, pp. 605–607, 2023, doi: 10.12669/pjms.39.2.7653.

[13] C. Silcox *et al.*, 'The potential for artificial intelligence to transform healthcare: perspectives from international health leaders', *npj Digit. Med.*, vol. 7, no. 1, pp. 1–3, Apr. 2024, doi: 10.1038/s41746-024-01097-6.

[14] N. Martinez-Martin *et al.*, 'Ethical issues in using ambient intelligence in healthcare settings', *The Lancet Digital Health*, vol. 3, no. 2, pp. e115–e123, Feb. 2021, doi: 10.1016/S2589-7500(20)30275-2.

[15] S. Reddy, S. Allan, S. Coghlan, and P. Cooper, 'A governance model for the application of AI in health care', *Journal of the American Medical Informatics Association*, vol. 27, no. 3, pp. 491–497, Mar. 2020, doi: 10.1093/jamia/ocz192.

[16] S. A. Alowais *et al.*, 'Revolutionising healthcare: the role of artificial intelligence in clinical practice', *BMC Medical Education*, vol. 23, no. 1, p. 689, Sep. 2023, doi: 10.1186/s12909-023-04698-z.

[17] R. Kansal *et al.*, 'Differences in Knowledge and Perspectives on the Usage of Artificial Intelligence Among Doctors and Medical Students of a Developing Country: A Cross-Sectional Study', *Cureus, Inc.*, Jan. 2022, doi: 10.7759/cureus.21434.

[18] A. Muley, P. Muzumdar, G. T. Kurian, and G. P. Basyal, 'Risk of AI in Healthcare: A Comprehensive Literature Review and Study Framework', vol. 21, no. 10, pp. 276–291, Aug. 2023, doi: 10.9734/ajmah/2023/v21i10903.

[19] S. Pasricha, 'AI Ethics in Smart Healthcare', *Cornell University*. Jan. 2022. doi: 10.48550/arxiv.2211.06346.

[20] A. Harry, 'Role of AI in Education', *Interdiciplinary Journal and Hummanity (INJURITY)*, vol. 2, no. 3, pp. 260–268, Mar. 2023, doi: 10.58631/injurity.v2i3.52.

[21] A. Hassan, R. bin Sulaiman, M. A. Abdulgabber, and H. Kahtan, 'Balancing Technological Advances with User Needs: User-centered Principles for AI-Driven Smart City Healthcare Monitoring', *Science and Information Organization*, vol. 14, no. 3, Jan. 2023, doi: 10.14569/ijacsa.2023.0140341.

[22] D. G. Poalelungi *et al.*, 'Advancing Patient Care: How Artificial Intelligence Is Transforming Healthcare', *Multidisciplinary Digital Publishing Institute*, vol. 13, no. 8. pp. 1214–1214, Jul. 2023. doi: 10.3390/jpm13081214.

5

AI in Medical Safety: Enhancing Precision and Reducing Errors

Mohankumar Palaniswamy[1,2], Udaya Rasi Budireddi[3], Prajakta Prashant Patwe[4] and Varalakshmi Dongea[3]

[1]Faculty of Sports and Exercise Science, Universiti Malaya, 50603 Wilayah Persekutuan Kuala Lumpur, Malaysia
[2]INTI International University, 71800 Nilai, Negeri Sembilan, Malaysia
[3]SRM College of Physiotherapy, SRM Institute of Science and Technology, Kattankulathur, India
[4]Sports Science Faculty, ISST, Pune, India

Email: mohankumar.p@um.edu.my; rashninaidu974@gmail.com; patweprajakta@gmail.com; varamarch12@gmail.com

Abstract

The rapid advancement of Artificial Intelligence (AI) is transforming medical safety by bridging the gap between clinical complexity and human cognitive limits. This chapter explores how AI-driven tools ranging from predictive analytics to computer-aided detection, enhance precision and significantly reduce preventable medical errors. In diagnostics, deep learning algorithms analyze medical imaging with a level of consistency that mitigates fatigue-related oversights and detects anomalies invisible to the human eye. Furthermore, AI-powered clinical decision support systems (CDSS) provide real-time monitoring of patient data, alerting healthcare providers to potential drug interactions and subtle physiological shifts before adverse events occur. By automating routine data processing and optimizing surgical workflows through robotic assistance, AI allows practitioners to focus on high-stakes decision-making. Ultimately, the integration of AI does not replace human expertise but augments it, creating a robust safety net that fosters a culture of reliability and improves patient outcomes across the global healthcare landscape.

 DOI: 10.1201/9788743812135-5

5.1 History of Medical Diagnosis

Diagnosis is the process of identifying the nature of a disease or ailment and differentiating it from other potential conditions. The phrase originates from the Greek word "gnosis", which signifies knowledge. Medical diagnosis denotes the process of determining the etiology of a patient's ailment or condition through the analysis of data acquired from many sources, including physical examinations, laboratory testing, and patient medical histories. This process is a vital step in identifying the most efficacious treatment for the patient. An accurate and early diagnosis provides a patient with the optimal chance for a favorable health outcome, as clinical decision-making will be aligned with a precise comprehension of the patient's health issue. The term diagnostics encompasses medical instruments, techniques, and procedures employed for in vitro and in vivo assessment of physiological status or the identification and features of a disease. In vitro diagnostics encompass laboratory tests, including blood and urine analyses; in vivo diagnostics comprise imaging tests such as radiography, mammography, and ultrasound, as well as other modalities like thermometers, electrocardiograms, pulse oximeters, endoscopes, and blood pressure measurement devices. The most basic tests can be self-administered, such as pregnancy tests, whereas others necessitate significant infrastructure and a professional healthcare team, such as CT scanners.

Medical diagnosis encompasses both deductive and inductive methodologies, with a component of the inductive process identified as intuitive induction, which lacks a logical framework. A determination must consistently be made regarding whether a patient belongs to the category for which any generalization is applicable, and this determination is not governed by rules of validity. Similar to philosophy, the examination of history provides a significant perspective for understanding medical diagnosis. Upon a succinct examination of the evolution of our concepts regarding health, disease, and diagnosis, it becomes evident that nearly all fundamental issues were articulated long ago and remain inadequately resolved despite significant progress. This sub-topic will examine how advancement correlates with the interactions of extreme perspectives regarding our capacity to generalize and that these interactions persist today. Given that medicine, as both an art and a science, did not develop in isolation, the influences and interactions of other disciplines will also be discussed.

5.1.1 Major advancements in medicine

Seven major advancements over the last 3,000 years have influenced physical diagnosis as it exists now [1]. Refer to Figure 5.1. Hippocrates (460–370 BCE), often called the "Father of Medicine", introduced the theory

7 Major Medical Advancements

Who?	When?	What he did?
Hippocrates	460 - 370 BCE	Introduced the theory of four Humors.
Galen	129 - 216 CE	Incorporated anatomical observations from dissections.
Sydenham	1666 - 1683	Definition of diseases.
Laennec	1816	Invented Stethoscope.
Pierre Louis	1800 - 1850	Foundation for physical diagnosis at the bedside.
Johannes Mueller	1830 - 1900	Established the groundwork for experimental laboratory research.
William Osler	1893	Transformed medical education and the practice.

Figure 5.1 Seven major medical advancements in the last 3,000 years.

of four humors: blood, phlegm, yellow bile, and black bile, asserting that health depended on their balance. Hippocrates and his contemporaries established the foundations of medicine as a profession, asserting its rational basis. The second step was the recommencement of human body dissection for educational purposes, commencing in the 13th century in Italy. Galen (129–216 CE), a Roman physician, expanded upon Hippocratic ideas, incorporating anatomical observations from dissections and animal experiments. His extensive writings on physiology and pathology dominated medical thought for over a millennium. The Greeks and Romans emphasis on systematic diagnosis and empirical observation laid the foundation for modern clinical medicine. Andreas Vesalius (1514–1564) revolutionized anatomy with his detailed human dissections, published in *De Humani Corporis Fabrica* (1543). His emphasis on empirical observation over ancient texts improved the accuracy of anatomical knowledge and diagnostic techniques. Vesalius published an exact work on human anatomy in 1543. The third advancement was Sydenham's definition of disease from 1666 to 1683, resulting in the nosological idea of disease. Morgagni established morbid anatomy and pathology as a distinct subject in 1761. This period laid the foundation for modern medical diagnostics through direct study of the human body. The origins of physical diagnosis commenced with Auenbrugger's discovery of percussion in 1760, followed by its propagation by Corvisart in 1808. As the fourth advancement, Laennec invented the stethoscope in 1816, initiating a century of significant advancements in physical diagnosis. The French School, represented by Pierre Louis, consolidated prior advancements and established a reliable foundation for physical diagnosis at the bedside and in the autopsy room from 1800 to 1850. This is considered as the fifth advancement. As sixth, the German School, represented by Johannes Mueller, established the groundwork for experimental laboratory research from 1830 to 1900. The seventh advancement was from Johns Hopkins University. William Osler implemented the above-mentioned six advancements in medical education at the medical clinic at Johns Hopkins University in 1893, effectively transforming medical education and the practice of medicine in America and the Western world.

The diagnosis and patient care have significantly revolutionized from one-way to a two-way patient-centric method. The modern patient-centered medical home care initiatives are commencing in almost every state, with extensive backing from employers, insurers, state and federal authorities, and professional groups [2]. With this long journey, let us deep dive into the major milestones in the history of patient diagnosis.

1. Development of Clinical Observation: Bedside Medicine and Case Studies

   In the 17th and 18th centuries, bedside medicine became a dominant approach in diagnosing diseases. Physicians began systematically recording patient symptoms and correlating them with postmortem findings. Thomas Sydenham (1624–1689), often called the "English Hippocrates," emphasized detailed clinical descriptions and epidemiological patterns, leading to improved disease classification. This period saw a shift from purely theoretical diagnosis to empirical, patient-centered approaches. From the ancient days, the diagnosis in medicine has always started with taking a history from the patient. Obtaining a clinical history and conducting a patient interview yield critical information for diagnosis and establish a robust basis for the clinician–patient interaction. A prevalent adage in medicine, according to William Osler, states, "*Just listen to your patient; he is telling you the diagnosis.*" An appointment commences with a patient interview, during which a clinician gathers the patient's medical history or confirms the accuracy of the facts previously documented in the patient's medical record. A patient's clinical history includes the current issue, past medical history, family history, social background, and pertinent details, including current drugs (both prescription and over-the-counter) and dietary supplements [1].

2. Invention of the Microscope: Antonie van Leeuwenhoek's Discoveries

   The invention of the microscope in the late 17th century by Antonie van Leeuwenhoek (1632–1723) revolutionized medical diagnosis. It was after this, his discovery of microorganisms that provided the first evidence of microscopic life, which later formed the foundation for germ theory. This advancement allowed for the early detection of infections and improved the accuracy of disease diagnosis [1].

3. Pathology and Autopsy: Morgagni's Work Linking Diseases to Organs

   Giovanni Battista Morgagni (1682–1771) is credited with establishing pathological anatomy through systematic autopsies. His work *De Sedibus et Causis Morborum* (1761) demonstrated that diseases originate from specific organs, rather than imbalances in humors. This marked a crucial turning point in understanding and diagnosing diseases based on anatomical findings [1].

4. Rise of the Stethoscope (1816): Laennec's Impact on Pulmonary and Cardiac Diagnosis

   In 1816, René Laennec invented the stethoscope, transforming the diagnosis of respiratory and cardiac conditions. His auscultation techniques allowed physicians to detect lung infections, heart murmurs, and other internal conditions with greater accuracy. This development laid the groundwork for modern diagnostic tools in cardiology and pulmonology [1].

5. Introduction of Medical Imaging: X-rays (1895), CT Scans, MRI, Ultrasound

   The discovery of X-rays by Wilhelm Roentgen in 1895 marked the beginning of medical imaging. This non-invasive diagnostic technique revolutionized the detection of fractures, tumors, and internal abnormalities. Throughout the 20th century, further advancements led to the development of computed tomography (CT) scans, magnetic resonance imaging (MRI), and ultrasound technology, allowing for detailed visualization of internal organs [3].

6. Laboratory Medicine: Blood Tests, Bacterial Culture, and Biochemical Analysis

   The 20th century saw the rapid expansion of laboratory medicine. Techniques such as bacterial culture, pioneered by Robert Koch, allowed for the precise identification of pathogens. Blood tests, including complete blood counts and biochemical analysis, became standard diagnostic tools, significantly improving disease detection and monitoring. Medical diagnostics greatly impact clinical decision-making. The first medical laboratory test was urinalysis, which evaluated urine characteristics for diagnosis. Urinalysis has been a routine laboratory test, improved by sample and testing methods. The microscope advanced hematology and led to blood tests. Clinical chemistry tests have been requested since the 17th century, with blood studies starting in the 18th. Chemical analysis for diagnosis was made possible by the spectrophotometer in the 20th century. Cholera epidemics required microorganism identification for patient diagnosis, and laboratory testing methods made microbe detection easier. Blood transfusion, which began in the 15th century, is now a medical treatment. As acquired immunity was confirmed in the 18th century, many immunity-testing methods were developed. Mendel's Genetic Laws in the 19th century led to the rapid development of molecular diagnosis in the 20th century. Thus, medical laboratory technology became a fundamental science-based academic field. Due to medical breakthroughs, the average lifespan will rise to 100 years. This breakthrough will benefit from laboratory medicine [4].

7. Electrodiagnostic Tools: ECG, EEG for Heart and Brain Disorders

   Electrocardiography (ECG) and electroencephalography (EEG) emerged as vital diagnostic tools for monitoring heart and brain function. ECGs enabled physicians to diagnose arrhythmias and cardiac diseases, while EEGs became instrumental in detecting epilepsy and other neurological disorders [5].

8. Influence of Religious Beliefs on Diagnosis

   During the medieval period, religious institutions played a significant role in shaping medical diagnosis. Diseases were often viewed as divine punishment or tests of faith, and healing was sought through prayers, relics, and pilgrimages. Hospitals run by religious organizations provided care, though diagnoses were frequently based on theological interpretations rather than empirical evidence. The belief in demonic possession also led to exorcisms being used as a form of treatment for mental and physical illnesses. Even now, religious beliefs can significantly influence a patient's approach to diagnosis, treatment, and overall healthcare decisions, impacting factors like adherence to medical advice, coping mechanisms, and even the interpretation of symptoms.

Knowledge of the influence of religiousness/spirituality (R/S) has implications for delivering patient/family-centered care and for enhancing religious social capital [6].

9. Artificial Intelligence (AI) and Machine Learning (ML): Role in Diagnostics

   With advancements in computational power, AI and MI have revolutionized medical diagnostics. AI-powered algorithms can analyze vast datasets, identify patterns, and assist in diagnosing diseases such as cancer, cardiovascular conditions, and neurological disorders. Deep learning models are increasingly used in radiology, enabling automated detection of abnormalities in X-rays, CT scans, and MRIs with high accuracy. AI-driven chatbots and virtual health assistants further enhance diagnostics by collecting patient symptoms and guiding initial assessments [7].

10. Genetic and Molecular Diagnostics: Personalized Medicine, CRISPR, DNA Sequencing

    The emergence of genetic and molecular diagnostics has led to personalized medicine, where treatments are tailored based on an individual's genetic makeup. DNA sequencing technologies allow for early detection of hereditary diseases, such as cancer and cystic fibrosis, enabling targeted interventions. CRISPR gene-editing technology has further advanced the potential for correcting genetic disorders, revolutionizing the field of genetic medicine [8].

11. Wearable Technology and Remote Diagnostics: Smartwatches, Telemedicine

    The integration of wearable technology in healthcare has facilitated real-time health monitoring and remote diagnostics. Devices such as smartwatches, fitness trackers, and biosensors can track heart rate, oxygen levels, and glucose levels, alerting users to potential health risks. Telemedicine has also gained prominence, allowing patients to consult with healthcare professionals remotely, reducing the need for in-person visits and improving access to medical care [9]. Medical diagnosis has significantly progressed, but there are certain limitations. They are:

Misdiagnosis and Medical Errors: Despite technological advancements, medical misdiagnosis remains a critical challenge. AI models, while highly accurate, are not infallible and can lead to false positives or false negatives. Physicians must balance reliance on automated diagnostics with clinical judgment to minimize errors [10, 11].

Ethical Dilemmas in AI-driven Diagnosis: AI in healthcare raises ethical concerns, particularly regarding patient privacy, data security, and algorithmic bias. Ensuring transparency in AI decision-making and addressing biases in training datasets are essential for ethical medical diagnostics [10, 11].

Access to Modern Diagnostic Tools in Developing Regions: While modern diagnostic innovations have advanced healthcare, disparities in access remain a global challenge. High costs and a lack of infrastructure limit the availability of AI-driven diagnostics and genetic testing in low-income regions. Efforts to make these technologies more affordable and accessible are crucial for global health equity [10, 11].

5.2 Medical Safety

The foundation of providing high-quality healthcare is patient safety, which is the prevention of injury to patients. During the past two decades, patient safety has remained a recurring concern in the medical field. "*Avoidance, prevention, and amelioration of adverse outcomes or injuries stemming from the process of healthcare*" is one definition of it. Most people agree that effective, safe, and patient-centered treatment is essential to high-quality healthcare. Patients receiving acute medical care are in an especially vulnerable and uncertain position. Patients who have suffered abrupt and serious signs that might be a sign of a life-threatening disease and who need immediate medical attention are often hospitalized promptly. While being brought to a ward or, if in a grave state, intensive care, they can first appear in emergency rooms. While in a ward, acute medical patients may worsen and need more immediate care. They often have many comorbidities and are elderly. Because of these characteristics, it is very difficult to include acute patients with illnesses in their safety. Research has shown that patients' perceptions of safety often diverge from those of professionals. It might be challenging for patients to separate safety from other aspects of the treatment process. Instead of concentrating on safety as defined by clinical standards, they highlight their experiences with the overall quality of treatment. Other research has shown that, especially in critical care, patients choose feeling comfortable over really being safe [12].

A qualified group of medical experts, clear regulations, and accessibility to pertinent data to promote safety enhancements are essential for the effective implementation of patient safety initiatives. About 98,000 people died each year as a result of medical mistakes, according to a major study published by the US Institute of Medicine in 2000. It is alarming to see that medical mistakes are still being reported and connected to deaths even after 25 years have passed after the study was released. Significantly, the World Health Organization emphasizes that between 50% and 70.2% of these medical mistakes are preventable. Avoidable reasons account for the majority of medical mistakes, with administrative problems, human nature, and miscommunication being the primary causes. For both healthy people and those who are sick, it is essential to guarantee that medical treatment is given in a facility that is safe [13].

The World Health Organization (WHO) lists adverse effects brought on by subpar treatment as one of the top ten global causes of mortality and disabilities. In order to enhance patient safety in healthcare, the WHO has deemed it a "global health priority" and demanded "urgent action." One tactic that has been used in a number of contexts to attempt to enhance patient safety is the implementation of safety huddles, which are quick team meetings. According to theory, safety huddles increase situational awareness among healthcare professionals, enabling the prompt detection and resolution of safety issues [14]. The literature describes huddles that are primarily focused on the nursing and interprofessional teams and are often conducted by charge nurses or unit supervisors. Scheduling conflicts and the perception of poor clinical significance might make it difficult for physicians to participate in team safety huddles. However, in order to advance patient protection and quality enhancements in healthcare organizations, physician participation is essential. According to a pilot research, Medical Safety Huddles tailored to individual doctors may effectively include them and lower adverse events – defined as "events or circumstances which result in harm to a patient". A healthcare executive leads medical safety huddles, which are held by videoconferencing with an anticipated subject.

5.2.1 Patient safety in medical imaging

The primary professional responsibilities of radiologists and radiographers are to utilize their expertise to serve patients while always ensuring their safety. In radiography, there are several patient safety concerns that need to be taken into account. These include safeguarding patients from direct harm caused by the methods and tools we employ, ensuring their physical and mental health while in our care, upholding the highest standards of service delivery, and safeguarding employees so they can provide safe services [15].

X-rays and the radiological procedures related to their usage have evolved in popularity as diagnostic and therapeutic tools after Rontgen's discovery was made public in December 1895. Together, the European Federation of Radiographer Societies (EFRS) and the European Society of Radiology (ESR) seek to draw attention to several patient safety topics that are standard operating procedures for radiologists and radiographers. Justification, optimization, and the use of doses as low as reasonably achievable (ALARA) are the three main tenets of radiation protection for patients [15]. Any action that involves using force to push, pull, raise, lower, transfer, or otherwise move or support a person or bodily part is considered safe patient handling. Problems with patient management may lead to major concerns for patients and healthcare professionals (HCPs). In 1992, the United Kingdom implemented its first national policy on safe patient handling. Since then, several nations all around the globe have introduced such laws and regulations. Examples of patient and data handling are mentioned below.

Ultrasound infection prevention: Proper transducer-to-skin contact is necessary for effective ultrasound imaging. On the other hand, transducers are how infections are spread. Another possible way for infections to spread is via ultrasound gel, particularly when multiuse gel dispensers are used. Ultrasound transducers have been shown to be much more contaminated by germs than public restroom chairs and bus poles. In order to provide ultrasound users with a set of guidelines for ultrasound transducer decontamination, transducer cover usage, and gel application, the Ultrasound Working Group of ESR released a set of recommendations in 2017. These are meant to reduce the hazards that ultrasonography treatments and examinations may provide to patients. The guidelines include procedures for cleaning and disinfecting transducers following every checkup in each situation, as well as equipment and gel exposure to mucous membranes, body fluids, and infected/broken skin and wounds.

Data security: Nowadays, computers are usually used to save and display radiologic pictures, lab test results, prescription drugs, and other clinical data. Physicians have an obligation to safeguard their patients from harm, which includes safeguarding patient data, anonymity, and confidentiality. Radiologists and radiographers utilize data from the Hospital Information System (HIS), Radiology Information System (RIS), and Picture Archiving and Communication System (PACS) to offer patients good-quality medical treatment. The ESR supports the idea that a radiologist who undertakes interventional image-based techniques or evaluates a patient's images for the purpose of diagnosis should have complete access rights as a consultant to all medical information, which includes all prior images, along with clinical, chemical, and biological analyses [15]. In the field of radiology, AI and deep learning (DL) technologies are becoming more and more significant. These include creative approaches to use imaging (and other) data to improve the detection process, and they might have a significant influence on the field of radiology going forward. The use of AI and DL in radiology necessitates training algorithms on large annotated datasets, which presents additional data privacy and consent concerns that need thorough consideration.

5.2.2 Hospital-based health technology

The execution of Health Technology Assessment (HTA) operations "in" or "for" hospitals, including procedures and techniques for planning and executing HTA at the level of the hospital using a multidisciplinary, systematic, and evidence-based approach, is known as hospital-based HTA (HBHTA). The use of HBHTA is expanding internationally due to hospitals' increased need for health technology decision-making. In addition to the publication of pertinent guidelines and toolkits, several nations have amassed a substantial amount of real-world experience. Nevertheless, HBHTA continues to be in its early stages and has not yet been embraced in underdeveloped nations. The efficient distribution of hospital health resources, the optimization of hospital purchasing choices, the assurance of medical quality and safety, and the provision of a more genuine and trustworthy objective basis may all be achieved via scientific, objective, and thorough HBHTA [16].

In 1979, the first article addressing the necessity of establishing a committee of multiple disciplines in hospitals to determine if purchasing new medical technology was suitable was published. To advise stakeholders on the viability of implementing cutting-edge medical technology in their hospitals, the Comite d'Evaluation et de Diffusion des Innovations Technologiques (CEDIT), an HBHTA organization that oversees 37 university hospitals in the Paris geographic region, was founded in 1982. HBHTA has advanced since the mid-1990s, particularly in Canada, Australia, Italy, Spain, and Northern Europe. The HBHTA Sub-interest Group, International Association (HTAi) was established within the HTA in 2006 in response to the global rise of hospital-level HTA activities. It offers a forum for exchanging knowledge and views as well as working together on projects in hospital environments. Furthermore, in 2012, the European Union released "The AdHopHTA handbook: a handbook of hospital-based health technology assessment" and provided funding for a European initiative on implementing hospital-based health technology assessment (AdHopHTA). The guidebook offers a set of standards of excellence in HBHTA that are supported by empirical evidence [17].

In contrast to HTA at the national and geographical levels, HBHTA aims to structure HTA action to guide decisions made by management in hospitals while taking into account the unique problem of setting up tasks in hospitals. It also goes beyond simply creating context-specific and scientifically sound documents. New technology is often introduced at hospitals. The implementation of research-based management and the decision-making process in hospitals greatly depends on HBHTA's ability to support hospital executives in evaluating and analyzing the necessity and viability of new technologies, improving the accuracy of health resource reservation, optimizing buying choices, and ensuring medical quality and safety. This is demonstrated by professionals with international advanced experience [18].

5.2.3 Safety precautions in healthcare

Healthcare professionals should be learning more about the development of MI algorithms. New AI tools have grown as a result of massive data collection, but their effectiveness depends on high-quality data that is precise, clinically relevant, and validated in a variety of contexts. Health institutions should consider how to securely incorporate these new tools into their workflow while the regulatory framework for AI tools is being formalized [19]. The priorities for digital clinical safety can be considered in two parts: first, the intrinsic safety of technologies, and second, the extrinsic ability of technologies to drive safety. Embracing these two components requires digital clinical safety to become part of the healthcare culture, with everyone understanding their role in digital clinical safety. Implementing AI and ML tools with care can help fulfill the promise of avoiding unfavorable outcomes. Health Information Technology (HIT) improves patient safety by reducing medication errors, reducing adverse drug reactions, and improving compliance with practice guidelines [20]. There should be no doubt that HIT is an important tool for improving healthcare quality and safety. A comprehensive framework for organizations looking to improve patient safety outcomes when using health information technology includes nine components. They are mentioned in Figure 5.2.

5.2.4 Data management and challenges in healthcare IT

Data management in digital health can be defined as "*people's ability to manage their own health information and data, to ensure the confidentiality and*

Figure 5.2 Framework for organizations to improve patient safety outcomes while using HIT.

security of this data, and to request health services effectively using this data". At the very least, a fundamental understanding of data collection, storage, and normalization is necessary for data management in the context of digital health. By guaranteeing efficacy, efficiency, accessibility, security, and customization, the digital health environment serves as a tool to enhance health and healthcare delivery [21]. When it comes to data security, the healthcare industry is among the most vulnerable. Cybercriminals place a high value on healthcare data, which includes personal health records, diagnostic data, and treatment plans. This personal information is frequently stolen during data breaches in healthcare institutions, and it may subsequently be sold on the dark web, used for identity theft, or utilized as a form of blackmail [22].

Data breaches in healthcare have an effect on patient trust in addition to financial expenses. Patients may conceal important health information due to a breach out of fear of disclosure, which could have a negative impact on their health. Because of this betrayal, it is even more important to have strong security measures in place. In particular, automation provides a means of handling the enormous volume of data while preserving the privacy, availability, and integrity of medical records, hence reducing the dangers connected with human error.

Complicatedness of Compliance: Healthcare firms have a complicated network of regulations to follow in order to protect patient information, in addition to safeguarding sensitive data. Important laws like the General Data Protection Regulation (GDPR) in Europe and the Health Insurance Portability and Accountability Act (HIPAA) in the US provide strict rules for healthcare institutions on how to manage, retain, and distribute personal health data [23, 24]. Serious financial fines and harm to one's reputation may arise from noncompliance with these constantly changing restrictions. Today's healthcare settings, where systems are becoming more dispersed and cloud-based, make compliance even more difficult. Maintaining compliance across these scattered environments becomes a major challenge when healthcare firms turn to cloud solutions for increased scalability and flexibility.

5.3 Digital Health

Advanced medical technologies, disruptive innovations, and digital communication have all progressively become inseparable from delivering best practice healthcare under the umbrella term "Digital Health". By the 2010s, medical knowledge was still expanding quickly, making the digitization of healthcare unavoidable. A variety of technologies, such as smartphone-connected ECG and genome sequencing, are now widely accessible thanks to Digital Health. The rise of digital health interventions and the rapid advancement of digital technologies have significantly influenced health practices. When referring to health-related technology, the terms "Digital Health" and "eHealth" (electronic health) are among the most inclusive since they cover nearly any hardware or software program that uses the binary system – information stored as zeroes and ones, instead of an analog system for data collection, storage, manipulation, and transmission [25]. The World Health Organization (WHO) has defined digital health (DH) as *"the field of knowledge and practice associated with the development and use of digital health technologies to improve health."* Digital healthcare refers to instruments and services that employ information and communication technologies (ICTs) to enhance and optimize health and lifestyle management, as well as play a role in the prevention, diagnosis, and treatment of diseases. Digital health interventions are being adopted with encouraging results in both high-income and low- and middle-income nations, with differences in how they are implemented and how they turn out. Significant clinical effects were demonstrated by high-quality Randomized Controlled Trials from wealthy nations [26]. Innovative adaptations of accessible technology have improved health in low- and middle-income nations, indicating the promise for affordable digital solutions in environments with limited resources. Digital health interventions show promise for managing rheumatic diseases. Tailoring these interventions to local infrastructure and emphasizing patient engagement are crucial for successful adoption.

In the health care ecosystem, digital health has become a comprehensive phrase that includes electronically recorded data as well as technical and communications infrastructure and applications. The tools required to build a healthy future are being redefined and re-engineered by revolutionary developments in digital health, which are revolutionizing biomedical science, medicine, and health. Current developments in self-management, healthcare, and biomedical science include cloud computing, AI, ML, blockchain, digitally mediated diagnostics and therapy, telemedicine, and consumer-facing mobile health applications. These advancements hold promise for improving outcomes, encouraging more involved patients, and promoting earlier diagnoses and therapies.

Digital health technology's (DHTs) have significantly altered the healthcare sector, bringing with them a number of advantages as well as important hazards that need to be well controlled. With a greater variety of intelligent and networked gadgets, DHT broadens the definition of eHealth to encompass digital consumers. It also covers other applications of digital technology for health, including robots, AI, including ML, big data analytics, the Internet of Things, and advanced computing [27]. Safe and successful use of DHTs in healthcare settings requires limiting access to sensitive patient data, ensuring security, and keeping up-to-date backup systems. With the correct guidelines, instruction, and design advancements, DHTs can successfully safeguard patient data and raise the standard of patient care [28].

DHT is becoming more and more involved in the administration and provision of healthcare. It is a means of gathering data in the actual world to describe patients, their treatment paths, and how they react to other clinical interventions. New procedures and insights that were previously unattainable through the architecture of the traditional health system have been made possible by DHT, encompassing real-time patient self-monitoring, innovative diagnostic and disease surveillance systems, and virtual care, in addition to being used as interventions [29].

In clinical treatment, pharmaceutical-related damage, such as adverse drug events (ADEs) and prescription errors, poses a substantial burden. Several steps in the medication process can lead to unsafe medication practices, such as prescribing errors, which account for almost 50% of medication errors (e.g., incorrect dosage, contraindication, and drug–drug interactions (DDIs) overlooked), dispensing errors, administration errors, and inadequate monitoring (e.g., hypokalemia among diuretic users due to inadequate renal and electrolyte monitoring). ICT is used in DHT to improve patient outcomes. DHT treatments include automated medication-dispensing systems, telemedicine, mobile health (mHealth) apps, electronic prescriptions, computerized provider order entry (CPOE) or clinical decision support systems (CDSS), and phone or text message reminders. DHT may help to improve medication use monitoring and support clinical judgments. With a significant decrease in ADEs and medication errors, DHT treatments offer a financially feasible way to enhance drug safety [30, 31].

5.3.1 Challenges in digital health

Medical decisions that do not involve medical professionals and put patients' lives in peril can result from the misread data from digital health devices and untrustworthy internet sources. Unauthorized third parties may obtain sensitive patient health information via devices that make data accessible to patients and stakeholders. There has been evidence of remote hacking of medical devices. In order to give consumers high-quality, trustworthy information, more focus must be placed on validating health sensors, other digital health equipment, and smartphone apps [32].

In the rapidly evolving digital era, hospitals must effectively handle health information innovation. A multihospital health system can enhance its management and prioritization of digital health initiatives by implementing an experience-based codesign (EBCD) methodology [33]. An implementable, efficient approach to managing requests for digital health projects, including setting priorities and monitoring projects from inception to completion, was developed by the EBCD. The most important health initiatives will probably be given priority thanks to this result of the example EBCD process. For the general population, this means future digital health services will be better, quicker, and more effective.

5.3.2 Ethics in digital health

Innovation in digital health faces several ethical and policy challenges. Five requirements must be fulfilled for digital health applications and products to result in noticeable innovation and health effects, whether at the individual or population level [34]. Refer to Figure 5.3.

First, data is crucial to digital health. Therefore, one of the main requirements for the creation of novel diagnostic, treatment, and monitoring technologies in this field is having access to adequate volumes of data. Second,

Figure 5.3 Requirements for health applications and products to end with innovation.

the key to innovation in digital health is compliance with current regulatory requirements for data security, privacy, and defense. The advancement of this subject can therefore be significantly aided or hindered by legal frameworks. The whole spectrum of ethical concerns in data processing, however, is not covered by legislative provisions. Additionally, they don't address all of the valid worries that data subjects may have. Third, the accurate identification of accountability for data uses and their effects on people, families, and communities should be guaranteed by strong and open accountability procedures. Additionally, accountability creates channels for informing data subjects about pertinent health information. Fourth, Evidence of efficacy and safety is a crucial prerequisite for digital health to succeed. Licensed digital health apps and products must pass rigorous evaluation procedures and satisfy cost-effectiveness standards before they can be paid for by public health systems and insurance companies. Nonetheless, this does not imply that unlicensed programs and products cannot include supporting data. Meeting these conditions will promote the fifth criterion for digital health innovation, which is trust in regulators and developers. This will help healthcare providers adopt digital health and ensure equitable benefit sharing from innovations in digital health.

5.4 Automation in Healthcare

A major factor in improving the overall quality of care provided to patients is the automation of digital healthcare systems. Automation is defined as *"applications of robotics, artificial intelligence, machine learning, machine vision, and similar emerging and mature digital technologies that will allow human work to be substituted by computer capital"* [35]. Automation has completely transformed the healthcare sector and made it more economical for the sector to conduct daily operations. Because automation eliminates human mistakes and weariness, it can assist offer precision and consistency and may even lower the number of infections, patient problems, and fatalities. In addition, automation can benefit physicians, hospitals, and professionals financially by lowering costs and increasing efficiency [36]. Automation has progressed science, which has improved the quality of healthcare. The ability to keep previous health records and provide them electronically is only two examples of how automation has outperformed other aspects. Automation is expected to be fulfilled by the advancement and application of AI in healthcare, which could influence the delivery of healthcare services. The ability to distribute it across various settings enhances both the hospital's and the patient's service delivery [37]. In the rapidly evolving field of healthcare, the combination of automation and AI has emerged as a powerful force that has the potential to fundamentally alter patient care [38]. These two transformative factors are not just new technological updates; rather, they signify a profound change that is altering the healthcare industry as a whole.

AI has proven to have impressive qualities in clinical decision making, including the ability to predict and categorize illnesses, as well as to offer insights and recommendations. There is mounting empirical evidence that knowledge-based clinical decision support systems, namely AI-based decision support systems (DSS), have the potential to improve practitioner performance [39]. AI has proven effective in a variety of medical imaging use cases, including the diagnosis of diabetic retinopathy from retinal fundus photos, the prediction of cardiovascular risk factors, the detection of mitosis in breast cancer histology images, and the dermatologist-level accuracy of skin cancer classification.

AI, which is a broad category of advanced computer-based analytical tools created by mimicking human intelligence, has potential applications in healthcare, such as the identification of medical conditions and the forecasting of health outcomes. A type of AI called ML is distinct from standard mathematical algorithms in that it incorporates the concept of "learning" from the input of sizable datasets. Usually, an algorithm is trained to complete a certain task, and its performance is then verified with a fresh dataset.

Big data sets are needed for ML algorithms. As healthcare becomes more digitally connected, electronic health records (EHRs) generate vast amounts of data that can be used to build AI algorithms. Using electrocardiogram (ECG) data to train AI models could help doctors diagnose acute coronary syndrome (ACS) [40].

5.4.1 Healthcare automation's possibility

Automation is the use of technology in the healthcare industry to streamline and expedite procedures [41]. This has a big effect on the administrative and operational parts of healthcare delivery and offers a number of substantial benefits, such as:

Streamlined workflows: Healthcare professionals can focus on patient care by using automation to eliminate tedious, manual tasks like scheduling appointments and billing.

Enhanced accuracy: The possibility of human error in data entry and record-keeping is decreased by automated systems, which can have detrimental effects on patient safety.

Efficiency and cost reduction: Automation reduces the time and resources needed to complete different tasks, which results in cost savings and more effective healthcare operations.

Data management: Large volumes of patient data are kept secure, organized, and available using automation techniques.

Monitoring of the workflow is necessary for effective automation and optimization. Recently, the automation of health care workflows using contemporary computing technology has been a national priority. A workflow monitoring tool (WMOT) can show its effectiveness by boosting situational awareness, facilitating clinical forecasts, and facilitating better administrative and medical decision-making. Workflows in the healthcare industry are increasingly becoming automated. WMOT consists of four components: (1) goal orientation; (2) thorough and robust data collection; (3) integrated and extensible analysis; and (4) subject experts [42].

5.4.2 Security automation

Security automation refers to the use of technology to carry out security tasks without direct human intervention. In healthcare IT, this encompasses a range of functions, including threat detection, incident response, patch management, and compliance reporting. By reducing the administrative load on IT teams, automation enables healthcare organizations to concentrate on more complex security duties while guaranteeing that basic procedures are completed quickly and precisely. In healthcare, where data breaches and cyberattacks can have devastating consequences, the need for automated security tools is even more pronounced. Automation in security allows healthcare organizations to respond to incidents faster, manage vulnerabilities more efficiently, and ensure that security protocols are consistently followed across diverse IT environments. Automation offers a number of important advantages, especially in terms of improving efficiency and security. Among its main benefits is its capacity to lessen the operational strain on IT staff. Electronic health records (EHRs) and mobile health apps are only two examples of the networked systems that are making healthcare environments more complex [43]. In such a setting, manually managing security can be very taxing. Routine processes like patching, monitoring, and access control can be greatly accelerated and improved by using automated solutions.

5.4.3 Advances in security automation

The future of automated security is bright as long as the healthcare sector keeps embracing digital change. New technologies like blockchain, quantum computing, and AI are going to completely change how healthcare companies handle security and compliance. For instance, AI-driven security systems are getting more advanced, allowing automatic reactions to security events and predictive threat identification. AI and ML algorithms are already being used to analyze vast amounts of data from healthcare IT environments, identifying potential threats before they escalate. In the future, these tools are expected to become even more advanced, offering real-time threat analysis and response capabilities that can mitigate risks faster and more effectively.

Personalized treatment plans, more operational efficiency, and better diagnostic accuracy are just a few of the many advantages that AI provides. However, new vulnerabilities are created when it is implemented in healthcare systems. Implementing strong access control procedures, securing data via encryption, and defending against hostile attacks are all necessary to ensure AI security. Healthcare businesses can protect patient information and avoid data breaches and illegal access by addressing these issues. By detecting anomalies, ML is essential to improving security. ML algorithms are able to spot odd patterns or behaviors that could point to system flaws or possible security risks. Real-time monitoring and early anomaly identification depend on this capability to enable prompt actions and avert possible security incidents [44]. Because of their flexibility, ML models may continuously learn from fresh data, offering constant defense against changing threats. It takes a complete strategy that incorporates frequent updates, thorough validation, and ongoing monitoring to apply AI and ML security measures effectively.

5.5 Error Reduction with AI

5.5.1 Diagnostic accuracy with AI

Diagnostic accuracy relates to the ability of a test to discriminate between the target condition and health. AI refers to the science and engineering of making intelligent machines, through algorithms or a set of rules, which the machine follows to mimic human cognitive functions, such as learning and problem-solving. AI systems function in a purposeful, intelligent, and adaptable way because they can either foresee problems or address them as they arise. Healthcare systems can accomplish their "quadruple aim" with AI by standardizing and democratizing a future of connected and AI-augmented care, precision therapies, precision diagnostics, and, eventually, precision medicine.

Over the past ten years, AI in healthcare has expanded significantly and has the potential to revolutionize the way that treatment is provided. The best examples of AI in healthcare are when ML techniques are used to mimic fundamental clinical decision-making in order to monitor the health of individual patients, when advanced analytics are used to sort through massive data sets in order to achieve clinical efficiencies, or when natural language processing (NLP) is used to perform surveillance and forecast outbreaks. Beyond these fundamental tasks, AI encompasses a variety of areas. Expert rule-based systems, robotic process automation, NLP, ML, and deep learning (DL) systems are the subfields of AI in healthcare. AI programs that possess expert-level abilities to solve certain problems through knowledge-based decision-making are referred to as expert systems, knowledge-based, and/or reason-based systems. Expert systems are being created for use in healthcare settings. Expert systems are made to mimic the clinical judgment and reasoning of experts using artificial neural networks. This allows them to either replace professionals with AI or transfer their expertise to others. Expert systems have been applied in a number of healthcare settings, including improving first responder performance, diagnosing conditions like various headaches and arrhythmias, forecasting the course of illnesses like hepatitis and wound healing, and optimizing radiotherapy treatment regimens [45].

Diagnostic imaging is one of the medical domains where AI has demonstrated revolutionary promise. Recent developments in AI-powered technology have created new opportunities to enhance echocardiography procedures. AI algorithms improve image quality, automate measurements, and aid in cardiovascular disease detection. These technologies match the diagnostic abilities of skilled echocardiographers, improve consistency, and decrease manual errors. By providing notable advancements in patient care, workflow efficiency, diagnostic accuracy, and tele-echocardiography, AI holds the potential to completely transform echocardiography. AI's incorporation into standard clinical practice is becoming more and more essential as the technology develops.

AI-assisted diagnostic technologies have shown promise in increasing the accuracy and efficacy of cancer diagnosis, particularly in endometrial cancer patients. The quality of patient care is improved by this invention, which also signals a shift in oncology toward more customized and effective treatment modalities. AI holds great promise for enhancing oncology diagnosis by specifically detecting and classifying endometrial cancer. All of the studies' combined results indicate steady progress in the successful use of AI in medical diagnostics. In particular, deep learning algorithms such as convolutional neural networks (CNNs) have shown remarkably high detection accuracy for endometrial cancer. It has been demonstrated that these technologies can carry out diagnostic tasks on par with human experts.

AI has made great strides in processing and understanding complex medical data, enabling faster and more precise patient diagnosis than ever before. Furthermore, because AI is especially adept at identifying various cancer kinds and distinguishing benign from malignant cases, these studies have demonstrated encouraging results for AI in prioritizing pathologist evaluations, which could result in an earlier cancer diagnosis and better patient outcomes. Because it has a significant impact on the prognosis of patients and treatment decisions, the highest level of diagnostic accuracy is essential in the field of oncology [46]. ML and applied AI can be used in several fields at once and offer faster and more accurate task performance. With the rapid advancement of technology and computer capacity, AI and robotics are at the forefront of medical progress. AI has the potential to significantly increase the accuracy and efficiency of radiation oncology operations, and mistake prevention is most successful when data transfer procedures are automated. AI will also increase the effectiveness of treatment, decrease transcription errors, increase the learning curve for new programs, automate the radiation therapy process by creating templates, detect troublesome patterns, fix possible mistakes, track fixes, and standardize the procedure in the most efficient manner. Moreover, by comparing treatment plans and delivery to preprogrammed templates, AI can be utilized to validate them [47].

Numerous innovative opportunities for enhancing patient care are presented by the application of AI in pathology. Ruiqian Artificial Intelligence Assistive Cytology Diagnostic System (AICyte), a new automated cervical cytology screening system, was created to answer the crucial question of whether or not an automated system might be used as an initial screening tool. AICyte significantly increases reading speed when pathologists use it for the initial screening of cervical liquid-based cytology sections. It also has the same sensitivity as manual work, but it also has improved specificity and accuracy [48].

For effective workflows and patient safety in the operating room, accurate surgical tool identification is essential, especially when it comes to avoiding issues like retained surgical instruments. Models of AI have demonstrated the ability to automate this procedure. The healthcare industry is rapidly being impacted by AI. Surgical instruments can be successfully classified from images using publicly available large language models (LLMs) – ChatGPT-4, ChatGPT-4o, and Gemini – and a specialized commercial mobile application called Surgical-Instrument Directory (SID 2.0). In broad classification tasks, ChatGPT-4o achieved 89% accuracy (precision = 0.92). While accurate instrument identification still needs work, accessible, affordable AI systems utilizing public LLMs can meet or surpass specialist smartphone applications for simple classification tasks. This lays the groundwork for the development of more precise and affordable surgical instrument recognition systems, which could improve patient safety and operating room efficiency, especially in environments with limited resources [49].

5.5.2 Medical errors

Medical errors include a wide spectrum of issues that are made as we deliver patient care, such as inaccurate diagnoses, pharmaceutical errors, surgical errors, and miscommunication. This may contribute to various other undesirable outcomes like prolonged hospital stay, more medical expenses, and, in the worst cases, morbidity and death. There are many evidences in the literature stating that medical errors have a significant impact on health outcomes. For example, there was a retrospective study conducted that analyzed more than 34,000 admissions, and 3.7% experienced adverse events, out of which 2.6% had permanent disability, and 13.6% led to mortality [1].

5.5.2.1 Types of medical errors

Medical errors are broadly categorized into errors of omission and errors of commission. Errors of omission arise when desired interactions are not executed, while errors of commission occur when an incorrect action is performed. The following are some of the specific medical errors.

- Diagnostic errors: They can significantly influence patient outcomes. Diagnostic mistakes may arise from cognitive distortions, insufficient information extraction, or systemic issues. Responsible human aspects include bias in cognition and temporal constraints.
- Medication errors: They are prevalent and can cause harm to the patient. Medication errors are caused by a variety of factors, such as illegible writing, unclear communication, and a lack of medication knowledge across medical professionals. Responsible human aspects include inadequately prepared electronic health records and disruptions in communication.
- Surgical errors: Surgical errors may result in devastating results for patients. Surgical mistakes, such as wrong-site operations, inappropriate procedures, and equipment breakdowns, can arise as a result of disagreements, insufficient preoperative preparation, or burnout among surgical team members. Responsible human factors include failures in team communication and fatigue.
- Communication errors: They can happen at any point during health care delivery and can cause negative effects. These errors may be the consequence of insufficient documentation, poor handovers, or misinformation between healthcare providers. Responsible human factors include improper handover procedures and presumptions.
- System errors: System errors are fundamental flaws within healthcare systems that result in medical errors. Insufficient employee numbers as a subject, poor handover protocol, and insufficient technology exhibit systematic problems that may elevate the probability of errors. Responsible human factors include the intricate nature of healthcare systems and the lack of training.
- Hospital-acquired infections: One area where AI shows potential is in the detection and diagnosis of infectious diseases. There has been great progress in the area of healthcare-associated infection (HAI) monitoring and prediction thanks to the inclusion of ML-based models. This might be a game-changer for patient safety and infection management.

Responsible human factors include unsafe hygiene and improper use of devices [50].

- Equipment errors: The design issues in medical equipment, improper handling, human error, and device malfunction are prevalent sources of medical errors. A considerable quantity of medical equipment has been implanted in patients (e.g., pacemakers, defibrillators, and nerve and brain stimulators), which may fail and result in fatal outcomes. Equipment malfunctions may arise from discrepancies among manufacturers, insufficient testing and servicing, ineffective design, and inadequate maintenance. Errors regarding tube and catheter connections, such as using catheters for inappropriate reasons, administering the incorrect line via a pump, and incorrectly positioning feeding tubes into the lung, are prevalent. These undesirable occurrences might have fatal consequences if a misconnection is not promptly rectified [51]. Responsible human factors include inadequate maintenance and improper handling.
- Patient falls: A number of factors, such as blood loss, drug side effects, post-anesthesia effects, hypoglycemia, altered mental state, advanced age, mobility disability, and insufficient personnel, may exacerbate the risk of falls in a healthcare environment. Responsible human factors include inadequate supervision and incorrect use of assistive or mobility devices [52].

5.5.2.2 Error analysis methods

In medical practice, errors are often categorized based on origin and outcomes. The severity of medical errors based on origin and outcomes is broadly sub-classified into four and five categories. They are presented in the Figure 5.4.

5.5.3 AI in healthcare

AI is transforming healthcare by markedly decreasing medical mistakes and enhancing patient safety. Through the use of extensive data, AI can discern trends, forecast future dangers, and enhance clinical decision-making with exceptional precision. AI significantly enhances diagnosis accuracy by using ML algorithms to assess medical imaging, laboratory findings, and patient histories for the early detection of illnesses such as cancer, heart disease, and infections. This reduces the probability of misdiagnosis, a primary contributor to medical mistakes. AI is a broad area of computer science that focuses on creating intelligent machines that can carry out tasks that normally call for

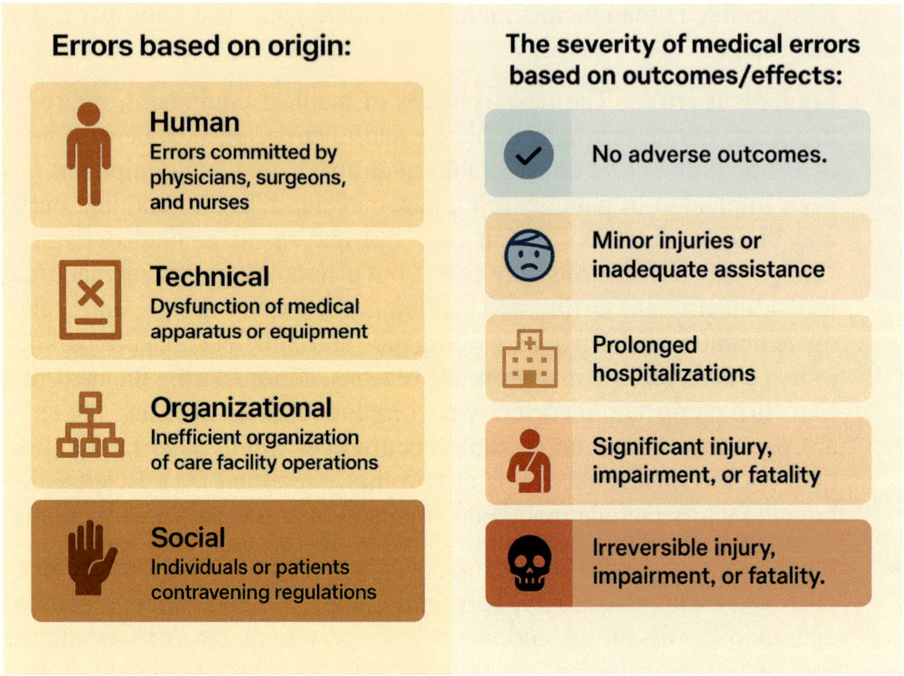

Figure 5.4 Severity of medical errors based on origin and outcomes.

human intelligence. The general pattern for artificially intelligent healthcare systems is as follows: system begins with a vast amount of data, on which ML algorithms are used to extract information. This knowledge is then utilized to provide a meaningful output that addresses a clearly defined issue in the medical system. Applications of AI in the field of medical sciences include matching patient symptoms to an appropriate physician, patient diagnosis, drug discovery, a bot assistant that can translate languages, transcribe notes, and organize images and files. AI is revolutionizing the healthcare sector by improving clinical outcomes, patient engagement, and service delivery, especially through hybrid chatbots. In domains like mental health support, chronic disease management, and diagnostics, these chatbots use AI and human input to deliver intelligent, tailored interactions [53].

The four primary categories of AI in healthcare are prescriptive, predictive, analytical, and expressive applications. AI can diagnose common health issues, save time, lessen the burden of skilled medical personnel, and lower treatment costs – all of which can help alleviate the scarcity of professional healthcare specialists. AI analyzes data using clever algorithms, and robotic process automation (RPA) increases accuracy and efficiency by automating repetitive operations. By increasing the accuracy of diagnoses, speeding up administrative work, cutting down on operation times, and enhancing patient care, these technologies are rapidly transforming the healthcare industry. Furthermore, recently implemented AI platforms like PathAI and Buoy Health have helped automate several medical procedures, especially diagnosis and treatment [54]. The availability of resources, technological compatibility, and the technical proficiency of healthcare personnel are some significant aspects that affect the adoption of AI systems in the industry. Results-wise, AI was found to be a valuable tool for automating medical diagnosis and treatment, handling claims and payments, and organizing medical records. As a result, the use of AI in healthcare improves care delivery by increasing the automation of healthcare services.

Real-time alerts and recommendations are provided by AI-driven clinical decision support systems (CDSS), which enable healthcare professionals to comply with best practices and prevent medication errors or inappropriate treatment protocols [55]. AI enables timely interventions by facilitating predictive analytics, which entails the identification of patients at heightened risk for negative outcomes such as sepsis, hospital-acquired infections, or accidents. AI reduces prescription mistakes in pharmaceutical administration by validating patient data against drug interactions, sensitivities, and doses, thereby ensuring the safe delivery of pharmaceuticals. Furthermore, robotic process automation (RPA) reduces human error by automating repetitive administrative tasks, assuring accurate documentation, and decreasing the probability of mistakes due to weariness or supervision. AI significantly enhances surgical precision using robots, hence reducing complications and increasing accuracy. Moreover, AI systems may scrutinize clinical notes and extract relevant information to ensure thorough and accurate recordkeeping using NLP.

5.5.3.1 Preventing medical errors through AI

AI has evolved to be a viable tool for preventing medical errors. Clinical and scientific decision-making is increasingly supported by sensor-based digital health technologies (sDHTs). Many advantages come from the digital clinical measurements they produce, such as increased patient-relevant data, better patient access, lower costs, and increased participation throughout health care ecosystems. Evidence-based medicine (EBM) has emerged as a key method for improving patient outcomes and medical care. EBM will likely rely on medical professionals' proficiency with digital health and AI technology as innovation spreads throughout healthcare companies [56].

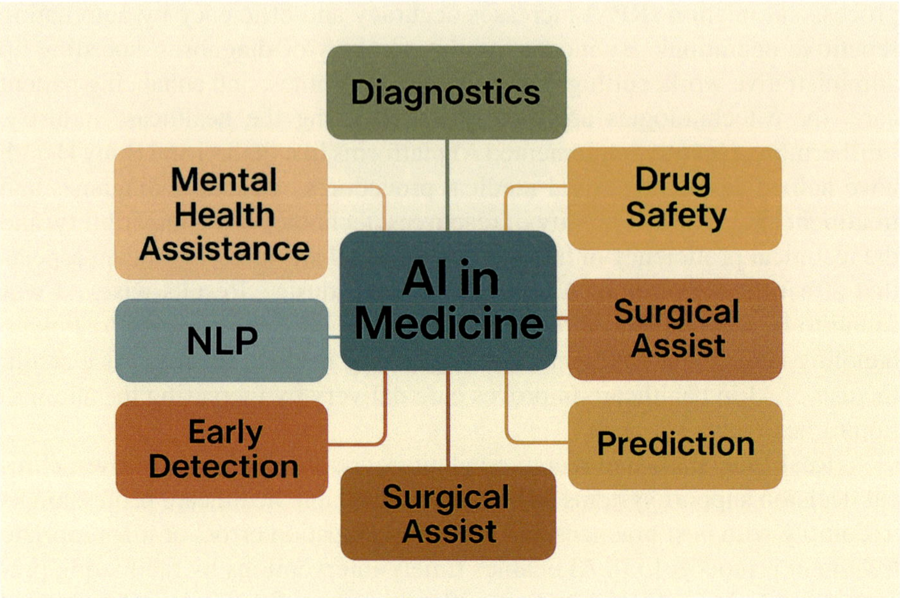

Figure 5.5 AI in preventing medical errors.

The quality and personalization of healthcare could be significantly improved by developments in AI and DHT. The following are some key aspects where AI can be used for preventing medical errors. Kindly refer to Figure 5.5.

- Diagnostic errors: This is the most common type of medical error. AI tools and software aid healthcare professionals for making appropriate and timely diagnosis. For example, in breast cancer imaging, AI can identify mammographic anomalies with accuracy equivalent to that of radiologists, and several commercial software solutions have emerged in recent years [57]. Thus, AI can help in early detection and intervention.
- Drug safety: Patient harm is largely caused by medication errors. AI technology may help healthcare practitioners reduce prescription errors by offering decision assistance. Based on a patient's medical history, current prescriptions, allergies, and probable drug interactions, AI algorithms may recommend suitable pharmaceutical doses.
- Surgical assist: AI-assisted surgical technologies are constantly used to augment precision and minimize the risk of errors during surgical procedures. Surgical robots coupled with AI algorithms may aid surgeons

in executing complicated surgeries with enhanced precision. AI might change surgical education and practice, ensuring the best patient care [58].

- Prediction: Predictive analytics may be implemented by AI to identify patients who are at a higher risk of adverse events and medical errors. AI algorithms may be able to identify patterns and risk variables associated with specific adverse events by analyzing a variety of patient data, such as clinical records, vital signs, and laboratory findings. AI has been used to improve the diagnosis of illness [59].
- Early detection: AI-driven monitoring systems may instantly evaluate patient data, encompassing vital signs, telemetry, and laboratory findings, to detect early signals of deterioration or prospective consequences. The potential of AI to improve diagnostic precision, reduce detection time, and enable real-time monitoring of disease epidemics has been demonstrated [60].
- Natural language processing (NLP): The extraction and analysis of information from unstructured clinical narratives, such as physician notes and discharge summaries, are facilitated by NLP approaches. The ability of ML prediction models to forecast potential data abnormalities before they develop into substantial problems has been examined. This proactive strategy reduces the probability of data integrity violations and enables the prompt execution of remedial measures.
- Mental health assistance: Because patients want rapid and easy feedback, the use of AI in mental health therapies is expanding. New insights on the topic have been made possible by recent developments in AI, which allow technology to deduce connections to emotions from a wider range of data sources [61].

5.5.3.2 Challenges and limitations of AI in healthcare

AI technologies hold considerable potential in the healthcare sector, especially in addressing the persistent challenge of medical errors. While there have been notable advancements in AI systems, their integration within the healthcare sector faces considerable challenges and constraints. There is also a need for further research for finding solution and solving the problems. One of the gaps in literature is how AI make decision and solve an issue. AI tools do not provide reasoning and evidence from literature in support of their decision like healthcare professionals do. And also, healthcare providers may not accept AI. The intrinsic limitations of ML, the drawbacks of ethics and the law, and societal resistance have all impeded the advancement of AI. Potential challenges associated with AI in the healthcare sector:

- AI diagnosis does not consistently outperform human diagnosis.
- AI programs can present challenges in comprehension and may exhibit excessive ambition.
- Bias.
- Challenges in execution.
- Concerns regarding transparency and potential risks associated with data sharing.
- Concerns regarding regulations.
- Ensuring the availability and accessibility of data.
- Errors in diagnosing illnesses.
- Societal challenges.

5.5.3.3 Ethical issues in AI

- Data sharing: Ethics in data sharing dismantles AI in informed consent, privacy and data protection, ownership, neutrality, and openness [62].
- Fairness: The most prevalent ethical concern is the unfairness resulting from bias in data sources. All data sets will exhibit bias to some degree, influenced by gender, sexual orientation, ethnicity, or sociocultural, environmental, or economic variables [63].
- Clinical practice: The integration of AI into healthcare practice presents novel issues for physicians. While a completely rule-oriented robot may seem more dependable at first, an ethical individual is more trustworthy in scenarios necessitating intricate clinical practice judgments. AI often exacerbates biased results, irrespective of the particular clinical interactions [64].

5.5.3.4 Legal issues in AI

- Security: Security is the paramount concern in the integration of AI within the medical sector, necessitating the most stringent evaluation.
- Hardware protection: All AI products need computers, phones, and wristbands to work. Three main hardware security vulnerabilities must

be highlighted [65]. First, cost, temperature, and electromagnetic interference will impact even the greatest physically unclonable operations. Second, physicians and engineers struggle to employ AI that combines numerous technologies due to the complexity and professionalism of medical knowledge and IT. Third, address AI network security.

- Software protection: Despite doing well in the first design examination, the AI system generally performs poorly in targeted design confrontations [66]. If the attacker knows everything about the trained neural network model (training data, model architecture, hyperparameters, number of layers, activation function, and model weights), all phases of AI algorithm construction will be targeted.
- Human factors: Software code represents modern AI. Engineers will make mistakes managing thousands of programs. AI systems may be improved via updates and upgrades. However, AI errors in medical applications may endanger patients.
- Estimating human genetic assets: The legal regulations safeguarding patient privacy in DNA collection, transmission, and storage need improvement.
- Social acceptance: Healthcare professionals in developing countries express significant apprehension over the potential replacement by AI in the future.

5.6 Conclusion

5.6.1 Quality improvement

There is always an opportunity to increase quality. This needs to be accepted and capitalized to become ingrained in routine practice, so that every chance for introspection on performance, results, and patient interactions is used to impact learning and, when necessary, to bring about change.

Errors: They occur in all human endeavors. Errors should be avoided at all costs, but when they do occur, they should be accepted. Departments should be encouraged to have a no-blame culture.

Continuing professional development (CPD): Based only on our knowledge from formal training, we cannot presume that it is suitable to practice for the rest of our lives. To adequately serve our patients and adjust our practices to new advances, technology, and evolving situations, we must pursue ongoing education.

Peer review: Everyday operations in healthcare departments already include several possibilities for peer assessment of our work. For example, reviewing previous study observations when a new study is being reported, reviewing imaging quality when a study is being reported, reviewing several studies and how they have changed over time when holding multidisciplinary team conferences, reviewing studies from elsewhere entities imported for the opinions of specialists or subspecialists, etc.

Clinical audit: Since 1997, medical facilities have been required by European Union guidelines to conduct clinical audits. Clinical auditing is a straightforward yet effective method for assessing present procedures and, where necessary, offering recommendations for their modification and improvement. Clinical audit basically entails comparing our actions to a standard and, where necessary, modifying our actions to match that standard.

External review: In many nations, it is legally required for healthcare departments to undergo external evaluations that evaluate their operations in comparison to established standards.

Risk management: Regardless of the laws in any nation, the professionals who work in healthcare departments should bear the primary responsibility for managing and reducing risk in such departments. Peer review and group accountability are essential components of successful risk management.

5.6.2 Prevention of hospital-acquired infections

The Centers for Disease Control and Prevention (CDC) states that broad guidelines for preventing the spread of illness should be part of basic infection control in healthcare institutions [67]. A few of the tenets are listed below.

- Maintain good hand hygiene by properly cleaning your hands or by using an alcohol-based disinfection solution.
- When necessary, put on personal protective equipment.
- Teach patients the proper way to cough and sneeze, as well as how to use masks while dealing with contagious diseases.
- Recognize problems pertaining to patients' solitary and make sure staff members are aware of them.
- Make sure the patient's surroundings and the items are properly cleaned via sterilization and disinfection.

- Carefully handle textiles and wash clothing, and dispose of them in accordance with hospital standards.
- Make sure that safe injection practices are followed, including the "one needle, one syringe, one use" guideline.
- Make sure that sharps are stored and disposed of properly.

It is essential to remember that the details given during shift transitions will impact the care delivered during the entire shift, and that key information may be overlooked, resulting in voids in treating patients. It is advised to communicate important information using the SBAR (situation, background, assessment, and recommendation) technique with the appropriate modifications [68]:

- Situation: What is the patient's or the scenario's current state? Find out the main complaint of an emergency patient. Find out what the inpatient's current issue is.
- Background: What is the setting or clinical history? What transpired during this inpatient stay, or what is the pertinent medical history?
- Evaluation: What do I believe to be the issue? Request the most recent observations and pertinent clinical results.
- Suggestion: How would I go about fixing it? What must be done right now? Are there any tasks that need to be done? How crucial is it?

5.6.3 Data security

Organizations involved in radiology must ensure that rules and regulations pertaining to the safeguarding of medical data are in place. Currently, local laws, hospital management policies, or national authorities mostly control access to databases like electronic patient records (EPR) and PACS. The new General Data Protection Regulation (GDPR), which has been in effect across the European Union (EU) since May 25, 2018, protects citizens of the EU with respect to the availability, analysis, and free flow of their private information. The rule seeks to maintain the advantages of digital image processing for public health and research while safeguarding the privacy of private health information. "Data protection by design and by default" is now a fundamental premise under the new GDPR [69].

The enhancement of error avoidance in healthcare will be augmented by AI's ability to learn and adapt from real-time data as it evolves. However, the effective incorporation of AI requires continuous cooperation among technology developers, physicians, and healthcare institutions to ensure ethical use, mitigate biases, and safeguard patient privacy. Ultimately, AI is a powerful tool that enhances human knowledge, therefore improving treatment quality, elevating patient outcomes, and minimizing medical mistakes. However, there are challenges associated with AI usage, such as issues of bias, lack of trust, and transparency. The medical community can make the most of AI's potential to improve patient care, reduce errors, and save lives by easing these limitations and encouraging developers of AI to work with healthcare practitioners. To overcome existing challenges and ensure full integration of AI-driven solutions into the healthcare ecosystem, further research and development are required.

5.6.4 Digital health

WHO emphasizes that digital health can be beneficial to achieving the Sustainable Development Goals by making health and well-being services accessible with high standards for all people globally. The primary emphasis in the field of digital health is on health, not technology. The idea of health placed more focus on the population's and individuals' health and well-being than on illnesses and patients. It is clear that the concept of technology places more emphasis on how technology should be used than on its technical features. In the realm of digital health, mHealth seemed to be a dominant concept. It was intimately associated with AI and, through it, with genomics. Digital health is the appropriate use of technology to improve community and individual health and well-being, and to improve patient care by processing clinical and genetic data intelligently.

References

[1] H. K. Walker, "The Origins of the History and Physical Examination," in *Clinical Methods: The History, Physical, and Laboratory Examinations*, Boston, Butterworths, 1990.

[2] P. A. Nutting, W. L. Miller, B. F. Crabtree, C. R. Jaen, E. E. Stewart and K. C. Stange, "Initial lessons from the first national demonstration project on practice transformation to a patient-centered medical home," *Annals of Family Medicine,* vol. 7, no. 3, pp. 254-260, 2009.

[3] J. H. Scatliff and P. J. Morris, "From Roentgen to magnetic resonance imaging: the history of medical imaging," *Journal of health policy analysis and debate,* vol. 75, no. 2, pp. 111-113, 2014.

[4] H.-J. Lee, S.-H. Oh, and C. L. Chang, "Origins and History of Laboratory Medicine," *Lab Med Online,* vol. 7, no. 2, pp. 53-58, 2017.

[5] V. Mishra, N. M. Gautier and E. Glasscock, "Simultaneous Video-EEG-ECG Monitoring to Identify Neurocardiac Dysfunction in Mouse Models of Epilepsy," *Journal of Visualized Experiments,* vol. 29, no. 131, p. 57300, 2018.

[6] M. E. Lyon, L. J. D'Angelo, Y. I. Cheng, R. H. Dallas, P. A. Garvie, J. Wang, and A. P. C. C., "The influence of religious beliefs and practices on health care decision-making among HIV positive adolescents," *AIDS Care,* vol. 32, no. 7, pp. 896-900, 2020.

[7] B. Mittelstadt, "Principles Alone Cannot Guarantee Ethical AI," SSRN, 5 November 2019. [Online]. Available: https://ssrn.com/abstract=3391293. [Accessed 5 May 2025].

[8] J. A. Doudna and E. Charpentier, "Genome editing. The new frontier of genome engineering with CRISPR-Cas9," *Science,* vol. 346, no. 6213, p. 1258096, 2014.

[9] R. P. Hirten, M. Danieletto, K. Landell, M. Zweig, E. Golden, R. Pyzik, S. Kaur, H. Chang, D. Helmus, B. E. Sands, D. Charney, G. Nadkarni, E. Bagiella, L. Keefer, and Z. A. Fayad, "Remote Short Sessions of Heart Rate Variability Biofeedback Monitored With Wearable Technology: Open-Label Prospective Feasibility Study," *JMIR Mental Health,* vol. 11, p. e55552, 2024.

[10] D. D. Farhud and S. Zokaei, "Ethical Issues of Artificial Intelligence in Medicine and Healthcare," *Iranian Journal of Public Health,* vol. 50, no. 11, pp. i-v, 2021.

[11] R. McNerney, "Diagnostics for Developing Countries," *Diagnostics,* vol. 5, no. 2, pp. 200-209, 2015.

[12] E. Sutton, G. Martin, H. Eborall, and C. Tarrant, "Undertaking risk and relational work to manage vulnerability: Acute medical patients' involvement in patient safety in the NHS," *Social Science & Medicine,* vol. 320, p. 115729, 2023.

[13] Y. Guner, K. Yilmaz, D. Yurtseven, and T. Mümin, "Determination of Medical Faculty Clinical Students' Attitudes Towards Patient Safety: A Mixed Design Study," *Safety and Health at Work,* vol. 15, pp. 404-411, 2024.

[14] M. Guo, M. Bayley, P. Cram, R. Dunbar-Yaffe, C. Fortin, K. Go, L. Linett, J. Matelski, A. Mayo, J. Pelc, L. R. Robinson, L. Rotteau, J. Wolfstadt and C. Soong, "Protocol for a stepped wedge cluster randomized quality improvement project to evaluate the impact of medical safety huddles on patient safety," *Contemporary Clinical Trials Communications,* vol. 30, p. 100996, 2022.

[15] E. S. o. R. and E. F. o. R. S., "Patient safety in medical imaging: A joint paper of the European Society of Radiology (ESR) and the European Federation of Radiographer Societies (EFRS)," *Radiography,* vol. 25, pp. e26-38, 2019.

[16] Z. Dai and X. Liao, "Hospital-based health technology assessment: The next frontier for traditional Chinese medicine hospitals," *Journal of Traditional Chinese Medical Sciences,* vol. 8, pp. 110-114, 2021.

[17] M.-P. Gagnon, M. Desmartis, T. Poder and W. Witteman, "Effects and repercussions of local/hospital-based health technology assessment (HTA): a systematic review," *Systematic Reviews,* vol. 3, p. 129, 2014.

[18] M.-P. Gagnon, "Hospital-Based Health Technology Assessment: Developments to Date," *Pharmaco Economics,* vol. 32, pp. 819-824, 2014.

[19] P. Ross and K. Spates, "Considering the Safety and Quality of Artificial Intelligence in Health Care," *The Joint Commission Journal on Quality and Patient Safety,* vol. 46, no. 10, pp. 596-599, 2020.

[20] Y. K. Alotaibi and F. Federico, "The impact of health information technology on patient safety," *Saudi Medical Journal,* vol. 38, no. 12, pp. 1173-1180, 2017.

[21] M. Palaniswamy, "ESG and SDG in healthcare," in *ESG Innovation for Sustainable Manufacturing Technology: Applications, designs and standards*, Kuala Lumpur, IET, 2024, pp. 305-339.

[22] D. H. Fehmi and E. D. Yardan, "Data management in the digital health environment scale development study," *BMC Health Services Research,* vol. 23, p. 1249, 2023.

[23] K. M. Miller, K. Lukic, and B. Skiera, "The impact of the General Data Protection Regulation (GDPR) on online tracking," *International Journal of Research in Marketing,* 2025.

[24] H. Subramanian, A. Sengupta, and Y. Xu, "Patient Health Record Protection Beyond the Health Insurance Portability and Accountability Act: Mixed Methods Study," *Journal of Medical Internet Research,* vol. 26, p. e59674, 2024.

[25] G. J. Thomas and D. S. Bond, "Review of innovations in digital health technology to promote weight control," *Current Diabetes Reports,* vol. 14, no. 5, p. 485, 2014.

[26] A. Santosa, J. W. Li and T. C. Tan, "Randomized controlled trials of digital health interventions for rheumatic disease management: a systematic review," *Systematic Reviews,* vol. 103, pp. 136-147, 2025.

[27] E. Pyper, S. McKeown, J. Hartmann-Boyce, and J. Powell, "Digital Health Technology for Real-World Clinical Outcome Measurement Using Patient-Generated Data: Systematic Scoping Review," *Journal of Medical Internet Research,* vol. 25, p. e46992, 2023.

[28] A. Hasman, J. Mantas and H. F. Marin, "Digital health and health informatics," *International Journal of Medical Informatics,* vol. 186, p. 105404, 2024.

[29] J. P. Bakker, S. J. McClenahan, P. Fromy, S. Turner, B. T. Peterson, B. Vandendriessche, and J. C. Goldsack, "A Hierarchical Framework for Selecting Reference Measures for the Analytical Validation of Sensor-Based Digital Health Technologies," *Journal of Medical Internet Research,* vol. 27, p. e58956, 2025.

[30] W. N. Insani, N. Zakiyah, I. M. Puspitasari, M. Y. Permana, K. Parmikanti, E. Rusyaman, and A. A. Suwantika, "Digital Health Technology Interventions for Improving Medication Safety: Systematic Review of Economic Evaluations," *Journal of Medical Internet Research,* vol. 27, p. e65545, 2025.

[31] N. K. Mensah, G. Adzakpah, J. Kissi, H. Taylor-Abdulai, S. B. Johnson, P. A. Agbeshie, C. Opoku, J. Abakah, E. Osei, A. Y. Agyekum, and R. O. Boadu, "Health Professionals' Ethical, Security, and Patient Safety Concerns Using Digital Health Technologies: A Mixed Method Research Study," *Health Services Insights,* vol. 26, no. 17, p. 11786329241303379, 2024.

[32] E. Vayena, T. Haeusermann, A. Adjekum, and A. Blasimme, "Digital health: meeting the ethical and policy challenges," *Swiss Medical Weekly,* vol. 16, no. 148, p. w14571, 2018.

[33] A. S. Black, S. Naicker, A. Tariq, P. Le, R. Donovan, M. Jones, S. Canaris, R. Warne, C. Ballantine, and S. M. McPhail, "Applying Experience-Based Co-Design principles to improve digital health demand management processes in a large metropolitan multi-hospital health system," *Health Policy and Technology,* vol. 13, no. 4, p. 100905, 2024.

[34] F. Fatehi, M. Samadbeik, and A. Kazemi, "What is Digital Health? Review of Definitions," *Studies in Health Technology and Informatics,* vol. 275, pp. 67-71, 2020.

[35] V. P. Gupta and A. K. Arora, "Automation in Healthcare Services," in *Applications of Deep Learning and Big IoT on Personalized Healthcare Services*, IRMA International, 2020, p. 19.

[36] S. M. Mohammad, "Implementation of automation in applications of healthcare, private, and public sectors in IT," *International Journal of Innovations in Engineering Research and Technology,* vol. 7, no. 5, pp. 364-372, 2020.

[37] A. Ingole and S. Sonwane, "Robotics And Automation in Healthcare," in *2024 International Conference on Healthcare Innovations, Software and Engineering Technologies (HISET)*, Karad, India, 2024.

[38] W. Y. Leong, Y. Z. Leong, and W. S. Leong, "Advancements in healthcare architecture through 5G technology," in *International Conference on Engineering Technologies and Applications (ICETA 2024)*, Taipei, 2024.
[39] M. Soori, F. K. G. Jough, R. Dastres, and B. Arezoo, "AI-Based Decision Support Systems in Industry 4.0: A Review," *Journal of Economy and Technology,* 2024.
[40] P. Z. Chan, M. A. I. B. Ramli and H. S. J. Chew, "Diagnostic Test Accuracy of artificial intelligence-assisted detection of acute coronary syndrome: A systematic review and meta-analysis," *Computers in Biology and Medicine,* vol. 167, p. 107636, 2023.
[41] P. Nimkar, D. Kanyal, and S. R. Sabale, "Increasing Trends of Artificial Intelligence With Robotic Process Automation in Health Care: A Narrative Review," *Cureus,* vol. 16, no. 9, p. e69680, 2024.
[42] D. T. Y. Wu, L. Barrick, M. Ozkaynak, K. Blondon, and K. Zheng, "Principles for Designing and Developing a Workflow Monitoring Tool to Enable and Enhance Clinical Workflow Automation," *Applied Clinical Informatics,* vol. 13, no. 1, pp. 132-138, 2022.
[43] A. A. A, G. M A, S. V, A. M, C. R, and M. M, "Securing electronic health records using blockchain-enabled federated learning for IoT-based smart healthcare," *Clinical eHealth,* 2025.
[44] A. S. Ansari, G. Altuwaijri, F. Alodhyani, M. I. E.-K. Ghembaza, S. M. D. Paramb, and M. S. Mohammadi, "A Detailed Review of Current AI Solutions for Enhancing Security in Internet of Things Applications," *Computers, Materials and Continua,* vol. 83, no. 3, pp. 3713-3752, 2025.
[45] K. Basu, R. Sinha, A. Ong, and T. Basu, "Artificial Intelligence: How is It Changing Medical Sciences and Its Future?" *Indian Journal of Dermatology,* vol. 65, no. 5, pp. 365-370, 2020.
[46] E. Huynh, A. Hosny, C. Guthier, D. S. Bitterman, S. F. Petit, D. A. Haas-Kogan, B. Kann, H. J. W. L. Aerts, and R. H. Mak, "Artificial intelligence in radiation oncology," *Nature Reviews Clinical Oncology,* vol. 17, no. 12, pp. 771-781, 2020.
[47] C. B H, E. S, and R. A, "AI-Generated Image-Based Mnemonics: Enhancing Learning Efficiency in Radiation Oncology," *International Journal of Radiation,* vol. 120, no. 2, pp. e678-679, 2024.
[48] X. Bai, J. Wei, D. Starr, X. Zhang, X. Wu, Y. Guo, Y. Liu, X. Ma, Y. Wei, C. Li, M. L. Zilla, W. Zhang, X. Zeng and C. Zhao, "Assessment of Efficacy and Accuracy of Cervical Cytology Screening With Artificial Intelligence Assistive System," *Modern Pathology,* vol. 37, no. 6, p. 100486, 2024.

[49] S. A. Haider, O. A. Ho, S. Borna, C. A. Gomez-Cabello, S. M. Pressman, D. Cole, A. Sehgal, B. C. Leibovich, and A. J. Forte, "Use of Multimodal Artificial Intelligence in Surgical Instrument Recognition," *Bioengineering,* vol. 12, no. 1, p. 72, 2025.

[50] A. A. Godbole, P. M. Mehra, S. Banerjee, P. Roy, N. Deb, and S. Jagtap, "Enhancing Infection Control in ICUS Through AI: A Literature Review," *Health Science Reports,* vol. 8, no. 1, p. e70288, 2025.

[51] E. S. Kirkendall, K. Timmons, H. Huth, K. Walsh, and K. Melton, "Human-Based Errors Involving Smart Infusion Pumps: A Catalog of Error Types and Prevention Strategies," *Drug Safety,* vol. 43, no. 11, pp. 1073-1087, 2020.

[52] J. Kim, E. Lee, Y. Jung, H. Kwon, and S. Lee, "Patient-level and organizational-level factors influencing in-hospital falls," *Journal of Advanced Nursing,* vol. 78, no. 11, pp. 3641-3651, 2022.

[53] J. N. Kok Wah, "Revolutionizing e-health: the transformative role of AI-powered hybrid chatbots in healthcare solutions," *Frontiers in Public Health,* vol. 13, p. 1530799, 2025.

[54] M. A. Mohammed, M. A. Mohammed and V. A. Mohammed, "Impact of Artificial Intelligence on the Automation of Digital Health System," *International Journal of Software Engineering & Applications,* vol. 13, no. 6, pp. 23-29, 2022.

[55] G. D. Giebel, P. Raszke, H. Nowak, L. Palmowski, M. Adamzik, P. Heinz, M. Tokic, N. Timmesfeld, F. Brunkhorst, J. Wasem, and N. Blase, "Problems and Barriers Related to the Use of AI-Based Clinical Decision Support Systems: Interview Study," *Journal of Medical Internet Research,* vol. 27, p. e63377, 2025.

[56] G. Wagner, M. Ringeval, L. Raymond, and G. Pare, "Digital health competences and AI beliefs as conditions for the practice of evidence-based medicine: a study of prospective physicians in Canada," *Medical Education Online,* vol. 30, no. 1, p. 2459910, 2025.

[57] H.-E. Kim, H. H. Kim, B.-K. Han, K. H. Kim, K. Han, H. Nam, E. H. Lee and E.-K. Kim, "Changes in cancer detection and false-positive recall in mammography using artificial intelligence: a retrospective, multireader study," *The Lancet Digital Health,* vol. 2, no. 3, pp. e138-148, 2020.

[58] D. A. Hashimoto, G. Rosman, D. Rus, and O. R. Meireles, "Artificial Intelligence in Surgery: Promises and Perils," *Annals of Surgery,* vol. 268, no. 1, pp. 70-76, 2018.

[59] J. Chen, D. Remulla, J. H. Nguyen, A. Dua, Y. Liu, P. Dasgupta, and A. J. Hung, "Current status of artificial intelligence applications in urology

and their potential to influence clinical practice," *BJU International,* vol. 124, no. 4, pp. 567-577, 2019.

[60] F. Epelde, "How AI Could Help Us in the Epidemiology and Diagnosis of Acute Respiratory Infections?" *Pathogens,* vol. 13, no. 11, p. 940, 2024.

[61] C. A. Lovejoy, V. Buch and M. Maruthappu, "Technology and mental health: The role of artificial intelligence," *European Psychiatry,* vol. 55, pp. 1-3, 2019.

[62] B. D. Mittelstadt and L. Floridi, "The Ethics of Big Data: Current and Foreseeable Issues in Biomedical Contexts," *Science of Engineering Ethics,* vol. 22, no. 2, pp. 303-341, 2016.

[63] R. J. Geis, A. P. Brady, C. C. Wu, J. Spencer, E. Ranschaert, J. L. Jaremko, S. G. Langer, A. B. Kitts, J. Birch, W. F. Shields, R. v. d. H. v. Genderen, E. Kotter, J. W. Gichoya, T. S. Cook, M. B. Morgan, A. Tang, N. M. Safdar and M. Kochli, "Ethics of Artificial Intelligence in Radiology: Summary of the Joint European and North American Multisociety Statement," *Canadian Association of Radiologists Journal,* vol. 70, no. 4, pp. 329-334, 2019.

[64] K. Tobia, A. Nielsen, and A. Stremitzer, "When Does Physician Use of AI Increase Liability?" *The Journal of Nuclear Medicine,* vol. 62, no. 1, pp. 17-21, 2021.

[65] Y.-F. Pu, Z. Yi and J.-L. Zhou, "Defense Against Chip Cloning Attacks Based on Fractional Hopfield Neural Networks," *International Journal of Neural Systems,* vol. 27, no. 4, p. 1750003, 2017.

[66] L. Jiang, Z. Wu, X. Xu, Y. Zhan, X. Jin, L. Wang, and Y. Qiu, "Opportunities and challenges of artificial intelligence in the medical field: current application, emerging problems, and problem-solving strategies," *Journal of International Medical Research,* vol. 49, no. 3, p. 3000605211000157, 2021.

[67] C. Boev and E. Kiss, "Hospital-Acquired Infections: Current Trends and Prevention," *Critical Care Nursing Clinics of North America,* vol. 29, no. 1, pp. 51-65, 2017.

[68] M. S. Achrekar, V. Murthy, S. Kanan, R. Shetty, M. Nair, and N. Khattry, "Introduction of Situation, Background, Assessment, Recommendation into Nursing Practice: A Prospective Study," *Asia-Pacific Journal of Oncology Nursing,* vol. 3, no. 1, pp. 45-50, 2016.

[69] A. Tang, R. Tam, A. Cadrin-Chenevert, W. Guest, J. Chong, J. Barfett, L. Chepelev, R. Cairns, R. J. Mitchell, M. D. Cicero, M. G. Poudrette, J. L. Jaremko, C. Reinhold, B. Gallix, B. Gray, and R. Geis, "Canadian Association of Radiologists White Paper on Artificial Intelligence in Radiology," *Canadian Association of Radiologists Journal,* vol. 69, no. 2, pp. 120-135, 2018.

6

Leveraging AI for Enhancing Safety in Healthcare

Chia Chao Kang[1] and Wendy Wai Yeng Yeo[2]

[1]School of Artificial Intelligence and Robotics, Jalan Sunsuria, Bandar Sunsuria, 43900 Sepang, Selangor Darul Ehsan, Malaysia
[2] School of Pharmacy, Monash University Malaysia, Jalan Lagoon Selatan, 47500 Bandar Sunway, Selangor Darul Ehsan, Malaysia

Email: chiachao.kang@xmu.edu.my; Wendy.Yeo@monash.edu

Abstract

As healthcare systems become increasingly complex, ensuring patient safety remains a major challenge. Preventable adverse events such as diagnostic errors, medication mistakes and procedural complications are continued to affect millions of patients yearly. This chapter examines how Artificial Intelligence (AI) is emerging as a powerful tool to address these safety concerns in the healthcare system. It explores the application of AI in improving diagnostic accuracy through medical imaging and decision-support systems. AI also helps in enhancing medication management as well as supporting adherence and strengthening procedural safety through surgical robotics and real-time patient monitoring. The chapter also discusses the growing role of predictive analytics, wearable technologies and remote monitoring systems in enabling earlier detection of health deterioration along with more personalized care. In a nutshell, AI provides promising opportunities to build safer, more responsive and patient-centered healthcare systems for the future.

6.1 Introduction

According to the World Health Organization (WHO) (2023), approximately one in ten patients experience adverse events due to medication errors, unsafe

 DOI: 10.1201/9788743812135-6

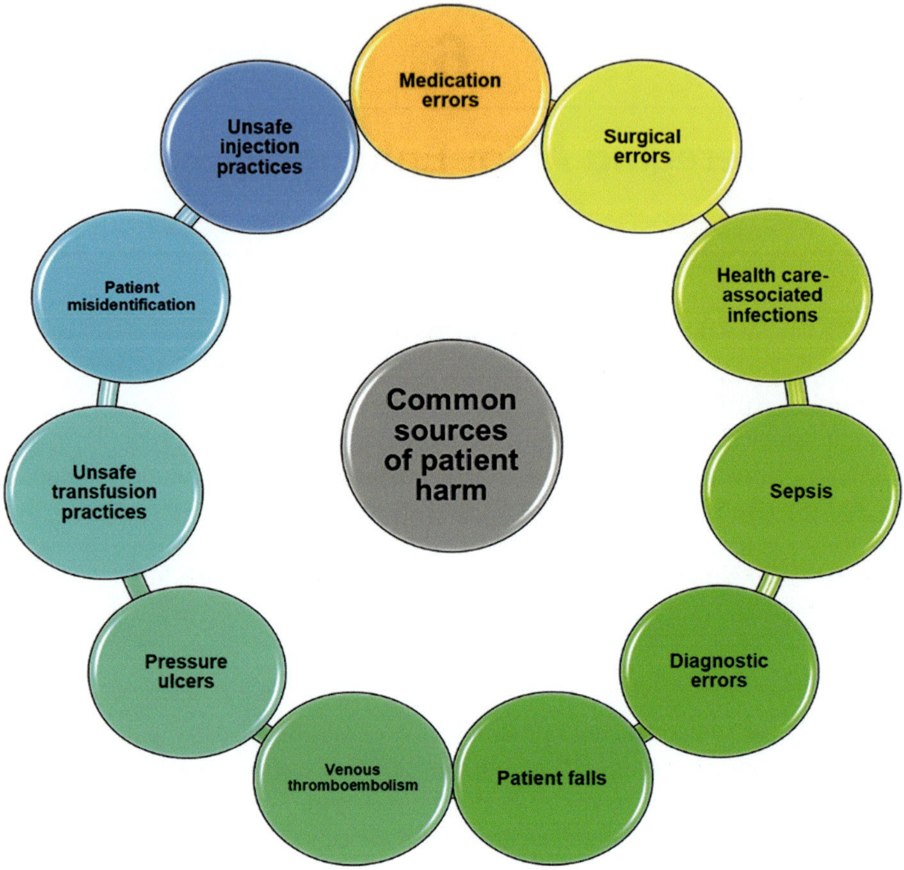

Figure 6.1 The list of common sources of patient harm in the healthcare system.

surgical procedures, diagnostic errors, patient misidentification, and others in healthcare, resulting in over 3 million deaths reported yearly due to unsafe care [1] (Figure 6.1). Factors identified contributing to patient harm include complex interventions, poor workflows, resource shortages, as well as human factors and behavior. In addition, patient-related issues, environmental challenges, technological errors, and their misuse further compound the risks.

Based on the findings from the Pennsylvania Patient Safety Reporting System (PA-PSRS), as the largest repository of patient safety data in the United States and one of the largest in the world, error related to procedure, treatment, and/or test was the most common event type across all reports [2] (Figure 6.2). Nevertheless, patient safety can be improved by identifying the

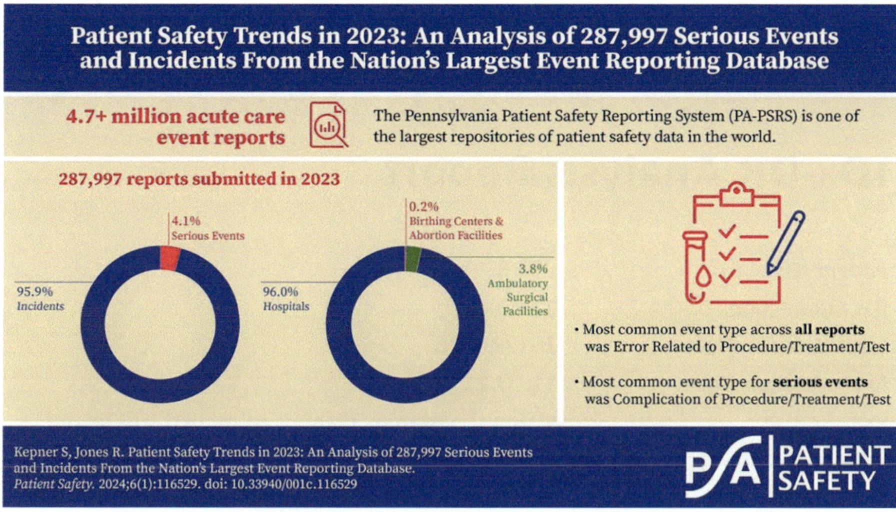

Figure 6.2 Patient safety trend in 2023.
Source: [https://www.pslhub.org/learn/patient-safety-in-health-and-care/patient-safety-trends-in-2023-an-analysis-of-287997-serious-events-and-incidents-from-the-nation%E2%80%99s-largest-event-reporting-database-22-april-2024-r11429/].

contributing factors and events that result in medical errors, developing multifaceted prevention protocols, and implementing these strategies at various healthcare levels. Herein, the integration of artificial intelligence (AI) into healthcare and medical technologies is pivotal in developing effective patient safety measures at various healthcare levels to ensure patients' well-being and optimal outcome.

6.2 Leveraging AI for Advancements in Healthcare Safety and Medical Technologies

6.2.1 Diagnostic accuracy and decision support

With the recent advancement in AI technologies, diagnostic accuracy in healthcare safety has improved, particularly in medical imaging analysis. For instance, in retina diseases, the AI algorithms can efficiently process large volumes of imaging data, as well as identify patterns and trends associated with these conditions [3]. These systems are also capable of detecting abnormalities and analyze subtle patterns and indicators of diseases [4]. The AI-based retina detection, such as age-related macular degeneration, diabetic retinopathy, and glaucoma, helps healthcare professionals in making more informed diagnoses and planning by providing clear rationales for predictions [5–7]. Figure 6.3 exhibits an example of a report generated using the

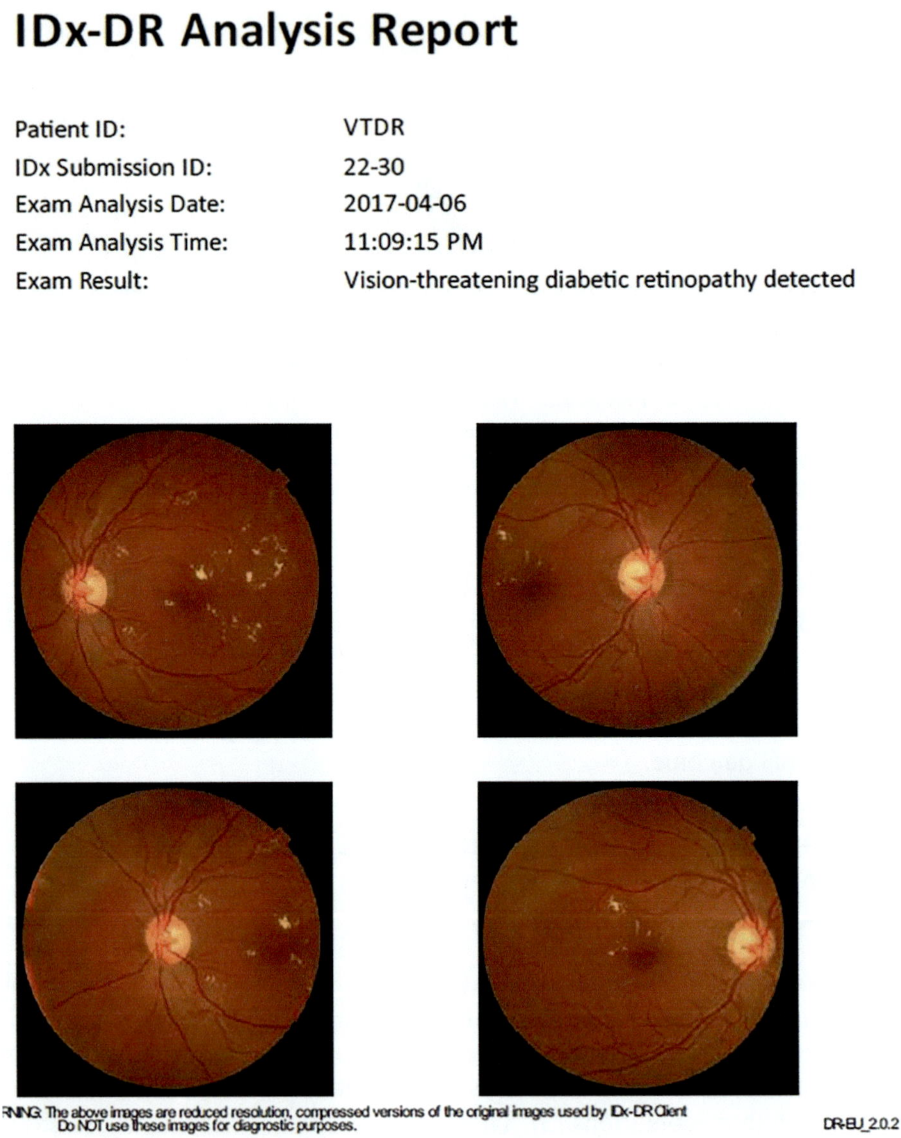

Figure 6.3 An example of a report generated from IDx-DR, an AI-based software system that uses an algorithm for autonomous detection of diabetic retinopathy, designed as a screening tool for primary care providers. Source: [https://www.healthvisors.com/en/idx-dr/].

IDx-DR, the first FDA-approved AI-based software system for diagnostic screening of diabetic retinopathy. This technology aids in minimizing diagnostic errors while optimizing workflows, which eventually improve patient outcomes. Furthermore, the integration of AI with patient history improves clinical decision-making and disease diagnosis, thereby enabling more personalized treatment [8].

6.2.2 Medication management and safety

In pharmacy practice, high volume of patient data involving medical records, laboratory results, and medication profiles often relies heavily on manual processes that cause high risk of human errors, inefficiencies, and delays. This necessitates the use of AI technologies such as AI algorithms and machine learning for effective analysis [9]. The data-driven analysis can be utilized to predict and detect adverse drug event interactions which remain a leading cause of morbidity and mortality around the world [10]. Various AI models are employed to identify potential drug–drug interactions by assessing the safety and efficacy of medicines, besides making informed recommendations. A recent study explored various AI-based chatbots, including ChatGPT-3.5, ChatGPT-4, Microsoft Bing AI, and Google Bard, in moving forwards of enhancing the accuracy and efficiency of clinical decision-making. These tools provide different levels of sensitivity, specificity, and accuracy attributed to different large language models (LLMs) in analyzing drug–drug interactions and providing management recommendations, which contribute to improving patient safety [11].

Additionally, AI solutions play a crucial role in improving medication adherence, as poor adherence to prescribed treatments often contributes to disease progression, increased hospitalizations as well as higher healthcare costs. A study by Labovitz and colleagues reported that the use of an AI platform on mobile devices revealed an absolute improvement of 67% for medication adherence among stroke patients undergoing direct oral anticoagulant therapy [12]. This finding highlights the potential of the AI platform as a real-time medication management tool to enhance adherence and influence patient behavior in taking medications, while strengthening the doctor-patient relationship [12]. Meanwhile, a recent report showed that an AI-supported, pharmacist-led medication adherence program for hypertension, cholesterol, and diabetes effectively improved disease control and reduced costs through data-driven patient engagement [13]. Hence, AI is essential in improving medication adherence for effective medication management and safety in addressing issues such as complicated dosing schedules, complex regimens, forgetfulness, lack of medication counselling, and others. Furthermore, the

Figure 6.4 MEMS®Cap Smart Pill Bottle enhances medication compliance by tracking medications intake and capturing essential study data which enable a seamless experience for patients and valuable non-compliance insights for researchers in clinical trial settings. Source: [https://aardex.aardexgroup.com/smart-pill-bottle-case-study].

innovative AI-powered smart pill bottles can transform compliance monitoring in clinical trials by tracking adherence, providing reminders to patients, and at the same time, generating valuable data to improve patient compliance and study outcomes, as shown in Figure 6.4.

6.2.3 Procedural safety and monitoring

With rapid advancements in modern technology, the use of AI in real-time monitoring and surgical assistance is widely used, bringing benefits to both healthcare professionals and patients. These AI technologies are reshaping and transforming the healthcare system in a new era of safety, efficiency, and precision, spanning from preoperative planning to post-op care [14]. According to the Report by Market Research Future (MRFR), it is estimated surgical robots market size will be worth USD 21.41 billion by 2030 at 19.87% compound annual growth rate (CAGR) during the forecast period [15]. For example, AI-powered surgical robots such as the da Vinci surgical system assist surgeons by providing real-time feedback and adjusting for tremors during delicate operations. This not only enhances patient safety but increase efficacy and safety of surgeries, enabling greater precision and consistency in complex surgeries [16]. Figure 6.5 illustrates various AI-assisted surgical systems that minimize errors, reduce risks of complications, and reduce invasiveness in procedures by combining advanced robotics, real-time data analysis, and machine learning algorithms to support surgeons in performing precise and efficient procedures.

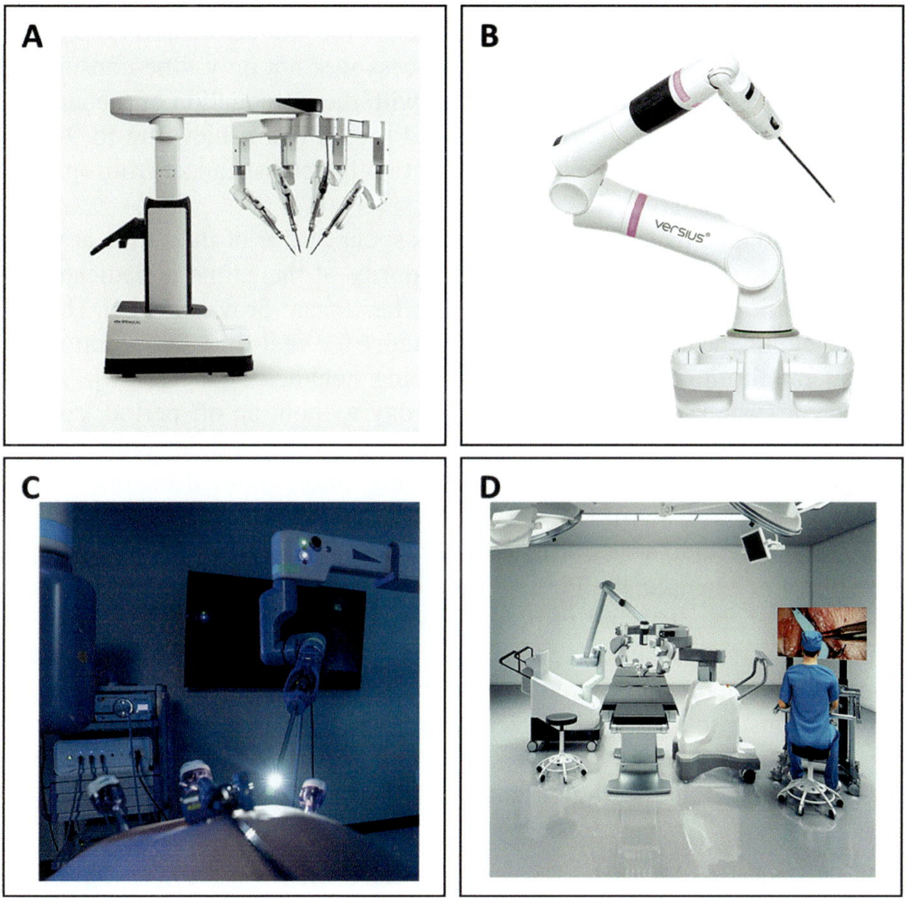

Figure 6.5 AI-assisted surgical robotics. (A) Da Vinci Xi: A widely used multiport robotic system offering advanced instrumentation, featuring Firefly® fluorescence imaging and integrated table motion. (B) Versius: Features patented V-Wrist technology, enabling portability, modularity, and 360° wrist rotation. (C) Senhance® Surgical System: Provides performance-guided robotic-assisted surgery, maintaining time and cost efficiency comparable to traditional laparoscopy. (D) MUSA-3: A microsurgical robotic system combining a surgeon console, robotic arm cart, and trusted surgical instruments.

Besides that, the integration of AI in medical procedures plays a crucial role in identifying early warning signs of complications, enabling timely interventions and improving patient safety. Deep learning algorithms, for example, are applied to analyze the long-term ECG data for the detection of cardiac arrhythmia cases [17]. A separate study utilizes the fast AI framework and the 1-cycle policy, which are automated for diagnosis and detection of metastases in the pathological tissue of breast cancers from whole slide images [18]. Traditionally, the pathologists had to undergo hours of examining histological slides to identify and detect the characterization of lymph nodes for breast cancer. This manual process was not only time-consuming but also prone to human error. However, with the introduction of the current AI-powered model, this current proposed model can achieve up to 97.4% accuracy, aiding the pathologists in predicting the breast cancer from spreading with precise analysis.

It is notable that hospital physicians spent 25.5% of their time at work in direct contact with patients, as the majority of their time is dedicated to documentation and interaction with other healthcare providers [19]. Hence, the development of autonomous AI systems for real-time and continuous patient monitoring is crucial for enhancing healthcare safety [20]. These intelligent systems operate 24 hours per day without an off period, continuous with monitoring and responding to patient vitals and detecting critical changes in health conditions. By leveraging autonomous decision-making capabilities, AI can swiftly identify early warning signs of medical emergencies such as cardiac arrest or respiratory distress, allowing for timely interventions. For example, the Philips' IntelligVue Guardian allows clinicians to track clinical, predict, and respond proactively to address the challenge of manually calculating the early warning score (Figure 6.6). Besides that, intelligent ICU systems now employ autonomous AI to monitor multiple patients simultaneously to alert the emergency response team before they escalate to life-threatening situations by integrating real-time data from pervasive sensing technologies, as shown in Figure 6.7.

6.3 Mitigating Human Error with AI-Enhanced Workflows

6.3.1 Error reduction in clinical environments

The AI has rapidly evolved from a futuristic concept to a practical tool that is transforming the current healthcare system. One of the main advantages of AI is the ability to process large volumes of data within a short period of time with high accuracy, and hence it becomes a suitable tool for automating

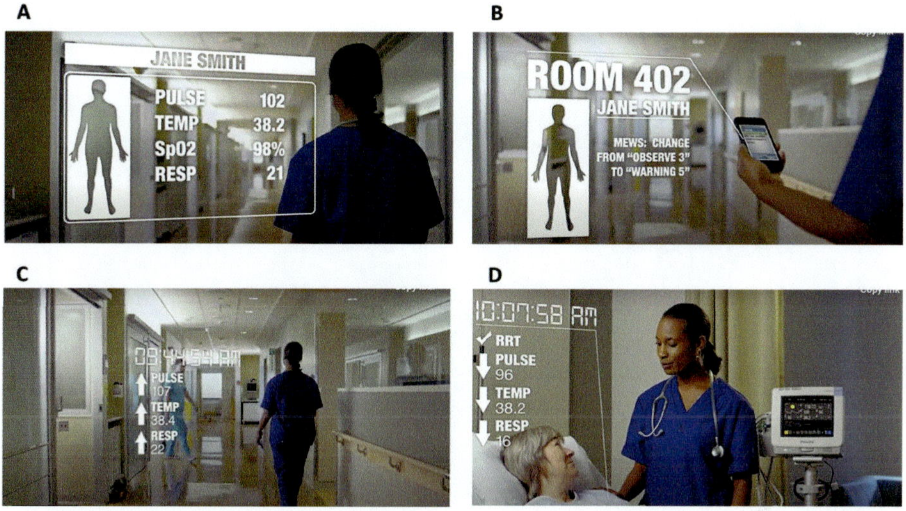

Figure 6.6 The IntelliVue guardian solution with early warning scoring is a patient monitoring system that integrates software, clinical decision support algorithms, and mobile connectivity to accurately identify patients at risk for timely and effective interventions. (A) The patient data is automatically calculated in the form of an early warning score by closely monitoring each patient's early warning score system. (B and C) If early signs of patient decline occur, the system sends an alert directly to the clinicians' mobile devices. (D) The healthcare providers take appropriate action to stabilize the patient's condition to prevent further deterioration.
Source: [https://www.philips.com.my/healthcare/clinical-solutions/automated-early-warning scoring/intellivue-guardian-ews].

routine tasks that are time-consuming and prone to human error. A recent study has shown that AI can significantly enhance nurses' work-life balance by automating administrative responsibilities and others [22]. Through automation of repetitive tasks, AI not only allows human resources to focus on more strategic activities but also mitigates human errors in clinical environments by leveraging real-time data and streamlining daily routines.

For example, AI can minimize manual errors, such as providing automated prescriptions, ensuring proper dosage calculations for patients, and preventing drug interactions [23]. This automated process can avoid many mistakes caused by distractions or incomplete information. The automated process also maintains detailed records and identifies deviations for correction. Therefore, this will enhance the clinical workflows, such as assigning and sequencing tasks based on urgency and resource availability. Besides that, automated systems can minimize errors from overworked staff and distribute

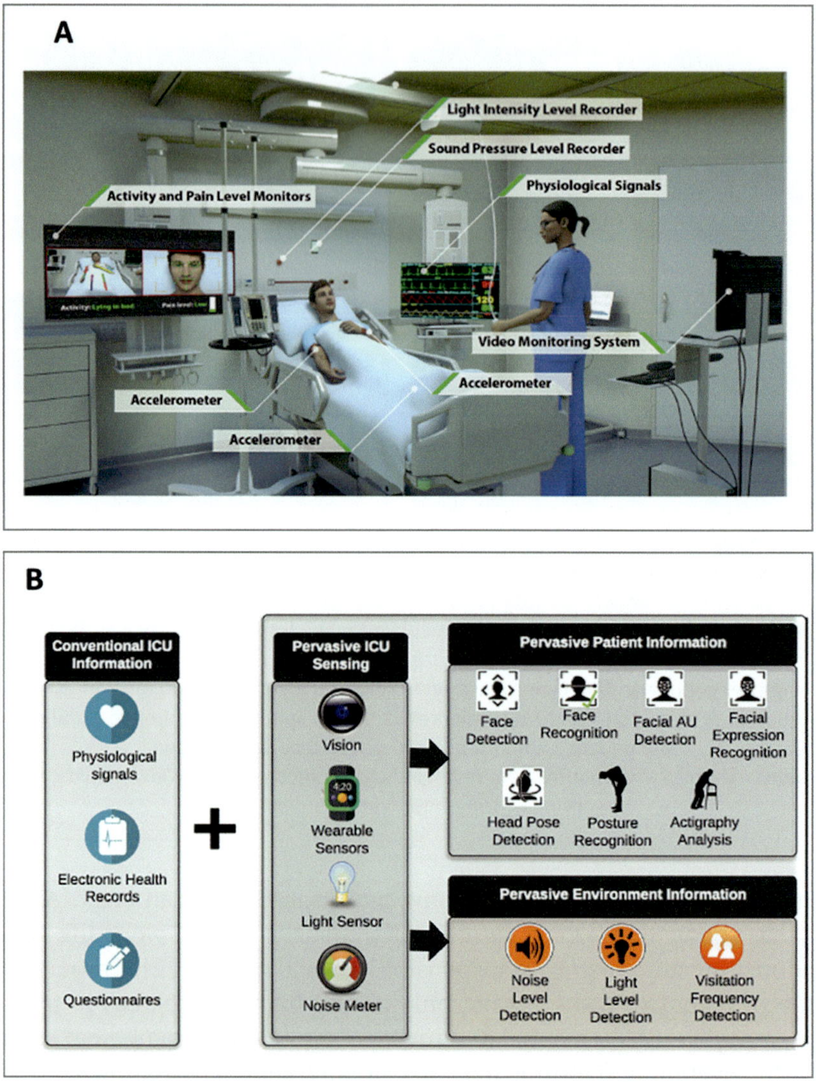

Figure 6.7 (A) The intelligent ICU utilizes pervasive sensing to collect data from patients and their environment. The system includes wearable accelerometer sensors, a video monitoring system, a light sensor, and a sound sensor for continuous monitoring. (B) The Intelligent ICU information complements conventional ICU information. Pervasive information is provided by performing face detection, face recognition, facial action unit detection, head pose detection, facial expression recognition, posture recognition, extremity movement analysis, sound pressure level detection, light level detection, and visitation frequency detection. Face detection icon, face recognition icon, facial AU detection icon, facial expression recognition icon, and head pose detection icon: © iStock.com/bitontawan. Adapted from [21], which is published under the terms of the Creative Commons Attribution 4.0 International License.

workloads evenly to reduce rushed decisions and overlooked details to ensure accurate patient records and allow clinicians to focus on care deliver [24, 25].

The AI technologies are also reshaping patient care across various dimensions, with AI-powered intelligent virtual assistants being utilized for patient support through telehealth sessions. These virtual assistants are able to provide immediate support for queries, scheduling appointments, or follow-up reminders, which help to relieve healthcare providers' workloads [26]. This helps reduce the likelihood of miscommunication as well as ensure patients adhere to prescribed care plans and provide timely guidance for common symptoms. There are several health chatbots at current market, such as Youper, Babylon Health, Florence, and others, which assist in symptom checking, medication reminders, and mental well-being support to provide personalized health insights and offer recommendations based on real-time data. Overall, AI-enhanced workflows greatly reduce the likelihood of human error in clinical settings by offering assistance, automating processes, and optimizing care delivery at all levels. These systems tackle issues such as fatigue and cognitive strain while enabling healthcare providers to attain improved results with a lower incidence of avoidable errors.

6.3.2 AI-driven predictive analytics for preventative care

Nowadays, AI-driven predictive analytics for preventative care is one of the important approaches for clinical decision support. The AI is capable of analyzing medical images, including X-rays and CT scans, with speed and precision, assisting in the early detection of diseases which may be difficult to identify using traditional methods [27, 28]. Moreover, the subtle patterns in patient data that may signal complications or deterioration can be identified earlier. Besides that, AI-driven predictive analytics also improve diagnostic consistency and reduce oversight due to human limitations by using algorithms that analyze genetic markers and family history, particularly in individuals with a higher risk of cancer. All these insights allow healthcare providers to proactively identify potential errors and offer appropriate treatments, aiding in minimizing adverse events and associated errors [29]. Additionally, leveraging patient history and biometric data together with medical imaging to detect and predict diseases, AI integration can bring forward toward the development of precision medicine [8].

Besides, AI-powered wearable devices and IoT tools are widely recognized for their role in enabling real-time, continuous health monitoring and alerts, which can potentially reduce emergency interventions and improve patient outcomes. A recent study reported that a deep-learning model capable of predicting cardiac arrhythmia on average 30.8 min before the onset appears using AI and electrocardiogram information gathered through wearable devices, with an accuracy of 83% [30]. Meanwhile, another study demonstrated an advanced AI-driven glucose monitoring and controlling system using a closed-loop insulin delivery system, which integrates real-time glucose monitoring for precise and personalized diabetes management [31]. Duckworth and colleagues explored the use of explainable machine learning to predict hypoglycemia and hyperglycemia in type 1 diabetes individuals up to 60 minutes in advance, while also automatically identifying key factors that contribute to increased risk based on their continuous glucose monitoring data [32].

Notably, the AI system continues evolving and learn from human experts and real-world cases by collecting feedback, learning from feedbacks, and refining their performance over time and experience. Thus, the AI system has the capability to provide more optimize clinical decision-making across various settings by combining dialog, visualization, collaboration, as well as deliver hidden data into actionable insights for improved patient care [33]. Overall, the integration of AI-powered predictive analytics with real-time health monitoring offer great potential in managing chronic conditions, minimizing medical risks, and ultimately improving healthcare efficiency and enhancing precision medicine.

6.4 Current Trends and Future Prospects of AI in Healthcare

Exploring how the integration of AI with wearable health technology could further improve patient monitoring and safety for early diagnosis of cardiovascular diseases [17]. For instance, devices such as the portable KardiaMobile from AliveCor, USA is a smartphone-connected ECG recorder for personal use (Figure 6.8A). It allows detection of up to six of the most common arrhythmias, including atrial fibrillation, bradycardia, tachycardia, sinus rhythm with premature ventricular contractions, sinus rhythm with wide QRS, and sinus rhythm with supraventricular ectopy. This medical-grade device operates by placing it in the palm of the hand, offers greater convenience compared to traditional transtelephonic monitoring and routine in-person evaluations.

Such advancements in wearable devices, with the integration of AI-driven algorithms with IoT enabling personalized health recommendations by identifying subtle patterns and trends in cardiac activity that may go undetected by traditional diagnostic methods. This technology facilitates

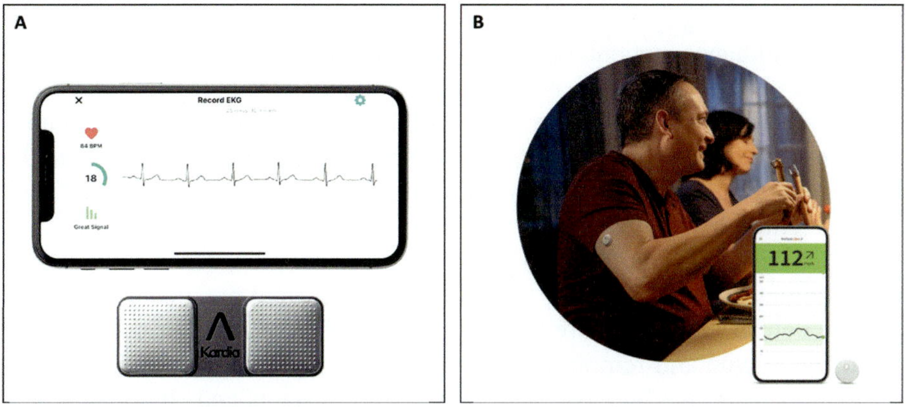

Figure 6.8 Wearable medical devices (A) KardiaMobile is a clinically validated, FDA-cleared device which records medical-grade electrocardiogram (EKG) in just 30 seconds, providing instant analysis directly on your phone from the comfort of your home. (B) FreeStyle Libre 3 system, a continuous glucose monitor, allowing individuals to check their glucose levels at any time.

earlier intervention and better management of cardiovascular conditions by enabling continuous monitoring and real-time alerts, and hence significantly improves patient safety. Moreover, the data collected from these devices can contribute to large-scale health databases, driving innovation and research in preventive cardiology. This synergy between AI and wearable health technology underscores a transformative shift toward proactive, patient-centered care in cardiovascular health management.

In addition, the development of small and lightweight medical devices, such as continuous glucose monitors (CGMs) integrated with AI algorithms with IoT, is advancing healthcare safety. For example, the world's smallest and thinnest sensor, Abbot's FreeStyle Libre 3 system (Figure 6.8B), is a CGM system consisting of a sensor and an app. The sensor is applied painlessly to the back of the upper arm and streams glucose readings automatically to the smartphone at any time. The LibreLinkUp app allows up to 20 people to remotely track glucose data and trends from a smartphone. This device provides customizable alerts and alarms for hypo- or hyperglycemic events. Furthermore, the FreeStyle Libre system tracks changes in glucose levels, which aid in informed food choices and daily activities, thereby reducing emergency situations and enhancing patient safety.

Overall, these emerging AI technologies, such as KG monitoring and diabetic CGMs, significantly enhance patient safety through advanced remote monitoring systems [34]. AI-integrated remote monitoring tools significantly enhance patient safety, providing early warnings for abnormal health conditions and thus enabling early detection of potential issues and timely medication intervention. With the real-time monitoring advantages, combined with adjustable settings for proactive risk management, reduce the likelihood of human error that potential in creating safer, more efficient, and patient-centered healthcare systems [35].

Besides supporting early prevention and personalized care at home, AI technologies have the potential to transform the current practice of medicine and the delivery of healthcare by strengthening the patient's safety measures via telemedicine and remote healthcare settings [36]. The extensive patient data can be leveraged via AI-powered virtual assistants and chatbots, which provide various functionalities in ensuring safer and more efficient care for patients in remote locations or underserved areas [37]. This includes the function of answering medical queries, scheduling appointments, and guiding medication adherence, moving forward, improving patient engagement and compliance. The AI-integrated remote monitoring tools improve the quality of care in addition to increase accessibility for patients, which play crucial roles for advancing equitable and efficient healthcare delivery.

The future of AI in healthcare safety is poised for transformative innovations and leveraging cutting-edge technologies to enhance patient care, reduce risks, and improve outcomes, as shown in Figure 6.9. These emerging AI technologies will enable more precise, proactive, and scalable safety solutions in the healthcare system.

6.5 Conclusion

The integration of AI technologies has revolutionized healthcare safety with applications spanning from imaging, diagnostics, predictive analytics, medication management, telemedicine to personalized treatment. Its ability to process vast amounts of data and identify different disease patterns has enabled timely interventions, improved patient monitoring, and more accurate diagnoses. Furthermore, AI in remote and telehealth settings is transforming healthcare safety by enabling proactive and efficient care while bridging gaps in access and enhancing trust in virtual healthcare delivery. This has greatly minimized the risk of diagnostic errors, medication mistakes, and procedural complications. Ultimately, AI is set to drive advancement in diagnostics, treatments, and healthcare practices, paving the way for a more innovative and efficient healthcare system in the future.

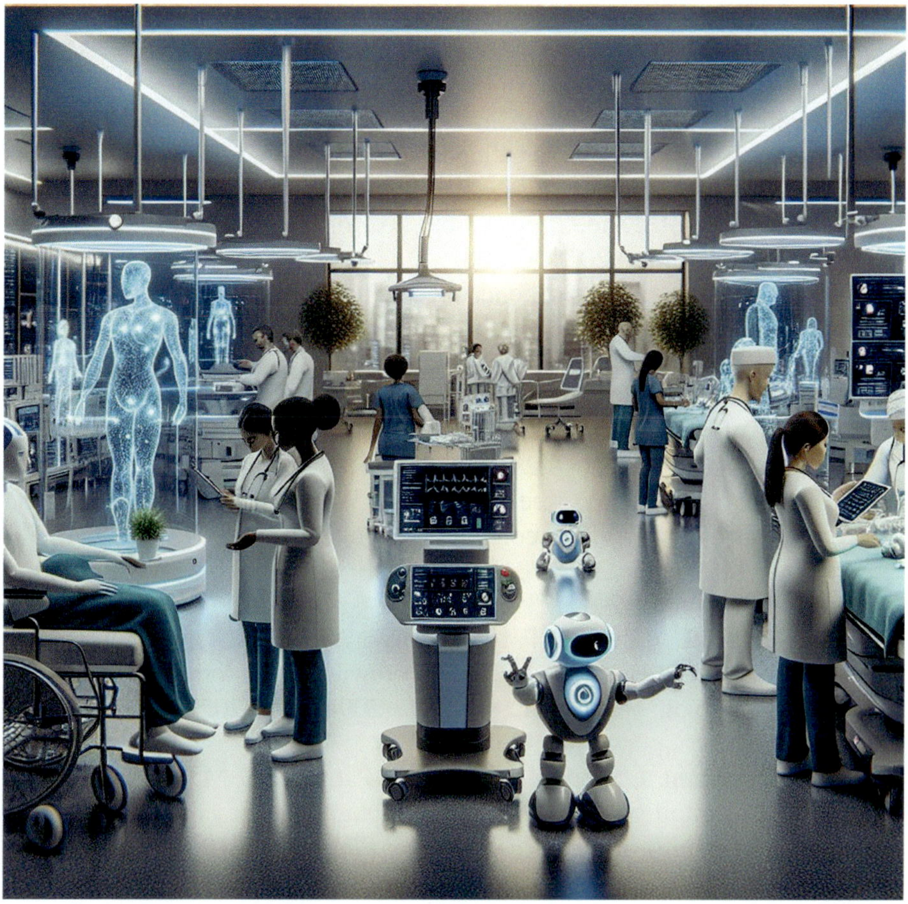

Figure 6.9 Future of AI in healthcare (Microsoft Co-Pilot. (2025). Image generated using Microsoft Co-Pilot).

References

[1] World Health Organization. (n.d.). Patient safety. Retrieved November 22, 2024, from https://www.who.int/news-room/fact-sheets/detail/patient-safety.

[2] S. Kepner and R. Jones, "Patient Safety Trends in 2023: An Analysis of 287,997 Serious Events and Incidents From the Nation's Largest Event Reporting Database," in "Patient Safety," 2641-4716 2689-0143, 2024, vol. 6.

[3] U. P. S. Parmar *et al.*, "Artificial Intelligence (AI) for Early Diagnosis of Retinal Diseases," (in eng), *Medicina (Kaunas),* vol. 60, no. 4, Mar 23 2024, doi: 10.3390/medicina60040527.

[4] M. Fatima, P. Pachauri, W. Akram, M. Parvez, S. Ahmad, and Z. Yahya, "Enhancing retinal disease diagnosis through AI: Evaluating performance, ethical considerations, and clinical implementation," *Informatics and Health,* vol. 1, no. 2, pp. 57-69, 2024/09/01/ 2024, doi: https://doi.org/10.1016/j.infoh.2024.05.003.

[5] D.-K. Hwang *et al.*, "Artificial intelligence-based decision-making for age-related macular degeneration," *Theranostics,* vol. 9, no. 1, pp. 232-245, 2019, doi: 10.7150/thno.28447.

[6] S. Qummar *et al.*, "A Deep Learning Ensemble Approach for Diabetic Retinopathy Detection," *IEEE Access,* vol. 7, pp. 150530-150539, 2019, doi: 10.1109/access.2019.2947484.

[7] X. Chen, Y. Xu, D. W. Kee Wong, T. Y. Wong, and J. Liu, "Glaucoma detection based on deep convolutional neural network," 2015: IEEE, doi: 10.1109/embc.2015.7318462. [Online]. Available: https://dx.doi.org/10.1109/embc.2015.7318462

[8] C. C. Kang, T. Y. Lee, W. F. Lim, and W. W. Y. Yeo, "Opportunities and challenges of 5G network technology toward precision medicine," *Clin Transl Sci,* vol. 16, no. 11, pp. 2078-2094, Nov 2023, doi: 10.1111/cts.13640.

[9] S. H. Chalasani, J. Syed, M. Ramesh, V. Patil, and T. M. Pramod Kumar, "Artificial intelligence in the field of pharmacy practice: A literature review," (in eng), *Explor Res Clin Soc Pharm,* vol. 12, p. 100346, Dec 2023, doi: 10.1016/j.rcsop.2023.100346.

[10] N. P. Tatonetti, P. P. Ye, R. Daneshjou, and R. B. Altman, "Data-Driven Prediction of Drug Effects and Interactions," *Science Translational Medicine,* vol. 4, no. 125, pp. 125ra31-125ra31, 2012, doi: 10.1126/scitranslmed.3003377.

[11] F. Y. Al-Ashwal, M. Zawiah, L. Gharaibeh, R. Abu-Farha, and A. N. Bitar, "Evaluating the Sensitivity, Specificity, and Accuracy of ChatGPT-3.5, ChatGPT-4, Bing AI, and Bard Against Conventional Drug-Drug Interactions Clinical Tools," *Drug, Healthcare and Patient Safety,* vol. Volume 15, pp. 137-147, 2023, doi: 10.2147/dhps.s425858.

[12] D. L. Labovitz, L. Shafner, M. Reyes Gil, D. Virmani, and A. Hanina, "Using Artificial Intelligence to Reduce the Risk of Nonadherence in Patients on Anticoagulation Therapy," (in eng), *Stroke,* vol. 48, no. 5, pp. 1416-1419, May 2017, doi: 10.1161/strokeaha.116.016281.

[13] C. Worrall, D. Shirley, J. Bullard, A. Dao, and T. Morrisette, "Impact of a clinical pharmacist-led, artificial intelligence–supported medication adherence program on medication adherence performance, chronic disease control measures, and cost savings," *Journal of the American Pharmacists Association : JAPhA.,* vol. 65, no. 1, p. 102271, 2025, doi: 10.1016/j.japh.2024.102271.

[14] A. Amin *et al.*, "Future of Artificial Intelligence in Surgery: A Narrative Review," *Cureus,* 2024, doi: 10.7759/cureus.51631.

[15] K. Dey, "Surgical Robots Market Research Report Information By Product Type (Instrument & Accessories, Robotic Systems, and Services), By Application (Gynecologic Surgery, General Surgery, Cardiac Surgery, Urologic Surgery, Colorectal Surgery, and Head And Neck Surgery), By Control Mechanism (Direct Telemanipulator and Computer Control) By End User (Hospitals and Ambulatory Surgical Centers) and Region (North America, Europe, Asia-Pacific, and Rest of the World)—Forecast till 2032," 2021. Accessed: 26 February 2025. [Online]. Available: https://www.marketresearchfuture.com/reports/surgical-robots-market-3025

[16] Q. Fan, Z. Fu, and D. Xiong, "Advantages and prospects of robotic surgery for colorectal cancer," *Intelligent surgery,* vol. 8, pp. 1-7, 2025, doi: 10.1016/j.isurg.2025.01.001.

[17] N. E. Almansouri *et al.*, "Early Diagnosis of Cardiovascular Diseases in the Era of Artificial Intelligence: An In-Depth Review," *Cureus,* 2024, doi: 10.7759/cureus.55869.

[18] A. Vulli, P. N. Srinivasu, M. S. K. Sashank, J. Shafi, J. Choi, and M. F. Ijaz, "Fine-Tuned DenseNet-169 for Breast Cancer Metastasis Prediction Using FastAI and 1-Cycle Policy," (in eng), *Sensors (Basel),* vol. 22, no. 8, Apr 13 2022, doi: 10.3390/s22082988.

[19] M. Weigl, A. Müller, A. Zupanc, and P. Angerer, "Participant observation of time allocation, direct patient contact and simultaneous activities in hospital physicians," *BMC Health Services Research,* vol. 9, no. 1, p. 110, 2009, doi: 10.1186/1472-6963-9-110.

[20] S. A. Alowais *et al.*, "Revolutionizing healthcare: the role of artificial intelligence in clinical practice," (in eng), *BMC Med Educ,* vol. 23, no. 1, p. 689, Sep 22 2023, doi: 10.1186/s12909-023-04698-z.

[21] A. Davoudi *et al.*, "Intelligent ICU for Autonomous Patient Monitoring Using Pervasive Sensing and Deep Learning," (in eng), *Sci Rep,* vol. 9, no. 1, p. 8020, May 29 2019, doi: 10.1038/s41598-019-44004-w.

[22] M. K. K. Rony *et al.*, "The role of artificial intelligence in enhancing nurses' work-life balance," *Journal of Medicine, Surgery, and*

Public Health, vol. 3, p. 100135, 2024/08/01/ 2024, doi: https://doi.org/10.1016/j.glmedi.2024.100135.
[23] O. Khan, M. Parvez, P. Kumari, S. Parvez, and S. Ahmad, "The future of pharmacy: How AI is revolutionizing the industry," *Intelligent Pharmacy,* vol. 1, no. 1, pp. 32-40, 2023/06/01/ 2023, doi: https://doi.org/10.1016/j.ipha.2023.04.008.
[24] H. Shamszare and A. Choudhury, "Clinicians' Perceptions of Artificial Intelligence: Focus on Workload, Risk, Trust, Clinical Decision Making, and Clinical Integration," (in eng), *Healthcare (Basel),* vol. 11, no. 16, Aug 16 2023, doi: 10.3390/healthcare11162308.
[25] K. J. Ruskin, A. C. Ruskin, and M. O'Connor, "Automation failures and patient safety," *Current Opinion in Anesthesiology,* vol. 33, no. 6, pp. 788-792, 2020, doi: 10.1097/aco.0000000000000935.
[26] A. Haleem, M. Javaid, R. P. Singh, and R. Suman, "Telemedicine for healthcare: Capabilities, features, barriers, and applications," (in eng), *Sens Int,* vol. 2, p. 100117, 2021, doi: 10.1016/j.sintl.2021.100117.
[27] L. Pinto-Coelho, "How Artificial Intelligence Is Shaping Medical Imaging Technology: A Survey of Innovations and Applications," (in eng), *Bioengineering (Basel),* vol. 10, no. 12, Dec 18 2023, doi: 10.3390/bioengineering10121435.
[28] M. Khalifa and M. Albadawy, "Artificial Intelligence for Clinical Prediction: Exploring Key Domains and Essential Functions," *Computer Methods and Programs in Biomedicine Update,* vol. 5, p. 100148, 2024/01/01/ 2024, doi: https://doi.org/10.1016/j.cmpbup.2024.100148.
[29] A. Choudhury and O. Asan, "Role of Artificial Intelligence in Patient Safety Outcomes: Systematic Literature Review," (in eng), *JMIR Med Inform,* vol. 8, no. 7, p. e18599, Jul 24 2020, doi: 10.2196/18599.
[30] M. Gavidia *et al.*, "Early warning of atrial fibrillation using deep learning," (in eng), *Patterns (N Y),* vol. 5, no. 6, p. 100970, Jun 14 2024, doi: 10.1016/j.patter.2024.100970.
[31] S. Medanki *et al.*, "Artificial intelligence powered glucose monitoring and controlling system: Pumping module," (in eng), *World J Exp Med,* vol. 14, no. 1, p. 87916, Mar 20 2024, doi: 10.5493/wjem.v14.i1.87916.
[32] C. Duckworth *et al.*, "Explainable Machine Learning for Real-Time Hypoglycemia and Hyperglycemia Prediction and Personalized Control Recommendations," (in eng), *J Diabetes Sci Technol,* vol. 18, no. 1, pp. 113-123, Jan 2024, doi: 10.1177/19322968221103561.
[33] K. B. Johnson *et al.*, "Precision Medicine, AI, and the Future of Personalized Health Care," (in eng), *Clin Transl Sci,* vol. 14, no. 1, pp. 86-93, Jan 2021, doi: 10.1111/cts.12884.

[34] Z. Guan *et al.*, "Artificial intelligence in diabetes management: Advancements, opportunities, and challenges," *Cell Reports Medicine,* vol. 4, no. 10, p. 101213, 2023, doi: 10.1016/j.xcrm.2023.101213.

[35] F. Tsvetanov, "Integrating AI Technologies into Remote Monitoring Patient Systems," 2024 2024, vol. 37: MDPI, p. 54, doi: 10.3390/engproc2024070054. [Online]. Available: https://dx.doi.org/10.3390/engproc2024070054

[36] J. Bajwa, U. Munir, A. Nori, and B. Williams, "Artificial intelligence in healthcare: transforming the practice of medicine," (in eng), *Future Healthc J,* vol. 8, no. 2, pp. e188-e194, Jul 2021, doi: 10.7861/fhj.2021-0095.

[37] Z. Ni *et al.*, "Implementation of Chatbot Technology in Health Care: Protocol for a Bibliometric Analysis," (in eng), *JMIR Res Protoc,* vol. 13, p. e54349, Feb 15 2024, doi: 10.2196/54349.

7

AI in Hospital Management, Patient Management, Diagnosis, and Treatment

Neha Kuthiala[1] Mohankumar Palaniswamy[2,3] Harikrishnan Ranganathan[4] and Chandrakumar Kadirvelu[5]

[1]University of Alberta, Edmonton, Canada
[2]Faculty of Sports and Exercise Science, Universiti Malaya, 50603 Wilayah Persekutuan Kuala Lumpur, Malaysia
[3]INTI International University, 71800 Nilai, Negari Sembilan, Malaysia
[4]School of Physiotherapy, Sri Balaji Vidyapeeth, Pondicherry, India
[5]SRM College of Physiotherapy, SRM Institute of Science and Technology, Kattankulathur, India

Email: kuthialaneha0312@gmail.com; mohankumar.p@um.edu.my; hariptsbv@gmail.com; chandrak5@srmist.edu.in

Abstract

Artificial Intelligence (AI) is fundamentally reshaping healthcare by optimizing the continuum of care, from administrative efficiency to bedside precision. In hospital management, AI-driven predictive analytics streamline resource allocation, bed management, and staffing, reducing operational bottlenecks. Simultaneously, patient management is enhanced through remote monitoring and personalized engagement tools that ensure adherence to care plans and improve long-term outcomes. In the clinical realm, AI's impact on diagnosis is profound; deep learning algorithms analyze complex medical imaging and genomic data with unprecedented speed, identifying pathologies at their earliest stages. This precision extends to treatment, where machine learning models facilitate personalized medicine by tailoring therapeutic interventions to an individual's unique biological profile and real-time physiological data. By integrating these four pillars, AI creates a cohesive, data-driven ecosystem

 DOI: 10.1201/9788743812135-7

that minimizes human error, maximizes institutional throughput, and significantly elevates the standard of patient-centric care.

7.1 Safety in Healthcare

The World Health Organization (WHO) said in 2017 that "Medication without harm," its third worldwide patient safety challenge, will concentrate on pharmacological safety with the goal of lowering the worldwide incidence of drug mistakes by 50% in 5 years. Medication error is defined as *"any preventable event that may cause or lead to inappropriate medication use or patient harm while the medication is in the control of the healthcare professional, patient, or consumer. Such events may be related to professional practice, health care products, procedures, and systems, including prescribing, order communication, product labeling, packaging, and nomenclature, compounding, dispensing, distribution, administration, education, monitoring, and"* [1]. Medication errors may happen at any point throughout the prescription, compounding, dispensing, handling, tracking, and usage of medications.

The WHO defines patient safety (PS) as the prevention of medical mistakes and the harm they cause to patients while they are receiving treatment. Injuries, fatalities, or disabilities may result from unsafe medical procedures [2]. The necessity to enhance patient safety culture (PSC) in the global healthcare sector has been acknowledged as a result of the increase in these accidents. Collaboration, institutional and cultural understanding, disclosure of mistakes and risk consciousness, gender and demography, job experience, and number of employees were all thought to have a major influence on PS. Perceptions of PS were also correlated with individual factors, such as the maturity and competence of medical personnel. Globally, the term "patient safety culture" refers to the dedication of medical facilities to patient well-being. It is defined as "*the product of individual and group values, attitudes, perceptions, competencies, and patterns of behavior that determine the commitment to, and the style and proficiency of, an organization's health and safety management*" [3].

Insecure medical practices cause injuries, impairments, and even mortality to millions of people annually around the globe. The International Nuclear Safety Advisory Group coined the phrase "safety culture" in reference to the flawed procedures that led to the 1986 Chernobyl nuclear power plant accident [4]. Since then, several highly reliable, safety-critical sectors, including nuclear power and aviation, have adopted the idea, which is now seen as essential to the company's safety record. The emphasis on creating a culture of safety has shifted more recently to the healthcare sector, where it is now one of the main tenets of the PS movement. Initiatives to enhance and evaluate safety culture multiplied as the significance of safety culture in healthcare was more recognized, highlighting the necessity for thorough evaluation methods. The expansion of this field has coincided with growing external demand on healthcare companies to conduct routine safety culture evaluations from regulatory bodies, accrediting bodies, and other safety authorities.

PSC has become a crucial component of excellent healthcare delivery, highlighting the beliefs, mindsets, and activities inside healthcare organizations that promote the safety of patients above all else. The notion of high-reliability organizations (HROs) has attracted interest due to its capacity to constantly provide safe and dependable services, even in complicated and high-risk settings. In the past few years, the significance of PSC has been emphasized due to its essential function in risk mitigation, mistake prevention, and enhancement of care quality delivery [5]. A successful PSC enables healthcare professionals to articulate safety concerns, cooperate proficiently within multidisciplinary teams, and participate in ongoing learning and enhancement initiatives. Moreover, firms with a strong PSC exhibit a commitment to openness, responsibility, and patient-focused care, encouraging credibility and respect across patients and shareholders. As part of the programs, the National Center for Patient Safety created a PSC module that was given to all veterans affairs workers via the All Employee Survey (AES). Preliminary studies indicated good accuracy, design, and category validation for a 20-issue including four measures: (1) recognizing hazards and Culture, (2) failure disclosure and prevention, (3) supervisor interactions and confidence, and (4) team cohesiveness and participation [6]. The 20 issues are mentioned in Table 7.1.

According to multiple investigations, factors at the company and a person's levels, including safety voice, perceived manager support for safety, safety climate, resilience-related factors, and perceived business support for safety, may have an impact on employees' safety practices and safety outcomes in healthcare facilities [7].

Safety Climate: Looks at how workers see the safety techniques, rules, and protocols in their companies. Safety environment is linked to workplace accidents and predicts dangerous conduct. A positive safety atmosphere in the workplace is essential for safe operations [8].

Perceived Business Support for Safety: Employee perceptions of an organization's dedication to helping and caring for its staff are related to perceived organizational support. Reduced levels of risky behaviors, unfavorable safety outcomes, as well as an increase in workers' organizational engagement, might result from perceived organizational support for safety.

Table 7.1 Patient safety culture and their items.

PSC scales	Items within the scale
Failure disclosure and prevention	Mistakes have led to positive changes here.
	We are given feedback about changes put into place based on event reports.
	We discuss ways to prevent errors from happening again in this unit.
Recognizing hazards and culture	We take the time to identify and assess risks of PS.
	I will not be punished if I report a PS problem or unsafe act.
	Safety education and training provided to me are enough to accomplish my job safely.
	Staff will freely speak up if they see something that may negatively affect patient care.
Team cohesiveness and participation	Employees in my workgroup do what is right, even if they feel it puts them at risk.
	Members in my workgroup can bring up problems and tough issues.
	People support one another in my unit.
	People treat each other with respect in my workgroup.
	The people I work with cooperate to get the job done.
	Disputes or conflicts are resolved fairly in my workgroup.
	My workgroup members communicate well with each other.
Supervisor interactions and confidence	Supervisors set challenging and yet attainable performance goals for my workgroup.
	My direct supervisor communicates the reasoning behind decisions that have an impact on my work.
	My supervisor listens to what I have to say.
	My supervisor treats me with respect.
	I have trust and confidence in my supervisor.
	My supervisor does not engage in favoritism.

More job satisfaction, fewer accidents, dedication to work-safe procedures, and a strong appreciation for colleagues' safety efforts are all linked to more favorable attitudes [9].

Perceived Manager Support for Safety: The degree to which supervisors promote safe work methods among their subordinates is known as supervisor support for safety. Reduced rates of unfavorable safety outcomes are associated with increased supervisor safety assistance. A higher risk of physical injuries at work is substantially correlated with a lack of supervisor safety assistance. The safety voice intentions of workers might be influenced by a supervisor's dedication to safety [10].

Safety Voice: The term "safety voice" refers to workers' opinions of possible risks at work and their advocacy for safety to avert injuries. This idea conveys actions of awareness to others about dangerous working circumstances and safety concerns to prevent accidents and harm. Acts intended to lower injury risks, eliminate hazards, and raise an organization's overall safety standards are referred to as safety voice [11].

Resilience: A resilient system has four capabilities: learning, reacting, predicting, and regulating. Resilience engineering is a strategy for managing organizational safety by fostering the cultural, intellectual, and social skills necessary for staff members to predict, regulate, react, and learn how to work securely within a secure limit. Resilience in healthcare systems, which are intricate adaptive systems, refers to the systems' capacity to modify their operation prior to, during, or after unintended occurrences and changes [12]. The term "individual resilience" describes the personal traits that allow an individual to endure hardship and tragedy. It also considers the capacity to recover from adversity or failure, which is a stress-coping skill. Resilience is the ability to successfully adjust to hardship and tragedy while continuing to function well [13].

In the past, the following research tools have been used to evaluate PSC: the Hospital Survey on Patient Safety Culture (HSPSC), the Safety Attitudes Questionnaire (SAQ), the Patient Safety Climate in Health Care Organizations (PSCHO), the Modified Stanford Instrument (MSI-2006), and the Scottish Hospital Safety Questionnaire (SHSQ) [14]. Refer to Table 7.2. The primary purposes of safety culture assessment in the healthcare industry are to: (1) recognize safety culture to pinpoint areas that require enhancement and increase patient safety consciousness; (2) examine patient safety interventions and monitor changes over time; (3) carry out both inside and outside benchmarking; and (4) satisfy orders or legal requirements. There are still several issues with measuring and addressing safety culture that need to be taken into account, such as variations in definitions, instruments, dimensions, and the rate of response [15].

The **Hospital Survey on Patient Safety Culture** (HSPSC), created in 2004 by the Agency for Healthcare Research and Quality (AHRQ) inside the US Department of Health and Human Services, gained widespread usage. This instrument is centered on reporting incidents, patient safety, and

Table 7.2 Dimensions of patient safety culture in different tools.

Survey	PSC dimensions
HSPSC	Assistance from management for patient safety
	Cooperation among units
	Cooperation between units
	Learning within the organization and ongoing development
	Nonpunitive reactions to mistakes
	Openness in communication
	Recommendations and dialogue on mistakes
	The anticipation and behaviors of the staffing manager or supervisor that support patient safety
	The frequency of recorded incidents
	Transitions and handoffs
	Views of patient safety generally
SAQ	Circumstances of work
	Contentment at work
	Identification of stress
	Organizational views
	Safety environment
	Teamwork mindset
PSCHO	Fear of being held accountable
	Overall focus on PS unit safety regulations
	Resources of the organization
	Senior managers' involvement
	Shame-related fear
	Unit endorsement and acknowledgment of safety initiatives
MSI	Disgrace and the consequences of reporting
	Leadership in the organization for safety
	Leadership of the unit for safety
	Learning habits for safety
	projected level of security

Survey	PSC dimensions
SHSQ	Collaboration between hospital departments
	Cooperation across hospital departments
	Handoffs to hospitals
	Nonpunitive reactions to mistakes
	Openness in communication
	Organizational development and enhancement
	Perceptions of safety overall
	Recommendations and dialogue on mistakes
	recruitment
	Reporting incident frequency
	Supporting patient safety via hospital management
	The expectations and conduct of supervisors

mistakes. Staff attitudes on medical mistakes, reporting adverse events, and other patient safety-related topics may be evaluated using this survey. Despite being mainly designed for hospital usage, the initial survey has been improved with many iterations. The safety culture among patients in public pharmacies, nursing homes, outpatient clinics, and ambulatory settings has been assessed by this study. Arabic, Spanish, French, and Dutch are among the languages in which the HSPSC is accessible. The 42-item hospital questionnaire evaluates 12 composites that are regarded as subscales [16]. Additionally, the instrument asks users to simply indicate the number of occurrences that have happened over the last 12 months and to offer an overall grade on the safety of patients for their work area or unit. Among the 12 composites, "Supervisor/manager expectations and actions promoting safety," "Organizational Learning and Continuous Improvement," and "Teamwork within Hospital Unit," are frequently used and are built on established recommendations for tracking PSC in healthcare facilities [17]. Later, the AHRQ created an enhanced form of the HSPSC that includes 18 items about the employment area or unit, 4 items about their relationship with the manager or supervisor, 6 items about interactions, 3 items about the number of events reported, 1 item about the patient safety guide, and 11 items about their hospital.

Table 7.3 Major parts of the SAQ.

Major parts	Representation
Safety climate	Views of a proactive and resolute dedication to safety
Teamwork climate	Perceived level of staff cooperation
Job satisfaction	Satisfaction with the job experience
Stress recognition	Recognition of the impact of stress on performance
Perceptions of management	Acceptance of the management action
Working conditions	Perceived level of logistical assistance and workplace setting suitability

Sexton and associates at the University of Texas in the United States created the **Safety Attitudes Questionnaire** (SAQ). The SAQ is made up of six major parts, as mentioned in Table 7.3. The Safety Climate, Teamwork Climate, Job Satisfaction, Stress Recognition, Perceptions of Management, and Working Conditions are the six areas that the SAQ examines regarding the caregiver attitudes on safety culture [18]. The SAQ's main benefit is its adaptability to various healthcare environments. 30 elements are regarded as standard in all situations out of the 60 elements or items used in the full version of the SAQ. A five-point Likert scale, from strongly agree to strongly disagree, is used in the poll. This survey may include six more questions in addition to the thirty standard items, three of which are devoted to demographic research. The five-point Likert scale may also be used to respond to the statements used by the short-form SAQ. English, Swedish, Dutch, Norwegian, German, Arabic, and Chinese are among the languages in which the abbreviated version is readily available [19].

The 32-item **Safety Attitude Questionnaire in Chinese** (SAQ-C) measures five aspects of PSC: working environment, job fulfilment, opinions about administration, safety climate, and collaboration climate. Strongly disagree, somewhat disagree, neither agree nor disagree, slightly agree, and strongly agree were the five Likert answer options for all patient safety concerns. The survey's second component gathered demographic data that is thought to influence opinions about patient safety. Gender, age, education, profession, position, job status, site of employment, number of workdays per week, years spent at the institution, and whether the employee typically had direct patient contact were among the demographic details [20].

According to Singer *et al.* [21], the Stanford Safety Instrument was used to help construct the **Patient Safety Climate in Health Care Organizations**

(PSCHO). The 38 elements of the PSCHO tool are used to evaluate interconnected organizational subjects, work groups, and social aspects. A two-page form is used to score the items on a Likert scale. PSCHO is regarded as the first instrument to measure the safety environment in businesses outside of hospitals and examine safety components. Numerous healthcare institutions may use the management and clinical staff information gathered from this survey. The performance of various hospital unit types may be compared using PSCHO, which has completed psychometric testing. This tool's previous iteration has been altered in terms of duration and multilingual compatibility.

The primary goal of the **Scottish Hospital Safety Questionnaire** (SHSQ), which was created for the clinical staff of the Scottish National Health Service (NHS), is to assess the safety results and atmosphere for both patients and employees. The SHSQ consists of four main parts: 44 questions about the hospital survey (HSPSC), 10 items about employee security behavior, 2 items about self-reported employee and patient injuries, and 7 items about demography [22].

Thirty-two distinct questions covering five areas were intended to be evaluated by the **Modified Stanford Instrument**-2006 (MSI-2006) regarding the PSC in Healthcare Facilities Survey. These elements include, but are not limited to, problems with awareness of oneself, embarrassment, and asking for assistance. The MSI-2006 instrument has been modified to make it easier to evaluate the opinions of a variety of hospital employees, such as nurses, managers, technicians, direct care workers, and health professionals. Since support service workers are a vital component of the medical facility and healthcare environment, this test also contains evaluations of other factors. With the goal of producing reliable and relevant data over an extended period, MSI-2006 was created for a variety of medical settings [23].

7.1.1 Health Information Technology

A growing elderly population, rising pollution levels, and people's sedentary lives are some of the primary causes of the healthcare industry's expansion. Different approaches are used by academicians and entrepreneurs to acknowledge this expansion, possibility, and medical care delivery. Health Information Technology (HIT) is the concept of leveraging cloud-based services via the internet, networked systems, etc., in the healthcare industry. To provide care and services more efficiently, it mostly makes use of patient-related electronic medical records, details, and data. The lack of internet access in certain areas, the absence of rules, regulations, and standards, as well as the absence of sufficient infrastructure and knowledgeable employees, are some of the many difficulties and problems associated with the use of information technology. HIT is recognized as the most potential instrument for raising the overall standard of medical systems' performance, security, and excellence. By eliminating medical malpractice, cutting medical expenses, expanding access to reasonably priced treatment, and lessening administrative hassles, it improves the quality of care. Another significant technology that partners with HIT is the information and communications system (ICT). ICT is the infrastructure that enables HIT.

7.1.1.1 Classification of HIT

Electronic Health Records: EHRs are vast computer libraries that organize health-related data for individuals or populations in a logical manner. They enable the storage and exchange of digital records among several healthcare providers. A wide range of data may be found in EHRs, such as demographics, medical history, prescription and allergy information, immunization records, laboratory test outcomes, radiographic images, vital signs, and individual characteristics like age and weight [24].

Telemedicine: Telemedicine is the practice of providing therapeutic treatments to patients who are in various places by using electronic communication and information technology. Healthcare professionals may utilize telemedicine as a technique to expand conventional medical procedures outside of a conventional clinic. Furthermore, telemedicine offers a fresh approach to helping individuals lead healthy lives, particularly considering the COVID-19 epidemic. It makes it easier for patients to participate in healthcare decision-making [25].

Digital Health Resource: This idea involves storing material in a digital format. A digitized medical library is a computer-accessible collection and storage of digital information. Medical practitioners, students, patients, and researchers may find health and scientific knowledge via digital health to improve, update, evaluate, or analyze the way healthcare is delivered. This offers several benefits, including the ability to be accessed at any time and from any location with an internet connection, requires less storage space, and maintenance expenses are far cheaper than those of conventional libraries. We must create new tools and technologies that allow efficient, automatic semantic categorization and search to handle the constantly increasing volume of electronic publications [26].

Health and Hospital Information: Health information systems and storage are the most controversial topics. Most national hospitals, particularly public hospitals and healthcare institutions, rely on manual operations rather than IT. A quick availability of patient data could influence the quality of medical treatment. These days, patient intake and enrolment are the main software application areas for information systems in contemporary healthcare firms. Hospitals must use automation in medical record administration, patient billing, general accounting, outpatient management, patient care divisions, guidance for decisions, managerial reporting, office automation, and specialized systems to satisfy the demands of contemporary medicine.

7.1.2 ICT and HIT-based platforms in India

Integrated Illness Surveillance Program (IDSP): Sickness screening information sharing is made possible by the Integrated Illness Surveillance Program (IDSP). Launched in India on November 2004, the National Health Mission (NHM) encompasses the IDSP initiative and is now operational across all Indian states and Union Territories. This plan's primary goals include the Rapid Reaction Teams' (RRT) detection and reaction to virus outbreaks, as well as a distributed lab-based, IT-enabled disease system management for diseases that are susceptible to epidemics. An epidemic signal dashboard is available on the IDSP website to assist you in monitoring infections [27].

Mother and Child Tracking System (MCTS): Developed by the National Informatics Center, this crucial online resource was first made available in 2009. This initiative was started by the Health and Family Department to use technological advances to provide a range of medical services to expectant mothers and children. The MCTS Portal generates a 16-digit identification number for the purpose of registering and tracking expecting moms and their kids until they turn five. The user-friendly layout of this platform makes it simple for healthcare administration to keep an eye on the quality of service. These treatments include vaccinations, postpartum care, and prenatal care. The system may notify the recipients and healthcare providers on a periodic schedule when a service is set to expire.

Electronic Health Management Information System (eHMIS): eHMIS is an internet-based digital initiative developed by the National Health Mission to collect, aggregate, and evaluate medical-related records from the most distant medical institutions all the way up to the national scale. This facility-based aggregation system lowers flow process mistakes and speeds up data transfer from facility levels to the government level. Having a dashboard, analyzing the information at all levels, and a variety of visualization

Table 7.4 HIT tools and its applications.

Technology	Usage
Automated medication dispensing (ADC)	Cut down on mistakes in critical care units.
Barcode medication administration (BCMA)	Cut down on drug and laboratory blunders.
Clinical decision support (CDS)	Operational enhancements include clinical outcome forecasting, computerization, and reminders.
Computerized physician order entry (COPE)	Minimize medical mistakes that are inappropriate for an integrated clinical decision support setting.
Overall electronic medical record (OEMR)	Security concerns, policy creation, and information about patients have all been addressed.
Patient data management systems (PDMS)	Shorten patient waiting periods for doctor's appointments and improve patient care.
Patient portals	Enhances the doctor-patient interaction, minimizes the amount of chart labor, and prevents data breaches.
Retained surgical item detectors	Not recommending keeping operating instruments.
Telemedicine – Telemonitoring	Juniors may get care for severely sick patients under the guidance of experts.
Telemedicine – Virtual visits	Everyone receives therapy at the appropriate moment, and it is achievable to get therapy anywhere.

instruments further facilitate data use. The eHMIS tool aids lawmakers in their decision-making processes [28]. Some of the HIT tools and its applications are mentioned in the Table 7.4.

7.1.3 Mobile health

The incorporation of mobile has transformed medical care. Mobile sensing is used to monitor human behavior, physiology, surroundings, and interactions. It utilizes the widely used sensors included into smartphones and smartwatches. The fundamental foundation of mobile health (mHealth) sensing techniques was proposed in recent publications [29]. These approaches employ noninvasive mobile sensing devices to gather information for identifying human activities and determining an individual's health status. Personalized health: personalized medicine is a patient-centered approach that involves tailoring interventions, therapies, products, and/or procedures to each patient based on their anticipated reaction or likelihood of contracting an illness. Consequently, the purpose of customized medicine is to optimize and maximize each patient's reaction to therapy by detecting, monitoring, and anticipating their present state of health.

7.1.4 Barriers to health information technology (HIT) adoption

Poor Internet Availability: Any informatics system that wants to share and exchange information efficiently must have access to the internet. Without adequate internet access, it is challenging to provide the finest healthcare services [30].

Lack of Professionals: To run or administer the information system, each new technology needs the use of skilled and knowledgeable experts.

Social and Cultural Barriers: The shift to a digital health information system is challenging as people are more used to their conventional methods and daily schedule. Organizational Barriers: Because the existing strategy is practical and there is a dearth of supporting evidence, such as surveys or proof models of better results, businesses are hesitant to invest in new technology.

In spite of these barriers, artificial intelligence (AI) is revolutionizing the patients' overall experience with Healthcare. They are mentioned in the Figure 7.1. below.

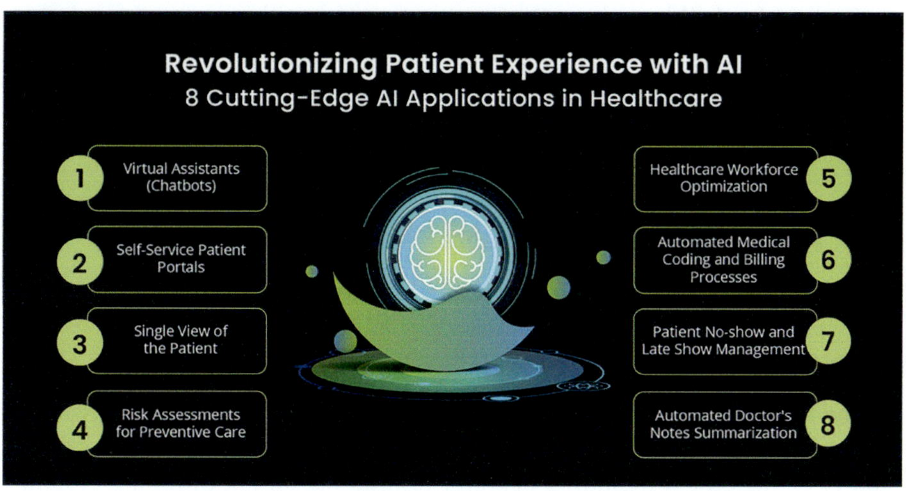

Figure 7.1 AI in patient experience with healthcare [31].

7.2 AI in Hospital Management

The process of globalization, complexity, and shifts in organization define the setting for healthcare delivery in the twenty-first century. The formidable forces have created a tough landscape for the sector as it endeavors to transform the aspirational objective of universal health coverage "ensuring that all individuals may receive health services without financial distress" into a practical reality. The convergence of these factors has resulted in an unprecedented influx of investment into healthcare, necessitating professional management and administration, alongside clinical expertise, to ensure the efficient allocation of resources across primary, secondary, and tertiary care. External factors, including international workforce shortages, cross-border mobility, and fierce competition for proficient health professionals, alongside internal factors such as multigenerational personnel and evolving organizational and governance structures in healthcare, will significantly influence the capacity to achieve human resources for health objectives [32].

Artificial intelligence (AI) and associated technologies are becoming more ubiquitous in both industry and society, and are starting to be used in healthcare. These technologies possess the capacity to revolutionize several facets of patient care and administrative procedures inside provider, payer, and pharmaceutical entities. Numerous research findings indicate that Art, enhancements in computational capacity, and innovations in AI algorithms. The confluence of these elements has created new opportunities for improving the efficiency, accuracy, and overall effectiveness of hospital management methods [33]. The importance of AI in hospital administration is highlighted by its ability to tackle enduring difficulties in the healthcare sector, including resource limitations, escalating prices, and the growing need for tailored and efficient healthcare services. The revolutionary influence of AI promises to augment the capacities of healthcare workers and revolutionize the whole spectrum of patient care [34]. Refer to Figure 7.2.

7.2.1 AI applications in hospitals

The three primary fields include AI's role in optimizing logistics and resource management, its application in automating administrative tasks, and its contribution to enhancing patient flow and scheduling.

AI for hospital logistics and resource management: Predictive inventory management for medical supplies, medications, and equipment; efficient facility management including heating, ventilation, air conditioning systems,

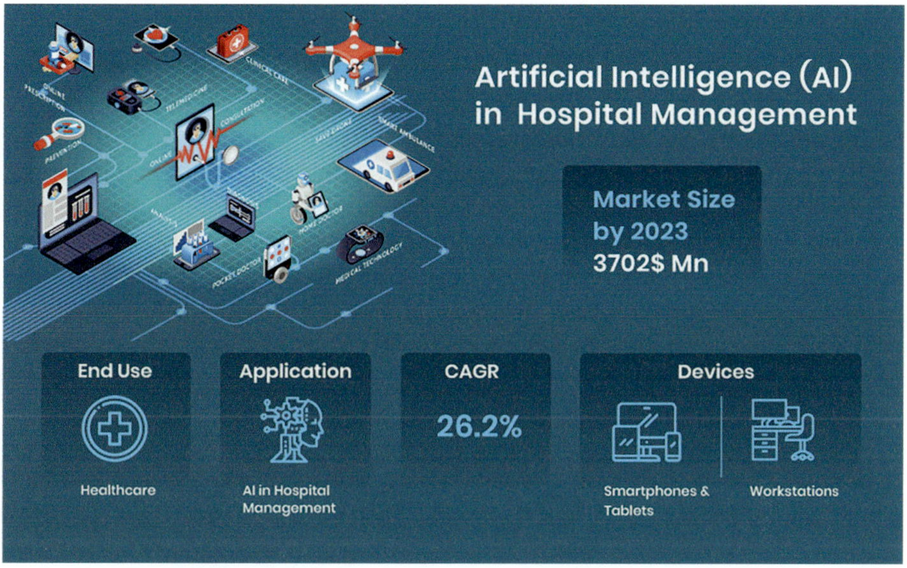

Figure 7.2 Effect of AI in hospital management [35].

and predictive maintenance; optimization of resource allocation for staff and materials; and supply chain optimization and management during emergencies and health crises [36].

Automating administrative tasks with AI: Management of patient data encompasses electronic medical records (EMRs) and the analysis of unstructured data; automation of billing and claims processing to ensure accuracy and compliance; implementation of AI-driven scheduling systems for appointments and procedures; automation of document management and processing; automated communication and reminders to enhance patient engagement; and monitoring of data security and compliance [36].

AI in patient flow and scheduling optimization: Enhancement of patient flow via predictive analysis of admissions, discharges, and transfers; implementation of dynamic scheduling systems for appointments and procedures to reduce no-shows and cancellations. Reduction in waiting times can be achieved through improved triage processes and real-time patient wait time prediction. Additionally, enhancing patient experience involves providing accurate information and integrating telehealth services for virtual consultations [36].

7.2.2 AI in clinical applications

The rapid development of AI in the last few years has piqued interest in exploring its potential uses in various healthcare operations. Applying AI to the discipline of cardiology, electrophysiology, and electrocardiogram (ECG), although it is noninvasive, cheap, and simple to record and preserve, the 12-lead ECG is a regularly utilized modality. Incorporating AI into this century-old apparatus turns it into a cutting-edge tool. AI-ECG has the potential to improve healthcare in every way, from screenings and preventative measures to diagnosis, treatment, and outcome prediction. Expertise and education are necessary for the interpretation of ECGs. It is common practice to use rule-based automated diagnosis when a cardiologist is not available. Traditional rule-based algorithms, however, may not always provide sufficient results in terms of accuracy. Some AI models have been created with diagnostic performance equivalent to that of cardiologists, and AI-ECG, which stands for artificial intelligence in electrocardiograms, may assist in increased diagnostic accuracy. New gadgets are also being made possible by the AI-ECG technology. As a means of stratification, wearable technologies like implanted loop recorders (ILRs) and ECG-compatible mobile phones and smartwatches may screen the general population for cardiovascular illness and identify high-risk populations [37]. Implementing a feature analysis framework to decrease features from collected cardio-mechanical signals produced by a continuous wavelet transform, the researchers also discovered that AI was helpful for the categorization of aortic stenosis (AS). Several machine learning (ML) algorithms were evaluated in terms of their performance, and a new two-dimensional convolution neural network (2D-CNN) was created using continuous wavelet transform (CWT) coefficients as input pictures. Accuracy results showed that the feature selection and classification framework worked as intended, which bodes well for using AI for AS classification [38].

7.2.3 AI in orthopedics

To alleviate osteoarthritis, a new intra-articular (IA) injection with appropriate beta-lapachone-loaded IA formulations was required. Scientists suggested combining poloxamers with hyaluronic acid. An optimum formulation was generated using AI, considering the experimental findings of several hydrogels. This AI-designed formulation showed encouraging results in an in-vivo assessment for the treatment of osteoarthritis, with outstanding rheological qualities and a significant reduction in the release of degradative and proinflammatory chemicals [39]. In this instance, using a rapid area

CNN to diagnose meniscus tears, they showed that it accurately detected the two meniscal horn locations, the existence of a meniscal tear, and the trajectory of the tear [40]. In a similar research, French researchers used MRI images to train a CNN that could specifically locate normal and torn menisci and determine the tear's direction. Although the model worked as expected, the researchers recommended adding 3D data or expanding the database to get better results, particularly for unusual cases of multiple tears or severely damaged menisci [41].

7.2.4 AI in drug development and discovery

Many biopharmaceutical companies like Bayer, Roche, and Pfizer have worked with IT companies to develop a platform for finding treatments in areas such as immuno-oncology and cardiovascular illnesses. AI in virtual screening (VS) is used to improve drug screening procedures. AI shall speed up the finding of new possible medications, finding a novel treatment for certain illness, particularly, finding a new therapies for complicated disorders. Recent research has proved that AI in drug screening showed a major improvement in simplifying the drug development process [42]. By addressing challenges in the enormous chemical space of over 10^{60} molecules and simplifying the development process, AI is essential in drug discovery. Faster drug development results from AI's involvement in confirming therapeutic targets, identifying hit and lead compounds, and improving drug structures. Managing the size, expansion, variety, and ambiguity of data in drug research datasets is one of the difficulties for AI. Though they might underperform in complicated biological property projections, quantitative structure–activity relationship (QSAR) models provide fast predictions. Conventional ML methods may find it difficult to handle the large drug development datasets. For some drug characteristics, deep learning (DL) models outperformed conventional ML in predictivity. VS and structure-based techniques using in silico procedures improve the selection of medicinal compounds effectively. Predictive models, molecular similarity, and in silico techniques, among other parameters, help to forecast chemical structures. Improving chemical screening techniques, notable systems, including deep VS, exhibit outstanding performance in docking receptors and ligands [43].

7.2.5 AI in bioactivity prediction

By evaluating the affinity of drug compounds toward target proteins or receptors, the prediction of bioactivity is very essential for drug development.

To produce the intended therapeutic reaction, drug molecules have to bind strongly with the target protein. AI-based approaches forecast drug-target interactions using many strategies, including feature-based and similarity-based. KronRLS and SimBoost are ML algorithms that assess drug–protein similarity to establish drug-target binding affinity. Predicting bioactivity considers drug characteristics from fingerprint data, logical methods in computer science (LMCS), and simplified molecular input line entry system (SMILES). Network-based techniques not depending on 3D protein structures have improved performance for deep learning algorithms such as DeepDTA and protein and drug molecule interaction prediction (PADME) [44]. Platforms such as PADME forecast drug-target interactions depending on drug and target protein characteristics using feed-forward neural networks. Mode of action by network analysis (MANTRA) identifies shared mechanisms of action and biological pathways by grouping substances according to gene expression patterns. Drug metabolism sites are found using tools such as SMARTCyp, fast metabolizer (FAME), and XenoSite. Software tools such as CypRules, MetaSite, MetaPred, and WhichCyp enable the identification of certain CYP450 isoforms implicated in drug metabolic pathways. Numerous authorized medications' clearance routes have been correctly predicted using support vector machine (SVM)-based models [43].

7.2.6 AI in toxicity prediction

Avoiding negative consequences depends on the prediction of toxicity in pharmacological compounds; many approaches and methods are used in this regard. Often starting with cell-based in vitro tests, then moving on to animal investigations, which may be expensive. Web-based technologies such as LimTox, pkCSM, admetSAR, and Toxtree may assist in saving expenses in toxicity forecasting. Advanced AI techniques forecast toxicity using compound similarity or input characteristics. Similarity ensemble approach (SEA) predicts negative effects by evaluating safety target prediction for marketed medications versus unintentional targets. Built using machine learning, eToxPred precisely forecasts the synthesis viability and toxicity of tiny organic compounds. PrOCTOR and other AI techniques forecast drug toxicity and spot possible clinical trial failures by means of molecular characteristics, protein targets, and pharmacological attributes. PrOCTOR also finds FDA-approved medications that subsequently exhibit negative consequences. Based on deep learning, Tox_(R)CNN assesses drug cytotoxicity via a deep convolutional neural network technique [45].

7.3 AI in Patient Management

The precision medicine is an evolving treatment and prevention strategy for diseases that considers individual variability in genes, environment, and lifestyle. This approach will allow healthcare professionals to more precisely forecast prevention and treatment methods for a specific condition and target them toward a particular group of people. Incorporating AI into healthcare would be an option to accomplish precision medicine, since this approach uses the cognitive proficiencies of healthcare professional [46]. AI applications in medicine are progressively on the rise, and it may transform vividly the delivery of healthcare services [47].

AI aids in the analysis of wide-ranging datasets in research, enabling the identification of patterns, prognosis, and generating prediction models which facilitate early intervention. The integration of AI in healthcare could revolutionize patient care and outcomes. AI resources bolster the contemporary paradigm shift toward patient-centered, precision treatment strategies. It can aid in developing customized treatment plans and in clinical decision-making. The extensive availability of high-performance computing, along with the accessibility to a huge amount of data created because of the upsurge in digitalization, created the platform for the abundant implementation of AI technologies in present-day healthcare. AI-powered chatbots and virtual therapists can provide incessant support, for a wider population at affordable costs, reducing social stigma, and improving accessibility. AI can detect risk factors and deliver appropriate interventions, potentially plummeting the strain on healthcare delivery systems in the prevention of diseases [48–50]. A general workflow of AI assistance in patient management is mentioned in Figure 7.3.

The role of AI technology is enhancing in the management of biological, psychological, and social aspects of health. At the same time, AI is applied for the delivery of a comprehensive bio-psychosocial model of management of health. For instance, the Biopsychosocial AI-Driven Digital Twin (BADT) framework integrates biological (genetic markers, physiological measures), psychological (cognitive assessments), and social (environmental) factor data streams into a unified system that changes constantly in line along with the patient's health condition. This model provides predictive analytics for risk assessment, early diagnosis, and simulation of individualized treatment plans using AI and machine learning [52]. The application of AI in biological (physical), psychological (mental), and social aspects of patient management is depicted below and in Figure 7.4.

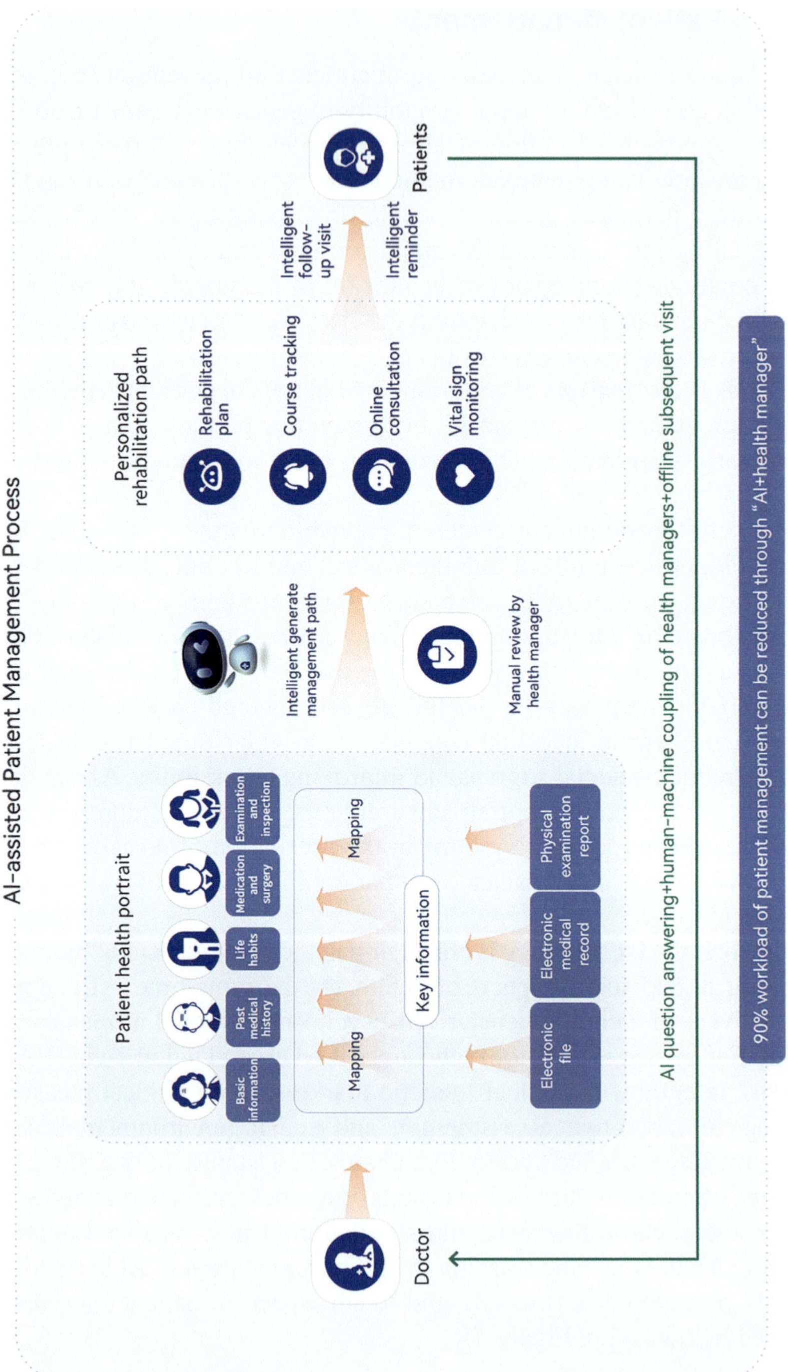

Figure 7.3 AI in patient management [51].

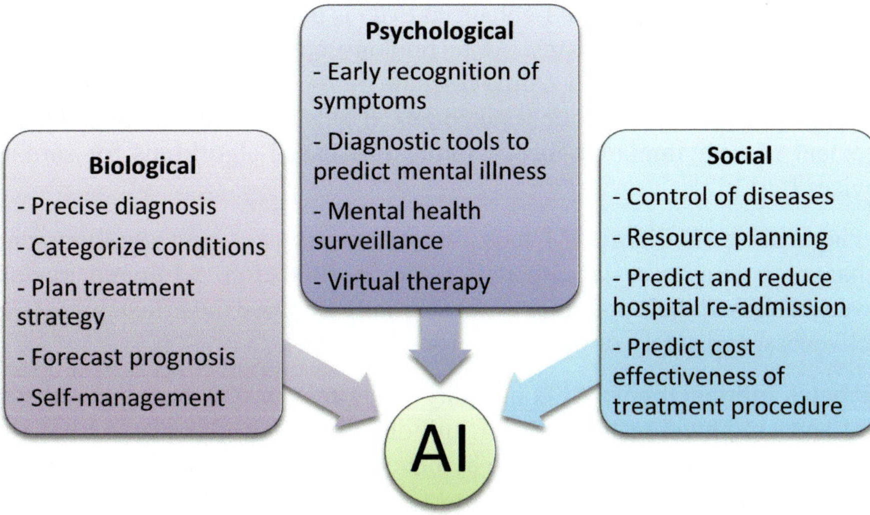

Figure 7.4 Integration of AI in bio-psychosocial aspects of patient management.

7.3.1 AI in managing physical aspects of health

AI could aid in various stages of patient care, such as prevention, diagnosis, treatment, monitoring, and rehabilitation. Its role in the management of patients with certain conditions is provided below.

Cancer: It could identify the individuals with high risk for developing colorectal cancer liver metastases (CRLM). AI models have also been established as equivocal or superior to proficient radiologists in detecting CRLM on computer tomography (CT) and magnetic resonance scans, or detecting them from the noninvasive analysis of exhaled air of the patients. Besides aiding in rapid histopathological examination, AI precisely assists in forecasting response to chemotherapy, early local tumor progression followed by excision, and patient survival following chemotherapy or surgery [49]. AI exerts a vital role in all aspects of glioma, covering tumor segmentation, diagnosis, differentiation, levelling, treatment response, estimation of clinical outcomes (prognosis and relapse), molecular topographies, clinical classification, and medication discovery [53]. Similarly, AI enhances risk prediction, diagnosis, and prognostication of hepatocellular carcinoma [54].

Pain management: AI-based interventions are used for pain recognition, prediction, and self-management [55].

Cardiovascular diseases: AI-enhanced ECG is used in diagnosing and managing cardiovascular illnesses. AI technology could substantially enhance precision and efficiency in cardiovascular treatment, which in turn would result in more favorable patient outcomes. It aids in the detection and management of arrhythmia by incorporating rule-based algorithms for cardiac devices [56] [57].

Perioperative medicine: AI aids forecasting surgical case durations and enhances post-anesthesia care unit resource allocation. AI-driven models have established their potential to substantially improve the efficacy, cost-effectiveness, and safety of operative procedures [58].

Diabetes management: AI could play a key role in transforming diabetes care and enlightening the lives of millions of people globally. AI has the potential to augment diabetes care by precisely predicting, categorizing, and managing diabetes and comorbidities in a personalized manner for a specific individual [46, 50].

7.3.2 AI in managing mental aspects of health

AI provides probable solutions for enhancing mental health through customized interventions, early recognition of symptoms, and virtual therapy avenues. AI-powered diagnosis can be an indispensable tool in mental healthcare. AI applied to precisely predict and categorize persons with schizophrenia, unipolar and bipolar disorder, risk of suicide, or psychological distress [59–61]. Moreover, neural network and deep learning approach help to recognize posts relevant to mental illness in social media [62], which could predict mental illness and classify it. At present chat-bot-based therapy is provided by AI tools such as Woebot, Wysa, Talkspace, and BetterHelp. Similarly, many emotional health apps such as Moodfit, Happify, Headspace, and DBT coach also use AI technology. Smartwatches incorporated with AI-based tools aid in monitoring alterations in sleep patterns, physical activity, and heart rate, providing valuable inputs for mental health surveillance [48].

7.3.3 AI in managing social aspects of health

Some AI built with social intelligence could comprehend and interact with human beings; at the same time, it can be used for social control of the disease. Healthcare professionals can optimize prescription choices and dosages by using AI algorithms to produce personalized recommendations for each patient based on social and lifestyle preferences and past medical history.

AI systems can continuously analyze socio-demographic variables, including geographic distribution, disease prevalence, and population demographics. This can help with prevention or treatment by identifying patients who are more likely to develop specific illnesses. Additionally, edge analytics can identify anomalies and forecast future healthcare events, guaranteeing that resources like vaccines are available where they are most required. Similarly, AI can be used to predict patients at greater risk for readmissions to the hospital based on their medical history and social history. This could help in incorporating appropriate strategies to avert readmissions and eventually reduce healthcare expenses [50]. Interestingly, AI can forecast the cost-effectiveness of operative procedures [58].

7.3.4 Challenges and prospects

Although AI is used in patient management, there are few challenges, such as safety, regulation, ethical issues, data access, privacy concerns, algorithm bias, lacking human empathy and comprehension, and paucity for extensive validation studies [58, 63]. It is critical to deliberate challenges in incorporating AI to warrant responsible and effective administration. There is a need to consider appropriate measures for data protection, trust building, patient education, collaboration among stakeholders, and overcoming algorithm biases [48, 50]. Apart from that, more large-scale, prospective, randomized controlled trials (RCTs) and rigorous studies relevant to AI in the healthcare system are required to standardize AI data and to ameliorate generalizability and the interpretability of results [54, 55]. With successful incorporation, AI is anticipated to enhance healthcare, resulting in better patient outcomes, greater efficiency, and access to customized management and quality care. However, healthcare professionals must undergo appropriate training to incorporate these technologies and maintain ethical principles efficiently. Nowadays, there is a surge in AI models that are interpretable and can offer clarifications for their recommendations. This enhances transparency and provides healthcare professional and clients to comprehend the rationale for AI-provided insights and choices. At the same time, establishing trust and educating patients are essential to the effective use of AI in healthcare [50].

7.4 AI in physiotherapy

Physiotherapy, also known as physical therapy, has evolved significantly since its origins in ancient civilizations. From early practices of massage and hydrotherapy to modern techniques incorporating advanced technologies, the field has continuously adapted to meet changing patient needs. Today, AI is at the forefront of innovation in physiotherapy, revolutionizing how practitioners diagnose conditions, develop treatment plans, and engage patients in their recovery process [64]. The roots of physiotherapy can be traced back to ancient civilizations, where therapeutic exercises and manual techniques were used for healing. In ancient Greece, Hippocrates advocated for manual therapy, while traditional Chinese medicine incorporated therapeutic exercises. The modern foundation of physiotherapy was laid in the 19th century by Per Henrik Ling, a Swedish Physiologist who developed "medical gymnastics" [65]. The early 20th century saw the formalization of physiotherapy as a profession, driven by events such as the poliomyelitis epidemic and World Wars. These events highlighted the need for structured rehabilitation services, leading to the establishment of professional organizations like the American Physical Therapy Association (APTA) in 1921 [66].

7.4.1 Technology integration in physiotherapy

One of the most prominent trends in physiotherapy is the integration of advanced technologies. Wearable devices, smart sensors, and motion capture systems have become integral to physiotherapy practice, providing real-time data on patient movements and progress. These technologies offer physiotherapists unprecedented insights into patient conditions, allowing for more accurate assessments and tailored treatment plans. A study by Rodgers *et al.* [67] in 2019 explored the use of wearable devices in physiotherapy, demonstrating how these technologies can provide real-time feedback on patient movements and progress. The researchers found that wearable sensors improved the accuracy of movement analysis and enabled more personalized treatment plans. Wearable technology has emerged as a game-changer in physiotherapy. These devices can continuously monitor various physiological and biomechanical parameters, offering a window into the patient's condition beyond the confines of the clinic. This continuous data collection enables physiotherapists to track patient progress more effectively and make data-driven decisions about treatment adjustments.

7.4.1.1 Telehealth and remote rehabilitation

The COVID-19 pandemic accelerated the adoption of telehealth services in physiotherapy, allowing practitioners to provide virtual consultations and remote monitoring. This trend has persisted beyond the pandemic, offering increased accessibility and convenience for patients [68]. In 2017,

Cottrell *et al.* [69] conducted a systematic review on the effectiveness of telerehabilitation for musculoskeletal conditions. Their findings showed that telerehabilitation was as effective as in-person care for many conditions, supporting the continued use of remote physiotherapy services beyond the pandemic. Telerehabilitation, or virtual physiotherapy, uses specialized software and technology to deliver care to clients remotely. These virtual visits can take place over video conferencing platforms, phone calls, or even through email and text communications. This approach has proven particularly beneficial for patients in remote areas or those with mobility issues, ensuring continuity of care despite physical limitations.

7.4.1.2 Personalized and evidence-based practice

The integration of AI-driven analysis of patient-specific data has enabled the creation of highly customized treatment plans [64]. This trend toward personalization aligns with the broader movement in healthcare toward precision medicine, where treatments are tailored to individual patient characteristics. A recent study by Rica Hartmann *et al.* [70] investigated the use of AI algorithms in developing personalized exercise programs for patients with chronic low back pain. The AI-driven approach resulted in significantly better outcomes compared to standard care, highlighting the potential of AI in creating tailored treatment plans. Evidence-based physiotherapy practice (EBPP) has become increasingly important, combining the best available scientific research with clinical expertise and patient values. This approach ensures that treatments are not only personalized but also grounded in robust scientific evidence, leading to improved patient outcomes.

7.4.1.3 Interdisciplinary collaboration

Physiotherapists are increasingly working alongside professionals from other medical disciplines to provide comprehensive care [71]. This interdisciplinary approach allows for a more holistic treatment of patients, addressing not just physical symptoms but also considering psychological, social, and environmental factors that may impact recovery. Research by Jack Seaton *et al.* [72] examined the impact of interprofessional collaboration in physiotherapy practice. The study found that physiotherapists working in interdisciplinary teams achieved better patient outcomes and reported higher job satisfaction compared to those working in isolation. Collaboration between physiotherapists and other healthcare professionals, such as physicians, occupational therapists, and dieticians, enables a more comprehensive approach to patient care. This teamwork allows for the exchange of expertise and knowledge, leading to more effective treatment strategies and improved patient outcomes.

7.4.2 AI integration in physiotherapy

The integration of AI in physiotherapy represents a significant leap forward for the field. AI technologies are being applied in various aspects of physiotherapy, from diagnosis and treatment planning to patient monitoring and rehabilitation. A practice-based review by Gopal Nambi *et al.* [73] explored the various applications of AI in physiotherapy. The authors identified several promising areas, including AI-assisted diagnosis, predictive analytics for injury prevention, and virtual reality-based rehabilitation programs. The review emphasized the potential of AI to enhance clinical decision-making and improve patient outcomes.

Enhanced Diagnosis and Treatment Planning: AI algorithms can analyze vast amounts of patient data, including medical history, imaging results, and real-time movement data from wearable devices. This analysis can help physiotherapists make more accurate diagnoses and develop more effective treatment plans. For example, AI can identify subtle movement patterns that might be indicative of underlying issues, allowing for earlier intervention and more targeted treatments.

Personalized Exercise Programs: AI can generate personalized exercise programs based on a patient's specific condition, progress, and goals. These programs can be dynamically adjusted based on real-time data from wearable devices, ensuring that patients are always working at the optimal level for their recovery.

Predictive Analytics: AI-powered predictive analytics can help physiotherapists anticipate potential complications or setbacks in a patient's recovery. By analyzing patterns in patient data, AI can flag potential issues before they become serious, allowing for proactive interventions.

Virtual Reality and Gamification: AI is also being integrated with virtual reality (VR) technologies to create immersive rehabilitation experiences. These VR environments can make therapy sessions more engaging and motivating for patients, potentially improving adherence to treatment plans.

Remote Monitoring and Telehealth Enhancement: AI can enhance telehealth services by providing more sophisticated remote monitoring capabilities. For example, AI algorithms can analyze video feeds of patients performing exercises at home, providing feedback on form and progress without the need for in-person visits.

7.4.3 AI in physiotherapy diagnosis

AI is transforming physiotherapy in several key areas. AI technologies are revolutionizing diagnostic capabilities in physiotherapy, offering unprecedented accuracy and efficiency in identifying musculoskeletal abnormalities and predicting patient outcomes. This transformation is evident across three key areas: medical imaging analysis, movement analysis, and predictive analytics.

7.4.3.1 Medical imaging analysis

AI-powered tools have significantly enhanced the interpretation of medical imaging, including X-rays, MRIs, and CT scans. These systems can detect subtle abnormalities that might be overlooked by human observers, leading to earlier and more precise diagnoses [74]. For instance, a 2024 study by Suman Rani *et al.* [75] demonstrated that a deep learning algorithm could detect knee osteoarthritis from X-ray images with 92.3% accuracy, surpassing the performance of experienced radiologists. This technology not only expedites diagnosis but also aids in treatment planning and monitoring disease progression. In sports medicine, AI has shown promise in identifying and classifying muscle injuries. A study by Mohsen Sadr *et al.* [76] in 2025 utilized a convolutional neural network (CNNs) and recurrent neural networks (RNNs) to analyze and predict the injury patterns in athletes using biometric data and motion videos from training sessions. They found that RNN is more capable than CNN in predicting sports injuries. This level of precision allows physiotherapists to tailor rehabilitation programs more effectively, potentially reducing recovery times and improving outcomes.

7.4.3.2 Movement analysis

Machine learning algorithms have transformed the analysis of gait patterns and joint movements, enabling the detection of subtle abnormalities that may indicate underlying conditions or injury risks [77]. Advanced AI-driven systems now use computer vision technology to perform detailed movement analysis and posture evaluation with unprecedented precision. A groundbreaking study by Radu Ilesan *et al.* [78] employed wearable sensors and AI algorithms to analyze gait patterns in patients with Parkinson's disease. The system could detect early signs of gait disturbances up to two years before clinical diagnosis, potentially allowing for earlier intervention and improved patient outcomes. Similarly, in sports rehabilitation, AI-powered motion capture systems are being used to assess athletes' movement patterns and identify potential injury risks. For example, Attila Schulc *et al.* [79] developed an AI system that analyzes an athlete's jumping and landing mechanics, predicting ACL injury risk with 87% accuracy.

7.4.3.3 Predictive analytics

AI's ability to leverage historical data for identifying early signs of neurological disorders and forecasting disease progression has significantly enhanced physiotherapists' ability to develop proactive treatment plans. By analyzing vast amounts of patient data, including medical histories, treatment outcomes, and recovery patterns, AI systems can predict potential complications and suggest preventive measures. A recent study by Dresser and Kohn [80] demonstrated the power of predictive analytics in stroke rehabilitation. Their AI model, trained on data from stroke patients, could predict recovery trajectories within the first week of treatment. This allowed physiotherapists to tailor rehabilitation programs more effectively, resulting in improved functional outcomes and reduced hospital stays. In the field of sports medicine, predictive analytics is being used to prevent injuries and optimize performance. Freitas *et al.* [81] developed an AI system that analyzes an athlete's training load, sleep patterns, and biomechanical data to predict injury risk. In a study involving professional soccer players, the system successfully predicted noncontact injuries, allowing for timely interventions and injury prevention strategies. These advancements in AI-driven diagnostics are transforming physiotherapy practice, enabling more accurate diagnoses, personalized treatment plans, and improved patient outcomes. As these technologies continue to evolve, they promise to further enhance the field of physiotherapy, leading to more efficient and effective patient care.

7.4.4 AI in treatment planning and execution

AI is indeed revolutionizing treatment planning in physiotherapy, offering personalized interventions, real-time progress monitoring, and optimized therapy sessions. This transformation is enhancing patient care and outcomes in unprecedented ways. AI's ability to analyze vast amounts of patient-specific data has led to the development of highly customized exercise programs in physiotherapy. This personalization goes beyond traditional methods, taking into account a wide range of factors to create truly tailored interventions. AI algorithms can process and analyze various types of patient data, including medical history, imaging results, baseline performance metrics, genetic factors, and demographic information. By considering these diverse data points, AI can create exercise programs that are uniquely suited to each patient's needs, capabilities, and goals. A 2024 study [82] demonstrated the effectiveness of AI in recommending safe, personalized exercises for patients with musculoskeletal disorders (MSDs). The study found a 90.5% agreement rate among physiotherapists that AI-recommended exercises posed no risk to patients. This high level of safety and personalization showcases AI's potential in creating individualized exercise plans without compromising patient well-being.

Progress Monitoring: Real-time tracking of patient metrics has transformed how physiotherapists assess and manage recovery progress. AI-enabled devices and systems provide continuous data collection and analysis, allowing for more accurate and timely interventions. AI-powered wearable devices and sensors play a crucial role in progress monitoring by tracking joint angles, range of motion, and muscle activity during exercises. They provide real-time feedback on technique to ensure correct movement and prevent injuries, and gather data on heart rate, oxygen levels, posture, and sleep patterns. The data collected by these devices is analyzed by AI algorithms to detect incremental improvements in patient performance, identify potential issues before they become serious problems, and provide quantified information about progress, keeping patients motivated.

Optimized Therapy Sessions: AI's ability to identify the most effective exercises for each individual has the potential to reduce therapy duration while maximizing outcomes. This optimization is achieved through sophisticated data analysis and machine learning algorithms. AI uses predictive analytics to estimate recovery timelines based on data from thousands of similar cases, set realistic expectations and milestones, and keep patients motivated throughout their recovery. AI systems can continuously adjust treatment plans based on real-time patient progress. This adaptive approach ensures that each therapy session is as beneficial and impactful as possible.

Gamification in Physiotherapy: AI-powered robotics are revolutionizing physiotherapy, creating more engaging, personalized, and effective rehabilitation experiences. These technologies are transforming traditional therapy approaches, enhancing patient outcomes, and improving the overall quality of care [83]. Gamification has emerged as a powerful tool in physiotherapy, leveraging AI to create engaging and motivating rehabilitation experiences. Gamified physiotherapy exercises increase patient motivation and adherence to treatment plans, provide immediate feedback and rewards for progress, and make repetitive exercises more enjoyable and less monotonous [84].

AI enhances gamified physiotherapy by adapting game difficulty based on patient performance, personalizing challenges to target specific rehabilitation goals, and providing real-time analysis of movement quality and progress. The integration of AI in gamification allows for more sophisticated and personalized interventions. AI algorithms can analyze patient data to adjust game parameters in real-time, ensuring that the difficulty level remains challenging yet achievable for each individual [85]. This adaptive approach not only maintains patient engagement but also optimizes the therapeutic benefits of each session.

VR in Physiotherapy: VR, combined with AI, is creating immersive and effective rehabilitation environments for physiotherapy patients. VR in physiotherapy offers realistic simulations of daily activities for practical training, increased patient engagement through immersive experiences, and safe environments to practice challenging movements [86]. AI enhances VR rehabilitation by analyzing patient movements in real-time to provide immediate feedback, adjusting virtual environments to match patient capabilities and progress, and collecting and analyzing data to optimize treatment plans. The effectiveness of VR in physiotherapy is supported by recent research. A study published in Nature Digital Medicine in 2024 highlighted that integrating AI with home-based VR rehabilitation can lead to improved outcomes for patients [85]. This approach allows for more accessible and continuous rehabilitation, potentially increasing the frequency and effectiveness of therapy sessions.

Robotics in Physiotherapy: The integration of AI-powered robotics in physiotherapy has opened new possibilities for rehabilitation, especially for patients with severe injuries or neurological conditions. Robotic systems in physiotherapy are used for gait training and analysis, assistance with repetitive movements, and precise control of force and range of motion. AI improves robotic physiotherapy by adapting assistance levels based on patient performance, analyzing movement patterns to provide personalized feedback, and predicting patient progress and adjusting treatment plans accordingly. The combination of gamification, VR, and AI-powered robotics is transforming physiotherapy by making treatments more engaging, personalized, and effective. As these technologies continue to evolve, they promise to enhance patient outcomes, reduce recovery times, and improve the overall quality of physiotherapy care. However, it's important to note that while these advancements offer exciting possibilities, they should be implemented thoughtfully, considering factors such as patient comfort, accessibility, and the need for human touch in therapy [87].

7.4.5 AI in patient engagement

AI-driven tools are revolutionizing patient engagement and treatment adherence through innovative technologies and personalized approaches. Here's an elaboration on the key areas of impact:

Real-Time Feedback: Wearable sensors integrated with AI provide immediate feedback on exercise performance, enabling patients to optimize their physical activity and rehabilitation efforts. These devices collect real-time data on various physiological parameters and movement patterns, which AI algorithms analyze to offer personalized insights. AI algorithms analyze patient data to create tailored exercise regimens, adjusting difficulty and intensity based on progress and health status. Wearable devices track metrics like heart rate, step count, and movement quality, providing instant feedback to users. AI systems dynamically adjust exercise goals based on patient performance and adherence, maintaining motivation and progress.

Automated Reminders: AI-powered apps send reminders for scheduled exercises and track adherence rates, significantly improving patient compliance with treatment plans. AI algorithms analyze patient behavior patterns to determine optimal times for sending reminders, increasing the likelihood of adherence. Apps automatically log completed exercises and medication intake, providing healthcare providers with accurate adherence data. AI-driven systems generate personalized motivational messages based on individual patient progress and preferences.

Virtual Health Assistants: Digital assistants use natural language processing to answer patient queries and offer encouragement, enhancing patient engagement and support. Virtual assistants provide round-the-clock support, answering patient questions and addressing concerns in real-time. AI-powered assistants analyze patient data to offer tailored health recommendations and lifestyle suggestions. Advanced NLP algorithms enable virtual assistants to provide empathetic responses and emotional support to patients [88]. Research showed that AI-driven virtual health assistants reduced hospital readmissions by 28% for chronic disease patients. These assistants offer personalized care experiences, empowering patients to take a more active role in managing their health. They also facilitate communication between patients and healthcare providers, fostering stronger patient-provider relationships [89]. Virtual health assistants are transforming patient support by improving advanced support, enhancing patient engagement and compliance, offering continuous health monitoring, and even providing mental health support [90]. They guide patients through testing procedures, treatment plans, and insurance claims, significantly reducing the workload of medical staff and improving treatment outcomes. The statistics of patient engagement and efficacy using AI is provided in Figure 7.5.

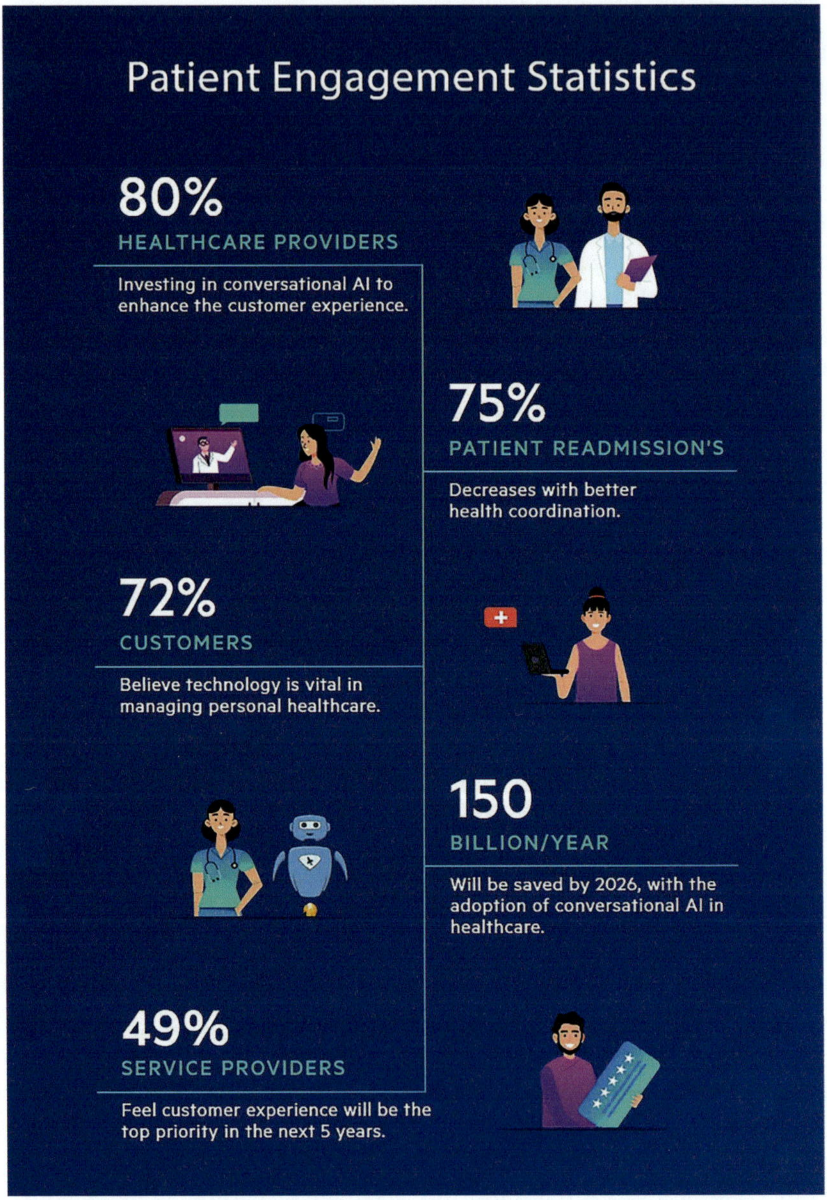

Figure 7.5 Statistics of patient engagement and efficacy using AI [91].

7.4.6 Challenges

The integration of AI and advanced technologies in physiotherapy presents both immense potential and significant challenges. While these innovations promise to revolutionize patient care, they also raise important ethical considerations and implementation hurdles.

Ethical Challenges: Data privacy and security are paramount concerns in the AI-driven physiotherapy landscape. As AI systems collect and analyze vast amounts of patient data, ensuring the confidentiality and protection of this sensitive information becomes crucial. There's a need for robust security measures and clear guidelines on data usage and storage. Algorithmic bias is another critical ethical issue. AI systems trained on limited or biased datasets may perpetuate or exacerbate healthcare disparities, potentially leading to unfair treatment recommendations or outcomes for certain patient groups. Ensuring the development of unbiased, inclusive AI models is essential for equitable care. The potential for job displacement and changing roles of physiotherapists also raises ethical questions. While AI can enhance efficiency, there's a need to balance technological integration with the irreplaceable human element of care, empathy, and professional judgment [92].

Implementation Challenges: Technological literacy among practitioners and patients is a significant hurdle. Physiotherapists need comprehensive training to effectively utilize AI tools, while patients may require education to engage with AI-driven therapies and remote monitoring systems [93]. The initial costs of implementing AI technologies can be substantial. Healthcare facilities must invest in infrastructure, software, and training, which may be challenging for smaller practices or resource-limited settings. Integration of AI systems into existing healthcare infrastructure presents technical challenges. Ensuring interoperability with current electronic health records and other medical systems is crucial for seamless adoption.

Future Developments and Outlook: Despite these challenges, the future of AI in physiotherapy is promising. We can expect to see more sophisticated AI-driven wearables and robotic systems for rehabilitation, enhancing the precision and effectiveness of treatments. Advanced machine learning algorithms may soon predict recovery times and optimize treatments in real-time, leading to more personalized and efficient care [94]. The integration of AI with virtual and augmented reality technologies could create immersive rehabilitation experiences, potentially improving patient engagement and outcomes. Additionally, the combination of AI with 3D printing for customized assistive devices or brain-computer interfaces for neurological rehabilitation could open up entirely new avenues for treatment. As these technologies evolve, we may see AI systems capable of analyzing larger, more diverse datasets, improving the accuracy and generalizability of AI models across different patient populations. This could lead to more equitable and effective care delivery.

In conclusion, while AI presents significant ethical and practical challenges in physiotherapy, its potential to enhance diagnostic accuracy, personalize treatment plans, and improve patient monitoring and engagement is undeniable. As the field continues to evolve, physiotherapists who successfully navigate these challenges and embrace these technologies will be well-positioned to provide cutting-edge, highly effective care to their patients. The key lies in addressing ethical concerns, overcoming implementation hurdles, and striking a balance between technological innovation and the human touch that remains at the heart of physiotherapy.

References

[1] N. "About Medication Errors," National Coordinating Council for Medication Error Reporting and Prevention, [Online]. Available: https://www.nccmerp.org/about-medication-errors. [Accessed 1 June 2025].

[2] W. H. O. "Global status report on road safety: time for action," World Health Organization, Geneva, 2009.

[3] B. Boussat, K. Kamalanavin and P. Francois, "The contribution of open comments to understanding the results from the Hospital Survey on Patient Safety Culture (HSOPS): A qualitative study," *PLoS One,* vol. 13, no. 4, p. e0196089, 2018.

[4] I. N. S. A. G. "Basic Safety Principles for Nuclear Power Plants," International Atomic Energy Agency, Vienna, 1999.

[5] K. J. Levine, M. Carmody and K. J. Silk, "The influence of organizational culture, climate and commitment on speaking up about medical errors," *Journal of Nursing Management,* vol. 28, no. 1, pp. 130-138, 2019.

[6] J. L. Sullivan, M. H. Shin, A. Ranusch, D. C. Mohr, C. Chen and L. J. Damschroder, "A Mixed Methods Study Exploring Patient Safety Culture at Four VHA Hospitals," *The Joint Commission Journal on Quality and Patient Safety,* vol. 50, no. 11, pp. 791-800, 2024.

[7] L. Omidi, M. Bahrami, K. M. Dolatabad, S. A. Zakerian and K. Azam, "Mindful organizing mediates the relations between group safety climate and safety-related behaviors among operating room team members," *Perioperative Care and Operating Room Management,* vol. 34, p. 100351, 2024.

[8] L. Omidi, H. Karimi, S. Mousavi and G. Moradi, "The Mediating Role of Safety Climate in the Relationship between Organizational Resilience and Safety Performance," *Journal of Health and Safety at Work,* vol. 12, no. 3, pp. 536-548, 2022.

[9] K. J. Mearns and T. Reader, "Organizational support and safety outcomes: An un-investigated relationship?," *Safety Science,* vol. 46, no. 3, pp. 388-397, 2008.

[10] B. Yanar, M. Lay and P. M. Smith, "The Interplay Between Supervisor Safety Support and Occupational Health and Safety Vulnerability on Work Injury," *Safety and Health at Work,* vol. 10, no. 2, pp. 172-179, 2019.

[11] G. E. Mathisen, T. Tjora and L. I. Vestly Bergh, "Speaking up about safety concerns in high-risk industries: Correlates of safety voice in the offshore oil rig sector," *Safety Science,* vol. 145, p. 105487, 2022.

[12] L. Omidi, G. Moradi, V. Salehi and M. Khosravifar, "A multi-criteria decision-making approach for prioritizing factors influencing healthcare workers' safety performance: A case of a women's hospital," *Journal of Safety and Sustainability,* vol. 1, no. 3, pp. 173-180, 2024.

[13] V. Salehi and B. Veitch, "Measuring and analyzing adaptive capacity at management levels of resilient systems," *Journal of Loss Prevention in the Process Industries,* vol. 63, p. 104001, 2020.

[14] A. Azyabi, W. Karwowski and M. R. Davahli, "Assessing Patient Safety Culture in Hospital Settings," *International Journal of Environmental Research and Public Health,* vol. 18, no. 5, p. 2466, 2021.

[15] L. A. Ellis, E. Falkland, P. Hibbert, S. Wiig, E. Ree, T. J. Schultz, C. Pirone and J. Braithwaite, "Issues and complexities in safety culture assessment in healthcare," *Frontiers in Public Health,* vol. 11, 2023.

[16] D. I. Aljabri, "Assessment of Patient Safety Culture in Saudi Hospitals: A Baseline Study in the Eastern Region," *Journal of King Abdulaziz University-Medical Sciences,* vol. 19, no. 1S, pp. 43-58, 2012.

[17] F. Alshammari, E. Pasay-an, M. Alboliteeh, M. H. Alshammari, T. Susanto, S. Villareal, M. C. Laami Indonto and F. Gonzales, "A survey of hospital healthcare professionals' perceptions toward patient safety culture in Saudi Arabia," *International Journal of Africa Nursing Sciences,* vol. 11, p. 100149, 2019.

[18] L. L. Gleeson, J. McNamara, E. Donworth, E. K. Crowley, A. Delaney, L. Sahm, D. O'Mahony, N. E. Russell and S. Byrne, "Healthcare provider perceptions of safety culture: A multi-site study using the safety attitudes questionnaire," *Exploratory Research in Clinical and Social Pharmacy,* vol. 9, p. 100228, 2023.

[19] J. B. Sexton, R. L. Helmreich, T. B. Neilands, K. Rowan, K. Vella, J. Boyden, P. R. Roberts and E. J. Thomas, "The Safety Attitudes Questionnaire: psychometric properties, benchmarking data, and emerging research," *BMC Health Services Research,* vol. 6, no. 44, 2006.

[20] H.-C. Cheng, A. M.-F. Yen and Y.-H. Lee, "Factors affecting patient safety culture among dental healthcare workers: A nationwide cross-sectional survey," *Journal of Dental Sciences,* vol. 14, pp. 263-268, 2019.

[21] S. Singer, M. Meterko, L. Baker, D. Gaba, A. Falwell and A. Rosen, "Workforce perceptions of hospital safety culture: development and validation of the patient safety climate in healthcare organizations survey," *Health Services Research,* vol. 42, no. 5, pp. 1999-2021, 2007.

[22] C. Agnew, R. Flin and K. Mearns, "Patient safety climate and worker safety behaviours in acute hospitals in Scotland," *Journal of Safety Research,* vol. 45, pp. 95-101, 2013.

[23] S. Zaheer, L. Ginsburg, Y.-T. Chuang and S. L. Grace, "Patient safety climate (PSC) perceptions of frontline staff in acute care hospitals: examining the role of ease of reporting, unit norms of openness, and participative leadership," *Health Care Management Review,* vol. 40, no. 1, pp. 13-23, 2015.

[24] A. Hoerbst and E. Ammenwerth, "Electronic Health Records: A Systematic Review on Quality Requirements," *Methods of Information in Medicine,* vol. 49, no. 4, pp. 320-336, 2010.

[25] J. Craig and V. Petterson, "Introduction to the Practice of Telemedicine," *Journal of Telemedicine and Telecare,* vol. 11, no. 1, pp. 3-9, 2005.

[26] S. K. Srivastava, "Adoption of Electronic Health Records: A Roadmap for India," *Healthcare Informatics Research,* vol. 22, no. 4, pp. 261-269, 2016.

[27] D. K. aut and A. K. Bhola, "Integrated disease surveillance in India: Way forward," *Global Journal of Medicine & Public Health,* vol. 3, no. 4, 2014.

[28] N. Menachemi and T. H. Collum, "Benefits and drawbacks of electronic health record systems," *Risk Management and Healthcare Policy,* vol. 4, no. 47, pp. 47-55, 2011.

[29] J. C. Sieverdes, F. Treiber, C. Jenkins and K. Hermayer, "Improving Diabetes Management With Mobile Health Technology," *The American Journal of the Medical Sciences,* vol. 345, no. 4, pp. 289-295, 2013.

[30] A. Annamalai, R. Vijayakumar, P. Vellaisamy and M. Nagarajan, "Impact of Health Information Technology Tools on Patient Safety in the Indian Healthcare Industry," *The Open Biomedical Engineering Journal,* vol. 17, p. e230925, 2023.

[31] A. Subramaniam, "Top 8 AI Use Cases in Healthcare for Driving Patient Engagement and Enhancing Patient Experience," Kanini, 17 July 2024. [Online]. Available: https://kanini.com/blog/how-is-artificial-intelligence-ai-transforming-patient-engagement/. [Accessed 28 June 2025].

[32] P. Turner, "The Changing Landscape of Healthcare," in *Talent Management in Healthcare*, Palgrave Macmillan, 2017, pp. 15-37.

[33] R. Najjar, "Redefining Radiology: A Review of Artificial Intelligence Integration in Medical Imaging," *Diagnostics (Basel),* vol. 13, no. 17, p. 2760, 2023.

[34] T. Davenport and R. Kalakota, "The potential for artificial intelligence in healthcare," *Future Healthcare Journal,* vol. 6, no. 2, pp. 94-98, 2019.

[35] R. S, "FABRIC Predicts by 2025, 42% of Hospital Management activities will be AI driven," Avira, [Online]. Available: https://www.avirainsights.com/PressRelease/ai-in-hospital-management. [Accessed 28 June 2025].

[36] S. M. Varnosfaderani and M. Forouzanfar, "The Role of AI in Hospitals and Clinics: Transforming Healthcare in the 21st Century," *Bioengineering (Basel),* vol. 11, no. 4, p. 337, 2024.

[37] T. Nakamura and T. Sasano, "Artificial intelligence and cardiology: Current status and perspective," *Journal of Cardiology,* vol. 79, no. 3, pp. 326-333, 2022.

[38] C. Yang, B. D. Ojha, N. D. Aranoff, P. Green and N. Tavassolian, "Classification of aortic stenosis using conventional machine learning and deep learning methods based on multi-dimensional cardio-mechanical signals," *Scientific Reports,* vol. 10, p. 17521, 2020.

[39] P. Diaz-Rodriguez, C. Marino, J. A. Vazquez, J. R. Caeiro-Rey and M. Landin, "Targeting joint inflammation for osteoarthritis management through stimulus-sensitive hyaluronic acid based intra-articular hydrogels," *Materials Science and Engineering: C,* vol. 128, p. 112254, 2021.

[40] V. Roblot, Y. Giret, M. Bou Antoun, C. Morillot, X. Chassin, A. Cotten, J. Zerbib and L. Fournier, "Artificial intelligence to diagnose meniscus tears on MRI," *Diagnostic and Interventional Imaging,* vol. 100, no. 4, pp. 243-249, 2019.

[41] V. Couteax, S. Si-Mohamed, O. Nempont, T. Lefevre, A. Popoff, G. Pizaine, N. Villain, I. Bloch, A. Cotten and L. Bossel, "Automatic knee meniscus tear detection and orientation classification with Mask-RCNN," *Diagnostic and Interventional Imaging,* vol. 100, no. 4, pp. 235-242, 2019.

[42] K.-K. Mak and M. R. Pichika, "Artificial intelligence in drug development: present status and future prospects," *Drug Discovery Today,* vol. 24, no. 3, pp. 773-780, 2019.

[43] X. Yang, Y. Wang, R. Byrne, G. Schneider and S. Yang, "Concepts of Artificial Intelligence for Computer-Assisted Drug Discovery," *Chemical Reviews,* vol. 119, no. 18, pp. 10520-10594, 2019.
[44] H. Ozturk, A. Ozgur and E. Ozkirimli, "DeepDTA: deep drug-target binding affinity prediction," *Bioinformatics,* vol. 34, no. 17, pp. i821-i829, 2018.
[45] D. Paul, G. Sanap, S. Shenoy, D. Kalyane, K. Kalia and R. K. Tekade, "Artificial intelligence in drug discovery and development," *Drug Discovery Today,* vol. 26, no. 1, pp. 80-93, 2021.
[46] Z. Guan, H. Li, R. Liu, C. Cai, Y. Liu, J. Li, X. Wang, S. Huang, L. Wu, D. Liu, S. Yu, Z. Wang, J. Shu, X. Hou, X. Yang, W. Jia and B. Sheng, "Artificial intelligence in diabetes management: Advancements, opportunities, and challenges," *Cell Reports Medicine,* vol. 4, no. 10, p. 101213, 2023.
[47] E. Sciarretta, R. Mancini and E. Greco, "Artificial Intelligence for Healthcare and Social Services: Optimizing Resources and Promoting Sustainability," *Sustainability,* vol. 14, no. 24, p. 16464, 2022.
[48] D. B. Olawade, O. Z. Wada, A. Odetayo, A. C. David-Olawade, F. Asaolu and J. Eberhardt, "Enhancing mental health with Artificial Intelligence: Current trends and future prospects," *Journal of Medicine, Surgery, and Public Health,* vol. 3, p. 100099, 2024.
[49] G. Rompianesi, F. Pegoraro, C. D. Ceresa, R. Montalti and R. I. Troisi, "Artificial intelligence in the diagnosis and management of colorectal cancer liver metastases," *World Journal of Gastroenterology,* vol. 28, no. 1, pp. 108-122, 2022.
[50] S. A. Alowais, S. S. Alghamdi, N. Alsuhebany, T. Alqahtani, A. I. Alshaya, S. N. Almohareb, A. Aldairem, M. Alrashed, K. B. Saleh, H. A. Badreldin, M. S. AI Yami, S. AI Harbi and A. M. Albekairy, "Revolutionizing healthcare: the role of artificial intelligence in clinical practice," *BMC Medical Journal,* vol. 23, p. 689, 2023.
[51] "AI-assisted Patient Management," Xunfei Healthcare, [Online]. Available: https://www.xunfeihealthcare.com/en/product/69.html. [Accessed 28 June 2025].
[52] S. A. Alimour and M. Alrabeei, "A Novel Model for Digital Twins in Mental Health: The Biopsychosocial AI-Driven Digital Twin (BADT) Framework," in *2024 11th International Conference on Software Defined Systems*, Gran Canaria, 2024.
[53] J. Luo, M. Pan, K. Mo, Y. Mao and D. Zou, "Emerging role of artificial intelligence in diagnosis, classification and clinical management of glioma," *Seminars in Cancer Biology,* vol. 91, pp. 110-123, 2023.

[54] J. Calderaro, T. P. Seraphin, T. Luedde and T. G. Simon, "Artificial intelligence for the prevention and clinical management of hepatocellular carcinoma," *Journal of Hepatology,* vol. 76, no. 6, pp. 1348-1361, 2022.

[55] M. Zhang, L. Zhu, S.-Y. Lin, K. Herr, C.-L. Chi, I. Demir, K. D. Lopez and N.-C. Chi, "Using artificial intelligence to improve pain assessment and pain management: a scoping review," *Journal of American Medical Informatics Association,* vol. 30, no. 3, pp. 570-587, 2023.

[56] M. A. Muzammil, S. Javid, A. K. Afridi, R. Siddineni, M. Shahabi, M. Haseeb, F. Fariha, S. Kumar, S. Zaveri and A. J. Nashwan, "Artificial intelligence-enhanced electrocardiography for accurate diagnosis and management of cardiovascular diseases," *Journal of Electrocardiology,* vol. 83, pp. 30-40, 2024.

[57] V. D. Nagarajan, S.-L. Lee, J.-L. Robertus, C. A. Nienaber, N. A. Trayanova and S. Ernst, "Artificial intelligence in the diagnosis and management of arrhythmias," *European Heart Journal,* vol. 42, no. 38, pp. 3904-3916, 2021.

[58] V. Bellini, M. Russo, T. Domenichetti, M. Panizzi, S. Allai and E. G. Bignami, "Artificial Intelligence in Operating Room Management," *Journal of Medical Systems,* vol. 48, no. 1, p. 19, 2024.

[59] S. V. Kalmady, R. Greiner, R. Agrawal, V. Shivakumar, J. C. Narayanaswamy, M. R. G. Brown, A. J. Greenshaw, S. M. Dursun and G. Venkatasubramanian, "Towards artificial intelligence in mental health by improving schizophrenia prediction with multiple brain parcellation ensemble-learning," *NPJ Schizophrenia,* vol. 5, no. 1, p. 2, 2019.

[60] T. T. Erguzel, G. H. Sayar and N. Tarhan, "Artificial intelligence approach to classify unipolar and bipolar depressive disorders," *Neural Computing and Applications,* vol. 27, pp. 1607-1616, 2016.

[61] B. L. Cook, A. M. Progovac, P. Chen, B. Mullin, S. Hou and E. Baca-Garcia, "Novel Use of Natural Language Processing (NLP) to Predict Suicidal Ideation and Psychiatric Symptoms in a Text-Based Mental Health Intervention in Madrid," *Computational and Mathematical Methods in Medicine,* vol. 2016, p. 8708434, 2016.

[62] G. Gkotsis, A. Oellrich, S. Velupillai, M. Liakata, T. J. P. Hubbard, R. J. B. Dobson and R. Dutta, "Characterisation of mental health conditions in social media using Informed Deep Learning," *Scientific Reports,* vol. 7, p. 45141, 2017.

[63] J. C. Ling Ong, B. J. Jie Seng, J. Z. Feng Law, L. L. Low, A. L. Hoon Kwa, K. M. Giacomini and D. S. Wei Ting, "Artificial intelligence,

ChatGPT, and other large language models for social determinants of health: Current state and future directions," *Cell Reports Medicine,* vol. 5, no. 1, p. 101356, 2024.

[64] A. S. Lundervold and A. Lundervold, "An overview of deep learning in medical imaging focusing on MRI," *Zeitschrift für Medizinische Physik,* vol. 29, no. 2, pp. 102-127, 2019.

[65] T. J. Terlouw, "Roots of Physical Medicine, Physical Therapy, and Mechanotherapy in the Netherlands in the 19th Century: A Disputed Area within the Healthcare Domain," *Journal of Manal and Manipulative Therapy,* vol. 15, no. 2, pp. e23-41, 2007.

[66] A. P. T. A. "Vision Statement for the Physical Therapy Profession," 25 September 2019. [Online]. Available: https://www.apta.org/apta-and-you/leadership-and-governance/policies/vision-statement-for-the-physical-therapy-profession. [Accessed 15 June 2025].

[67] M. M. Rodgers, G. Alon, V. M. Pai and R. S. Conroy, "Wearable technologies for active living and rehabilitation: Current research challenges and future opportunities," *Journal of Rehabilitation and Assistive Technologies Engineering,* vol. 6, p. 2055668319839607, 2019.

[68] S. Mani, S. Sharma, B. Omar, A. Paungmali and L. Joseph, "Validity and reliability of Internet-based physiotherapy assessment for musculoskeletal disorders: a systematic review," *Journal of Telemedicine and Telecare,* vol. 23, no. 3, pp. 379-391, 2017.

[69] M. A. Cottrell, O. A. Galea, S. P. O'Leary, A. J. Hill and T. G. Russell, "Real-time telerehabilitation for the treatment of musculoskeletal conditions is effective and comparable to standard practice: a systematic review and meta-analysis," *Clinical Rehabilitation,* vol. 31, no. 5, pp. 625-638, 2017.

[70] R. Hartmann, F. Avermann, C. Zalpour and A. Griefahn, "Impact of an AI app-based exercise program for people with low back pain compared to standard care: A longitudinal cohort-study," *Health Science Reports,* vol. 6, no. 1, p. e1060, 2023.

[71] C. G. Blum, R. Richter, R. Fuchs, F. Sandeck, K. Kunz and S. Heermann, "Interprofessional education in medical and physiotherapy studies for future collaboration," *Annals of Anatomy - Anatomischer Anzeiger,* vol. 240, p. 151850, 2022.

[72] J. Saeton, A. Jones, C. Johnston and K. Francis, "Facilitators of effective interprofessional collaborative practice for physiotherapy private practitioners: An interpretive descriptive study," *Journal of Interprofessional Education & Practice,* vol. 33, p. 100671, 2023.

[73] G. Nambi, M. Alghadier, S. H. Pakkir Mohamed and O. R. Aldhafian, "Clinical Usefulness of Artificial Intelligence in Physiotherapy – A

Practice-based Review," *SBV Journal of Basic, Clinical and Applied Health Science,* vol. 7, no. 4, pp. 184-188, 2024.

[74] P. Rajpurkar, E. Chen, O. Banerjee and E. J. Topol, "AI in health and medicine," *Nature Medicine,* vol. 28, pp. 31-38, 2022.

[75] S. Rani, M. Memoria, A. Almogren, S. Bharany, K. Joshi, A. Altameem, A. U. Rehman and H. Hamam, "Deep learning to combat knee osteoarthritis and severity assessment by using CNN-based classification," *BMC Musculoskeletal Disorders,* vol. 25, p. 817, 2024.

[76] M. M. Sadr, M. Khani and S. M. Tootkaleh, "Predicting athletic injuries with deep Learning: Evaluating CNNs and RNNs for enhanced performance and Safety," *Biomedical Signal Processing and Control,* vol. 105, p. 107692, 2025.

[77] S. Hwang, J. Kim, S. Yang, H.-J. Moon, K.-H. Cho, I. Youn, J.-K. Sung and S. Han, "Machine Learning Based Abnormal Gait Classification with IMU Considering Joint Impairment," *Sensors,* vol. 24, no. 17, p. 5571, 2024.

[78] R. R. Ilesan, C.-G. Cordos, L.-I. Mihaila, R. Flesar, A.-S. Popescu, L. Perju-Dumbrava and P. Farago, "Proof of Concept in Artificial-Intelligence-Based Wearable Gait Monitoring for Parkinson's Disease Management Optimization," *Biosensors,* vol. 12, no. 4, p. 189, 2022.

[79] A. Schulc, C. B. Leite, M. Csakvari, L. Lattermann, M. F. Zgoda, E. M. Farina, C. Lattermann, Z. Toser and G. Merkely, "Identifying Anterior Cruciate Ligament Injuries Through Automated Video Analysis of In-Game Motion Patterns," *Orthopaedic Journal of Sports Medicine,* vol. 12, no. 3, p. 23259671231221579, 2024.

[80] L. P. Dresser and M. A. Kohn, "Artificial Intelligence and the Evaluation and Treatment of Stroke," *Delaware,* vol. 9, no. 3, pp. 82-84, 2023.

[81] D. N. Freitas, S. S. Mostafa, R. Caldeira, F. Santos, E. Ferme, E. R. Gouveia and F. Morgado-Dias, "Predicting noncontact injuries of professional football players using machine learning," *PLoS One,* vol. 20, no. 1, p. e0315481, 2025.

[82] A. Griefahn, C. Zalpour and K. Leudtke, "Identifying the risk of exercises, recommended by an artificial intelligence for patients with musculoskeletal disorders," *Scientific Reports,* vol. 14, p. 14472, 2024.

[83] M. Palaniswamy, L. Wai Yie and B. Y. Suprapto, "Virtual and augmented reality in Industry 4.0," in *The Nine Pillars of Technologies for Industry 4.0*, Kuala Lumpur, The Institution of Engineering and Technology, 2020, pp. 61-78.

[84] F. M. Alfieri, C. d. Silva Dias, N. C. d. Oliveira and L. R. Battistella, "Gamification in Musculoskeletal Rehabilitation," *Current Reviews in Musculoskeletal Medicine,* vol. 15, no. 6, pp. 629-636, 2022.

[85] D. Tolks, J. J. Schmidt and S. Kuhn, "The Role of AI in Serious Games and Gamification for Health: Scoping Review," *JMIR Serious Games,* vol. 12, p. e48258, 2024.
[86] L. C. "Enhancing Therapy Through Gamification & AI," LENS Corporation, 20 July 2024. [Online]. Available: https://www.linkedin.com/pulse/enhancing-therapy-through-gamification-ai-lens-corporation-jsztc. [Accessed 20 June 2025].
[87] N. Lotz, "Getting fit is child's play: Gamification in rehabilitation and physiotherapy," REHACARE International, 12 October 2022. [Online]. Available: https://www.rehacare.com/en/media-news/emag/business/gamification-rehabilitation-physiotherapy. [Accessed 20 June 2025].
[88] U. Chaturvedi, S. B. Chauhan and I. Singh, "The impact of artificial intelligence on remote healthcare: Enhancing patient engagement, connectivity, and overcoming challenges," *Intelligent Pharmacy,* vol. In Press, 2025.
[89] A. "How virtual health assistants are transforming patient engagement," Aarogyapay, 23 January 2025. [Online]. Available: https://www.aarogyapay.com/how-virtual-health-assistants-are-transforming-patient-engagement/. [Accessed 20 June 2025].
[90] 1. "3 Ways AI Virtual Health Assistants Can Help Increase Patient Engagement," 100Plus, 20 September 2023. [Online]. Available: https://www.100plus.com/resource/3-ways-ai-virtual-health-assistants-can-help-increase-patient-engagement/. [Accessed 20 June 2025].
[91] N. A. "Conversational AI in Healthcare Improves Patient Engagement and Efficacy," Chatbots Life, 7 April 2021. [Online]. Available: https://blog.chatbotslife.com/conversational-ai-in-healthcare-improves-patient-engagement-and-efficacy-df470a68faeb. [Accessed 28 June 2025].
[92] B. Murdoch, "Privacy and artificial intelligence: challenges for protecting health information in a new era," *BMC Medical Ethics,* vol. 22, p. 122, 2021.
[93] G. Nambi, M. Alghadier, S. H. P. Mohamed, O. R. Aldhafian, N. A. Alshahrani and A. J. A. Albarakati, "Clinical Usefulness of Artificial Intelligence in Physiotherapy – A Practice-based Review," *SBV Journal of Basic, Clinical and Applied Health Science,* vol. 7, no. 4, pp. 184-188, 2024.
[94] K. Sharma, "Data Privacy and Security in AI-Driven Healthcare: A Critical Analysis," *International Journal of Sustainable Development in Computing Science,* vol. 5, no. 3, p. 416, 2023.

8

AI in Wearable Devices to Monitor Health Status

Mohankumar Palaniswamy[1,2] and Priyadarshini Mishra[3]

[1]Faculty of Sports and Exercise Science, Universiti Malaya, 50603 Wilayah Persekutuan Kuala Lumpur, Malaysia
[2]INTI International University, 71800 Nilai, Negari Sembilan, Malaysia
[3]Abhinav Bindra Sports Medicine and Research Institute, Odisha, India

Email: mohankumar.p@um.edu.my; drpriyadarshini.mishra@gmail.com

Abstract

The convergence of Artificial Intelligence (AI) and wearable technology is revolutionizing personal health management by shifting from reactive to proactive care. Wearable devices, equipped with advanced biosensors, continuously track physiological metrics such as heart rate variability, glucose levels, and sleep patterns. By applying machine learning algorithms to this continuous stream of high-frequency data, AI can identify subtle deviations from a user's baseline that may signal the onset of chronic conditions or cute medical events, such as arrhythmias or respiratory distress. These AI-driven wearables enhance diagnostic precision through real-time analysis, transforming raw data into actionable health insights. Furthermore, they facilitate personalized medicine by tailoring wellness recommendations to an individual's unique biological trends. Ultimately, AI-integrated wearables empower patients with self-monitoring tools while providing clinicians with longitudinal data, reducing hospital readmissions and fostering a more resilient, data-informed healthcare ecosystem.

 DOI: 10.1201/9788743812135-8

8.1 Digital Health Technology

Modernization calls for digital health. Innovation, clinical implications, and collaboration with cutting-edge technology have all contributed to the 20th-century changes, which have improved the health of the people and paved the way for the health system to include digitalization. In the modern digital economy, having a staff that is proficient in digital skills is absolutely essential. The realization of a digital health depends on resolving issues with infrastructure, affordability, and digital literacy. Electronic health records (EHRs), mobile health apps, wearable devices, telemedicine, telehealth, personalized medicine, electronic medical records (EMR), artificial intelligence (AI), blockchain, big data analytics, and the Internet of Things (IoT) are all part of digital health, which aims to improve healthcare delivery, public health, and overall wellness [1]. Refer to Figure 8.1.

The term "digital health (DH)" refers to an interdisciplinary field that includes all areas of medicine that make extensive use of digital tools. According to the World Health Organization, digital encompasses eHealth and other emerging fields like genomics, AI, virtual reality (VR), business analytics, big data, and blockchain, among others. Electronic health data, wearable technology, mobile health apps, and telemedicine are all part of DH. Aiming to facilitate computer-to-computer and network-to-network communication and data sharing, the internet was initially established in the 1980s. It has revolutionized several industries, healthcare included, throughout the years. Digital health solutions have the potential to transform healthcare delivery by enhancing health management and service accessibility.

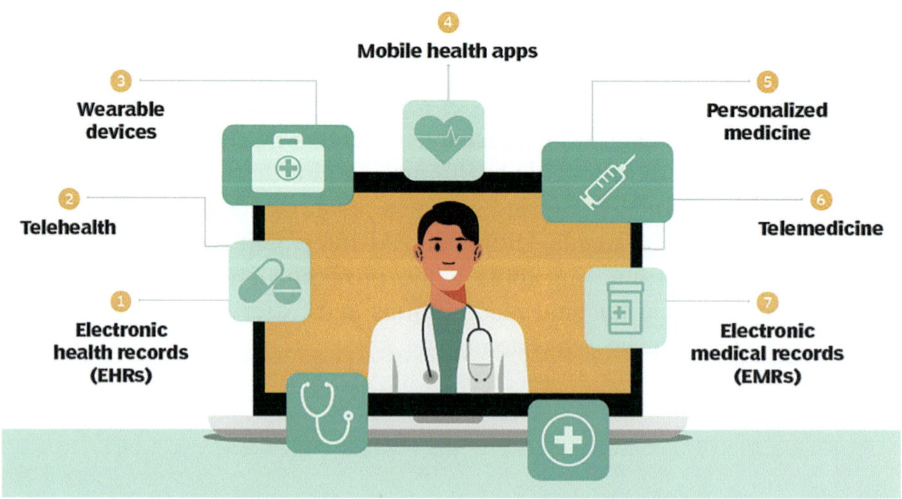

Figure 8.1 Fractions of digital health technology [2].

Software, hardware, sensors, and networks are all components of healthcare IT integration. It paves the way for health data management, telemedicine, distant care, and personalized treatment. Improved access to underserved areas, streamlined diagnosis, treatment planning, and patient management, wearable device empowerment, and cost savings from preventative care are all advantages. Data interoperability, privacy, the digital gap, and regulatory constraints are some of the obstacles that need to be addressed. Data breaches and improper use of protected health information are real possibilities due to privacy issues and incompatible data formats, which make data interoperability difficult. Inequalities in healthcare access are worsened by the digital divide. It is still not easy for digital health technology to comply with worldwide standards. Inequalities and compliance with global standards for digital health technologies remain complex [3].

8.1.1 Influence of digitization on patient

The field of digital health involves utilizing technology to enhance patient care in every aspect, from diagnosis to treatment and beyond. Better diagnosis and treatment, individualized attention, easier access to care, shorter hospital stays, fewer readmissions, lower healthcare costs, and more agency for healthcare providers are some of the most important outcomes. Tools for machine learning (ML) and AI enhance the precision of diagnoses, allowing for the prompt identification and treatment of diseases at an early stage. Patients are better protected by health informatics systems that lessen the likelihood of medication mistakes [4]. Patients with chronic diseases are better able to take charge of their own care when they get personalized treatment regimens developed from their unique medical records. Particularly for marginalized or far-flung communities, telehealth and telemedicine broaden access to medical treatment. Patients are more actively involved in their care when they use digital platforms to access their medical information and contact physicians more effectively. Reducing mistakes and superfluous procedures is the key to achieving cost efficiency. The use of real-time data, decision-making, and task execution time empowers health personnel, leading to the delivery of higher-quality treatment.

8.1.2 Healthcare adoption guidelines

Digital technologies are vital to long-term health systems and universal healthcare, and the global strategy recognizes that each country is responsible for its own digital health action plan within its unique environment. To be effective, digital health efforts need an integrated strategy. Digital health efforts can only reach their full potential when they are well-grounded in the larger health requirements and ecosystem, and when they are led by a solid strategy that unites leadership, financial, organizational, human, and technical resources. The efforts should be spearheaded by robust governance mechanisms. They tackle various health goals and are backed by standards and architecture. As digital public goods that may be adjusted to diverse nations and settings, the global approach supports the proper utilization of digital technology for health [5].

The global strategy promotes the appropriate use of digital technologies for health as digital public goods that are adaptable to different countries and contexts. It supports equity in access to digital resources and protects people, populations, healthcare professionals, and systems against misinformation, misuse of information, malicious cyber activities, fraud, exploitation, inappropriate use of health data, racism, and human rights violations within the framework established by international treaties binding Member States. The "digital determinants of health," such as literacy in information and communication technologies and access to equipment, broadband, and the internet, become more important as digital health becomes more prevalent. The global strategy emphasizes the need to ground digital foundations within national strategies and work with different sectors and stakeholders at all levels. The appropriate use of digital health takes into consideration health promotion and disease prevention, patient safety, ethics, interoperability, intellectual property, data security, privacy, cost-effectiveness, patient engagement, and affordability. It should be people-centered, trust-based, evidence-based, effective, efficient, sustainable, inclusive, equitable, and contextualized. We also recognize the urgent need to address the major impediments that least-developed countries face when implementing digital health technologies. This includes an appropriate enabling environment, sufficient resources, infrastructure to support digital transformation, education, human capacity, financial investment, and internet connectivity [6].

8.1.3 Digital tools working toward better health

Access, diagnostic accuracy, and the promotion of individualized treatment are three areas where digital health tools are reshaping the healthcare system. Some examples of these resources are AI-driven diagnoses, health monitoring applications, electronic health records (EHRs), and telemedicine platforms. Healthcare delivery is integrated with EHRs like Cerner and Epic Systems, which improves patient care coordination and decreases mistakes. Extending healthcare services, telemedicine systems such as HealthTap and Teladoc provide virtual consultations, encrypted messaging, and symptom screening driven by AI. Apps and wearables that measure health, such as smartwatches and fitness trackers, keep tabs on vital signals and promote better lifestyle choices. The ability of AI-powered diagnostic tools to analyze medical pictures and spot abnormalities greatly improves the speed and accuracy of diagnoses. Huma is one example of a remote patient monitoring (RPM) platform that provides real-time surveillance of vital signs, monitoring of symptoms, and insights enabled by AI for individualized care. Ada Health and other digital applications for mental health include features like guided meditation, mood monitoring, and the ability to access mental health resources. The availability of digital medicines, which include software-based treatments, for the management of diseases and illnesses is on the rise. Effective therapies for chronic illnesses are provided by these tools, which are evidence-based and FDA-cleared [7]. The advantages of digital health are provided in table 8.1. Refer figure 8.2 for a variety of digital tools available in personalized treatment.

8.1.4 e-Portals for digital health

Digital health encompasses a wide range of applications utilizing information technology and communications to manage health and wellness [8]. Key applications include:

- Telemedicine: By utilizing telecommunications, telemedicine offers remote healthcare services, helping both urban and rural people access healthcare.
- Point-of-Care Diagnostics (POCD): POCD allows for real-time illness management and monitoring by enabling accurate diagnoses in settings with limited resources using portable equipment.
- mHealth: By capitalizing on the massive smartphone market, mHealth makes digital health services more accessible through mobile platforms.
- Medical Virtual Assistants (MVAs): AI-powered medical virtual assistants (MVAs) help patients with health-related questions and administrative duties in the time between doctor's visits.
- Robot-Assisted Surgery: Potential future uses in micro-robotics aside, robot-assisted surgery improves surgical accuracy and patient recovery via minimally invasive approaches.
- Self-Monitoring Healthcare Devices: Wearable equipment that monitors physiological changes, letting users be proactive with their health monitoring.

Table 8.1 Advantages of digital health [9].

Features in digital health	Benefits
Healthcare equity and inclusivity	Improved access to healthcare services, especially in underprivileged regions, has been achieved through digital health initiatives. Catering to varied populations is made easier with multilingual platforms.
Empowerment and enhancement of health and patient	Patients are given more agency through digital health solutions since they provide them access to their health records and management tools. With the help of health applications and wearable tech, it is now possible to monitor vital signs, track progress, and make educated decisions.
Healthcare services simplified	More productivity and less red tape have resulted from the widespread use of digital technologies. Providers are able to access and exchange patient information effortlessly using electronic medical record (EMR) and health informatics systems, which eliminates paperwork and human mistakes.
Effective cost management in healthcare	Interventions in digital health lower healthcare expenditures. Streamlining operations and better allocating resources are two benefits of digital health technologies.
Enhanced quality of care and outcomes	Digital health interventions are facilitating personalized and evidence-based care. Access to real-time patient data, health analytics, and decision support tools ensures informed clinical decisions. This leads to improved treatment outcomes and patient safety.
Advancements in medical research and Innovation	Digital health platforms and data analytics help collect and analyze large-scale health data. The data-driven approach supports evidence-based decision-making, clinical trials, and the development of new treatments and interventions.
Preventive medicine	Preventive medicine will play a crucial role in the healthcare of the future. Regular screenings, health check-ups, health education, vaccination, and improved sanitation can make a significant difference in the prevention/early detection of noncommunicable diseases.
Personalized and precision medicine	Personalized and precision medicine is becoming a reality due to the translation of advances in genetic and molecular research. Digital health enables targeted screening, lifestyle modifications, and early interventions based on one's genetic profile.
Public health policies and initiatives	Policy interventions target risk factors, including tobacco use, air pollution, and sanitation. This requires close interaction among healthcare providers, policymakers, and communities.

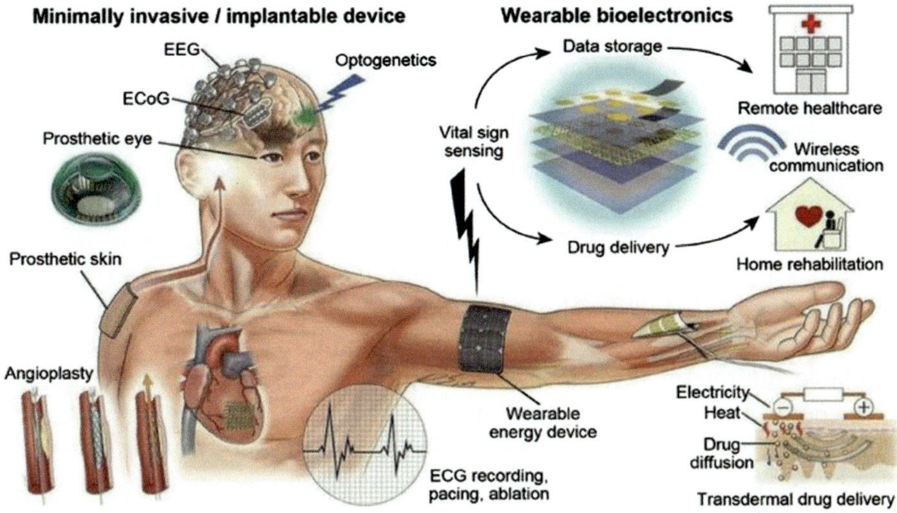

Figure 8.2 Digital tools in a personalized treatment [7].

- Electronic Health Records: The term "electronic health records" (EHR) refers to digital patient records that allow for improved healthcare management through increased accessibility and decreased test duplication.
- Health Service Aggregation: The term "health service aggregation" refers to web-based systems that link people with physicians and provide reviews and other information to help with healthcare decision-making.
- Big Data in Healthcare: Utilizes massive volumes of data produced by digital health services to enhance healthcare solutions and gain new insights; this is known as "big data" in healthcare.
- Blockchain in Healthcare: Enhances data storage, sharing, and privacy, promoting a value-based healthcare system and seamless information exchange.
- Targeted Advertising: Uses health data to deliver personalized product advertisements, raising ethical considerations regarding privacy.
- e-Pharmacies: Online pharmacies that expand access to medications, though their legal status remains uncertain.
- e-Learning in Healthcare: Facilitates consistent information sharing by giving healthcare workers easy access to ongoing professional development.

8.2 VR in Healthcare

Virtual reality (VR) is an image generated by a computer in a 3-dimensional plane that gives a feed of the task to an individual. VR has evolved with newer technologies & even reduced the financial burden by being affordable to be used by a larger number. Recent studies have reported VR to be an integral part of various therapeutic approaches in healthcare, as in disorders like phobias and anxiety disorder. Furthermore, it is a magical tool in rehabilitation, as well as a positive outcome in addressing Parkinson's disease, pain management, and developmental delay. VR products emerge as promising tools for medical care, offering the potential to establish markets with favorable returns on investment. The history of VR has evolved since the 18th century. A major milestone in the history of VR includes "Sword of Damocles" in 1968. The evolution started with stereoscopy in the 18th century by Sir Charles Wheatstone, with 2D imaging in 3 dimensions. Oculus significantly increased intense VR & Augmented Reality (AR) among various companies like Sony, Samsung, HTC & Google, making significant investments as it's a mine of $2 billion projects. AR has supportive evidence from the last two decades, helping the academic community, with evolution into VR-supported programs (gaming), aiding in better rehabilitation & training of patients with neuropsychology as a background [10]. Refer figure 8.3. VR has been found to unravel various pivotal mysteries of human memory, especially helpful for dementia patients. Pioneering works on nerve cells associated with spatial cognition have been conducted by John O'Keefe, May Britt Mosel, and Edvard by adapting the term "brain GPS." The evolution of technologies has set the background for 3D imaging across various sectors, including healthcare, military, and education. As VR progresses, its integration into critical sectors underscores its potential for revolutionizing practices, education, and training methodologies.

Teaching and Learning Process: 3D VR models are used to enhance the teaching mechanism & better learning. The technologies include various application-based and 3D VR models for learning in the field of anatomy & surgery. Photogrammetry is a technique that enables the simulation of 3D objects by deriving coordinates and spatial measurements from photographs. Incorporating these tools has resulted in noteworthy enhancements in the instruction of human anatomy. Medical students have expressed their perspectives on 3D-VR as an educational tool, emphasizing its superior advantages in comprehending human anatomy compared to conventional methods [11]. The neurosurgery research laboratory provides an ideal

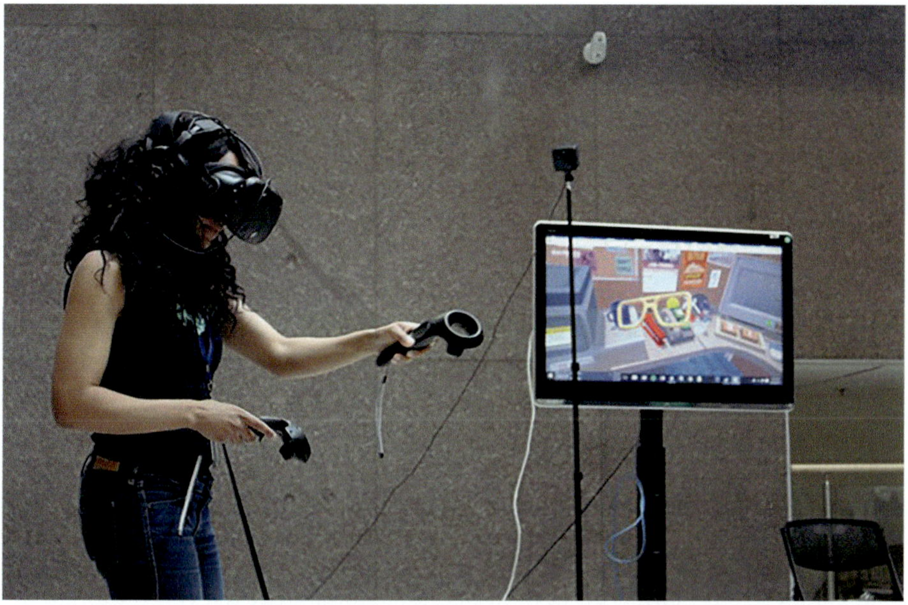

Figure 8.3 VR in gaming rehabilitation [10].

setting for gaining expertise in the intricate anatomy of microsurgery and mastering advanced surgical techniques essential for managing complex neurosurgical conditions. Trainees can utilize state-of-the-art equipment and instrumentation to simulate surgical procedures within this setting, enabling the refinement of visuospatial orientation and fine motor skills and the improvement of surgical techniques. Gonzalez-Romo *et al.* [12] proposed multimodal and integrated computerized teaching methods as a viable alternative to conventional cadaver dissection. The study introduced a metaverse, establishing a virtual neuroanatomy laboratory space as a centralized repository for neurosurgical anatomical resources. Motor imagery (MI), a cognitive process involving the mental rehearsal of body movements without physical execution, is a promising strategy for motor rehabilitation after a stroke. Using VR technology, action observation (AO) creates a simulated environment that reduces distractions, which may help make traditional motor imagery tasks easier. VR offers surgeons an immersive and interactive environment that complements fundamental surgical visualization by offering real-time visual cues and feedback during the procedure and enhancing surgical precision. Research has demonstrated that VR simulations can lead to a reduction of up to 53.7% in errors related to pedicle screw placement, highlighting its potential to augment surgical accuracy.

Diagnosis and Management: Integrating technologies such as VR and AR in surgeries addressing spinal deformities proves beneficial in preoperative planning. These technologies offer 3D visualizations of the patient's spinal alignment, providing precise osteotomy landmarks. The use of AR overlays aids surgeons in visualizing the final alignment before making surgical incisions, ensuring more accurate and reproducible surgical procedures. Research indicates that incorporating VR and AR in these surgeries improves patient outcomes, including reduced complications and revisions. VR technology has the potential to be used in teaching and training medical practitioners, particularly in intensive care units (ICUs), where complex treatment plans require theoretical understanding and preparedness for practice. In a randomized controlled trial conducted by Nas *et al.* [13], the efficacy of VR in teaching cardiopulmonary resuscitation was assessed among 381 participants. Wolff *et al.* [14] creatively created a VR training environment to improve conventional extracorporeal membrane oxygenation (ECMO) training methods. Colt *et al.* [15] developed a VR bronchoscopy simulation, which demonstrated dexterity, speed, and accuracy like experienced physicians. Chiang *et al.* [16] examined the effects of a 15-minute VR-based learning session on tracheostomy care in a prospective randomized research study including 60 healthcare personnel. After utilizing VR materials, participants experienced significant enhancements in self-efficacy, with favorable effects persisting for 3 to 4 weeks.

In ICU studies, stress is one of the main concerns affecting patients and medical staff. Nijland *et al.* [17] investigated the efficacy of VR in reducing perceived stress levels in a study that included 66 ICU nurses. The findings showed that 62% of ICU nurses who used VR relaxation during time off thought it was beneficial for lowering stress. Bodet-Contentin *et al.* [18] suggested that using VR to increase the efficacy of breaks might benefit 88 carers in the ICUs. In palliative care, VR as an adjunct to various management would be helpful to work on the psychological well-being of the patients. Further imparting an experience of relaxation & boosting emotional life along with offering a cognitive distraction for reducing symptoms like pain, anxiety & depression.

Recent studies [19, 20] have shown a positive correlation of creating a virtual environment in enhancing respiratory function through specialized breathing techniques. Studies showed that the Children's Hospital of

Illinois has developed over 400 clinical VR models (VRMs) for preoperative planning, initially applied in congenital cardiac surgery. These immersive experiences have since expanded to various surgical disciplines, particularly in cardiothoracic surgery, where proceduralists express increasing demand for such technology. VRM has been particularly beneficial in cases of brain tumors, where it aids in precise localization with high accuracy. Stereo electroencephalography (SEEG) has become more widely used for anatomical mapping in epileptic patients, and VR modeling has been essential in improving presurgical planning and patient education, especially in detecting centers of activity [21].

8.2.1 Future scope

VR technology has emerged as a valuable tool to enhance communication and facilitate shared decision-making in the medical context. It benefits patient communication, clinician training, and simulation, especially in high-risk medical settings like trauma, emergency, or surgical care [22]. VR simulations offer a realistic and effective alternative to traditional methods like role-playing, replicating clinical situations effectively in scenarios like the cardiac ICU. Researchers have developed various simulators for neurosurgical and pediatric surgery training, and VR has proven beneficial for patients [23]. For example, individuals with hand burns experienced significant improvements in their hand function, performance, and satisfaction when using VR compared to traditional rehabilitation. VR-based skills simulators extend to various medical procedures, including angiography, vascular access, percutaneous valve implantation, surgeries, and electrophysiology. Furthermore, enhancements in technology will lead to more precision and a better prognosis for various conditions [24]. The COVID-19 pandemic disrupted traditional medical practices, creating challenges for in-person visits. VR emerged as a pivotal solution, offering immersive rehabilitation experiences with minimal exposure risk. As telemedicine becomes more prevalent, VR facilitates virtual consultations with experts, overcoming time and space constraints. Research indicates that VR-based remote multidisciplinary meetings are feasible and engaging, highlighting telemedicine's enduring significance beyond the pandemic [25]. VR can enhance remote consultations, allowing patients to share real-time health data and engage in virtual consultations with healthcare professionals. VR can improve access to healthcare in underserved areas by bridging the gap between patients and healthcare providers. In future, it shall play a vital role in human–robot interaction (HRI). Refer figure 8.4.

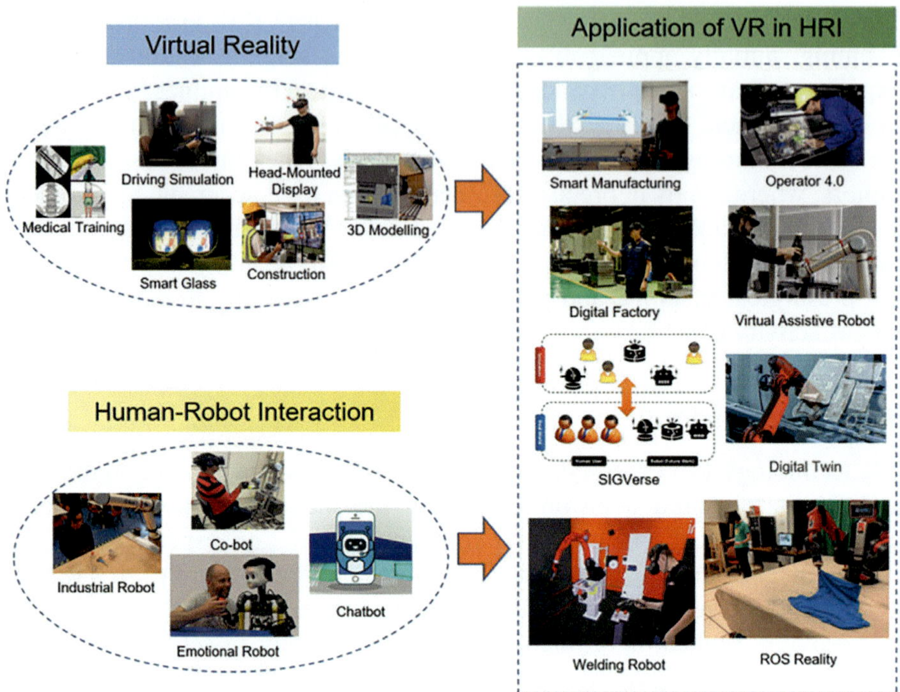

Figure 8.4 Applications of VR in human–robot interaction [26].

8.3 AI in Healthcare

AI is the call of the era. AI integrates ML, deep learning (DL), and natural language processing (NLP) to perform tasks that traditionally require human intelligence. Since its inception in 1951, AI has evolved significantly, leading to the development of the first AI program. Today, AI is transforming various fields, including healthcare, finance, and transportation. Academics have utilized AI to create intelligent tutoring systems and analyze vast datasets for patterns that humans would find challenging. In 1956, Professor McCarthy employed AI to simulate intelligent behavior and reflective thinking akin to that of humans, earning him the title of "father of AI" [27].

AI in healthcare tasks has seen significant advancements since the 20th century, driven by deep learning, computing power, and data analysis. Refer figure 8.5. It has been working to revolutionize healthcare by providing personalized health information, enabling virtual consultations, and facilitating remote monitoring. AI algorithms can offer tailored recommendations for maintaining good health, improving medication management, and enhancing

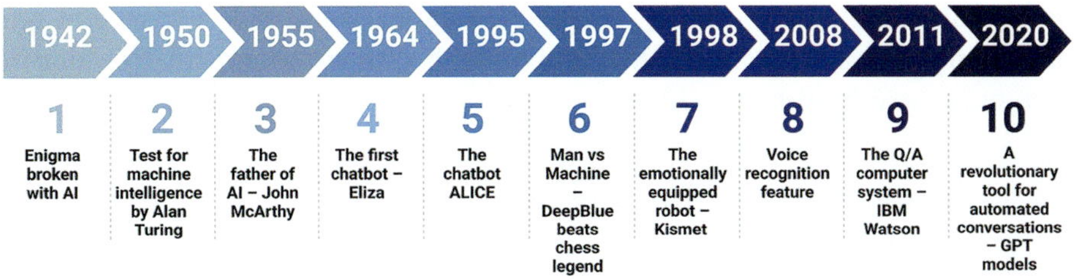

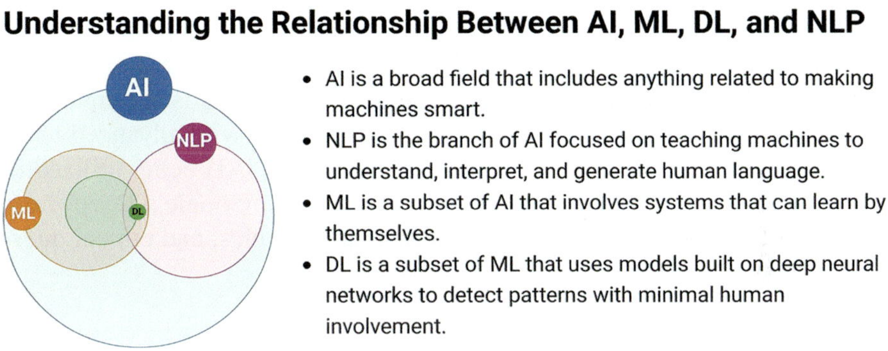

Figure 8.5 Relation between AI and other learnings [28].

transparency in healthcare. The COVID-19 pandemic has accelerated the use of AI in telemedicine and chatbot-enabled medical education for patients [29]. AI contributes to better assessment and management of client or patient complaints by automating processes and scheduling maintenance in advance. It also detects and prevents errors in medical records, providing real-time guidance and recommendations. Furthermore, AI assists healthcare professionals in staying updated with recent advancements across various fields by offering continuous professional development programs and simulated training opportunities.

Precision medicine, or personalized medicine, represents a tailored approach that customizes medical care to individual patients based on their unique characteristics. AI has emerged as a valuable tool in furthering personalized treatment, facilitating the analysis of complex datasets, predicting outcomes, and optimizing treatment strategies. AI has been utilized to forecast therapy responses, with studies demonstrating over 80% accuracy across various drugs. Additionally, AI plays a critical role in dose optimization and predicting adverse drug events, thereby enhancing patient safety and improving treatment outcomes. A novel system for dose optimization, Curate.AI, employs AI to dynamically adjust chemotherapy doses based on individual patient data [30]. Furthermore, predictive analytics and risk assessment are increasingly being leveraged in population health management to identify and guide health initiatives [31].

8.3.1 AI assistance in diagnostics

Medical diagnostics have markedly benefited from AI, which evaluates medical conditions or diseases by analyzing symptoms, medical history, and test results. Revolutionary advancements have empowered AI with the potential to enhance prediction accuracy, speed, and efficiency in the field of medical diagnosis [32]. The future of AI-based medical diagnostics is anticipated to be characterized by ongoing growth and development, with advanced technologies such as quantum AI (QAI) and general AI (GAI) being utilized in projects like OpenAI's Deep QA, IBM's Watson, and Google's DeepMind. However, challenges, including medical data quality, bias, and ethical questions, persist.

8.3.2 AI in genomic medicine

Predictive analytics is a promising technological advancement in the future of healthcare, enabling healthcare professionals to predict outcomes, events, and behaviors that may occur. By analyzing large quantities of data from various sources, predictive analytics can identify models and trends that can facilitate the successful implementation of targeted actions and programs, help healthcare professionals make better treatment decisions, and create personalized treatment plans for individual patients [33]. Personalized genetics represents a promising opportunity for the use of predictive analytics in the healthcare sector, as it allows healthcare professionals to identify individuals at increased risk for specific disorders and diseases well before the onset of symptoms. ML algorithms and data mining techniques can be employed to analyze historical data and accurately predict upcoming events or outcomes.

The most significant achievements of AI in the pharmaceutical field include the use of AI against tumors, which involved testing multiple treatments simultaneously. Exscientia aims to revolutionize the entire drug development process by utilizing ML to design new drugs, match patients with existing medications, and predict their behavior in the body. AI can significantly reduce the time and cost associated with drug development, as it assists pharmaceutical manufacturers in increasing the chances of success by minimizing the time and expenses involved in searching for new drugs.

Additionally, it can help identify individuals at risk of being readmitted to the hospital, enabling healthcare professionals to design tailored strategies to decrease the likelihood of repeated hospitalizations [34].

8.3.3 AI in publishing

AI is poised to revolutionize the publishing of scientific articles in journals by streamlining the peer-review process, enhancing the quality of peer review, and enabling new forms of publication. AI algorithms can automate the peer-review process, thereby reducing the workload on human reviewers and leading to faster publication times. Additionally, AI can enhance the quality of peer review by analyzing large amounts of data and identifying patterns that human reviewers may overlook. This results in a more thorough and accurate peer review process, ensuring the accuracy, validity, and reliability of scientific information. Moreover, AI can facilitate new forms of publication, such as interactive articles, which provide more engaging and accessible experiences for readers. Furthermore, AI can support reproducibility in scientific research by analyzing and validating scientific data, thereby improving the overall quality of scientific publications and reducing retractions due to errors or inaccuracies. Overall, AI has the potential to revolutionize the publishing process and improve the overall quality of scientific information [35].

8.4 Digital Implants

Traditional healthcare facilities and specialist-focused techniques are quickly giving way to dispersed patient-focused approaches in the healthcare industry. Among other innovations, sensors and intelligent wearables have shown promise in providing smart healthcare and distant medical services. Healthcare systems have seen the emergence and implementation of a wide range of digital health applications through these technologies, including smart medication, telemedicine, assisted living, remote and on-site resource tracking in hospitals, patient behavior modifications, and treatment adherence. For example, during COVID-19, smart gadgets such as smartphones, smart watches, smart bands, smart clothing, wireless blood pressure monitors, and smart glucometers were used for digital health screening [36].

Smart sensory devices are often used to automatically record health data, such as blood pressure, heart rate, and blood sugar level, which are then sent as electrical pulses for additional analysis. Numerous smart sensory devices have been utilized to record and convert medical data into electrical impulses that can be seen. Sensors, particularly biosensors and nanosensors, are progressively becoming vital tools for monitoring everyday life events in the medical industry for enhanced clinical diagnoses and tracking biological components. Smart wearables have the ability to provide health data and interact with other devices [37]. The widespread use of cellphones with sensors offers previously unheard-of chances to create workable and reliable health therapies [38]. For example, several health applications have made use of smart wearable technology, including smartwatches, wristbands, eyeglasses, headsets, earphones, body straps, foot and hand-worn devices, and smart jewelry.

8.4.1 Implants in dentistry

One technique to increase the predictability of restorative dentistry is digital dentistry, particularly when substituting all or a portion of the original teeth. CAD/CAM (computer-aided design/computer-aided manufacturing) is the most recent technology to join the restorative dentistry field. This technology, which was adapted from the automotive, aerospace, and even watchmaking industries, is widely used due to its benefits in terms of speed, precision, and efficiency. CAD/CAM gives restorative dentists and technicians a wider range of dental prosthesis solutions when combined with reliable implant technology. The main responsibility of the dental laboratory in restorative dentistry is to precisely replicate all of the technical and aesthetic specifications that the dentist has established in a restorative solution [39]. With the advent of digital laboratory laser scanning technology and related software, the dental lab was able to develop a digital dental environment that accurately displays a real three-dimensional (3D) virtual model. Digital technology has the potential to significantly simplify or even completely replace some of the most laborious and mechanical processes (such as waxing, investing, burnout, casting, and pressing) that are involved in the traditional fabrication of a dental restoration. This digital process will enable the dentist and technician to produce functional dental restorations using a precise and consistent process.

Instead of being linear, laboratory production may now be vertical thanks to digital technology. The present laboratory manufacturing process proceeds in a highly linear fashion, with day 1 being model fabrication, day 2 being waxing, day 3 being finishing, day 4 being ceramics, and so on. Based on this manufacturing technology, an all-ceramic or porcelain-fused-to-metal (PFM) restoration typically takes 5 to 7 working days to produce [39].

The customer will continue to provide impressions in the digital laboratory. However, it is possible to complete the same operation in two to three days rather than days or weeks. Following receipt in the laboratory, the imprint may be scanned, and the resulting data will be simultaneously sent to many digital manufacturing units. This may enable the completion of the model and the restorations, such as the final ceramic restoration, the framework, and the wax-up, simultaneously.

The producers of scanning equipment have significantly broadened the range of recommendations for the usage of their systems in dental offices since the devices' launch. Additionally, they have linked their software and hardware with the majority of dental labs. These include the CAD/CAM solutions Densys3D Solution (Densys), Lava Chairside Oral Scanner C.O.S. (3M ESPE), FastScan (IOS Technologies), E4D Dentist (D4D Technologies), Cadent iTero (Cadent Align Technology, Inc.), and CEREC (Sirona Dental Systems) [40]. Nowadays, there are a number of commercially accessible methods in dentistry for scanning and documenting intricate intraoral surfaces. These days, intraoral dental scanners often use three scanning principles: parallel confocal laser scanning, active wave-front sampling, and triangulation.

Following the registration of the bite and digital imprint, the process proceeds to the digital realm for scanning and production [39].

Step 1: File creation: For each patient, a file is generated in the program. The patient's name, ID number, dentist's name, date, tooth number, and preferred restoration type are entered by the operator.

Step 2: Scanning: The working model containing the die is scanned, digitally recorded, and imported into the computer's virtual lab using the CEREC 3D optical scanning equipment.

Step 3: Virtual model: After that, the 3D virtual model appears on the screen, where it may be seen from any angle and modified.

Step 4: Design: The neighboring teeth. contact regions, and lastly, the gum line margins of the preparation are used to establish the dimensions and boundaries of the finished restoration.

Step 5: Database selection: By looking at the adjacent dentition, the operator may choose the corresponding age of the tooth's intended design from a database menu that the computer will display. The computer will then suggest a restoration and restoration location based on this data and the established parameters.

Step 6: Virtual placement: Based on all of the information, the computer has positioned the restoration in the best possible way; nevertheless, the operator must manually position and shape the restoration to the ideal dental site using their expertise and understanding of form and function.

Step 7: Occlusion confirmation: One of the software's automatic features is its ability to suggest fossa-point connections on the proper triangle ridges. Each contact point's location and intensity are shown visually and color-mapped instantly on the screen, and they are readily adjustable to suit operator and clinical preferences.

Step 8: Anatomical customization: A variety of virtual carving and waxing tools also enable the creation of innovations and customization of elements. By simulating real laboratory techniques, they may be utilized to modify occlusal anatomy, shapes, and preferences.

Step 9: Milling: Once the final digital restoration has been planned, all that has to be done is equip a chamber with the specified dimension and color of ceramic or composite block, click a displayed option, and an identical reproduction of the design will be created in about 15 minutes.

Step 10: Polishing: Using staining and glazing methods suitable for the chosen ceramic, the milling repair may typically be tailored.

8.4.2 Implant in spinal cord

For patients whose pain is not being sufficiently relieved by previous medical or surgical treatments, spinal cord stimulation (SCS) is a tried-and-true treatment option. By guiding stimulator points into the epidural space and connecting them to a planted pulse generator, pain signals are disrupted by electrical stimulation of the spinal cord's dorsal horns. SCS has been shown to be effective in treating severe diabetic neuropathy, complicated regional pain syndrome, failed-back surgery syndrome, and persistent lower back and leg pain in clinical studies [41]. Patients may evaluate the effectiveness of SCS treatment with a temporary SCS device over the course of three to ten days, during which time professionals regularly monitor their patients' pain levels. A successful assessment is usually defined by the implanting physician as a 50% or more increase in quality of life or a decrease in discomfort. Patients who have successfully completed a SCS temporary evaluation (SCSeval), undertaken physical and psychological examination, and failed alternative treatment methods such as medicine, surgery, physical therapy, or psychiatric therapy are qualified to receive an everlasting SCS implant. The success rate, which indicates sufficient pain management to qualify for a permanent implant, was assessed for 5,037 patients with sufficient monitoring data and a known result for their SCSeval. 90.1% was the total success rate. A total of 3,649 individuals had conversions to permanent implants in the 6 months after a successful SCSeval [42].

8.4.3 Importance of smart implants

Global health challenges have never been greater due to the rise in long-term ailments and conditions like cancer, heart disease, insomnia, cognitive decline, psychological problems, and functional decline, as well as the expenses of treating long-term effects and lifestyle-induced sickness. The prospects of sustainable smart health treatments depends on innovations like harmless smart implants that concentrate on providing digital healthcare services centered on successful disease prevention, real-time medical information collections, early identification of illnesses, real-time tracking of long-term illnesses, patient-tailored medication, and less-invasive disease management, rather than depending on traditional treatments that are occasionally impacted by the constraints implemented, such as COVID-19 guidelines [43].

The management and identification of physiological problems, early illness identification, prognosis, and mitigation of smart health surveillance depend on widespread and inconspicuous digital health monitoring equipment, as well as – most importantly – sensor types and data modeling algorithms. The emergence and implementation of noninvasive smart implants in a path of care heavily relies on sensors, particularly biosensors and nanosensors. Electrocardiograms, Electromyography, blood pressure tracking, electroencephalography, photoplethysmography, heart sound, respiration, sleep, and mobility monitoring are more applications for biosensors and nanosensors. Through the utilization of microfabrication and nanofabrication of biocompatible materials, the incorporation of biosensors and nanosensors in noninvasive smart implants can be beneficial from a scientific and clinical standpoint for improved monitoring of biological, psychological, and pathological processes instantaneously, over long distances, and continuously [44]. Among other applications, noninvasive smart implants may be used in orthopedics, hip replacements, dental treatment, breast implants, pacemakers, cardiac resynchronization therapy devices, and cosmetic therapy.

8.4.4 Limitations of implants

The acceptance and use of noninvasive smart implants in healthcare is not without difficulties and restrictions, despite the technology's potential to advance ubiquitous and customized treatment. These obstacles are covered here.

Lack of policies and framework: The absence of defined laws and frameworks may pose certain difficulties for the practical deployment and viability of noninvasive smart implants, despite the technology's promised advantages in healthcare.

Limited memory: Before being sent to an external system, health data gathered by biosensors and nanosensors in noninvasive smart implants should be buffered within the electronic device. However, given the overall dimensions of a noninvasive smart implant, these devices are unable to hold large volumes of data at once.

Implant failure: Noninvasive smart implants often use electrical or electromechanical sensors, which have certain disadvantages such as susceptibility to misalignments, vulnerability to electromagnetic fields, reduced compactness, and the need for regular calibration, all of which increase the risk of implant failure.

Health hazard by implants: Researchers and healthcare professionals are still concerned about implanting gadgets that are electronic with radiating signals within the human body, despite the fact that noninvasive smart implant technology has a bright future and the potential to address many healthcare problems, including cancer diagnosis, routine checkups, and the prompt delivery of medications as needed by the body.

Data security and privacy: Patients' well-being is gathered using noninvasive smart implants, which may reveal private and sensitive health information. This might have disastrous effects on the anonymity and confidentiality of the individual's medical records. Noninvasive smart implants should take preventative and security norms and procedures into account to guarantee privacy and security.

Clinical challenges: Despite the fact that noninvasive smart implant research is still in its infancy, there are many obstacles to overcome before they can be used in practice. For instance, when to use them, where to keep them, and how. Even though the procedure is the least intrusive, these are challenging questions to apply in practice. Other issues include electrical supply, sensor size, immunological rejection, and heating.

8.5 Telerehabilitation

Telerehabilitation programs may assist patients recovering from workplace injuries in overcoming environmental and motivational hurdles to participating in exercise-based rehabilitation and follow-up programs. Telerehabilitation may help overcome time constraints caused by job and family responsibilities. Telerehabilitation programs are accessible at any time and from any location. In comparison to outpatient physical therapy, home exercise activities, oral physical activity training, and discharge instruction, exercise-based telerehabilitation programs – such as exercise directions via a digital avatar or video, Nintendo Wii games, exergames using digital sensor-based electronic devices, outpatient physical therapy paired with complex games, and home exercise regimens that include mobile health-based education or with other inspirational SMS text messaging – have demonstrated improved results for pain, mobility, psychological wellness, and overall wellness. Additionally, for patients who had upper or lower limb musculoskeletal disorders or who had undergone total knee arthroplasty (TKA), telerehabilitation programs showed higher success rates than outpatient physical therapy programs or at-home exercise programs. Furthermore, two randomized controlled studies demonstrated that online cognitive behavioral therapy and a digital self-management tool reduced post-traumatic stress disorder and depression symptoms more than other methods [45].

Despite the encouraging outcomes of these telerehabilitation programs, there remain a number of obstacles and enablers to the acceptance and deployment of eHealth initiatives. These obstacles and enablers fall into three general categories: (1) personal, (2) institutional and societal, and (3) technological [46]. Constrained digital affinity and abilities, minimal user enthusiasm, refusal to use gadgets, worries over privacy, lack of personal contact, technical challenges like weak sound or picture quality, software performance issues, slow internet connections, and financial constraints are the most commonly mentioned institutional, social, and technological obstacles. On the one hand, the enablers include strong user enthusiasm, value for money in comparison to analogue care, time savings, and program fulfilment. simplicity of use, and good sound and picture quality [47]. Stakeholders play a vital role in telerehabilitation. The four groups of stakeholders in telerehabilitation are: (1) individuals who need rehabilitation following an occupational accident; (2) healthcare providers who treat patients following an occupational injury; (3) administrative staff; and (4) people on the team responsible for designing and developing telerehabilitation services [45].

Few research has looked at how to administer or enhance stroke telerehabilitation using easily available technologies, such as text messages and phone calls. A team of New Zealand physiotherapists was interested in learning more about the experiences of participants in a six-month post-stroke telerehabilitation program. Hence, they came up with the creation of Augmented Community Telerehabilitation Intervention (ACTIV) [48]. Following a stroke, ACTIV is a six-month customized exercise program led by physiotherapists that aims to help participants reach a goal of their own. Enhancing and promoting continuous physical activity was the goal of ACTIV, which used a mix of in-person meetings, scheduled phone conversations, and quick messages to promote participation. Participants who finished at least half of the ACTIV program saw a substantial increase in physical activity, according to a simultaneous randomized controlled trial (RCT). After a stroke, telerehabilitation differs from what many people anticipate from physical therapy. There are many important responsibilities a physiotherapist may play in promoting and assisting improvement once the difference is acknowledged. Frequent short-term interactions seem to aid in the development of plans for post-rehabilitation improvement. In a therapeutic context, physiotherapists should consider the fact that most individuals find progress toward a more normal life to be significantly more significant than initial treatment objectives.

The viability of telerehabilitation was the subject of a thorough literature study by a team of French experts [49]. Reviewing and debating the use of cost-utility methodologies in financial assessments of telerehabilitation therapies was their goal. Following PRISMA criteria, a review of the literature was done on PubMed, Scopus, the NHS Economic Evaluation Database, the Cochrane Library, the Centres for Review and Dissemination databases, and ClinicalTrials.gov. They used the PICOS system to determine the inclusion criteria. They comprised research that assessed patients undergoing exercise-based telerehabilitation for rehabilitation therapy for all illnesses and ailments, consisted of a control group that received in-person rehabilitation, assessed efficacy through improvements in quality of life, and employed randomized and controlled clinical study designs. A variety of intervention types were evaluated. All the studies described the health statuses of the patients using a standardized health-related quality of life questionnaire and were based on randomized clinical trials. With telerehabilitation services, the average quality-adjusted life years gained ranged from –0.09 to 0.89. They concluded that telerehabilitation is an affordable solution for a sizable population across several illness domains. This conclusion was supported by another group of researchers from Spain. To ascertain the clinical and financial efficacy of internet-based tele-rehabilitation throughout the healing process of musculoskeletal illnesses, a systematic study was carried out in 2024 [50].

They concluded that, in addition to saving money and time, telerehabilitation should be considered in the treatment of musculoskeletal problems when the best in-person rehabilitation is not possible.

8.6 Human Augmentation

Assistive soft wearable robotic (SWR) technologies have advanced at an exponential pace over the last ten years, spanning a wide range of applications, including human augmentation, robot-facilitated treatment, mobility support, and accomplishing activities of daily living (ADLs), to mention a few [51]. Over the last ten years, soft mechatronic technologies have gained popularity, dependability, and efficiency, making them a desirable alternative to wearable robotics [52]. The paradigm of completely soft, clothing-like wearables that seem almost invisible to the user has gradually replaced stiff exoskeletons and isolated compliant ways of actuation. In both educational and business contexts, wearable robotic systems composed of soft, flexible materials are gradually obtaining popularity. While some applications use few or no stiff components as mounting points for the soft actuators, other SWRs are completely soft, monolithic, garment-like wearable devices composed of fabric, soft actuators, and other compliant materials. Four primary categories of wearable robots may be distinguished: military, industrial, consumer, and medical [53]. The majority of wearable technology seeks to enhance or help.

Wearable robots have applications in augmentation, support, and rehabilitation. Based on their main purposes, wearable soft robots may be categorized into four groups: manipulators, haptic devices, sensor suits, and exosuits. A robotic garment that can exert stresses and/or torques on human joints is sometimes referred to as a soft robotic exosuit. For healthy users, a soft manipulator may serve as an additional arm or finger, and for users with impairments, it can serve as a prosthesis. In contrast to stiff ones, soft haptic devices have been developed to provide people realistic feel, motion guidance, and direction signals when teleporting or using virtual items with less damage and a greater variety of adjustment options. The purpose of sensing suits is to measure human movements. The majority of wearable soft gadgets are attached to people via velcro and clothes. The mounting mechanism makes sure the gadget remains mostly fastened to the body, even if it may distort with joint mobility. Range of motion, patient convenience, protection, and generating force/torque capacity are the main functional criteria for building wearable soft robots. The actuation mechanisms have a significant impact on each of these attributes. The literature mentions three of the most widely used actuators. They are shape-memory alloy actuators, cable-driven actuators, and fluid-driven actuators [54].

8.6.1 Fluid-driven actuators

Fluidic actuators' compliance, simple design, and broad force range make them popular in wearable soft devices. Fluidic actuators create their outputs by transforming a sealed chamber composed of textiles or elastomers and applying pressure from hydraulic or pneumatic sources. Users may now carry handheld pneumatic sources on their backs or waists, thanks to recent developments. Exosuits with elastomer actuators have been used for ankle rehabilitation as well as shoulder and elbow assistance. They are also often found in other wearable technology, including haptic gadgets, wearable manipulators, and supportive gloves. The majority of elastomer actuators have an inflated chamber within and are composed of rubber or silicone. McKibben/PAMs, elastomers, and textiles/fabric-based actuators are the subclasses of fluidic actuators.

8.6.1.1 Pneumatic artificial muscles (PAM)/McKibben

PAM actuators may be utilized to deliver high tensile forces that closely mimic the mechanics of human muscles contracting, since they usually exhibit a uniaxial contraction force upon actuator pressurization. One famous PAM actuator is the McKibben muscle. A cylindrical shell that may expand radially and turns inextensible at a maximal threshold makes up McKibben muscles. An airtight, thin-walled rubber tube with hyper elastic qualities is housed within the shell, which is sealed on both sides with a pressurization entrance. The PAM actuator contracts overall and gains tensile strength as a result of the tube's expansion of the shell's radius under pressure.

8.6.1.2 Elastomeric fluidic actuators

Soon after the McKibben muscle started drawing interest from researchers in the use of compliant actuators, wearable robots started to adopt new kinds of soft actuators manufactured from hyper elastic elastomers and other polymers. Early research on the use of hyperelastic materials in actuator designs showed that the actuators may be used to support the human hand. When engaging with environments of a complicated or uncertain shape, elastomeric actuators are tolerant. The main benefit of systems with such high adherence is the actuator's underactuated, simple design. In the middle of the decade, silicone-based actuators were used in successful human aid rehabilitation cases. The vast majority of applications have concentrated on helping the hand or wrist since fluidic elastomer actuators typically produce less force, however some have also targeted the lower limbs.

8.6.1.3 Fabric-based inflatables and textiles

In order to create soft exosuits more garment-like with smaller form factors, many actuators utilized in SWR designs have recently shifted to fabric-based techniques, using soft actuators constructed from fabrics and various types of textiles and thin films. Since textiles sometimes lack the hyper elastic qualities of silicone-based actuators, geometric material programming is frequently given greater weight in aesthetic decisions. Novel materials that can produce a wide range of deformations and force transfers have been made possible by advancements in fabric-based inflatable textiles. Actuators based on fabric have also been developed to provide a bending or rotating motion by simulating bellows behavior.

8.6.2 Cable-driven actuators

Around the early 2010s, as the word "exosuit" gained greater recognition and definition, the design of new wearable robots that were less heavy and had a smaller appearance started to converge into mainstream adoption [51]. To support certain movements, cable-driven actuation may readily imitate the actions of the human musculoskeletal system. These systems remain one of the most widely used actuation techniques, having seen substantial development in the last ten years. To develop high-performing exosuits, a great deal of study has been done on controllability and anchor locations for applied loads. In order to enable appropriate force transfer to the targeted joint, the cables, also known as tendons, are attached to a place on the exosuit that interacts with the human body. Usually, the cables are a strap or tab composed of lightweight polymers or synthetic textiles that are not extendable. In order to replicate the musculoskeletal behaviors of a particular joint or location, the cable is wound around the body and supplied to a motor, which, when turned on, applies a tensile force to the anchor point. Wearable soft robots use cable-driven actuators to provide quick response, minimal inertia, and minimize large structures close to moving joints. Cable-driven actuators, which were first used in a lot of exoskeletons, move a joint by dragging cables across it using electric motors that are not close to the joint. Soft materials like textiles or elastomers are used as cable attachment points across joints in wearable soft robots. Wearable additional fingers, haptic gloves, and assistive gloves have all used these actuators. Exosuits for the hip, ankle, elbow, and shoulder have also made employing them. These devices use Bowden cables to guide tendons throughout the body. Bowden cables may convey force or energy by moving an inner cable in relation to a hollow outer flexible cable.

8.6.3 Shape-memory alloy actuators

Shape-memory alloy actuators are being created for wearable soft robots due to the need for quiet, lightweight, compliant actuators with high force capabilities. Shape-memory alloy actuators employ a crystal phase shift brought on by temperature variations or an induced magnetic field to produce force. They can be taught to remember their shape at high temperatures, and when subjected to heat, they may change shape and revert to that shape. At low temperatures, a two-way shape-memory alloy can also retain its form. Actuators of this kind are used in exosuits to support wrist and forearm muscle strength, in supportive gloves, and in haptic devices. With an input power of 150 W, a single shape-memory-alloy-based fabric muscle unit that weighs just 24 g may exert 100 N of force and assist in lifting a barbell weighing up to 4 kg to the desired position. Actuators made of shape-memory alloy are small, light, and capable of being powered directly by electricity. However, since it takes seconds to heat up and cool down, the heating and cooling period before deformation is lengthy. The cooling period may be significantly longer in the absence of an active cooling system.

8.6.4 WAXO

Ankle exoskeletons for human walking augmentation were developed and dubbed walking augmentation ankle exoskeleton (WAXO). Its interplay between several subsystems, including the user, the mechanical structure, and the sensory and control systems, is what distinguishes it from comparable devices [55]. Reducing the exoskeleton's distal bulk was the primary goal. As a result, the mechanical construction consisted of only two struts that were fastened to the boot's left and right sides. However, the actuation mechanism was mounted on the waist rather than the front of the shank in order to further reduce the additional distal bulk. The force was transferred from the actuation unit to the tip of each strut using two Bowden cables. The cables shift their orientation from vertical to the actuation direction when they travel through a lightweight, specially made brace that is fastened to the shank. A case that was fastened to the waist contained the electronics, including the motor driver. The gait cycle was tracked using a single force-sensitive resistor (FSR), which was positioned under the boot insole. The motor was controlled, and a graphical user interface was provided by an off-board personal computer (PC).

8.6.5 WB-PEXO

The Guardian® XO® is an alpha prototype created by Sarcos Robotics [56] that weighs 160 kg, has a human-like design, and offers 24 active degrees of freedom in this system. They are: the hips (flexion/extension, abduction/adduction, and axial rotation), knees (flexion/extension), ankles (flexion/extension), shoulders (flexion/extension and abduction/adduction), humerus (axial rotation), and wrist (axial rotation). With external joint torques applied at the main body joints, this whole-body powered exoskeleton (WB-PEXO), which was designed for occupational use, is meant to provide an operator with the capacity to safely carry and handle weights up to 90 kg. An intellectual property "Get-Out-Of-The-Way" control method that simulates human motions and increases joint torques is used to do this. The WB-PEXO has a number of configurable characteristics that may be changed for a particular operator, such as actuation gains, payload, and gravity adjustment. As a prototype, the WB-PEXO's control and hardware implementations are still being improved to provide even more advantages for the operator's musculoskeletal loading.

Actuator designs for SWR: It is necessary to first determine which actuation techniques will be used, which part or joints will get help, and how the forces will be transferred from the actuator to the user in order to offer efficient, pleasant, and reliable assistance, in addition to characterizing the functional restrictions for SWR's design. The actuator designs have been divided into four categories: curling/bending, contracting/tensile, extending/stiffening, and bellows/rotary.

The Finnish researcher's narrative review sought to examine the mechanics behind the integration of AI and brain-computer interface (BCI), analyze new developments in signal processing and acquisition methods, and evaluate AI-enhanced neural decoding methodologies [57]. The researcher looks at important applications in a range of fields, including cognitive improvement and medicinal applications:

Neuroprosthetics and motor restoration: People with tetraplegia might effectively utilize BCI devices to do basic everyday chores like utilizing a robotic arm to feed themselves. This real-world application demonstrates the technology's feasibility for daily usage while directly addressing the long-term stability issue [58].

Communication systems for severe motor impairments: By using imagined handwriting, BCIs may let a paralyzed person type at speeds similar to those of healthy-looking smartphone users. This development is an important step in helping clinical people regain their normal communication skills [59].

Stroke rehabilitation: There have been encouraging outcomes when BCI technology is used with therapy. For stroke therapy, researchers used BCI-driven motor imagery education in a randomized controlled experiment. According to their findings, patients who received BCI-based training showed noticeably better motor recovery than those who received conventional treatment, demonstrating how adaptive learning processes may improve neuroplasticity and recovery [60].

Cognitive rehabilitation: Researchers showed how noninvasive BCI devices might provide individualized brain stimulation to enhance working memory in senior citizens, going beyond motor applications. Their application demonstrated how BCI-AI technology may be used to improve cognitive capabilities in addition to restoring them, meeting more general therapeutic demands [61].

Workplace and human–computer interaction: A 2020 study showed how passive BCI devices might be used in business settings, going beyond medical uses. Their approach effectively inferred user conditions like workload and stress from brain signals, allowing for adaptable interfaces that maximize productivity and user enjoyment. This program demonstrates the practical applications of high-bandwidth computing capabilities [62].

Integration of assistive technology: A semi-autonomous BCI-controlled wheelchair system that can navigate challenging real-world situations was successfully built in 2020 by researcher Meng and his colleagues in the field of assistive robotics. This combination of AI-driven obstacle avoidance and neural control shows how integrating several technologies may result in assistive gadgets that are more reliable and easier to use [63].

Human augmentation is an interdisciplinary field that addresses methods, technologies, and their applications for enhancing the sensing, action, and/or cognitive abilities of a human. This is achieved through sensing and actuation technologies, fusion and fission of information, and AI methods. Three primary categories may be used to further categorize human enhancement. They are enhanced intellect, enhanced action, and enhanced senses [64].

In order to either surpass the strengths of current senses or make up for sensory deficits (mainly ocular and hearing), augmented senses use techniques and technology. In the first scenario, alternative healthy senses are used to augment or greatly increase the sensory signals for the compromised senses. For instance, haptic actuators may be used to communicate speech signals to a deaf person or to explain the environment to a blind person. In the second scenario, extra sensors are used to monitor signals that are beyond the range of the human senses and convert them into a format that is appropriate for human usage. Human senses may be enhanced by a variety of technologies beyond their inherent limitations. The user might have "eagle eyes" or night vision thanks to light sensors or microscopic cameras that can see far beyond the wavelengths of human eyesight.

Motion augmentation was one of the first applications of enhancing human activity. Prosthetic limbs, for example, let an amputated limb regain some of its functions. Action may now be enhanced in ways that go beyond the limitations of human muscular and cognitive abilities, thanks to modern digital technology. People who are disabled, for instance, may walk on robotic feet thanks to exoskeletons. Dual-arm power amplification systems and exoskeletons are helpful for a variety of jobs that are typically performed by humans but cannot yet be completely automated due to their need for human intelligence. One possible use is in manual goods handling, where exoskeletons allow people to move larger objects and relieve lower back strain. Virtual exoskeletons, in which a robot positioned at a distant location is controlled in tandem with the user's motions, are an extension of the exoskeleton idea.

A close relationship between an individual and a computer is accomplished by physiological and neurophysiological monitoring of the individual's cognitive state in augmented cognition, a kind of human-technology interaction. In order to adjust computer intelligence to the individual's situational demands, augmented cognition incorporates information gathered from the user. As a result, a closed loop is created between an individual and the technology interface. Since its inception, augmented cognition has been an interdisciplinary area of study that integrates knowledge from computer science, engineering, neuroscience, cognitive psychology, and human–computer interaction. In order to overcome and adapt to bottlenecks, restrictions, and prejudices in human cognition and the information processing chain, the research's ultimate objective is to increase individuals' cognitive capacities and smoothly develop a functional augmented cognition. Some researchers claim that augmented cognition can help humans manage data in ways that are related to working memory (supporting the concurrent handling of data from multiple sources), attention (steering attention), executive function (guiding recall of prior data so that newly acquired data can be assessed optimally), and sensory memory (improving sensory perception).

Additionally, one of the main goals of augmented cognition is often thought to be maximizing the user's cognitive burden while interacting with a computer.

Current human augmentation initiatives, commonly known as "Human 2.0," concentrate on developing physical and cognitive enhancements as an essential component of the human body [65]. The linked Internet of Things (IoT) devices are now driving advancements in human augmentation. These gadgets' functionality is mostly dependent on communication technology. These gadgets are often found near to the human body. Bio-integrated technologies, such as neurally controlled prosthetic limbs, may be used in more specialized applications. An individual's gadgets create an integrated ecosystem and should function as a whole, made possible by the right communication technology. The communication technique used may differ from conventional wireless protocols like bluetooth or Wi-Fi, depending on the kind of device. Augmented Human (AH) apps need an internet connection along with local communication. Design principles, which depend on user requirements and desires, are the main factors influencing technological issues associated with AH products. Users' top priorities for wearable IoT devices include reduced weight and size, improved dependability, and extended battery life.

Hybrid electronics: Flexible hybrid electronics (FHE) combines electric circuits with thinned malleable materials to create devices that are lightweight, thin, flexible, bendable, conformal, perhaps stretchy, and disposable. Compared to traditional electrical systems, which are composed of heavy and inflexible materials, FHE offers significant benefits. The effective integration of stiff, miniature chips with flexible/stretchable circuit links has been made possible by recent developments in soft mechanics and sophisticated materials. Wearable systems' wireless power transmission, memory, and signal processing are all improved by such FHE in AH applications. For instance, FHE permits bio-friendly devices on living tissues such as synthetic human skin or body organs with time-dynamic movements for real-time health parameter monitoring. Generally speaking, the use of FHE in AH makes the devices more wearable and function better, which makes it easier for people to use them.

Size of the devices: IoT wearables, also known as nanonetworks, may be implemented at the nanoscale thanks to advancements in nanotechnologies. These nanodevices make use of graphene's special qualities, which enable electronic components such as antennas, processors, receivers, transmitters, sensors, and actuators to significantly reduce in size. In the THz frequency range, communication is made possible by graphene-based micro antennas.

However, the large signal power limitations during propagation significantly restrict the communication distance in the THz frequency spectrum. Even in an air environment with low humidity, the communication distance will not be greater than 2 meters. However, if the communication takes place in a setting with an excessive amount of liquids, like the human body, the transmission distance will drop to several millimeters, creating new difficulties in facilitating communication across such networks. Since these graphene-based THz communication devices, such as antennas and transceivers, are based on current electrical technology, they can be readily included into contemporary communication gadgets like smartphones and are tiny enough to be incorporated into biological systems.

Energy efficiency: In wearables, the battery unit is usually the biggest factor influencing the devices' weight and dimensions. Therefore, while building wearables, developers have to strike a compromise between dimensions and autonomous functioning. Most gadgets have a short operating time between charges since size and weight are prioritized in their design. Nonetheless, consumers' expectations are still shifting in favor of completely self-sufficient gadgets that don't need maintenance or recharging. Recent studies have focused on extending battery life by increasing the devices' energy efficiency in order to meet these needs. Network operations, data collection, and processing account for a significant portion of wearable energy expenses.

Reliability: Before a device may be accepted for any important application, reliability concerns must be resolved. Nonetheless, there are concerns over the authenticity and dependability of current wearable technology. The accuracy and dependability of the vast majority of gadgets on the market have not been confirmed. Significant differences in accuracy were found in recent wearable studies, with error margins as high as 25%. In addition to device dependability, server platforms' enabling quality. Placement optimization may significantly reduce the potential negative consequences of a cloud server failure, which are well covered in the literature.

8.7 Risk and Management

Information devices like PCs, laptops, tablets, smartphones, and smartwatches have historically been susceptible to two different types of security attacks. In the beginning, the owner could be affected if the data stored on or via the device – for example, downstream, in the cloud – is hacked, destroyed, stolen, or altered. Furthermore, it is theoretically possible for malevolent hackers to physically harm the computer equipment. The central processing unit (CPU) may ultimately undergo harm from an application that overloads it. Similar outcomes might occur if the graphics processing unit (GPU) is under stress. A computer's motherboard might be effectively "bricked" by flashing the BIOS and/or firmware, rendering it unable to power on; cellphones have also been susceptible to similar problems [66]. In the past, people have rarely been physically harmed by breaches in the security of their computing devices. The 4Ds grid provides a threat summary of this scenario and is a tool used by security analysts and information technology system executives to investigate the risks of wearable device security. It queries if the danger is one of deception, distortion, damage, or disablement. Refer to Figure 8.6.

The disablement danger is located in the bottom left quadrant of the grid because a security breach may threaten the physical characteristics of either the person or the gadget. A hacker might disable the gadget by either causing damage to it or just remotely turning it off so that it stops working. On the other hand, the device may be compromised in a manner that impairs the wearer's physical capabilities, even to the extent of harm. Examples of

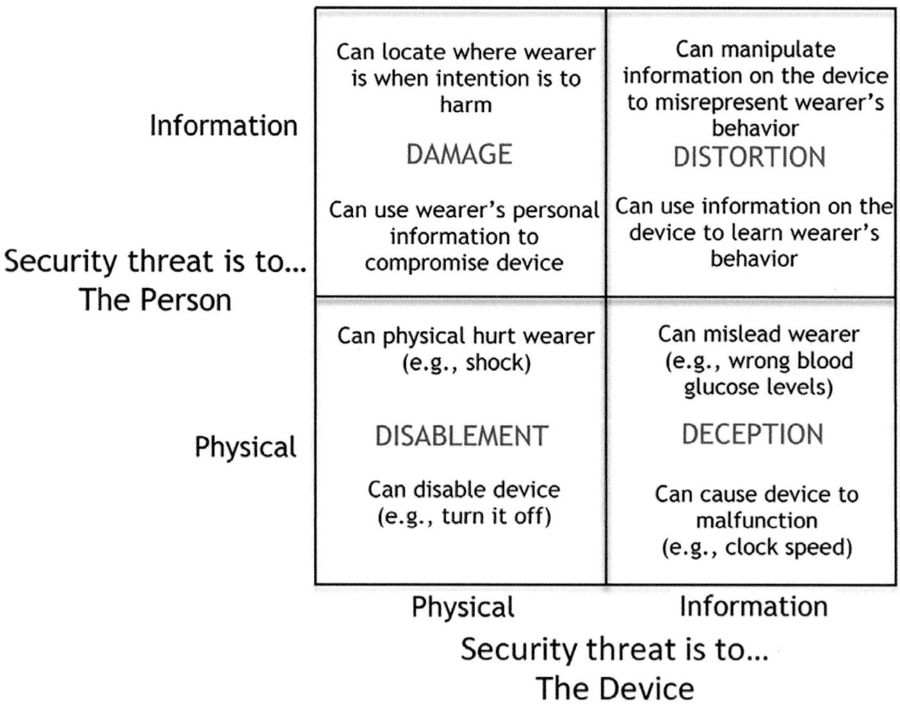

Figure 8.6 The 4D's risk grid [66].

this may include inflicting harm with a smart watch that shocks the user using its haptic mechanism or creating an unexpected failure in a powered exoskeleton arm that causes the wearer to drop what they are holding.

The damage quadrant includes security risks in which the wearer's data is at danger due to a physical breach of the device, instead of physical health. A person might lose all of their data, have it stolen, or have it altered by a simple gadget hack. Many wearable devices may serve as gateways to the bigger data kept on these kinds of gadgets since they will be linked to the wearer's other information systems, including PCs and cellphones. Additionally, the wearable might be utilized to track down a specific user with the goal of hurting them, their gadgets, or their belongings.

Deception is the subject of the bottom right cell of the grid, where an equipment security breach is digital but has a physical impact on the user. For instance, if the data from a medical device is maliciously altered, it may provide the user with inaccurate information about metrics like blood pressure or blood glucose. The user may be misled into a false feeling of security. As a result, they might react excessively to an inaccurate reading by altering their medicine dose. But, nothing was abnormal in reality.

The upper right quadrant shows distortion, where the breach is informative for both the wearer and the gadget. A third party may get malicious knowledge about a wearer's activity by breaking into a device's privacy settings. As a substitute, data on a wearer's device may be altered to provide misleading data regarding a person's actions, such as that they were following a prescription regimen when they weren't or leading a doctor to write a prescription for more medicine when the patient didn't need it.

There are two questions on the following decision-making tool that companies may use when thinking about wearable device security. First, what is the wearable's main purpose? Does it depend on mental capacity? Or does it function physically? Is the matter or the mind the main focus? What is the second capability that the wearable improves, in order to better educate the wearer? Or to carry out activities more effectively? This makes it possible to distinguish four different functions that wearable technology may fulfill. These responsibilities, known as the 4Ms, are shown in Figure 8.7. Companies should have a clear understanding of these responsibilities and how a wearable device's security might be breached, as well as the potential consequences for the user.

The wearable gadget that focuses on muscular duties, including lifting or transporting items or carrying out fine tasks with considerably more precision, is in the muscle quadrant. These tools, like smart gloves that allow surgeons to operate with more accuracy or exoskeleton arms that allow

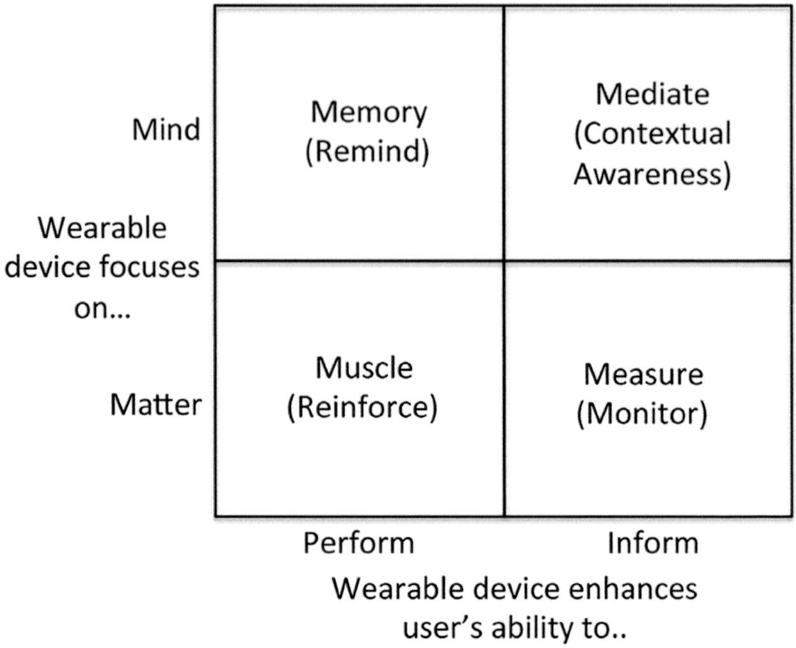

Figure 8.7 The 4M's of responsibility grid [66].

workers to lift much more weight, allow the user to do jobs more effectively than they could without them. The goal is to strengthen muscles, increase strength, increase endurance, or improve the capacity for finer, more precise labor. When the wearable's attention is on muscles, efforts to manipulate the device's functionality pose the biggest security risk. The user may sustain harm or become incapable of carrying out the job that the gadget was designed to support as a result. The user would be left carrying a load that was far heavier than they could typically handle if a modified exoskeleton lifting arm were designed to stall in the middle of the lift. The level of detail and refinement of a surgical smart glove may be switched off in the middle of the procedure, or its degree of precision could change in a manner that puts the patient at risk and leads to the surgeon making errors.

The consciousness is the subject of the remaining quadrants. Reminding wearers is one of the primary uses for wearable technology. This function, which falls under the memory quadrant, could be as straightforward as a smart watch alerting a couch potato at work to get up and move around if they haven't done so recently, or it could be more complicated, like using smart glasses or a headset to browse a database while working. The user may find it irritating to disable or alter the rate of "stand up" alerts on a smart watch. However, the repercussions may be far more severe if the data being sent into a smart headset is altered in a manner that deceives or perplexes the user.

The wearable gadget improves the wearer's capacity to stay informed about bodily characteristics in the measure quadrant. One example of this is medical equipment that measures and tracks physical indicators related to human physiology and biochemistry. An obstetrician may be informed of a fetal heartbeat via a band worn on the expectant mother's belly. It might be vulnerable to unlawful or evil hacking. The woman or the obstetrician may overreact by changing their treatment or underreact by taking no action when they need to take remedial action if the equipment made a significant measurement error and reported it wrongly. These two situations have the potential to be harmful and, in some cases, lethal.

Last but not least, if an electronic device in the mediate quadrant is compromised, it will not be able to notify the user when its primary emphasis is on the wearer's cognitive capacities. In other words, the gadget may not be successful in maximizing the wearer's contextual awareness. The Safelet is a smart wristband that notifies others of the wearer's location when they may be alone themselves in a potentially hazardous place at night. For instance, there may be severe repercussions if the gadget were to deceive the people receiving the signals into thinking the wearer was safe when they weren't. The Lechal shoe is a gadget that uses GPS data and a sequence of pulses within the shoe to steer the user. Its goal is to keep users from becoming lost in unfamiliar areas, especially in forests at night. It is aimed at the military, police, and the blind. By misinterpreting the user's context, compromised footwear may put the wearer in danger or lead to their loss.

8.7.1 The McCumber cube

One of the fundamental tenets of cybersecurity is that companies must use countermeasures to improve their security objectives during data states. Security objectives include data availability, confidentiality, and integrity. Data states include data transmission, processing, and storage. Countermeasures include proper experts, policy, and technology. Administrators may concentrate on each of these components separately before focusing on how they are related by using the McCumber cube, which is shown in Figure 8.8. The McCumber cube also serves as a reminder to administrators not to prioritize one of these factors above the others, since the information system's security depends on the cooperative management of all of them.

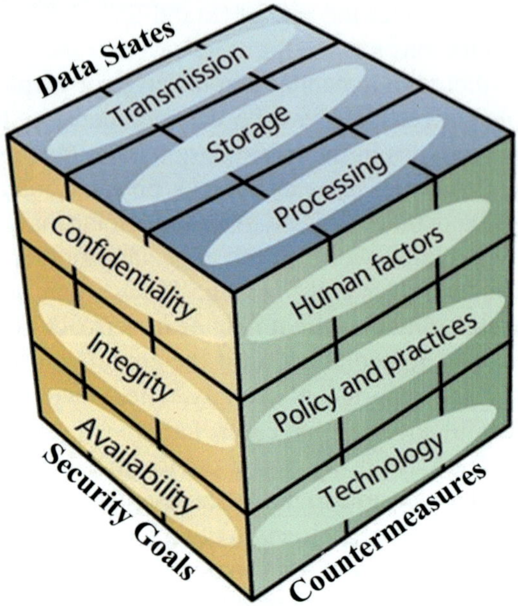

Figure 8.8 The McCumber cube [67].

References

[1] C. J. T. Butcher and W. Hussain, "Digital healthcare: the future," *Future Healthcare Journal,* vol. 9, no. 2, pp. 113-117, 2022.

[2] R. Awati, "What is digital health (digital healthcare)?," 25 March 2025. [Online]. Available: https://www.techtarget.com/searchhealthit/definition/digital-health-digital-healthcare.

[3] D. Jain, "Regulation of Digital Healthcare in India: Ethical and Legal Challenges," *Healthcare,* vol. 11, no. 6, p. 911, 2023.

[4] A. Z. Al Meslamani, "Why are digital health policies crucial?," *Journal of Medical Economics,* vol. 27, no. 1, pp. 167-169, 2024.

[5] I. J. B. d. Nascimento, H. Abdulazeem, L. T. Vasanthan, E. Z. Martinez, M. L. Zucoloto, L. Østengaard, N. Azzopardi-Muscat, T. Zapata and D. Novillo-Ortiz, "Barriers and facilitators to utilizing digital health technologies by healthcare professionals," *npj Digital Medicine,* vol. 6, no. 1, p. 161, 2023.

[6] A. Cuff, "The evolution of digital health and its continuing challenges," *BMC Digital Health,* vol. 1, no. 3, 2023.

[7] N. Kasoju, R. N S, R. Sasi, S. S, B. Soman, K. C, M. C V, H. V. P R and S. Behari, "Digital health: trends, opportunities and challenges

in medical devices, pharma and bio-technology," *CSI Transactions on ICT,* vol. 11, pp. 13-30, 2023.

[8] Y.-T. Shen, L. Chen, W.-W. Yue and H.-X. Xu, "Digital Technology-Based Telemedicine for the COVID-19 Pandemic," *Frontiers in Medicine,* vol. 8, p. 646506, 2021.

[9] N. D. A. "Digital Health in India," Nishith Desai Associates, Mumbai, 2025.

[10] D. C. Sharma, "Lab notes: Augmented video games can help in stroke recovery," Scroll.in, 19 February 2018. [Online]. Available: https://scroll.in/pulse/869168/lab-notes-augmented-video-games-can-help-in-stroke-recovery. [Accessed 16 April 2025].

[11] H. Sung, M. Kim, J. Park, N. Shin and Y. Han, "Effectiveness of Virtual Reality in Healthcare Education: Systematic Review and Meta-Analysis," *Sustainability,* vol. 16, no. 19, p. 8520, 2024.

[12] N. I. Gonzalez-Romo, G. Mignucci-Jimenez, S. Hanalioglu, M. E. Gurses, S. Bahadir, Y. Xu, G. Koskay, M. T. Lawton and M. C. Preul, "Virtual neurosurgery anatomy laboratory: A collaborative and remote education experience in the metaverse," *Surgical Neurology Intenational,* vol. 14, no. 90, 2023.

[13] J. Nas, J. Thannhauser, P. Vart, R.-J. v. Geuns, H. E. C. Muijsers, J.-Q. Mol, G. W. A. Aarts, L. S. F. Konijnenberg, F. D. H. Gommans, S. G. A. M. Ahoud-Schoenmakers, J. L. Vos, N. v. Royen, J. L. Bonnes and M. A. Brouwer, "Effect of Face-to-Face vs Virtual Reality Training on Cardiopulmonary Resuscitation Quality: A Randomized Clinical Trial," *JAMA Cardiology,* vol. 5, no. 3, pp. 328-335, 2020.

[14] G. Wolff, R. R. Bruno, M. Reiter, B. Kantzow, M. Kelm and C. Jung, "Virtual reality device training for extracorporeal membrane oxygenation," *Critical Care,* vol. 24, no. 1, p. 390, 2020.

[15] H. G. Colt, S. W. Crawford and O. Galbraith, "Virtual Reality Bronchoscopy Simulation: A Revolution in Procedural Training," *Chest,* vol. 120, no. 4, pp. 1333-1339, 2001.

[16] D.-H. Chiang, C.-C. Huang, S.-C. Cheng, J.-C. Cheng, C.-H. Wu, S.-S. Huang, Y.-Y. Yang, L.-Y. Yang, S.-Y. Kao, C.-H. Chen, B. Shulruf and F.-Y. Lee, "Immersive virtual reality (VR) training increases the self-efficacy of in-hospital healthcare providers and patient families regarding tracheostomy-related knowledge and care skills: A prospective pre-post study," *Medicine (Baltimore),* vol. 101, no. 2, p. e28570, 2022.

[17] M. J. W. H. Nijland, W. Veling, B. P. Lestestuiver and C. M. G. Van Driel, "Virtual Reality Relaxation for Reducing Perceived Stress of

Intensive Care Nurses During the COVID-19 Pandemic," *Frontiers in Psychology,* vol. 12, p. 706527, 2021.

[18] L. Bodet-Contentin, M. Letourneur and S. Ehrmann, "Virtual reality during work breaks to reduce fatigue of intensive unit caregivers: A crossover, pilot, randomised trial," *Australian Critical Care,* vol. 36, no. 3, pp. 345-349, 2023.

[19] M. Chessa, A. V. D. Bruaene, K. Farooqi, I. Valverde, C. Jung, E. Votta, F. Sturla, G. P. Diller, M. Brida, Z. Sun, S. H. Little and M. A. Gatzoulis, "Three-dimensional printing, holograms, computational modelling, and artificial intelligence for adult congenital heart disease care: an exciting future," *European Heart Journal,* vol. 43, no. 28, pp. 2672-2684, 2022.

[20] R. M. Ghosh, M. A. Jolley, C. E. Mascio, J. M. Chen, S. Fuller, J. J. Rome, E. Silvestro and K. K. Whitehead, "Clinical 3D modeling to guide pediatric cardiothoracic surgery and intervention using 3D printed anatomic models, computer aided design and virtual reality," *3D Printing in Medicine,* vol. 8, no. 11, 2022.

[21] T. N. Phan, K. J. Prakash, R.-J. S. Elliott, A. Pasupuleti, W. D. Gaillard, R. F. Keating and C. O. Oluigbo, "Virtual reality–based 3-dimensional localization of stereotactic EEG (SEEG) depth electrodes and related brain anatomy in pediatric epilepsy surgery," *Child's Nervous System,* vol. 38, pp. 537-546, 2021.

[22] M. Palaniswamy, L. Wai Yie and B. Y. Suprapto, "Virtual and augmented reality in Industry 4.0," in *The Nine Pillars of Technologies for Industry 4.0,* Kuala Lumpur, The Institution of Engineering and Technology, 2024, pp. 61-78.

[23] M. M. T. E. Kouijzer, H. Kip, Y. H. A. Bouman and S. M. Kelders, "Implementation of virtual reality in healthcare: a scoping review on the implementation process of virtual reality in various healthcare settings," *Implementation Science Communications,* vol. 4, no. 1, p. 67, 2023.

[24] C. T. Shiner, G. Croker, J. McGhee and S. G. Faux, "Perspectives on the use of Virtual Reality within a public hospital setting: surveying knowledge, attitudes, and perceived utility among health care professionals," *BMC Digital Health,* vol. 2, no. 18, 2024.

[25] C. K. Javvaji, H. Reddy, J. D. Vagha, A. Taksande, A. Kommareddy and N. S. Reddy, "Immersive Innovations: Exploring the Diverse Applications of Virtual Reality (VR) in Healthcare," *Cureus,* vol. 16, no. 3, p. e56137, 2024.

[26] Y. Lei, Z. Su and C. Cheng, "Virtual reality in human-robot interaction: Challenges and benefits," *Electronic Research Archive,* vol. 31, no. 5, pp. 2374-2408, 2023.

[27] J. Bajwa, U. Munir, A. Nori and B. Williams, "Artificial intelligence in healthcare: transforming the practice of medicine," *Future Healthcare Journal,* vol. 8, no. 2, pp. e188-194, 2021.

[28] S. A. Alowais, S. S. Alghamdi, N. Alsuhebany, T. Alqahtani, A. I. Alshaya, S. N. Almohareb, A. Aldairem, M. Alrashed, K. B. Saleh, H. A. Badreldin, M. S. Al Yami, S. Al Harbi and A. M. Albekairy, "Revolutionizing healthcare: the role of artificial intelligence in clinical practice," *BMC Medical Education,* vol. 23, p. 689, 2023.

[29] R. Hirani, K. Noruzi, H. Khuram, A. S. Hussaini, E. I. Aifuwa, K. E. Ely, J. M. Lewis, A. E. Gabr, A. Smiley, R. K. Tiwari and M. Etienne, "Artificial Intelligence and Healthcare: A Journey through History, Present Innovations, and Future Possibilities," *Life-Basel,* vol. 14, no. 5, p. 557, 2024.

[30] A. Blasiak, A. Truong, W. Jeit, L. Tan, K. Senthil Kumar, S. B. Tan, C. B. Teo, B. Kye, J. Tan, X. Tadeo, H. L. Tan, C. E. Chee, W.-P. Yong, D. Ho and R. Sundar, "PRECISE CURATE.AI: A prospective feasibility trial to dynamically modulate personalized chemotherapy dose with artificial intelligence.," *Journal of Clinical Oncology,* vol. 40, no. 16, p. 1574, 2022.

[31] D. B. Olawade, A. C. David-Olawade, O. Z. Wada, A. J. Asaolu, T. Adereni and J. Ling, "Artificial intelligence in healthcare delivery: Prospects and pitfalls," *Journal of Medicine, Surgery, and Public Health,* vol. 3, p. 100108, 2024.

[32] O. Oren, B. J. Gersh and D. L. Bhatt, "Artificial intelligence in medical imaging: switching from radiographic pathological data to clinically meaningful endpoints," *Lancet Digital Health,* vol. 2, no. 9, pp. e486-488, 2020.

[33] T. Davenport and R. Kalakota, "The potential for artificial intelligence in healthcare," *Future Healthcare Journal,* vol. 6, no. 2, pp. 94-98, 2019.

[34] C. Gallo, "Artificial Intelligence for Personalized Genetics and New Drug Development: Benefits and Cautions," *Bioengineering,* vol. 10, no. 5, p. 613, 2023.

[35] M. Dave and N. Patel, "Artificial intelligence in healthcare and education," *British Dental Journal,* vol. 234, pp. 761-764, 2023.

[36] I. Chitungo, M. Mhango, E. Mbunge, M. Dzobo, G. Musuka and T. Dzinamarira, "Utility of telemedicine in sub-Saharan Africa during the COVID-19 pandemic. A rapid review," *Human Behavior and Emerging Technologies,* vol. 3, no. 5, pp. 843-853, 2021.

[37] G. Gaobotse, E. Mbunge, J. Batani and B. Muchemwa, "Non-invasive smart implants in healthcare: Redefining healthcare services delivery

through sensors and emerging digital health technologies," *Sensors International,* vol. 3, p. 100156, 2022.
[38] M. Javaid, A. Haleem, R. Pratap Singh, S. Rab and R. Suman, "Significance of sensors for industry 4.0: Roles, capabilities, and applications," *Sensors International,* vol. 2, p. 100110, 2021.
[39] L. Culp, N. Y. Wong and C. E. Misch, "Digital Technology in Implant Dentistry," in *Dental Implant Prosthetics*, 2nd ed., Mosby, 2015, pp. 700-723.
[40] H. B. Aaronson and N. S. Birnbaum, "Digital Dental Impression Systems," *Inside Dentistry,* vol. 7, no. 2, pp. 84-90, 2011.
[41] A. K. Rock, H. Truong, Y. L. Park and J. G. Pilitsis, "Spinal Cord Stimulation," *Neurosurgery Clinics of North America,* vol. 30, no. 2, pp. 169-194, 2019.
[42] V. Venkatraman, R. Bharmi, F. Coletti, Z. F. Gellad, N. Lempel, R. Amit, N. Blank, J. Brown, C. Kumar, M. Fishman, R. Vallejo, D. Datta, B. B. Reeve, K. Chakravarthy, A. D. Sharan and S. P. Lad, "Real World Characterization of Chronic Pain, Success Rates and Implant Rates: Evidence from a Digital Health Platform of Patients Undergoing Spinal Cord Stimulation Evaluations," *The Journal of Pain,* vol. 24, no. 12, pp. 2228-2239, 2023.
[43] E. Mbunge, S. Jiyane and B. Muchemwa, "Towards emotive sensory Web in virtual health care: Trends, technologies, challenges and ethical issues," *Sensors International,* vol. 3, p. 100134, 2022.
[44] P. K. Dutta Pramanik, A. Solanki, A. Debnath, A. Nayyar, S. El-Sappagh and K.-S. Kwak, "Advancing Modern Healthcare With Nanotechnology, Nanobiosensors, and Internet of Nano Things: Taxonomies, Applications, Architecture, and Challenges," *IEEE Access,* vol. 8, pp. 65230-65266, 2020.
[45] L. Lange-Drenth, H. Schulz, I. Suck and C. Bleich, "Barriers, Facilitators, and Requirements for a Telerehabilitation Aftercare Program for Patients After Occupational Injuries: Semistructured Interviews With Key Stakeholders," *JMIR Formative Research,* vol. 8, p. e51865, 2024.
[46] L. Griebel, M. Pobiruchin and M. Wiesner, "Report on the MIE 2015 Workshop: Consumer Health Informatics – Barriers and Facilitators of eHealth Usage among Consumers," German Society for Medical Informatics, Biometry and Epidemiology, Berlin, 2015.
[47] H. K. Y. Almathami, K. T. Win and E. Vlahu-Gjorgievska, "Barriers and Facilitators That Influence Telemedicine-Based, Real-Time, Online Consultation at Patients' Homes: Systematic Literature

Review," *Journal of Medical Internet Research,* vol. 22, no. 2, p. e16407, 2020.

[48] N. L. Saywell, S. Mudge, N. M. Kayes, V. Stavric and D. Taylor, "A six-month telerehabilitation programme delivered via readily accessible technology is acceptable to people following stroke: a qualitative study," *Physiotherapy,* vol. 120, pp. 1-9, 2023.

[49] S. Baffert, N. Hadouiri, C. Fabron, F. Burgy, A. Cassany and G. Kemoun, "Economic Evaluation of Telerehabilitation: Systematic Literature Review of Cost-Utility Studies," *JMIR Rehabilitation and Assistive Technologies,* vol. 10, p. e47172, 2023.

[50] P. Molina-Garcia, M. Mora-Traverso, R. Prieto-Moreno, A. Diaz-Vasquez, B. Antony and P. Ariza-Vega, "Effectiveness and cost-effectiveness of telerehabilitation for musculoskeletal disorders: A systematic review and meta-analysis," *Annals of Physical and Rehabilitation Medicine,* vol. 67, p. 101791, 2024.

[51] C. Thalman and P. Artemiadis, "A review of soft wearable robots that provide active assistance: Trends, common actuation methods, fabrication, and applications," *Wearable Technologies,* vol. 1, p. e3, 2020.

[52] G. Bao, H. Fang, L. Chen, Y. Wan, F. Xu, Q. Yang and L. Zhang, "Soft Robotics: Academic Insights and Perspectives Through Bibliometric Analysis," *Soft Robotics,* vol. 5, no. 3, pp. 229-241, 2018.

[53] E. R. "Exoskeleton Companies and Organizations Directory," Exoskeleton Report, [Online]. Available: https://exoskeletonreport.com/exoskeleton-companies-and-organizations-directory/. [Accessed 5 April 2025].

[54] E. Q. Yumbla, Z. Qiao, W. Tao and W. Zhang, "Human Assistance and Augmentation with Wearable Soft Robotics: a Literature Review and Perspectives," *Current Robotics Reports,* vol. 2, pp. 399-413, 2021.

[55] Y. Bougrinat, S. Achiche and M. Raison, "Design and development of a lightweight ankle exoskeleton for human walking augmentation," *Mechatronics,* vol. 64, p. 102297, 2019.

[56] H. Park, S. Kim, M. A. Nussbaum and D. Srinivasan, "Effects of using a whole-body powered exoskeleton during simulated occupational load-handling tasks: A pilot study," *Applied Ergonomics,* vol. 98, p. 103589, 2022.

[57] T. Rudroff, "Decoding thoughts, encoding ethics: A narrative review of the BCI-AI revolution," *Brain Research,* vol. 1850, p. 149423, 2025.

[58] L. R. Hochberg, D. Bacher, B. Jarosiewicz, N. Y. Masse, J. D. Simeral, J. Vogel, S. Haddadin, J. Liu, S. S. Cash, P. v. d. Smagt and J. P. Donoghue, "Reach and grasp by people with tetraplegia using a neurally controlled robotic arm," *Nature,* vol. 485, pp. 372-375, 2012.

[59] U. Chaudhary, B. Xia, S. Silvoni, L. G. Cohen and N. Birbaumer, "Brain-Computer Interface-Based Communication in the Completely Locked-In State," *PLOS Biology,* vol. 12, no. 12, p. e3000089, 2018.

[60] F. Pichiorri, G. Morone, M. Petti, J. Toppi, I. Pisotta, M. Molinari, S. Paolucci, M. Inghilleri, L. Astolfi, F. Cincotti and D. Mattia, "Brain–computer interface boosts motor imagery practice during stroke recovery," *Annals of Neurology,* vol. 77, no. 5, pp. 851-865, 2015.

[61] R. M. G. Reinhart and J. A. Nguyen, "Working memory revived in older adults by synchronizing rhythmic brain circuits," *Nature Neuroscience,* vol. 22, pp. 820-827, 2019.

[62] L. R. Krol, P. Haselager and T. O. Zander, "Cognitive and affective probing: a tutorial and review of active learning for neuroadaptive technology," *Journal of Neural Engineering,* vol. 17, p. 049601, 2020.

[63] J. Meng, S. Zhang, A. Bekyo, J. Olsoe, B. Baxter and B. He, "Noninvasive Electroencephalogram Based Control of a Robotic Arm for Reach and Grasp Tasks," *Scientific Reports,* vol. 10, no. 1, p. 38565, 2020.

[64] R. Raisamo, I. Rakkolainen, P. Majaranta, K. Salminen and J. Rantala, "Human augmentation: Past, present and future," *International Journal of Human-Computer Studies,* vol. 131, pp. 131-143, 2019.

[65] R. Pirmagomedov and Y. Koucheryavy, "IoT technologies for Augmented Human: A survey," *Internet of Things,* vol. 14, p. 100120, 2021.

[66] A. J. Mills, R. T. Watson, L. Pitt and J. Kietzmann, "Wearing safe: Physical and informational security in the age of the wearable device," *Business Horizons,* vol. 59, no. 6, pp. 615-622, 2016.

[67] N. Mthembu, Artist, *SkidePlayer.* [Art]. CENGAGE, 2021.

9

Augmented Reality (AR)-Based Gamification Experience for Smart and Safe Sensitisation: An SDG14 Case Study Approach

Nassirah Laloo[1], Gomedhanand Ritlall[2], Mohammad Sameer Sunhaloo[1] and Tomal Chadeea[2]

[1]University of Technology, Mauritius
[2]Open University of Mauritius, Mauritius

Email: n.laloo@utm.ac.mu; viksii1014@gmail.com; ssunhaloo@utm.ac.mu; t.chadeea@open.ac.mu

Raising awareness about environmental and social issues is crucial in addressing some of the most pressing challenges of our time. Sensitisation is the foundation for encouraging individuals and communities to adopt more responsible behaviors and make informed decisions [1]. However, traditional sensitisation methods, such as lectures, pamphlets, or videos, often fail to capture attention and sustain engagement, especially among younger audiences. In this context, innovative technologies such as gamification and augmented reality (AR) offer a compelling alternative by providing interactive and immersive ways to educate and inspire action (Figure 9.1). Combined with AR, gamification presents an innovative way to educate and engage users effectively.

Gamification, which involves the application of game mechanics and game design elements in non-game contexts, has emerged as a powerful tool to influence behaviors, motivate participation, and facilitate learning [2] (Figure 9.2). When combined with AR, gamification takes on an even more dynamic role, focusing on player experience with immersive and interactive involvement that transcends the limitations of traditional methods. This combination provides users with a hands-on, experiential approach to learning and exploring new ideas in a safe and controlled environment (Figure 9.3).

 DOI: 10.1201/9788743812135-9

Figure 9.1 Technology for innovative and safe sensitisation.

By blending AR and gamification, we can create impactful solutions that educate and inspire action.

The integration of gamification and AR also enables users to simulate real-world challenges, such as cleaning marine debris or conserving

Figure 9.2 Interactive gameplay for enhanced player engagement.

Figure 9.3 Gamification approach.

underwater habitats, in a virtual setting. This safe, risk-free interaction allows for experiential learning while minimizing the physical and psychological risks associated with direct exposure to such challenges. The combination of engagement, safety, and learning makes AR gamification a promising tool for addressing SDG 14 and other global issues.

This chapter showcases the potential of AR-based gamification as an innovative framework for safe sensitisation, focusing on Sustainable Development Goal 14 (SDG 14), life below water. SDG 14 emphasizes the need to conserve and sustainably use oceans, seas, and marine resources, a critical mission given the increasing threats of overfishing, pollution, and climate change. The gamified AR experience discussed in this chapter addresses these issues by raising awareness about the importance of marine ecosystems and encouraging users to adopt behaviors that contribute to their preservation. Through a step-by-step walkthrough of the conceptualization, content creation, game mechanics, AR integration, and user testing, this case study demonstrates how AR gamification can make complex environmental issues accessible, engaging, and actionable.

9.1 Gamification as a Safe Sensitisation Approach

The core elements of a gamified experience include interaction, engagement, and immersion [3]. Safe sensitisation allows the creation and testing of sensitisation strategies in controlled and iterative cycles. Gamification as a tool for safe sensitisation enhances this process by providing a gamified and simulated version of real-world scenarios with real-time feedback and engaging experience. Developing a gamified sensitisation experience entails different steps (Figure 9.4). The sensitisation context and scope need to be well defined with clear goals. The audience and the focus group should be considered while designing and developing the experiences. Together with the fun aspect of gamification, an engaging experience in the form of storytelling may ensure more participation and outreach [4]. Also, different game mechanics and features should be considered to motivate the players [5]. These may include point systems, levels, badges, and other rewarding mechanisms. Application of vibrant visuals and intuitive, well-designed, user-friendly interfaces may increase player motivation [6]. Finally, the choice of the development tool is important in terms of its popularity, support, and required development efforts.

AR-based gamification provides a safe sensitisation platform both for the developers and the audiences. The developers can dare in their creativity and provide a prototyping environment for sensitisation that would be

Figure 9.4 Steps in developing a gamification experience.

practically impossible to reproduce. Moreover, the prototyping environment is risk-free compared to real-world scenarios and cheaper to develop, test, and deploy. The gamification approach to sensitisation creates engaging, controlled, and inclusive experiences. Complex issues can be presented in context to users without the real-world associated risks and dangers. With gamification, the environmental concepts can be presented in progressive levels. Tasks like ocean cleaning, coral planting, and sea creatures' rescue are made accessible and make the abstract concept of pollution impact more comprehensible with concrete visualization. Positive emotional engagement of gamification, such as success celebration, encouraging tones, and bright visuals, ensures sensitisation without guilt feelings and instead leaves the audiences with a feeling of contribution. With integrated AR, the audiences are encouraged as ambassadors of the cause by posing and sharing photos with augmented characters specific to the cause. The interactions often necessitate low physical strain from the players without dangerous move. Besides, the development process can consider ethical prototyping. The contents can be tested with relevant stakeholders and ensure experience-safe environments with no collection of personal data.

9.2 Game Design and Development Approach

The design and development of the game Bosun are presented to demonstrate how gamification offers a safe and efficient platform for sensitisation. The game focuses on raising awareness about marine conservation through interactive gameplay. Bosun is a 2D educational game with three levels designed to engage young minds and create awareness about the critical issues affecting the ocean, such as pollution, coral reefs destruction, and overfishing. Each level delivers a powerful message: small actions can lead to positive environmental change.

The game adopts a stylized and semi-abstract visual style, aimed at a young audience, with emphasis on education. Bright and cheerful colors are considered for a vibrant and visually engaging atmosphere while conveying a sense of environmental seriousness.

By integrating age-appropriate, inclusive interaction AR-based gamification, *Bosun* helps audiences of all ages understand and care about global issues like SDG14 safely. It allows sensitisation experiences in an environment where audiences can fearlessly learn, experience, empower themselves, and participate actively.

9.2.1 Pre-production

As part of the pre-production phase (Figure 9.5), a visual concept map, illustrated in Figure 9.6, was developed to brainstorm on the core elements of the education game Bosun. This exercise defined features related to the genre, theme, target audience, and gameplay mechanism in more detail. The game was structured into three progressive levels: beach cleaning, coral planting, and fish rescue.

9.2.2 Production Phase

9.2.2.1 Assets and scenes design

As part of the production phase, visual development focused on crafting an engaging and ecologically accurate underwater environment for Levels 1, 2, and 3 of the game. The hand-drawn concept sketches in Figures 9.7 to 9.15 depict a vibrant marine ecosystem, designed to reinforce the importance of biodiversity in ocean habitats visually. These early illustrations guided the creation of game assets by helping define the spatial arrangement, forms, and textures used at the different levels. The naturalistic details aim to create a sense of immersion and environmental appreciation in young players, while

Figure 9.5 Game design and development of SDG14 gamification experience.

supporting the educational goal of demonstrating the ecological role of clean beaches, corals, seaweeds, and responsible fishing in sustaining marine life.

9.2.2.2 Digital Vectorisation of Hand-Drawn Arts

This section illustrates how hand-drawn sketches are transformed into vibrant 2D digital artworks using Adobe Photoshop. Figures 9.16, 9.17, and 9.18 showcase the vectorisation of the level scenes, and Figures 9.19 to 9.24 illustrate the vectorisation of the game's assets. The initial concepts serve as the foundational sketches. The drawings were digitized through a thorough vectorisation process, which involves tracing, layering, and enhancing the original lines and forms using digital tools.

Adobe Photoshop provides an efficient platform for artists to bring their sketches to life with enhanced colors, gradients, textures, and lighting effects. The digital artwork was composed using a 16:9 aspect ratio, one of the most widely adopted screen formats. This ensures optimal compatibility and viewing experience across various digital devices and platforms, from desktop monitors to mobile screens.

Through this workflow, traditional artistic expressions are preserved while at the same time considering the flexibility and scalability of digital

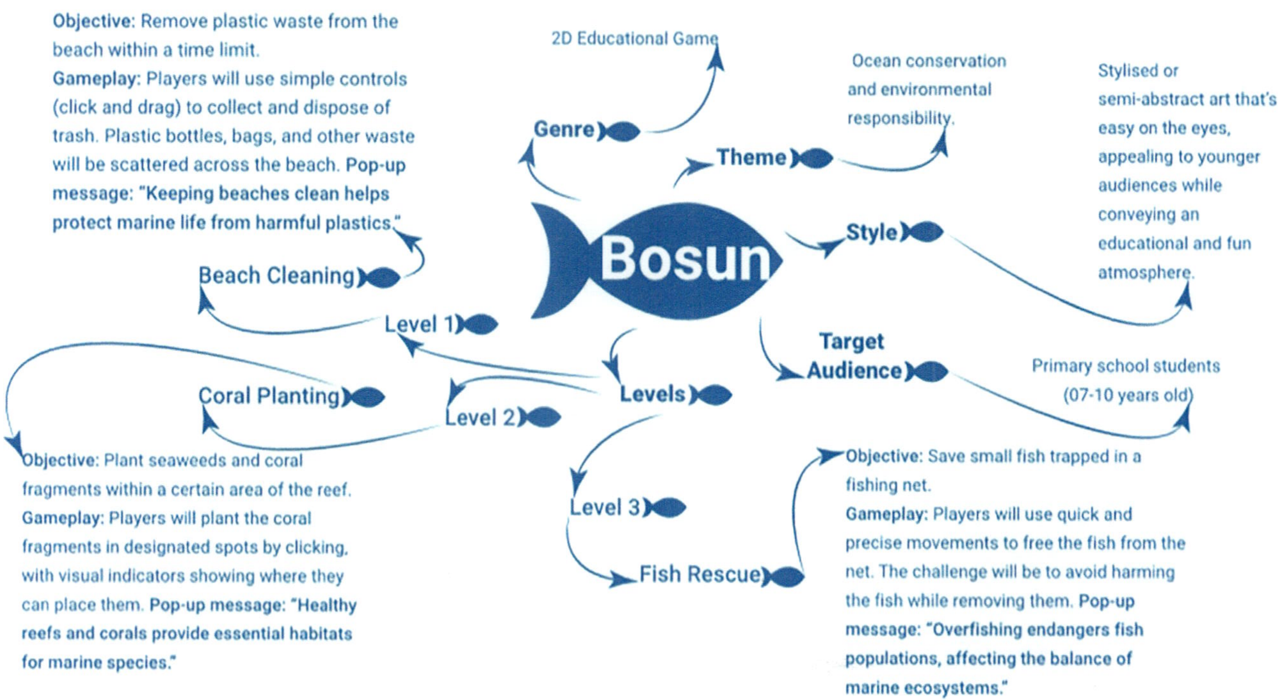

Figure 9.6 Early-stage conceptual mapping of Bosun, outlining its genre, target audience, core theme, visual style, and level structure.

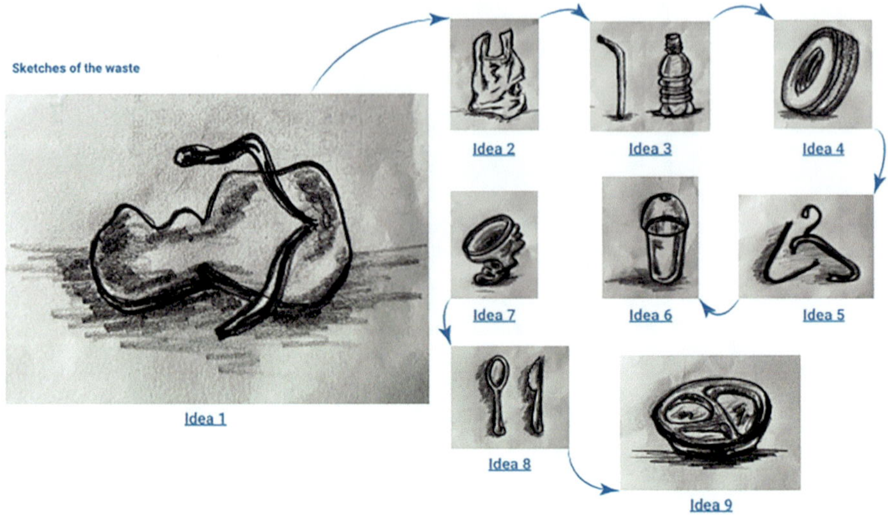

Figure 9.7 Level 1 asset design.

media. This process demonstrates the convergence of analogue artistry and digital design, which is especially relevant in game design, animation, and immersive content development.

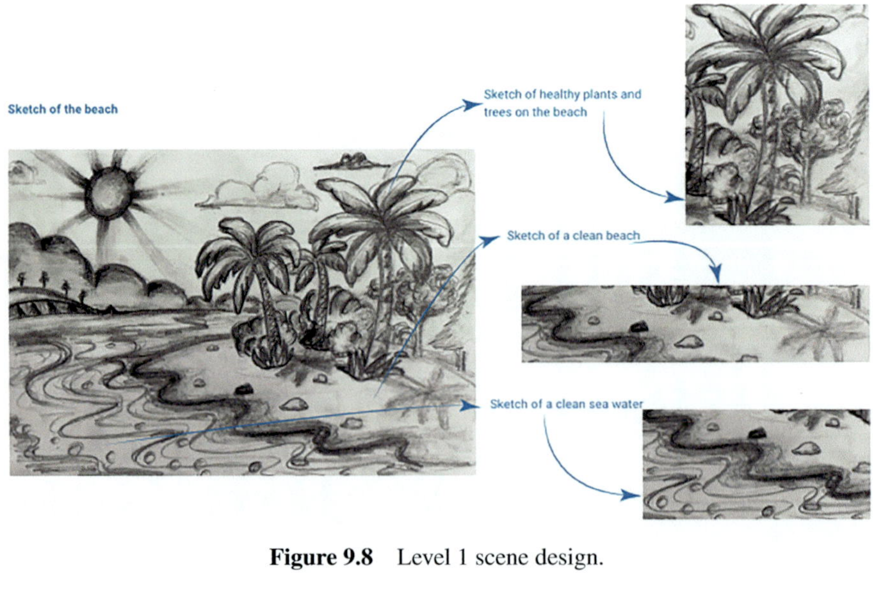

Figure 9.8 Level 1 scene design.

Figure 9.9 Level 2 asset design (1).

9.2.2.3 Development of the user interface components and game mechanics

The development of user interface (UI) components, sound design, and game mechanics are essential components in shaping the player experience and interaction. In the context of the underwater preservation scene design, this

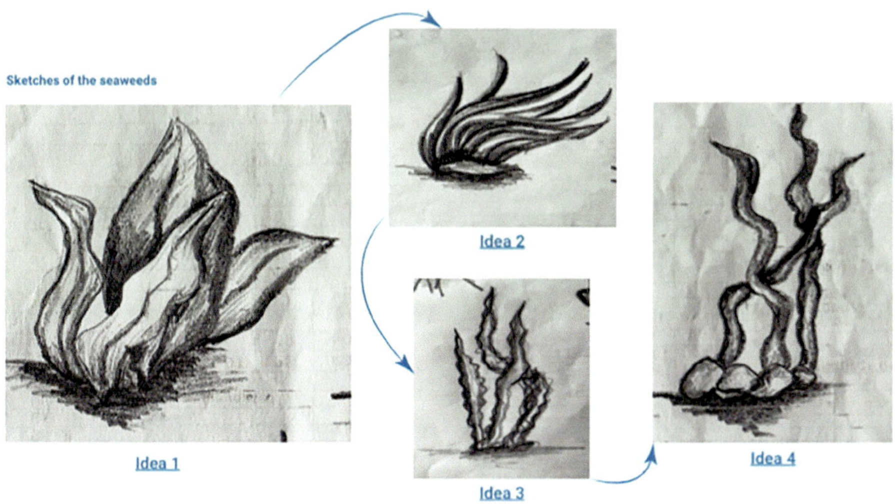

Figure 9.10 Level 2 asset design (2).

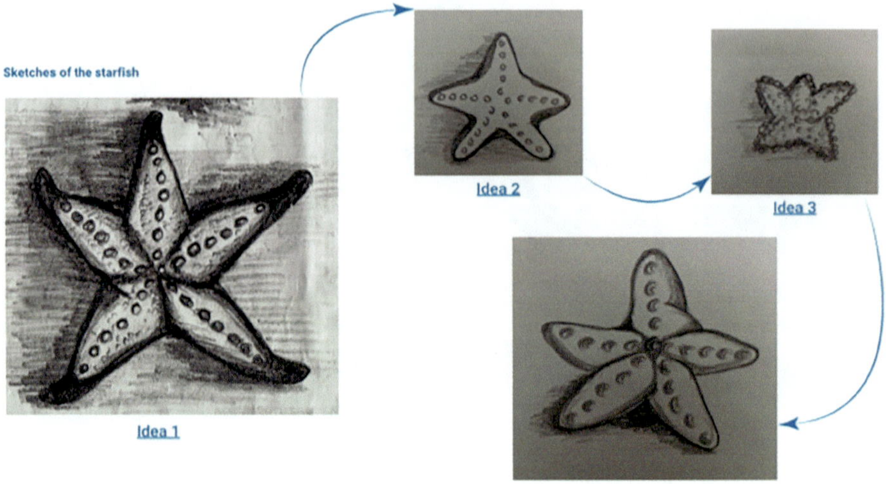

Figure 9.11 Level 2 asset design (3).

stage involves translating the visual assets, such as backgrounds, objects, and characters, into functional, interactive elements.

The digitally vectorized underwater environments, created using Adobe Photoshop, serve as a static backdrop and active interface layers. The assets are integrated into gameplay as interactive objects and are part of a resource-collection mechanic based on the game logic.

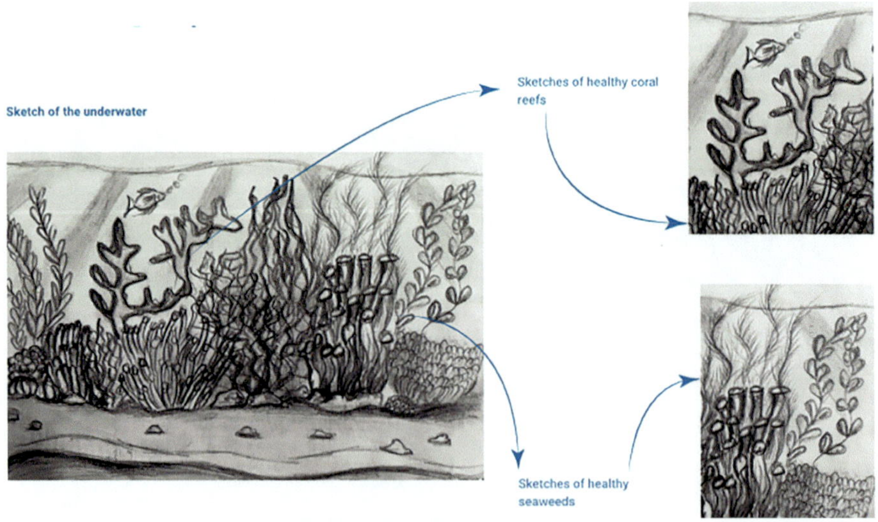

Figure 9.12 Level 2 scene design.

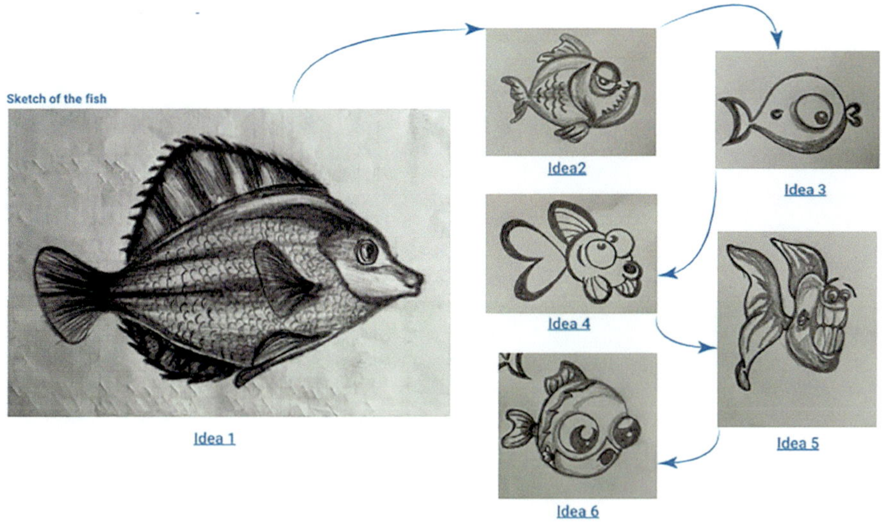

Figure 9.13 Level 3 asset design (1).

User interface elements (Figure 9.25 and Figure 9.26) such as score indicators, navigation cues, and interactive buttons are designed to harmonies visually with the game environment. In the underwater-themed games, translucent and bubble-like UI elements are used to maintain immersion and aesthetic consistency. The 16:9 aspect ratio adopted during scene development

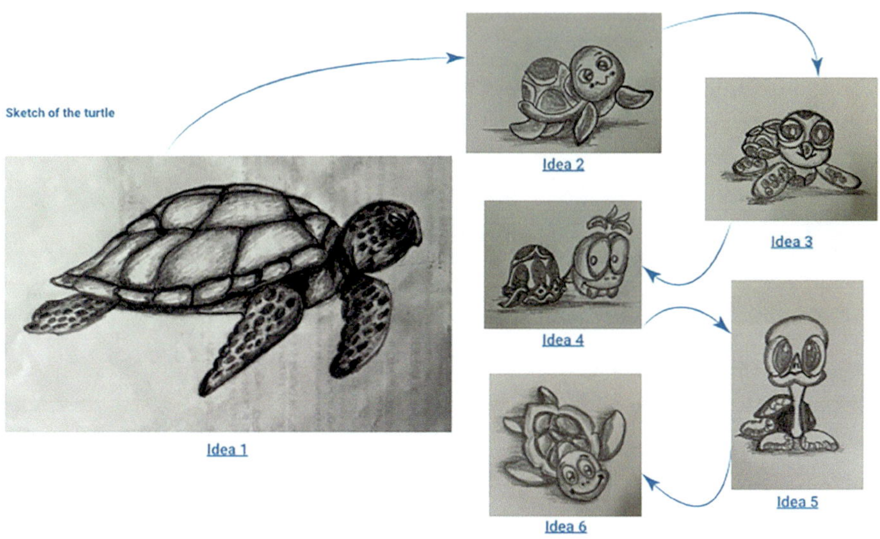

Figure 9.14 Level 3 asset design (2).

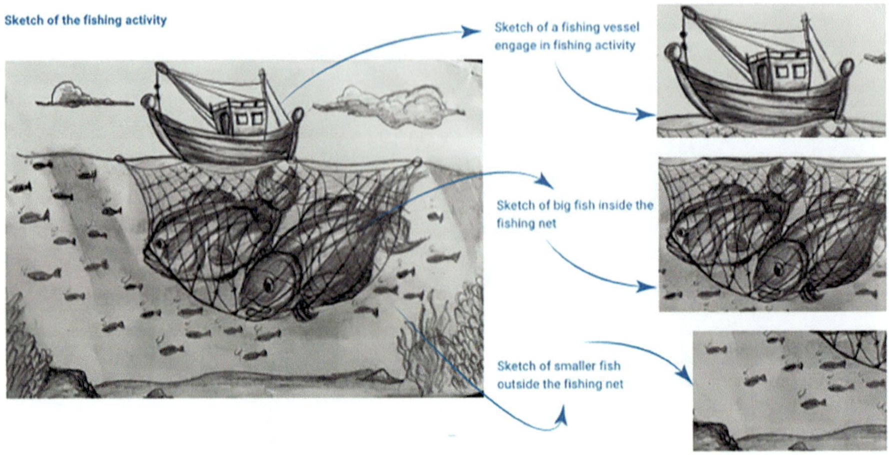

Figure 9.15 Level 3 scene design.

ensures that UI components scale properly across different screen sizes and resolutions, enhancing accessibility and user experience.

Simultaneously, the core game mechanics, including asset movement, collection, collision detection, item interaction, and environmental feedback, are mapped to the layout and constraints of the visual scene. The spatial positioning of objects within the digital artwork supports the design of logical gameplay pathways, objectives, and challenges.

By merging artistic design with interactive logic, this phase bridges creative vision with technical execution, leading to an engaging and intuitive gaming experience.

In level 1, as illustrated in Figure 9.27, plastic waste items are scattered across a virtual beach environment. The player is tasked with cleaning

Figure 9.16 Vectorisation of level 1 scene.

Figure 9.17 Vectorisation of Level 2 Scene.

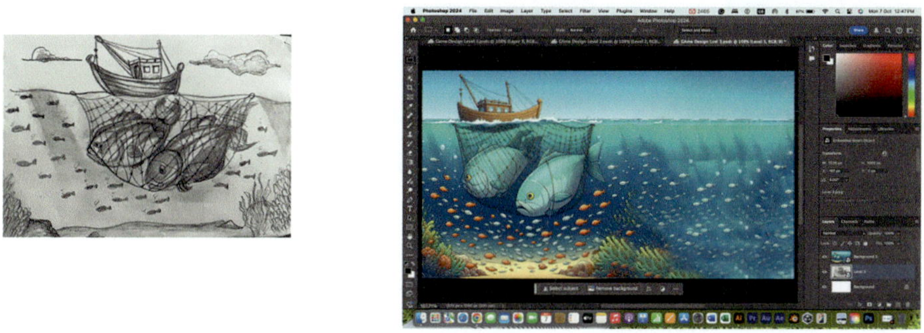

Figure 9.18 Vectorisation of level 3 scene.

Figure 9.19 Vectorisation of assets (1).

Figure 9.20 Vectorisation of assets (2).

the area within one minute by clicking on at least 100 objects. Successful completion of this task is required to advance to the next level. In level 2, seaweeds, coral fragments, and marine animals are placed across the screen.

Figure 9.21 Vectorisation of assets (3).

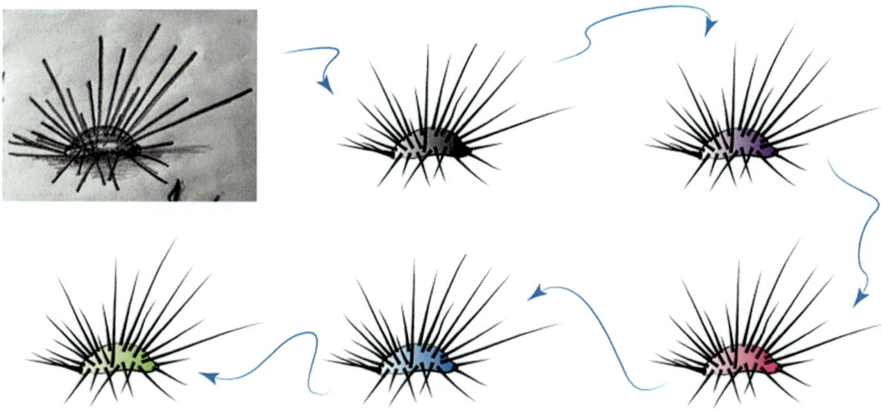

Figure 9.22 Vectorisation of assets (4).

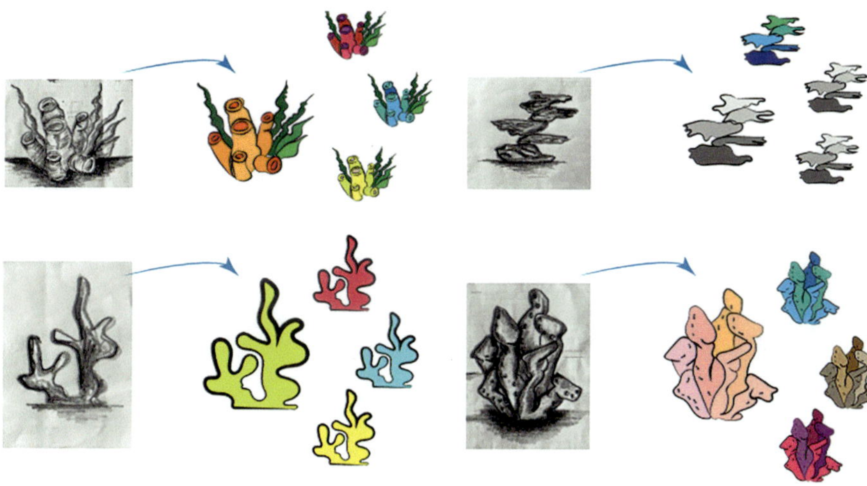

Figure 9.23 Vectorisation of assets (5).

As shown in Figure 9.28, the player's challenge is to drag and accurately position each element in its correct location within one minute. In level 3, undersized fish and sea turtles are trapped in a fishing net, as illustrated in Figure 9.29. The player's challenge is to rescue at least 100 of them by clicking and releasing them within one minute.

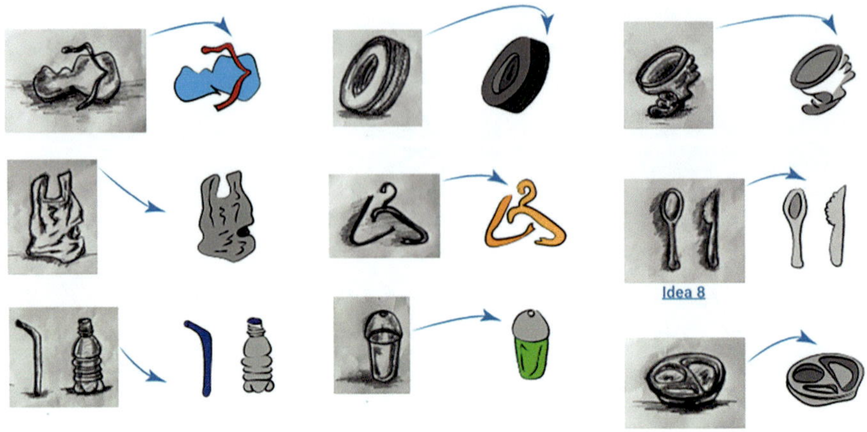

Figure 9.24 Vectorisation of assets (6).

9.2.2.4 Augmented reality integration in marine conservation gameplay

An AR layer was integrated into the game experience to enhance immersion and foster deeper engagement. This feature allows players to project creatures from the marine environment into their physical surroundings using mobile devices. By interacting with these AR visuals, players can simulate real-world conservation actions like rescuing undersized fish or cleaning

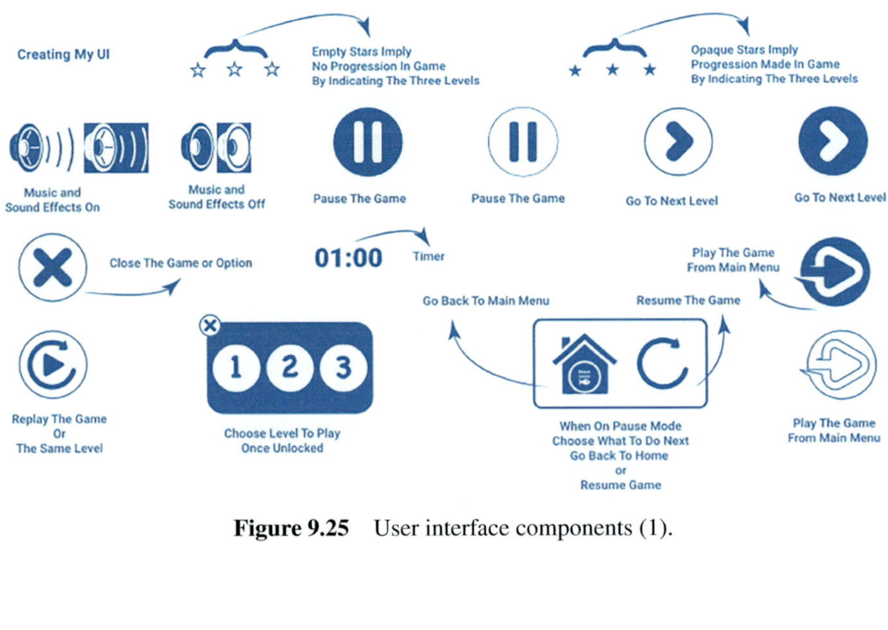

Figure 9.25 User interface components (1).

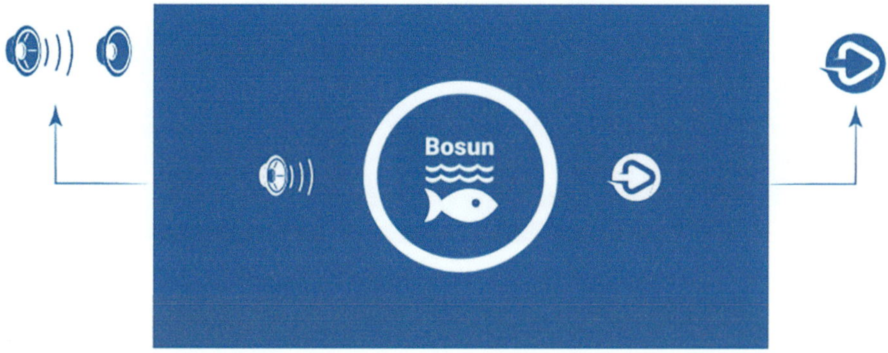

Figure 9.26 User interface components (2).

Figure 9.27 Level 1 gameplay mechanics.

Figure 9.28 Level 2 gameplay mechanics.

underwater habitats. Additionally, players can pose with virtual marine creatures for photos, which can be shared on social media, indirectly transforming them into ambassadors of ocean conservation. Figures 9.30 and 9.31 below demonstrate an experiential activity that celebrated International Music Day, where participants were encouraged to explore the harmony of underwater

Figure 9.29 Level 3 gameplay mechanics.

sounds and marine life in a clean and safe natural environment. This interactive dimension elevates the sensory experience and bridges the gap between digital learning and environmental awareness. In the context of SDG 14 (life below water), AR is a powerful tool for sensitisation, making abstract concepts such as biodiversity loss, overfishing, and habitat degradation more tangible and relatable to users. AR also supports experiential learning, which has been shown to improve knowledge retention and motivate responsible behavior among young audiences [8].

9.2.3 Deployment and game promotion

Following the development and testing phases, the deployment strategy focuses on making the game accessible to target audiences through online platforms and promotional campaigns. The game is accompanied by three visually

Figure 9.30 AR sea life and sound experience on International Music Day (1).

Figure 9.31 AR sea life and sound experience on International Music Day (2).

engaging posters designed for each level to capture interest and communicate the core message of marine conservation and sustainable practices. The visual concept of the posters is given in Figures 9.32, 9.33, and 9.34. These posters can be adapted for different platforms. A QR integration can further link to the gaming experience. The posters serve as both educational tools and marketing assets for digital and physical dissemination.

9.2.4 Safety features consideration

The AR gamification experiences in Bosun incorporate several technical features to support the physical, cognitive, and emotional well-being of players and at the same time adhering to the principles from ISO 9241-210:2019 [9].

Figure 9.32 Poster visual for level 3.

Figure 9.33 Poster visual for level 2.

Figure 9.34 Poster visual for level 1.

Interactions were assisted and restricted to flat surfaces within a limited play area to minimize excessive physical movement and ensure user safety. Marker-based AR was selected for its spatial reliability and safety, especially in controlled environments where printed markers clearly define the interaction zone. This ensures users know exactly where the experience begins and prevents excessive movement, contributing to a more focused and physically safe user experience. The AR experiences were showcased in the corridor of a metro station, a strategic location to attract a diverse audience and maximize public engagement.

The gameplay was time-limited with each level lasting 1 minute, minimizing screen fatigue and encouraging short, focused learning sessions. Touch-based interactions, such as tapping, dragging, and releasing, were considered for ease of use with limited motor strain and low-latency input needs. The user interface was designed with scalable vector graphics (SVG) with low cognitive load, featuring minimal text, clear visual cues, and intuitive navigation and feedback features. The interaction design was aligned with RETRO model principles to provide goal clarity and emotionally safe progression [10].

Accessibility features, including high-contrast artefacts, intuitive color-coded feedback, and minimal reliance on text, were considered. Audio elements were designed and tested to prevent sensory overload and ensure an appropriate experience environment.

9.3 Conclusion

This chapter has demonstrated how AR and gamification can be combined to support smart and safe sensitisation around marine conservation, aligning with the objectives of Sustainable Development Goal 14 (life below water). Through the integration of interactive digital experiences, educational gameplay, and immersive technologies, users were not only informed about environmental issues such as overfishing and habitat degradation. They were also empowered to engage actively and emotionally with the subject matter. The use of QR code-triggered AR, immersive soundscapes, and playful mechanics such as rescuing undersized fish exemplifies how experiential learning can enhance knowledge retention and inspire behavioral change. Additionally, the promotion strategies, including social media engagement and public-facing experiential events, extended the reach and impact of the initiative, positioning participants as ambassadors for marine sustainability. Overall, this approach showcases the potential of emerging technologies in advancing environmental education, advocacy, and action in a scalable and inclusive manner.

Acknowledgments

This work was carried out at the Immersive Media Lab of the University of Technology, Mauritius, an initiative that authors 1 and 3 co-founded. The lab focuses on innovative applications of immersive technologies, fostering research and development in this cutting-edge field. More information about the lab and its projects is available at https://www.utm.ac.mu/laboratories.

We extend our special thanks to the Open University of Technology, Mauritius, for their invaluable support in advancing this research.

References

[1] McKenzie-Mohr, D. (2011). *Fostering sustainable behavior: An introduction to community-based social marketing*. New society publishers.

[2] Sanchez, E., van Oostendorp, H., Fijnheer, J.D. and Lavoué, E. (2020). Gamification. In *Encyclopedia of Education and Information Technologies* (pp. 816-827). Cham: Springer International Publishing.

[3] Gunter, G., Kenny, R. F., & Vick, E. H. (2008). Taking educational games seriously: Using the RETAIN model to design endogenous fantasy into standalone educational games. Educational Technology Research and Development, 56(5–6), 511–537.

[4] Vega, E. and Camarero, C., 2024. Once upon a game: boosting brand storytelling through gamification. Journal of Product & Brand Management, 33(6), pp.717-732.

[5] Proulx, J.N., Romero, M. and Arnab, S., 2017. Learning mechanics and game mechanics under the perspective of self-determination theory to foster motivation in digital game based learning. Simulation & Gaming, 48(1), pp.81-97.

[6] Dakulagi, V., Yeap, K.H., Nisar, H., Dakulagi, R., Basavaraj, G.N. and Galindo, M.V., 2025. An overview of techniques and best practices to create intuitive and user-friendly human-machine interfaces. Artificial Intelligence and Multimodal Signal Processing in Human-Machine Interaction, pp.63-77.

[7] Lean, J., Moizer, J., Derham, C., Strachan, L. and Bhuiyan, Z., 2021. Real world learning: Simulation and gaming. Applied Pedagogies for

Higher Education: Real World Learning and Innovation across the Curriculum, pp.187-214.

[8] Moorhouse, N., tom Dieck, M.C. and Jung, T., 2019. An experiential view to children learning in museums with augmented reality. Museum Management and Curatorship, 34(4), pp.402-418.

[9] ISO – International Organization for Standardization. https://www.iso.org.

[10] Radianti, J., Majchrzak, T.A., Fromm, J. and Wohlgenannt, I., 2020. A systematic review of immersive virtual reality applications for higher education: Design elements, lessons learned, and research agenda. Computers & education, 147, p.103778.

10

A Blockchain-Based Framework for Securing Geospatial Terrain Data in Smart Manufacturing and Industry Logistics

Agnes Nalini Vincent[1], Nassirah Laloo[2], Mohammad Sameer Sunhaloo[2] and Uhoze Bagurubumwe[4]

[1]Amity Institute of Higher Education, Mauritius
[2,3]University of Technology, Mauritius
[4]Raise Agency, Mauritius

Email: vanalini@mauritius.amity.edu; n.laloo@utm.ac.mu; ssunhaloo@utm.ac.mu; nelsonbumwe@gmail.com

Abstract

Digital elevation model (DEM)-based terrain analysis is an important geographic information system (GIS) methodology that serves as the core aspect for spatial analysis applications in geomorphological studies. These analyses can be performed using cloud-based platforms like Google Earth Engines or ArcGIS online, or using a local GIS platform called quantum GIS (QGIS). The resulting terrain data must be disseminated. Geospatial data sharing and dissemination are crucial for promoting cooperation, effectiveness, efficiency, and optimized decision-making in a variety of industries. Geospatial terrain data plays a crucial role in site selection and industrial planning, automated logistics, autonomous vehicle navigation, and infrastructure resilience in manufacturing ecosystems. However, existing literature states that traditional systems lack mechanisms to detect tampering in elevation models, land surveys, or hydrological data. Because of this, manufacturing systems face risks such as flawed factory site selection, disrupted supply routes, or unsafe autonomous vehicle navigation, data tampering in production logs,

 DOI: 10.1201/9788743812135-10

counterfeit parts in supply chains, and a lack of real-time traceability. Hence, to manage the limitations of conventional terrain data storage and handling, this study proposes a blockchain-based framework to secure QGIS-processed terrain data, ensuring immutability and traceability for smart manufacturing applications. Blockchain distributed ledgers can permanently store high-resolution terrain data, minimize the chance of unintended alterations, and promote transparent, unrestricted collaboration. Using the country of the Republic of Mauritius as a case study toward tropical island states, this work demonstrated how elevation, slope, and aspect data extracted via QGIS can be securely stored and verified on a distributed ledger. Furthermore, this study incorporates an integration layer into the framework. The purpose of this integration layer is to enable real-time terrain alerts, smart contract-driven compliance checks, and to arrive at closed-loop feedback from IoT sensors. Thus, this proposed framework bridges blockchain-secured terrain data with manufacturing execution systems (MES) and IoT-enabled logistics networks.

10.1 Introduction

Terrain analysis is the quantitative study of Earth's topographic features and is the core function of Geographic Information Systems (GIS) [1]. Using computational and empirical techniques, it successfully offers a digital representation of the terrain. Terrain analyses positively influence research across multiple disciplines by providing a wealth of data on landforms and their characteristics. It is one of the essential techniques that further assist in ensuring success in studies related to the topography of the Earth. Terrain data offers critical insights for exploring the effects of climate change [6], climatic modeling [3, 20], planning of transportation [18], disaster risk mitigation [8, 9], urban development and smart cities [5, 15] leading to increasing reliance on geospatial data in the pursuit of the United Nations Sustainable Development Goals (SDG). Advancements in GIS, remote sensing, blockchain technology, and AI facilitate accurate terrain data modeling for policy formulation and infrastructure initiatives. Thus, security over data management and access is crucial to ensure informed decisions for a resilient and sustainable future. Reliable geospatial intelligence has a major impact on SDG 9 (industry, innovation, and infrastructure), 11 (sustainable cities and communities), 13 (climate action), and 15 (life on land). Use cases of terrain analysis include figuring out the terrain in a ground robot's future path in the field of robotics and autonomous ground vehicles [2], assessing the effect of terrain on the movement of off-road and unmanned ground vehicles [12], in study of soil erosion and land degradation, watershed and flood management, precision agriculture, urban planning and infrastructure development, disaster risk reduction and climate resilience, forestry and biodiversity conservation, defense and security applications, line of sight analysis, transportation and logistics, and promoting environmental protection. Furthermore, a variety of complex calculations, platforms, and analysis tools with strong and effective processing capabilities have facilitated research related to terrains.

Tampering with terrain data, whether intentional like a fraudulent act or accidental like processing flaws, can trigger cascading failures across systems reliant on geospatial accuracy. Few of critical interpretations of its impacts are environmental misinterpretation (example: false climate models), misclassified slopes, elevations or watersheds of earth surface leading to protected area encroachment (example: deforestation in flattened terrain models), sociopolitical manipulation (example: deliberate distortion of topographic maps that could fuel territorial conflicts), resource grabbing in in vulnerable regions, autonomous system failures (example: self-driving cars or drones relying on tampered terrain data may mis-navigate, causing accidents), and error in prediction by machine learning models when trained on fraudulent terrain data and infrastructure liability (example: engineers using falsified slope stability data may face lawsuits after collapses.

Securing the terrain data is more critical when considering "Smart Manufacturing" and "Industrial Logistics." It is essential to discuss the following cases to emphasize the need for securing terrain data using a blockchain framework: (i) terrain data affects factory site selection, logistics routes, and infrastructure resilience, (ii) tampered elevation geospatial data can disrupt supply chains such as port access, and road construction for raw material transport, (iii) accurate terrain models are an essential requirements for automated-guided vehicles (AGVs), drone deliveries, and warehouse placement and manufactures highly rely on these models, (iv) a factory in a flood-prone zone requires verified terrain data for disaster planning, (v) a mining company uses blockchain-secured elevation maps to automate haul truck routes, (vi) a port logistics firm relies on tamper-proof bathymetric (underwater terrain) data for cargo ship navigation.

In this context, the researchers investigated data accuracy and security-related issues that may arise during the data creation, collection, saving, and sharing processes and proposed an ethical GIS framework, which is a blockchain-based administration for terrain data generated by QGIS software while using DEM models as a raster base layer.

The digital representation of the surface of the earth devoid of vegetation or structures is known as a digital elevation model (DEM). DEMs offer three-dimensional representations of the Earth's surface. A digital illustration of the elevations/heights of a topographic surface, such as the Earth, in the form of a geo-rectified point-oriented or area-based grid, is called a DEM (digital elevation model). Data models, such as regular spaced grids, regular spaced points mesh, triangular irregular network (TIN), curves of iso-elevation (contour lines), have been identified to be useful for storing the Earth's terrain [22]. Out of all, the grid system is currently the most popular method. The most widely used DEMs make use of raster image file storage formats and rectangular grids, or arrays representations. Reliable sources such as NASA's Shuttle Radar Topography Mission (SRTM) provide high-resolution digital elevation models (DEM) [10]. SRTM DEMs are publicly accessible datasets. The SRTM DEM covers terrestrial areas between 56°S and 60°N latitude and offers elevation data with a spatial resolution of 90 meters (3 arc-seconds) [13]. Because of its accessibility and worldwide coverage, this dataset has been utilized extensively in hydrological, environmental, and geomorphological investigations that include Terrain analysis. The main input used by GIS algorithms to extract terrain features is DEM. DEMs that include slope gradient information are a reliable data source for performing terrain data analysis. The quantitative terrain features that characterize the Earth's surface are the foundation of digital terrain analysis (DTA), which can be performed using cloud-based platforms, namely ArcGIS, Google Earth Engine, or by using the software QGIS on a local machine. Slope, elevation, hillshade, viewshed, contour lines, ruggedness index, and aspect are important terrain characteristics. These measures determine the terrain dynamics and are essential in ecological habitat research, prediction of landslide, hydrological modeling, and military navigation. Salient GIS algorithms and techniques pertaining to DTA are Horn's techniques to determine slope and aspect, hillshade determination using azimuth and altitude parameters to replicate sun illumination, viewshed analysis using line-of-sight techniques, ruggedness index validation using vector dispersion, and contour lines production via isoline extraction.

The terrain features, when collected using DTA, need to be securely saved and disseminated to promote further research and collaborative work. Blockchain technology is a decentralized ledger technology that offers a unique method of storing and monitoring transactional data without the oversight and involvement of a central authority. A peer-to-peer network of computers called nodes makes up a typical blockchain. Each of these nodes runs blockchain software that enables each node to keep a copy of the data that has been digitally signed using cryptography [17]. Any changes made to the data are instantly shared across the network. Any modification to the data in this network needs to be examined and approved by most nodes through a consensus process. As a result, the data is trustworthy, accessible to anyone, and hence immutable [1]. Blocks can only be added to the current blockchain; once they are a part of the chain, they cannot be removed. According to the blockchain, it is an ever-expanding data structure that is built as an unchangeable list of records [17]. Ethereum is a blockchain-based platform designed to offer developers the opportunity to establish a secure blockchain using the Solidity programming language. Anybody creating a data management environment can code solidity programs or python programs to develop secure smart contracts, which are self-executing programs stored on a blockchain that enforce agreements automatically when certain conditions are met. They can also create decentralized applications with their own ownership rules and transaction formats [4]. Because blockchain technology ensures tamper-proof integrity and decentralized trust, it has the potential to completely transform the storage and sharing of terrain data.

Therefore, blockchain technology offers a revolutionary method for secure data exchange by providing a decentralized and unchangeable ledger to document transactions. Its fundamental features, including cryptographic hashing, distributed consensus protocols, and tamper-resistant data storage, effectively tackle security issues linked to conventional data sharing techniques [19]. The decentralized structure of blockchain removes single points of failure, thereby boosting resilience against cyberattacks and data breaches [16]. Technology's ability to ensure data integrity, confidentiality, and availability makes it an attractive choice for applications that require secure data sharing among multiple parties [21].

However, the primary challenge of blockchain is scalability, which affects a variety of variables, including latency, cost, capacity (the size of the blockchain), throughput (the number of transactions processed per second, or tps), and the block's finite size [11]. Since terrain data is big data, the use of blockchain technology for such data may raise an issue. This work considered tropical small island states and proposed a generalized framework for such island states by taking the island of Mauritius as a use case. Due to their smaller land areas, island states usually produce less landscape data than continental regions; yet blockchain scalability is still a complex problem that can be managed using light weight or hybrid blockchain technique [14].

The framework proposed by this study is being further advanced to not only secure DEM-generated terrain data, but to include an integration layer for APIs and IoT sensors connectivity to ensure real-time data flow and integration with manufacturing execution systems (MES). This integration layer is the main approach because terrain data processed by QGIS interfaces with: (i) Digital twins (for factory simulations, real-time terrain updates),

(ii) autonomous logistics (drones and AGVs) with geospatial data validated by blockchain, (iii) alerts are triggered by smart contracts if supply routes are at risk due to changes in the topography.

10.2 Material and Methods

Investigations on terrain analysis were conducted by considering the tropical island states, with the country of Mauritius as a case example. To achieve this purpose, this work used SRTM DEM 90 meters imagery raster data of Mauritius as the base DEM map. SRTM DEM raster was downloaded from the "Regional Centre for Mapping of Resource for Development" (RCMRD) geoportal [7]. The metadata of the DEM includes published date: September 6, 2017, data updated January 23, 2018, and is open-source data. The DEM image of Mauritius is exhibited as Figure 10.1.

The software used for DTA is QGIS long-term version 3.40 from the OSGeo4W package. In this work, values from the terrain layer derived from the base DEM raster layer were plotted at the current mouse point using the QGIS plugin's "Value tool" and were displayed in a table. This table, in turn, was saved as a data attribute table on the respective layers. A secure hash for this tabular data was created using the secure hash algorithm: SHA-256. To achieve this, the terrain data in table format was read into the python anaconda distribution. Using python programming, this data was then flattened into a single string by joining all cells in the fixed order of row-wise data, and then the hash value for this data was generated.

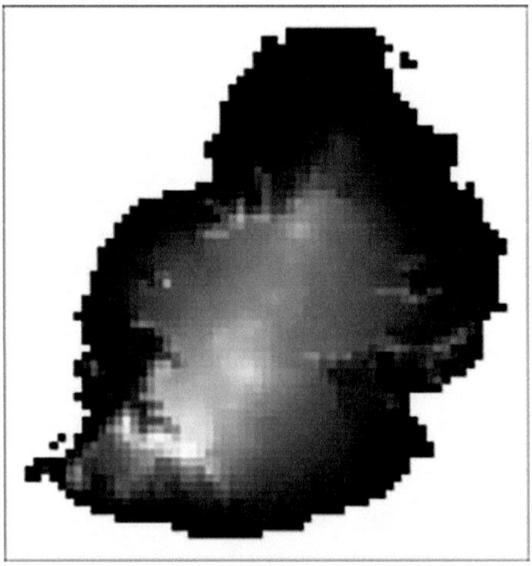

Figure 10.1 SRTM DEM 90 meters imagery raster data of Mauritius.

The process of the above framework (Figure 10.2) is explained in the following consecutive steps:

- *DEM Data Acquisition and Set Up of QGIS Software:* The initial step involves acquiring the DEM data of Mauritius from SRT and adding the DEM data as a raster layer to GIS software for conducting terrain data analysis. An example software tool used in this work is quantum GIS (QGIS)
- *Conduct of Terrain Data Analysis:* High-resolution DEM data of Mauritius was processed in QGIS to generate derivative layers. A QGIS Plugin called "Visual Tool" was used for this purpose.
- *Polygonize the DEM Data Layer:* The DEM layer is polygonized using the visual tool and conversion tool present under the raster menu of QGIS, and the derivative layers, such as slope layer, aspect value layer, elevation-contour layer, and hillshade layer, were developed. These derivative layers were developed by running the algorithms as follows: (1) slope algorithm in Geospatial Data Abstraction Library (GDAL) was run to produce the slope layer (2) Horn's formula was used to determine the aspect layer (3) GDAL contour algorithm found in processing tool box was used to generate the contour lines (4) gdaldem utility tool from the processing tool box was used to produce the hillshading layer information. Thus, respective derivative terrain layers for each terrain analysis were generated.
- *Export the Layers:* The layer contents residing as attribute table information in QGIS were exported as comma-separated value files (CSV) and were stored for further blockchain development.
- *Blockchain Structurization:* The software used for constructing and structuring a blockchain was the python programming language. The step-by-step execution for the construction of blockchain involved selection and import of necessary libraries, data loading into python environment, constructing the architecture of blockchain, concluding on the mechanism for hybrid encryption, generating and saving the blockchain and the keys, validating the blockchain by conducting an integrity check, and visualizing the blockchain data. Further, these blockchain data can be deployed as public blockchain to ensure immutability, decentralization, and enhanced security.
- *Introduction of an Integration layer:* This layer is established to connect to any manufacturing systems as per the scope of the industry, which is

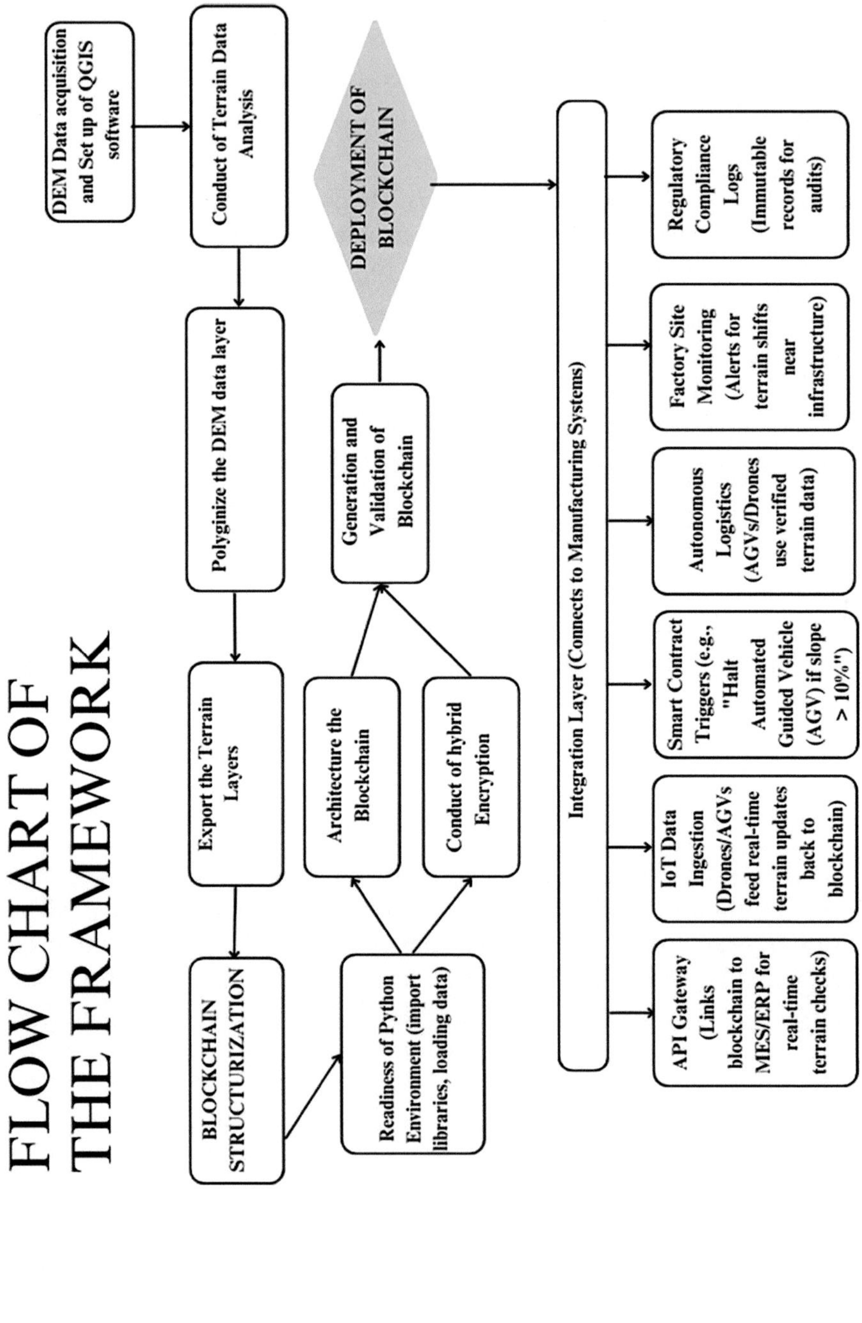

Figure 10.2 Flow chart of the blockchain-based framework for securing geospatial terrain data.

using the framework. Examples of connectivity to the integration layer include (i) API gateway to link to MES or real-time enterprise resource planning (ERP) systems, (ii) IoT device connectivity, (iii) smart contract trigger applications, (iv) connectivity to autonomous logistics systems, (v) site monitoring in factories/industries, and (vi) compliance mechanisms.

10.3 Results and Discussions

The DEM data of Mauritius that was formed based on SRTM data, is the study area. A slope map is a topographic map that displays elevation variations in detail. Slope maps are used by water control planners, landscape architects, and architects to assess a site. Predicting the flow of water is one of the most useful uses of a map. The slope tool in the raster terrain analysis module of the QGIS toolbox, which applies Horn's (1981) third-order finite difference method, was used to derive slope gradients. Using the user-specified slope values in degrees, this algorithm determined the maximum rate of change between each cell and its eight neighbors. The scaling parameter z-factor, which is the ratio of vertical units to horizontal, was adjusted to 1.0000 since the DEM's geographic coordinates (Lat/Long, WGS84) were x, y in degrees, and z was in meters. The slope map is shown in Figure 10.3.

Using the value tool, the slope, at respective coordinates were collected, and accounted as an attribute table of the layer. The distribution of slope value is illustrated in Figure 10.4.

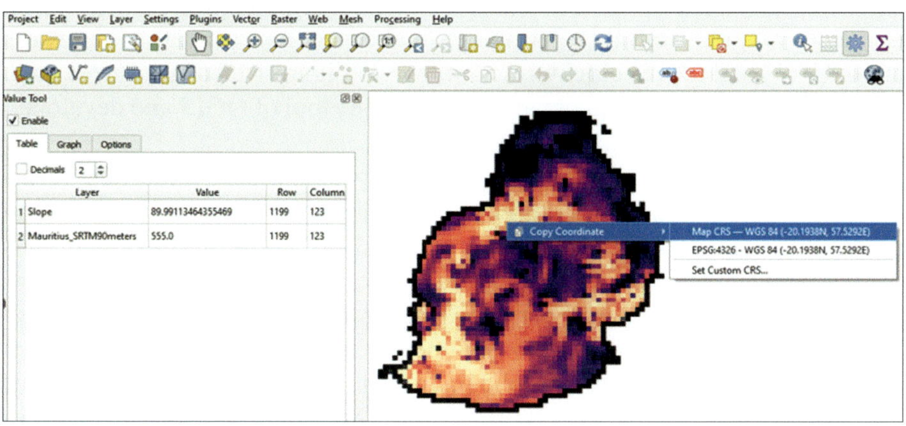

Figure 10.3 Slope map – The geoinformation layer of distribution of slope values.

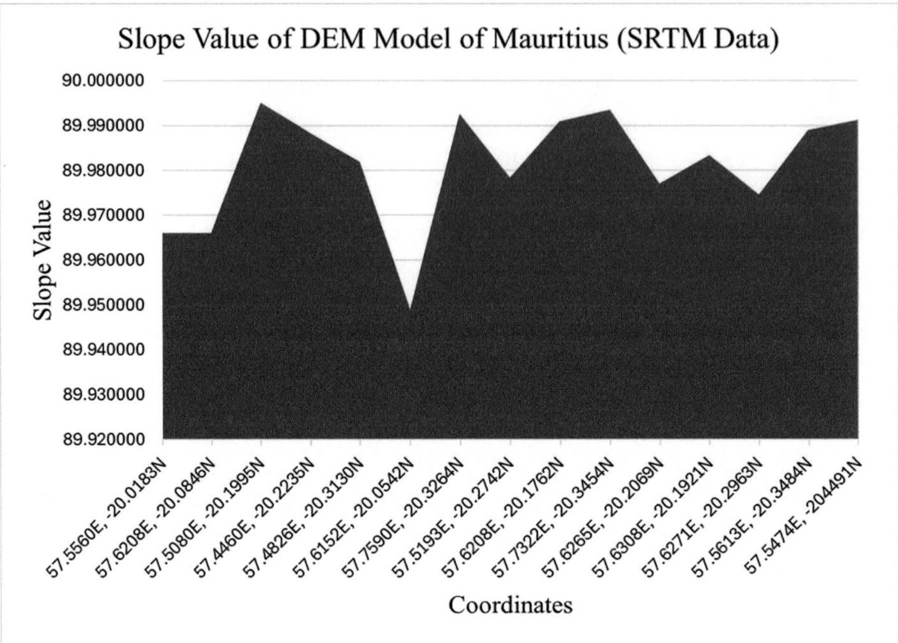

Figure 10.4 Distribution of slope of DEM model of Mauritius.

The next topographic derivative used for terrain analysis is the aspect value. Aspect value is an underlying terrain parameter that indicates the direction (compass) a slope faces. It is measured in degrees from 0° to 360°. The aspect of the input digital terrain model is computed using the aspect algorithm provided in the QGIS interface. The slope direction is expressed by values ranging from 0 to 360 in the final aspect raster layer, which starts at north (0°) and moves clockwise as shown in Figure 10.5 as an aspect map. This work captured the aspect values using value tool of QGIS and developed an attribute table of the layer.

To understand the distribution of the slope and aspect values, the resultant raster layers were polygonised (converting raster to vector data file) to obtain the attribute tables of the same. The distribution of slope value has been illustrated in Figure 10.6.

Contour lines are another topographic derivative for terrain analysis. Lines of constant elevation obtained from a digital elevation model (DEM) are represented by contour lines (isolines) in QGIS. The height of each contour line is indicated by the "elev" (elevation) value that is kept in each attribute table. The contour map for the area under study is shown in Figure 10.7.

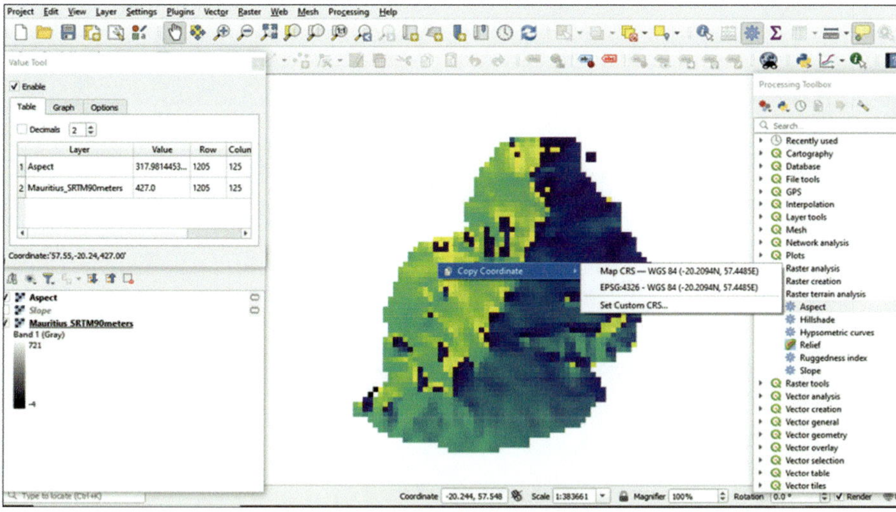

Figure 10.5 Aspect Map – The geoinformation layer of distribution of aspect values.

While sparse contours in the middle plateau indicated low-relief terrain ideal for agriculture, closely spaced contours in the northern sector were associated with places that were prone to landslides.

The elevation profile of Mauritius, derived from the SRTM dataset [23], is shown in Figure 10.8. The graph determines the frequency and variability of the island's relief by charting feature IDs against elevation values. The distribution shows a very diverse terrain; while most of the sampled points reside

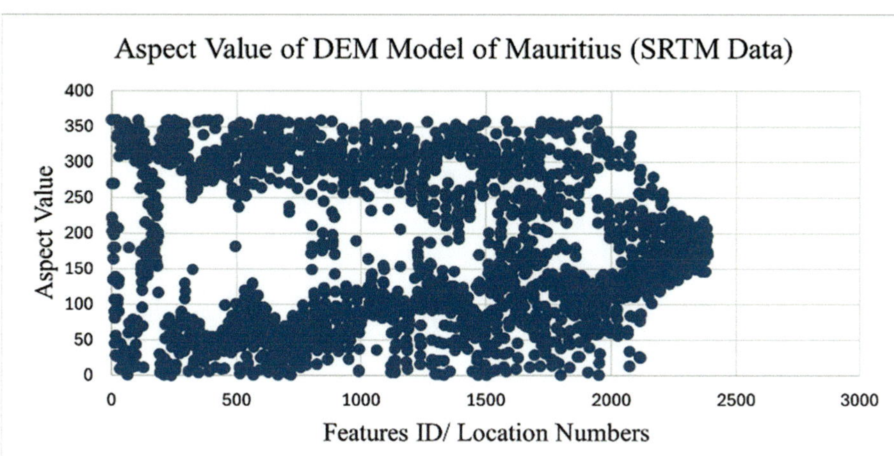

Figure 10.6 Distribution of aspect value of DEM model of Mauritius from SRTM Data [23].

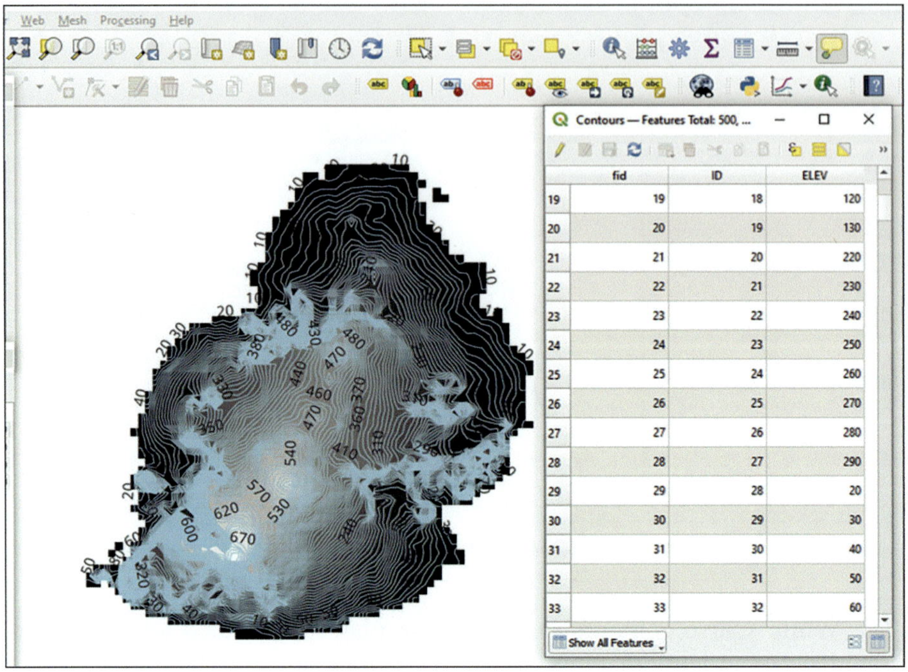

Figure 10.7 Contour Map – The geoinformation layer of distribution of contour lines.

at lower altitudes (<500 meters), the existence of spikes above 500 meters highlight the prominence of the inland mountain ranges.

In case of hillshade terrain analysis, a grayscale raster, brightness denotes exposure to the sun (black represents shadowing, white indicates

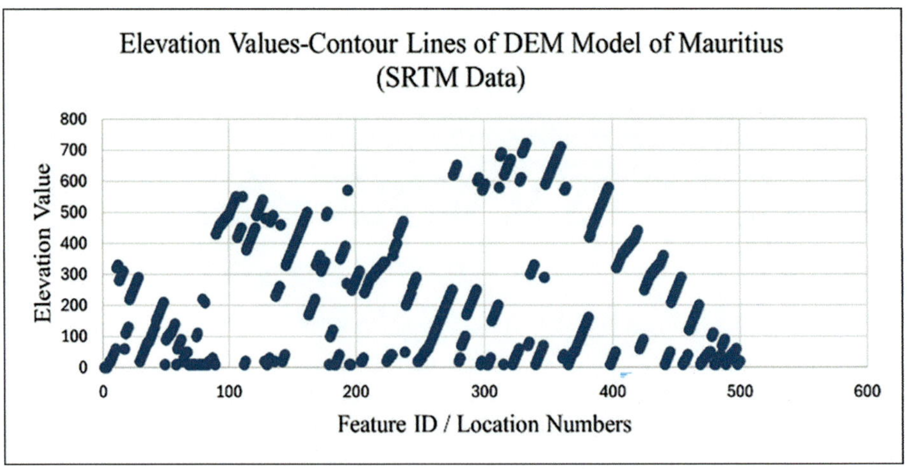

Figure 10.8 Distribution of elevation values of DEM model of Mauritius.

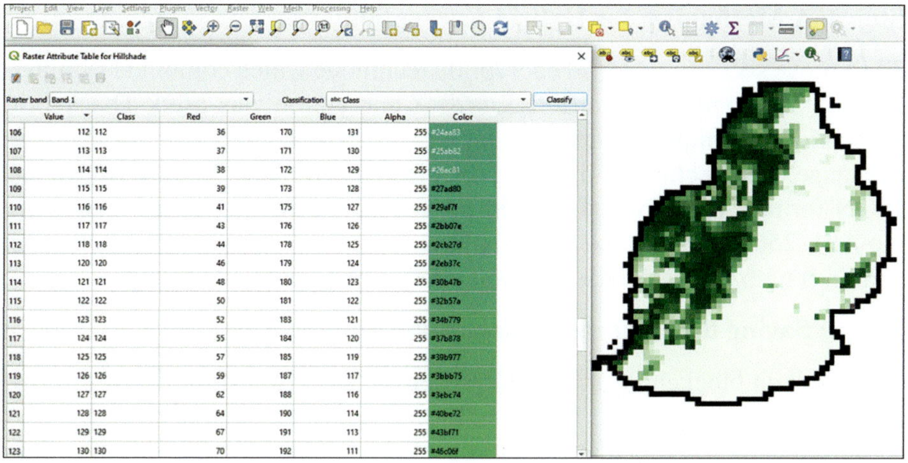

Figure 10.9 Hillshade Map – The geoinformation layer of distribution of hillshade.

illumination). The parameters of altitude (sun angle) and azimuth (sun direction) are used in this analysis. This DEM visualization is useful for studying hydrology, geomorphology, and mapping. Similarly, the hillshade terrain analysis was conducted, and the respective hillshade map is shown in Figure 10.9.

Thus, this study performed a terrain analysis for the considered DEM model and populated the respective attribute tables.

Blockchain implementation of terrain data collected as CSV files from DEM-STRM raster file using QGIS has been conducted using python software. The implementation steps of blockchain are as follows:

Step 1: Baseline Processing and Data Loading:

Slope.csv/aspect.csv/contour.csv files from were loaded into python environment using the Pandas library. To facilitate later blockchain integration, the CSV was parsed into a structured data frame as part of the initial processing.

Step 2: The Architecture of Blockchain Construction for Data:

The blockchain's blocks constituted an index as identifier of a sequential block, a timestamp which denoted the precise moment the block was created, terrain data readings (in a dictionary format), and the previous hash, which is the previous block's cryptographic hash. The block's contents were further hashed using SHA-256 (secured hash algorithm) to ensure integrity. A genesis block was used to initialize and establish the blockchain. The add_block () method was used to append future blocks to the genesis block. To ensure no tampering occurrence, the is_valid () method conducted cryptographic validation by confirming hash consistency along the chain.

Step 3: A Mechanism for Hybrid Encryption:

To improve security, a hybrid encryption technique which combined symmetric AES-256, and asymmetric RSA-2048 encryption was used. The hybrid encryption technique generated a public/private RSA key pair for safe key exchange. This technique involved data from each block being serialized as JSON format, which was followed by symmetric encryption of data using the AES-256 algorithm. Next, RSA-OAEP (optimal asymmetric encryption padding) with SHA-256 hashing was used to encrypt the AES key.

Step 4: Saving the Encrypted Blockchain and the Keys:

The resultant blockchain and the keys were stored as PEM files (private_key.pem, public_key.pem) and in binary format. Thus, the data is now stored as serialized python object that was possible using pickle module (pkl) of python resulting to pkl files (example: encrypted_blockchain.pkl), respectively.

Step 5: Validation and Decryption of the Blockchain Data:

RSA decryption was performed to extract the AES key from the encrypted packet. Original JSON data were recovered through AES decryption. An integrity check was conducted to confirm the hash consistency.

Step 6: Visualization of Blockchain:

Visualization strategies were used to improve interpretability. For example, the slope value plot (Figure 10.10) using "Matplotlib" library of python software was used to create a time-series graph of slope readings. The entire blockchain was visualized as graphs (Figures 10.10a and 10.10b). The structure of the entire chain (blockchain graph) was demonstrated as a visual via a directed graph (Figures 10.10a and 10.10b) that depicted block links using NetworkX of python software. To enhance understandability, the first 15 blocks were visualized as Figure 10.11. As a way forward, the work may involve "Geospatial Mapping," which could be an interactive Folium map that can be created using the dataset's coordinates, and the blockchain data can be deployed in blockchain network as public blockchain data to ensure immutability, transparency, decentralized access to data, and global collaboration for research purposes.

Thus, this framework proposed through this work demonstrates how DEM terrain data processed with QGIS and anchored on a blockchain with python software can transform geospatial intelligence in smart environments. By using terrain data collection and decentralized storage, the system ensures

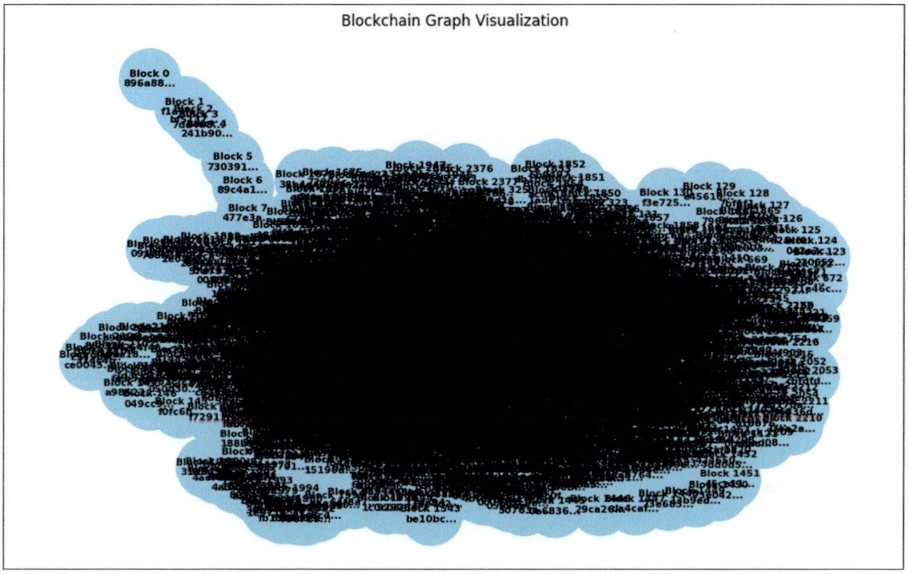

Figure 10.10a Blockchain graph visualization of the entire "slope terrain data" from DEM.

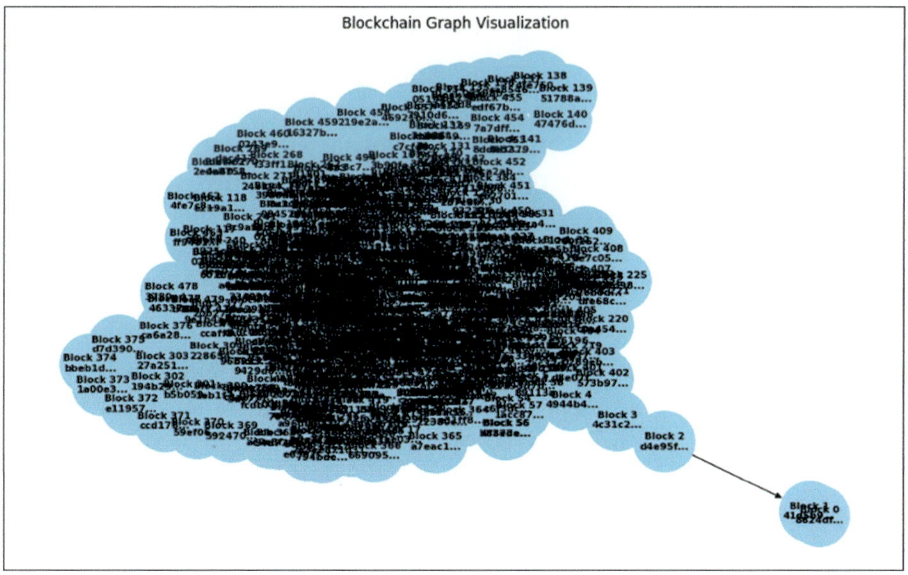

Figure 10.10b Blockchain graph visualization of the entire "aspect terrain data" from DEM.

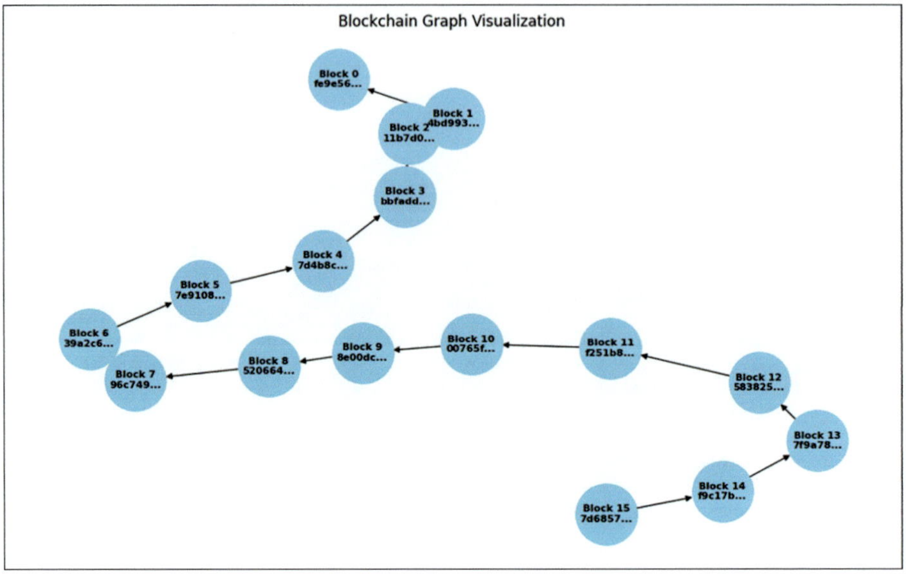

Figure 10.11 First 15 blocks of "slope terrain data" blockchain.

verifiable integrity of terrain datasets, which are crucial for applications like autonomous drone navigation, slope stability analysis, and flood modeling. Blockchain technology may make it possible for stakeholders (like local governments and environmental organizations) to access and share topography data while protecting privacy. Additionally, tokenized incentives for data producers (e.g., Ethereum-based tokens) can be used to improve real-time accuracy and encourage crowd-sourced geographic updates. This approach not only strengthens resistance to data manipulation in accordance with Industry 4.0 and smart city infrastructures, but also through integrated machine learning models, facilitating AI-driven terrain data analytics.

Step 7: After terrain data is encrypted and stored on a blockchain, based on the scope and requirement of the industry, the integration layer linking blockchain, MES, and IoT may be operationalized. Through various interfaces, the integration layer enables the following bidirectional data flow between production systems and the blockchain-terrain data landscape: (i) dynamic terrain validation during production scheduling is made possible by API-mediated interoperability with manufacturing execution systems (MES); (ii) continuous geospatial feedback loops from automated guided vehicles (AGVs) and environmental monitors are provided by embedded IoT sensor networks; and (iii) Ethereum-based smart contracts automatically enforce terrain-dependent operational constraints when processing real-time logistics data. The six functional modules that this study suggests for the integration layer of its design are as follows: (i) a RESTful API gateway for MES/ERP integration that uses OAuth2.0 authentication, (ii) light detection and ranging (LiDAR) data from site survey drones is processed by MQTT (message queuing telemetry transport)-based IoT edge computing nodes, (iii) terrain compliance guidelines encoded by hyperledger fabric smart contracts; (iv) navigation interfaces for autonomous mobile robots enabled by robotic operating systems (ROS); (v) terrain monitoring stations enhanced by computer vision; and (vi) on-chain auditing trails for ISO 9001 compliance paperwork.

10.4 Conclusion

In this study, terrain analyses were performed on the DEM data of Mauritius using QGIS software, and the output terrain data were stored on decentralized blockchain networks. Through this approach, this paper demonstrated how geospatial terrain data may be secured from unauthorized modifications while yet being accessible to verified stakeholders by utilizing blockchain's immutable ledger for terrain data storage and access. This study addressed important gaps pertaining to data integrity, and real-time decision-making by proposing a framework based on blockchain technology to secure terrain data processed by QGIS software for smart manufacturing applications. This research framework uses blockchain's distributed ledger technology to guarantee the immutable storage of terrain data models, reducing the possibility of issues like altered geospatial inputs, poor site selection, and interrupted autonomous logistics. Blockchain-secured terrain data is connected to manufacturing execution systems (MES) through the integration layer's integration of an API gateway and IoT sensor networks. This allows for: (i) automated compliance checks through smart contracts (such as flood-risk alerts for coastal factories), (ii) real-time terrain validation for supply chain logistics and autonomous vehicles (AGVs/drones), and (iii) closed-loop feedback from IoT devices (such as drones updating erosion data) to ensure data accuracy. Using the Republic of Mauritius as a case study, the framework demonstrated its applicability to tropical island states, where terrain volatility and climate risks necessitate resilient industrial planning. Future work will explore AI-driven anomaly detection in real-time terrain feeds, scalability optimizations for IoT deployments, and standardization of blockchain-geospatial APIs for Industry 4.0 ecosystems. This research advances the convergence of geospatial science and secure Industry 4.0 architectures, offering a replicable model for terrain-dependent sectors like mining, construction, and smart infrastructure.

References

[1] Berryhill, J., Bourgery, T., Hanson, A., Berryhill, J., Bourgery, T., & Hanson, A. (2018). *Blockchains Unchained BLOCKCHAIN TECHNOLOGY AND ITS USE IN THE PUBLIC SECTOR*. https://doi.org/10.1787/3c32c429-en

[2] Borges, P., Peynot, T., Liang, S., Arain, B., Wildie, M., Minareci, M., Lichman, S., Samvedi, G., Sa, I., Hudson, N., Milford, M., Moghadam, P., & Corke, P. (2022). A Survey on Terrain Traversability Analysis for Autonomous Ground Vehicles: Methods, Sensors, and Challenges. *Field Robotics*, *2*(1), 1567–1627. https://doi.org/10.55417/FR.2022049

[3] Brumatti, C. H. T., Schaefer, M., Villela, M. L. B., Lisboa-Filho, J., & Reis, J. C. S. (2023). *TerrainIntelGIS: A Geographic Intelligence System to Support Decision-Making in Environmental and Natural Disaster Scenarios*. 89–92. https://doi.org/10.5753/WEBMEDIA_ESTENDIDO.2023.235548

[4] Buterin, V. (n.d.). *Ethereum: A Next-Generation Smart Contract and Decentralized Application Platform.*

[5] Costa, D. G., Bittencourt, J. C. N., Oliveira, F., Peixoto, J. P. J., & Jesus, T. C. (2024). Achieving Sustainable Smart Cities through Geospatial Data-Driven Approaches. *Sustainability*, *16*(2). https://doi.org/10.3390/SU16020640

[6] Krishna Pasupuleti, M. (2024). Modeling Climate Impact and Urban Growth with Hadoop and ArcGIS: Advanced Geospatial Solutions. *Spatial Big Data Analytics: Leveraging Geospatial Tools for Research Innovation with Hadoop and ArcGIS*, 31–57. https://doi.org/10.62311/NESX/978-81-98048530

[7] *Mauritius SRTM DEM 90meters | RCMRD GMES & Africa Geoportal*. (n.d.). Retrieved May 19, 2025, from https://gmesgeoportal.rcmrd.org/datasets/rcmrd::mauritius-srtm-dem-90meters/about

[8] Mayomi, I., S., K. M., & Martins, A. K. (2014). Terrain Analysis for Flood Disaster Vulnerability Assessment: A Case Study of Niger State, Nigeria. *American Journal of Geographic Information System*, *3*(3), 122–134. https://doi.org/10.5923/J.AJGIS.20140303.02

[9] Miyamoto, T., Stricker, M., Ogishima, J., Iselborn, K., Nuske, M., & Dengel, A. (2023). Effect of Terrain Information on Multimodal Deep Learning for Flood Disaster Detection. *International Geoscience and Remote Sensing Symposium (IGARSS)*, *2023-July*, 448–451. https://doi.org/10.1109/IGARSS52108.2023.10282892

[10] Nwacholundu, U. V., Izuchukwu, J., Ebele, J., Onyedika, J., & Chinagorom, I. E. (2021). *Generating and analyzing Terrain characteristics from Shuttle Radar Topographic Mission (SRTM), DEM*. https://doi.org/10.30574/wjarr.2021.10.3.0272

[11] Pawar, M. K., Patil, P., & Hiremath, P. S. (2021). A Study on Blockchain Scalability. *Advances in Intelligent Systems and Computing*, *1270*, 307–316. https://doi.org/10.1007/978-981-15-8289-9_29

[12] Rada, J., Rybansky, M., & Dohnal, F. (2021). The Impact of the Accuracy of Terrain Surface Data on the Navigation of Off-Road Vehicles. *ISPRS International Journal of Geo-Information 2021, Vol. 10, Page 106*, *10*(3), 106. https://doi.org/10.3390/IJGI10030106

[13] Safanelli, J. L., Poppiel, R. R., Chimelo Ruiz, L. F., Bonfatti, B. R., de Oliveira Mello, F. A., Rizzo, R., & Demattê, J. A. M. (2020). Terrain Analysis in Google Earth Engine: A Method Adapted for High-Performance Global-Scale Analysis. *ISPRS International Journal of Geo-Information 2020, Vol. 9, Page 400*, *9*(6), 400. https://doi.org/10.3390/IJGI9060400

[14] Sanka, A. I., & Cheung, R. C. C. (2021). A systematic review of blockchain scalability: Issues, solutions, analysis and future research. *Journal of Network and Computer Applications*, *195*, 103232. https://doi.org/10.1016/J.JNCA.2021.103232

[15] Sarango-Ordóñez, J. P. (2024). Contribuciones de los sistemas de información geográfica (SIG) en la planificación urbana sostenible. *Multidisciplinary Collaborative Journal*, *2*(4), 1–15. https://doi.org/10.70881/MCJ/V2/N4/1

[16] Sathya, M., Atchiyya, C., Mareedu, N., Hanumanth, L., Vadla, R., & Krishna, V. (2024). *Secure and Transparent Medical Record Management System Using Python and Blockchain*. https://arxiv.org/abs/2408.02081v1

[17] Shen, C., & Pena-Mora, F. (2018). Blockchain for Cities - A Systematic Literature Review. *IEEE Access*, *6*, 76787–76819. https://doi.org/10.1109/ACCESS.2018.2880744

[18] Spear, B. D. (2004). Linking Spatial and Transportation Data. *Handbook of Transport Geography and Spatial Systems*, *5*, 309–326. https://doi.org/10.1108/9781615832538-018

[19] Trofimova, E. I. (2021). Blockchain for social memory institutions: Functional value and possibilities. *Scientific and Technical Libraries*, *1*(1), 115–124. https://doi.org/10.33186/1027-3689-2021-1-115-124

[20] Tsatsaris, A., Kalogeropoulos, K., Stathopoulos, N., Louka, P., Tsanakas, K., Tsesmelis, D. E., Krassanakis, V., Petropoulos, G. P.,

Pappas, V., & Chalkias, C. (2021). Geoinformation Technologies in Support of Environmental Hazards Monitoring under Climate Change: An Extensive Review. *ISPRS International Journal of Geo-Information*, *10*(2), 94. https://doi.org/10.3390/IJGI10020094

[21] Wu, L., Lu, W., Zhao, R., Xu, J., Li, X., & Xue, F. (2022). Using Blockchain to Improve Information Sharing Accuracy in the Onsite Assembly of Modular Construction. *Journal of Management in Engineering*, *38*(3). https://doi.org/10.1061/(ASCE)ME.1943-5479.0001029

[22] Xiong, L., Li, S., Tang, G., & Strobl, J. (2022). Geomorphometry and terrain analysis: data, methods, platforms and applications. *Earth-Science Reviews*, *233*. https://doi.org/10.1016/J.EARSCIREV.2022.104191

[23] Xiong, L., Tang, G., Yang, X., & Li, F. (2021). Geomorphology-oriented digital terrain analysis: Progress and perspectives. *Journal of Geographical Sciences*, *31*(3), 456–476. https://doi.org/10.1007/S11442-021-1853-9/METRICS

11

The Importance of Electromagnetic Security and Its Protection Assessment Technology

Wen Zheng[1] **and Leong Wai Yie**[2]

[1,2]INTI International University, 71800 Nilai, Negeri Sembilan, Malaysia

Email: i25031583@student.newinti.edu.my

Abstract

The rapid advancement of electronic technology, marked by applications like 5G communications, artificial intelligence, mobile internet, IoT, industrial internet, and unmanned systems, has significantly complicated electromagnetic environments. Consequently, ensuring electromagnetic security has become more crucial than ever. Electromagnetic security is closely linked to information security and is the cornerstone of cybersecurity. It directly impacts the safe and stable operation of information carriers and is vital for national defense, socio-economic stability, public health, and overall national security. Therefore, the entire society must prioritize electromagnetic security.

11.1 The Evolution of Electromagnetic Domain Awareness and Security Development

For many years, the industry has generally lacked a correct understanding of basic concepts such as electromagnetic interference (EMI), electromagnetic compatibility (EMC), and electromagnetic susceptibility. The basic

 DOI: 10.1201/9788743812135-11

concepts and their interrelationships are as follows: electromagnetic interference (EMI) is an electromagnetic phenomenon where electromagnetic disturbances cause mutual influences among electronic devices and lead to adverse consequences. EMI includes two aspects: electromagnetic emissions and electromagnetic susceptibility. EMI is an inherent property of a product, and it is predictable and distinguishable. Electromagnetic compatibility (EMC) refers to the coexistence state where devices can perform their respective functions together in a common electromagnetic environment. EMC sets limit requirements for EMI, specifying that the electromagnetic emissions of a system should not exceed the emission limit requirements, and the electromagnetic susceptibility should not exceed the susceptibility limit requirements. Electromagnetic compatibility is not measurable; it can only be obtained through design and evaluation [1]. Electromagnetic susceptibility (EMS) refers to the degree to which the performance of electronic devices is affected or fails under electromagnetic disturbance conditions. EMS can be determined through experiments and tests, and it is one of the important indicators for measuring the electromagnetic compatibility of devices.

With the transformation from mechanization to informatization, intelligence, and networking, human society has evolved from the tangible physical world into an intangible physical realm characterized by electromagnetic fields and waves. The understanding of the electromagnetic domain has evolved from electromagnetic compatibility to electromagnetic security, which can be roughly divided into three stages. The first stage is the narrow understanding of electromagnetic compatibility, where the goal of achieving electromagnetic compatibility is mainly realized by controlling electromagnetic interference, with the core issue being the resolution of self-interference within the system. The second stage is the improvement of electromagnetic environmental adaptability, which, based on effectively controlling electromagnetic interference, further controls the effects of the electromagnetic environment. The core issue here is the system's adaptability to the electromagnetic environment under conditions of "self-interference, mutual interference, and hostile interference." The third stage focuses on electromagnetic security under strong electromagnetic attacks. Based on paying attention to electromagnetic compatibility and electromagnetic environmental adaptability, this stage aims to enhance the system's security capabilities under strong electromagnetic attacks, with the core issue being the electromagnetic vulnerability under electromagnetic attack conditions.

11.2 Biological Effects and Prevention Methods in Electromagnetic Environments

The advancement of technology and the constant renewal of electronic appliances have brought convenience to people's lives, but at the same time, they have also created an invisible network of electromagnetic waves, leading to a gradual increase in the intensity of electromagnetic radiation (EMF) in the living environment. In 1996, the United Nations launched the International EMF Project, which aims to study the potential health effects of electromagnetic radiation and has established internationally recognized EMF exposure standards [2]. Multiple cross-sectional surveys have found that exposure to electromagnetic radiation is associated with symptoms such as poor sleep and fatigue [3, 4]. There have even been numerous self-reported cases of health issues due to exposure to electronic devices, which are referred to as electromagnetic field-induced environmental allergies [5].

After being exposed to a certain dose or duration of electromagnetic radiation, the human body can suffer varying degrees of harm. It can damage the central nervous system, causing symptoms such as dizziness, fatigue, and neurasthenia; it can trigger cardiovascular system disorders, such as arrhythmia and bradycardia, and increase the incidence of coronary heart disease; it can harm the eyes, causing damage to the cornea, lens opacity and aging, and cataracts; it can affect reproductive capabilities, leading to decreased male sexual function, female endocrine disorders, increased spontaneous abortion rates in pregnant women, and fetal developmental abnormalities; it can even induce the production of electric and magnetic fields within a biological body after exposure to electromagnetic radiation. When converted into thermal energy, this can raise the temperature of deep tissues within the body and increase the risk of cancer [6].

In daily life, we need to enhance our awareness of electromagnetic radiation protection. Household appliances and office equipment should not be placed too closely together, and it is advisable to avoid using them simultaneously for extended periods. When electrical appliances are not in use, it is important to turn off the power promptly to prevent the long-term accumulation of weak electromagnetic fields generated in standby mode. After devices such as microwave ovens and printers are turned on, it is better to stay at least 1 meter away. For long phone calls or conferences, it is recommended to use headsets or microphones. The human nervous and reproductive systems are the most sensitive to electromagnetic radiation, so it is essential to minimize frequent and intense contact between these sensitive areas and electromagnetic waves, maintaining a safe distance of more than half a meter whenever possible [7].

11.3 Information Security Protection Technology in Electromagnetic Environments

11.3.1 The electromagnetic security protection system based on the "OODA Loop"

The "OODA Loop" model, proposed by U.S. Air Force Colonel John Boyd, consists of four processes: observe, orient, decide, and action [8]. The electromagnetic security protection system based on the "OODA Loop" includes electromagnetic environment monitoring and direction-finding devices, leakage shielding devices, and UAV countermeasures in its front end. The back-end features application servers equipped with electromagnetic security protection software and database servers with electromagnetic spectrum databases, forming a monitoring system with one center and multiple perception nodes [9]. This protection system divides the electromagnetic security protection process of the core area of the space launch site into four loops: spectrum perception, situation analysis, assessment and warning, and risk disposal. It operates in an autonomous, cyclic, and feedback-driven manner, enabling rapid response from signal detection to anomaly handling. The principle is shown in Figure 11.1.

The spectral perception loop serves as the starting point of the "OODA Loop," which involves the monitoring equipment in the core area to sense and collect electromagnetic signals from the surrounding environment. The situation analysis loop analyzes the electromagnetic data collected by the spectral perception loop. Meanwhile, it integrates data from the central station and perception nodes, and in combination with the electromagnetic wave propagation model in the core area, employs algorithms such as interpolation to depict the electromagnetic spectrum situation map. The assessment and warning loop receives feedback data from the situation analysis loop and evaluates the risk level based on the built-in risk assessment mechanism. The risk disposal loop is the precision energy release phase. According to the input from the assessment and warning loop, it coordinates the equipment within the system to perform localization, classification, and counteraction, forming a closed loop for anomaly disposal and feeding the results back to the spectral perception loop. The Hainan Commercial Space Launch Site in China has established a regional perception network and countermeasures based on the "OODA Loop". It can detect typical electromagnetic security risks such as electromagnetic noise, interference, radiation leakage, and UAV harassment at the launch site. It can identify electromagnetic interference events within 1 minute and locate the interference source within 30 minutes. This has solved the previous problem of low efficiency and automation in detecting interference sources, which required professional personnel to carry equipment for

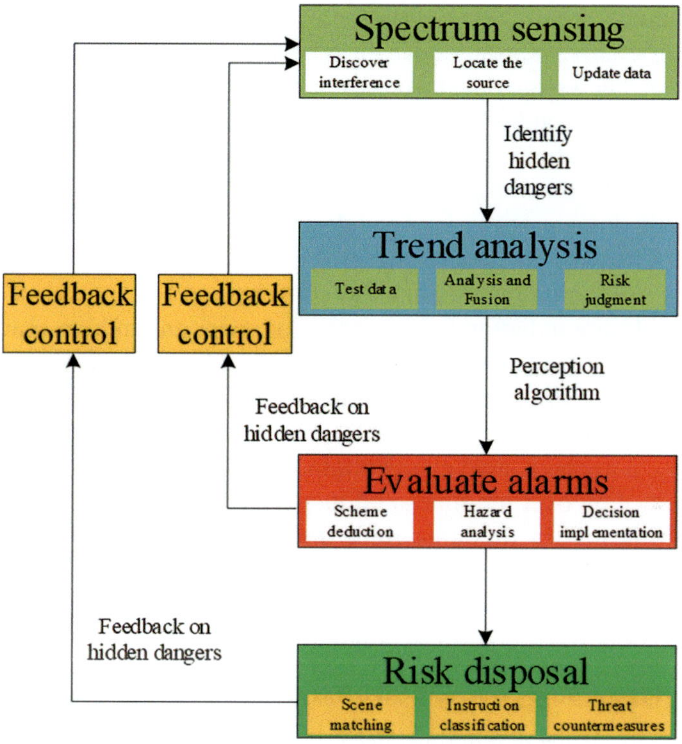

Figure 11.1 The principle of the OODA Loop in electromagnetic safety protection systems.

monitoring and was incapable of dealing with short-duration electromagnetic interference signals. This method has improved the efficiency of handling and enhanced electromagnetic security protection capabilities [10].

11.3.2 Shielding protection technology

Shielding protection technology employs specific technical methods to confine the effects and impacts of electromagnetic radiation within a designated spatial area. It is currently the most widely used technique for electromagnetic radiation protection [11]. Wang Baoguo *et al.* employed a single-sided shielding protection method for electromagnetic interference and network information protection in building environments. A single-sided conductive glass curtain wall can provide partial electromagnetic shielding for information and radio-frequency devices within a room. This reduces the likelihood of electromagnetic signals within the area being intercepted externally and diminishes the interference of external electromagnetic signals on indoor information devices, thereby bringing electromagnetic security risks within a controllable range. Additionally, the conductive glass curtain wall also has the capability to acquire voice and image data through communication reconnaissance means. Experiments were conducted to evaluate the electromagnetic protection effectiveness of the conductive glass curtain wall. The radiation field distribution in both longitudinal and transverse directions for a rectangular shielded body in a deep-shadowing scenario, considering multiple edge diffractions, was calculated. The experimental results are consistent with the classical theory's predictions of longitudinal attenuation convergence and transverse shell-like distribution. Using radiation field distribution maps and indoor–outdoor radio wave propagation models, they analyzed the shielding effectiveness and safety impact distance of single-sided shielding in specific engineering contexts. The layout of the Model room is shown in Figure 11.2. Simulations showed that for a 10 m × 3 m conductive glass curtain wall, shielding reduced the outdoor safety distance by over ten times and increased the indoor safety distance by 1.30–1.56 times. These findings guide the quantitative design of single-sided shielding projects. The method, now successfully applied, is gaining industry favor for its cost-efficiency [12].

11.3.3 Energy-selective electromagnetic protection technology

Under intense electromagnetic pulses, the focus of electromagnetic protection lies in severing the coupling pathways between the intense electromagnetic pulses and sensitive equipment, thereby reducing the electromagnetic

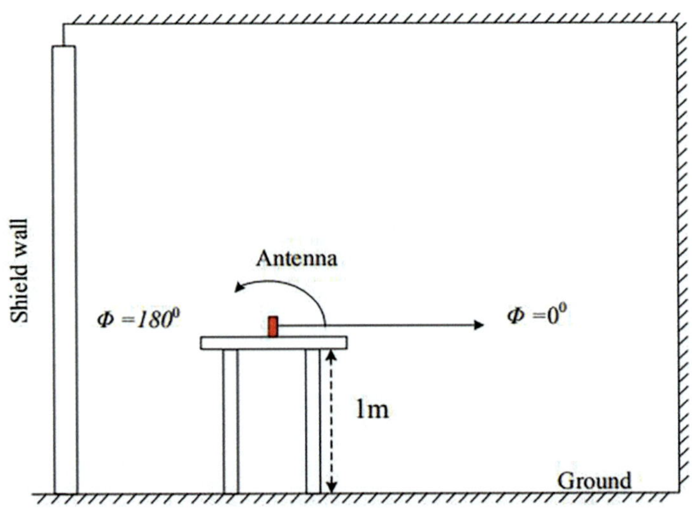

Figure 11.2 Layout of a single-sided shielding protection model room

energy received by the sensitive devices. Electromagnetic protection can be categorized into front-door protection and back-door protection based on the coupling pathways. Front-door protection primarily prevents high-power microwaves (HPM) from entering the system through the front-door paths, such as antennas and transmission lines. In contrast, back-door protection aims to prevent HPM from entering the system through back-door paths, including holes, gaps, and cable interfaces on the electronic equipment enclosures. Research on back-door protection is relatively comprehensive, and effective measures such as grounding and shielding can be employed to cut off the back-door coupling pathways. However, research on front-door protection is relatively limited [13]. Under instantaneous intense electromagnetic pulses, traditional protection methods face limitations, and front-door protection encounters challenges such as in-band operation, high power, and rapid response. To address these issues, Liu Peiguo *et al.* proposed an energy-selective electromagnetic protection method, which is a novel adaptive intense electromagnetic protection technology. The core principle of this method is the field-induced impedance transformation mechanism. By using impedance-sensitive materials or artificial electromagnetic structures, the method can sense the intensity of the electromagnetic wave energy in real-time and achieve adaptive impedance control. When the incident electromagnetic wave energy is below the safety threshold, the protection device maintains a high impedance, allowing the electromagnetic wave to transmit with low loss. Upon detecting an intense electromagnetic pulse, the nonlinear characteristics of the material or device trigger a sudden impedance drop. This impedance mismatch significantly attenuates the electromagnetic energy. This state transition occurs without external control and has a response time on the nanosecond scale. It overcomes the contradiction between the power capacity and the response speed of traditional protection devices. Moreover, it provides effective protection without affecting the normal operation of the equipment, thus solving the dilemma of "protection" and "compatibility" in front-door protection of electronic devices. This method offers a new approach for intense electromagnetic protection and is of great significance for enhancing the electromagnetic protection capabilities of electronic equipment [14]. The protection schematic diagram is shown in Figure 11.3.

11.3.4 Electromagnetic security cooperative suppression technology

The management and control of electromagnetic security is complex and diverse, and is a key issue in communication interference and related fields [15]. Shi Jia *et al.* have put forward the technology of electromagnetic

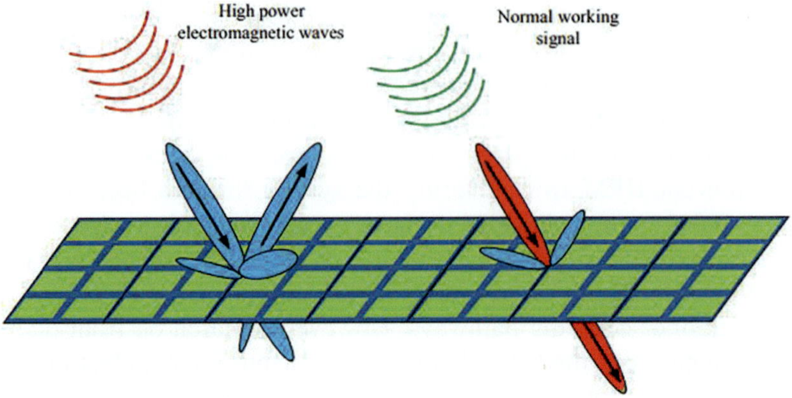

Figure 11.3 Schematic diagram of energy selection electromagnetic protection.

security cooperative suppression. They first built a radio wave propagation model for complex urban environments, and through simulation analysis, they revealed the characteristics of such environments. Then, to achieve effective electromagnetic suppression and avoid harmful interference, they designed a collaborative deployment strategy for electromagnetic suppression devices using potential game theory and proposed a power optimization method based on genetic algorithms. This enables collaborative multi-device operations and efficient delivery in complex electromagnetic environments, significantly enhancing the overall effectiveness of electromagnetic suppression systems. Simulation experiments show that the developed electromagnetic suppression device layout algorithm performs close to the theoretical optimum with lower computational complexity. Further analysis indicates that the new power optimization algorithm reduces transmission power by over 50% compared to traditional interference power allocation schemes, improving collaborative and precise control capabilities [16].

11.3.5 Low-radiation technology

Low-Radiation Technology is an integrated application of black-red isolation techniques, shielding, and filtering measures aimed at suppressing electromagnetic signal leakage through multilayered protection mechanisms. The primary consideration is the black-red separation technique, which separates radiation sources that may generate useful information from those that generate useless information. Signals that can be decrypted to reveal valuable information when intercepted are termed “red signals,” while those that cannot be decrypted are referred to as "black signals." Moreover, information exchange between black and red devices is strictly unidirectional, allowing only black devices to transmit information to red devices. This prevents black devices from becoming carriers of red signals and avoids coupling effects through connecting lines. Low-radiation technology has been successfully applied in computers used by confidential departments such as the Party, government, and military. The display cover of low-radiation computers is embedded with shielding glass, and the rear cover is equipped with a shielding plate to isolate electromagnetic radiation. Electromagnetic shielding layers are implemented on the front and rear covers and their seams. Shielding measures are also adopted for connecting lines to prevent signal coupling. Additionally, filters are installed at critical circuits or interfaces to suppress high-frequency stray signals and electromagnetic interference. Through the synergistic effects of physical isolation, electromagnetic shielding, and signal purification, this technology significantly reduces the risk of sensitive information being intercepted and is suitable for the protection of electronic devices in high-security scenarios.

11.3.6 Electromagnetic noise interference technology

Electromagnetic noise interference technology conceals useful information in electromagnetic leakage emissions by increasing the intensity and complexity of the electromagnetic leakage radiation noise. Even low-radiation emission products inevitably leak unconscious electromagnetic signals. To prevent adversaries from acquiring information, the interference device employs a wide frequency range and high amplitude to mask the information from two aspects simultaneously. For example, computer video information jammers are information security and confidentiality protection products developed to address the issue of electromagnetic leakage from computers. They provide multiple layers of protection for computer radiation information through spatial random number encryption technology, correlated interference, and noise confusion, thereby making it more difficult for adversaries to steal information. Spatial random number encryption technology: the electromagnetic radiation signals from classified computers are scrambled. Even if an adversary receives these signals, it is extremely difficult to decode the effective information they carry. Correlated interference technology refers to the ability of the interference device to generate signals that can track the computer's radiation information in real-time and maintain a high degree of correlation with it. This technology effectively overcomes the weakness of using pure white noise as an interference signal, which is easily demodulated, thereby reducing the likelihood of being cracked. Electromagnetic interference technology is currently relatively mature, easy to use, and has strong resistance to decryption. However, its level of protection is somewhat limited and is mainly used to protect information with lower levels of confidentiality [17].

11.3.7 Comparison of the advantages and disadvantages of various electromagnetic security protection technologies

NO.	Protection Technology	Advantages	Drawbacks	Scenarios Suitable for Application
1	"OODA Loop" Security Protection System	1. Fast response speed. 2. Multi-device collaboration to form a monitoring network covering the core area. 3. High degree of automation, active protection, and reduced manual intervention.	1. High cost. 2. Continuous improvement of system performance is required, which increases the cost of technological iteration. 3. Regular calibration of equipment is needed, resulting in a large amount of maintenance work.	Space launch site military base communication hub
2	Shielding Protection Technology	1. It has a relatively high cost-effectiveness ratio. 2. The shielding effect in a specific direction is significant. 3. It covers a wide frequency band, with better performance in the high-frequency range.	1. Ground reflection can reduce the shielding effectiveness. 2. High precision is required for deployment. 3. The environmental adaptability is limited.	Indoor protection. Localized sensitive area. Temporary protection
3	Energy-Selective Electromagnetic Protection Technology	1. Strong adaptive response, capable of automatically distinguishing electromagnetic energy without external control. 2. High power tolerance, suitable for protection against strong electromagnetic pulses.	1. In complex electromagnetic environments, signal overlap may lead to misjudgments. 2. Regular calibration of the devices is required, and the maintenance demands high technical expertise.	Electronic Warfare and Information Countermeasures. Space and Critical Infrastructure. Industrial Control Systems

		3. Compatible with both internal and external protection.	3. The protective performance significantly decreases in the high-frequency range.	
4	Electromagnetic Security Cooperative Suppression Technology	1. Efficient collaborative suppression, significantly enhancing the efficiency of suppression. 2. Precise control and management, avoiding collateral damage to whitelisted devices. 3. Multi-dimensional collaboration, achieving comprehensive coverage and suppression across the entire domain.	1. High computational complexity, requiring substantial computing resources, and limited real-time performance. 2. Dependent on the precision of environmental modeling, with potential errors in complex terrain conditions. 3. Limited adaptability to dynamic scenarios, and the need to enhance the rapid response capability to sudden electromagnetic interference.	Security for major events, electromagnetic management in densely built-up areas, and protection of communication hubs
5	Low-Radiation Technology	1. Source control, reducing the coupling risks of radiation sources at the source. 2. Unidirectional communication assurance, preventing information leakage caused by reverse communication.	1. High cost and high maintenance difficulty. 2. Limited flexibility, with the unidirectional communication design reducing the system's scalability.	Suitable for high-security scenarios

(*Continued*)

NO.	Protection Technology	Advantages	Drawbacks	Scenarios Suitable for Application
6	Electromagnetic Noise Interference Technology	1. Increase the difficulty of espionage and effectively conceal useful information. 2. Easy to deploy and quick to apply.	1. Limited protection level, mainly used for the protection of low-classification information. 2. Dependent on the intensity of interference, if the opponent uses advanced filtering or signal separation technology, the interference effect can be weakened.	General office environment, temporary combat scenarios

11.4 In Typical Scenarios: Electromagnetic Security Assessment Technology

11.4.1 Electromagnetic compatibility safety margin assessment technology for ships

With the widespread application of modern electronic technology, the increasing number of electronic, electrical, and electromechanical devices in systems has led to a deteriorating electromagnetic environment. To ensure electromagnetic compatibility (EMC), systems need to possess a certain safety margin. Cheng Weilan *et al.* developed Safety Margin Assessment Software based on data models to evaluate the electromagnetic compatibility (EMC) test data of ships at various stages. The software conducts comprehensive safety margin assessments, including low-frequency power safety margin assessment, peak power safety margin assessment, magnetic field radiation safety margin assessment, and electric field radiation safety margin assessment. The software identifies potential electromagnetic interference (EMI) risks, analyzes the weak links of incompatibility, determines the causes of EMI, and takes measures for reinforcement design to ultimately resolve EMC issues. It uses actual test data from overall experiments as the interference emission model, eliminating system errors caused by simplified boundary constraints during modeling, thus ensuring high credibility. The sensitivity model is based on the electromagnetic susceptibility characteristics of the equipment, eliminating the need for sensitivity threshold testing or safety margin assessment experiments, resulting in a cost-effective approach. This method is highly accurate and easy to implement, providing a new way to verify whether the safety margin of electromagnetic compatibility for ships meets the standards. The program has been put into use and has achieved good results [18]. The safety margin assessment process is detailed in Figure 11.4.

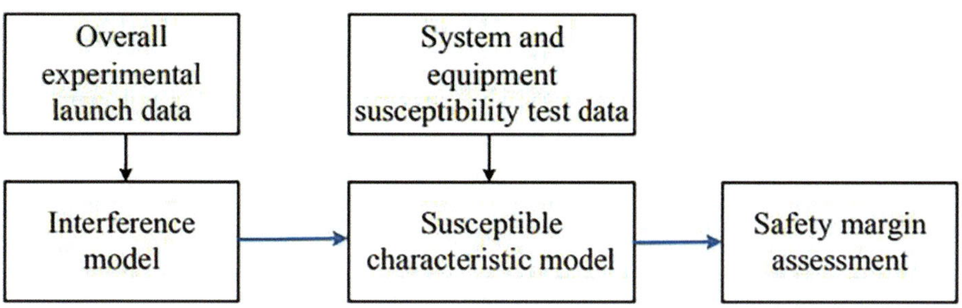

Figure 11.4 Safety margin assessment process.

11.4.2 Electromagnetic safety assessment technology for autonomous vehicles

As the automotive industry evolves toward new energy, intelligent, and connected vehicles, a significant number of electronic devices are employed and play crucial roles. Controllers, environmental perception sensors, computational processing controllers, and information transmission links are all vital components. Electromagnetic interference in any of these components can lead to severe accidents; assessing electromagnetic safety is particularly important [19, 20]. Autonomous vehicles place greater emphasis on interaction with the external environment. How to build effective interaction, activate various systems of the vehicle, and evaluate them accurately remains a new challenge in verifying the electromagnetic compatibility of automobiles. At present, most autonomous vehicles in the industry use a variety of sensors, such as LiDAR, millimeter-wave radar, and optical cameras, combined with multiple positioning methods like the Global Navigation Satellite System, Real-Time Kinematic, Inertial Navigation System, and high-definition maps to ensure driving safety [21]. Currently, there is no effective LiDAR signal simulation device available. Addressing the challenge of activating intelligent driving systems in autonomous vehicles within electromagnetic compatibility laboratories, Zhang Gaojie and his team conducted an exploration to establish a closed-scenario setup in an anechoic chamber, enabling the activation of vehicle intelligent driving functions through physical scanning by actual LiDAR devices.

Firstly, the experimental setup was conducted. A connected communication interaction was established within the laboratory, and movable and fixed obstacles were set up. Antenna orientation: The radiating antenna was positioned to avoid the vehicle's direction of travel to prevent the autonomous driving system from identifying it as an obstacle and failing to function. Due to the dispersed installation locations of the perception sensors on the autonomous vehicle, additional experimental directions were added to enhance coverage. The angles between the antenna orientation and the vehicle were selected as 45°, 135°, 225°, and 315°, respectively. Testing distance: the distance between the front end of the antenna and the vehicle reference point should be no less than 3 meters to prevent the autonomous driving system from identifying the antenna as an obstacle and failing to enter the autonomous driving mode. Connected communication: Wireless communication, satellite positioning, and roadside communication signals were placed to activate the functions of the autonomous driving system. Fixed obstacles: Triangular cones were placed 3.5–4 meters ahead of the vehicle on both sides. Movable obstacles: The track for the movable dummy was placed 5–10 meters ahead of the vehicle to achieve automatic reciprocating motion, thereby monitoring the working state of the vehicle's autonomous driving system sensors and the core computing unit.

Secondly, the experiments were initiated within the laboratory. Static start-up scenario: the vehicle was parked in the EMC laboratory. Upon entering the autonomous driving mode, the perception and positioning sensors were activated, and network communication was established. A target location was specified within the high-definition map. By manipulating the movable obstacles and varying the signal conditions, the controller was stimulated. Based on the vehicle's algorithm, real-time vehicle motion commands were computed. The perception information and decision-making commands during the immunity test were recorded. Dynamic Cruise Scenario: The autonomous driving controller was programmed to output commands that drove the vehicle at a constant speed on the chassis dynamometer in the EMC laboratory. A vehicle speed of 50 km/h was selected, and the vehicle's operating state during the immunity test was monitored. Monitoring Status: The human–machine interaction interface of the autonomous vehicle is designed to be more intuitive and clearer. It integrates multiple pathways, including audio and video, CAN network, Ethernet, cloud data interaction, and local vehicle hard disk storage, to extract and analyze a large amount of underlying data. The HMI interface is further enhanced for clarity. By monitoring these data streams, sensitive components are identified, interference sources are analyzed, and the product design is optimized to enhance electromagnetic safety performance.

Finally, the outfield road vehicle harness excitation method was selected for electromagnetic safety experiments to verify the consistency between indoor test results and real-vehicle road performance. An intelligent transportation test site was chosen, equipped with complete intelligent traffic lights, traffic signs, markings, dummies, nonmotorized vehicle models, differential GPS base stations, mobile communication devices, and roadside communication equipment. The harness excitation test system was installed on the vehicle, with the inverter connected to the vehicle's battery, supplying power to the test equipment. Centering on the autonomous driving system controller, interference was injected into the input and output lines of various component ports, including the controller and signal transceiver converters. When the connecting harness had multiple branches, the injection probe conducted tests on each branch at a distance from the excitation branch node. By combining the EMC laboratory and outfield methods to verify autonomous vehicles, the experimental results indicated that the electromagnetic safety verification

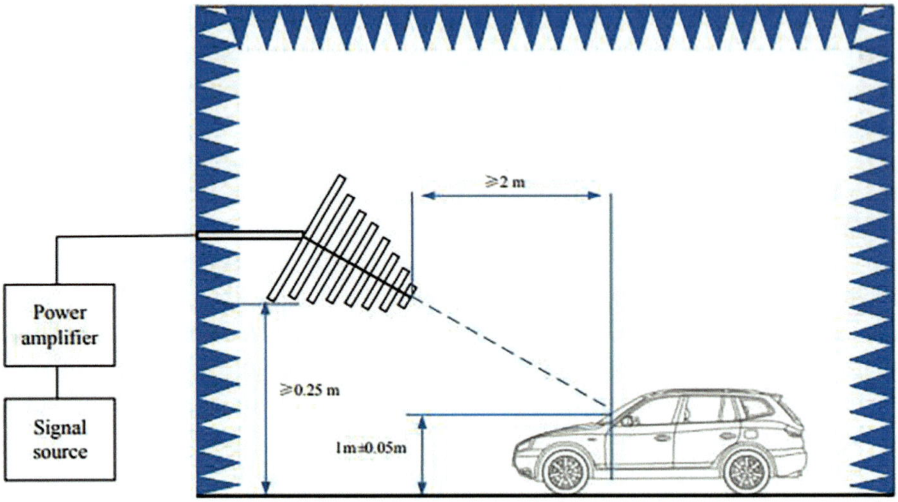

Figure 11.5 Layout diagram for vehicle radiated immunity testing.

method combining dynamic and static working conditions based on the EMC laboratory can effectively identify electromagnetic safety risks in intelligent vehicles, providing directions for enhancing product performance [22]. Layout diagram for vehicle radiated immunity testing is shown in Figure 11.5.

11.4.3 Safety margin assessment technology combining injection and irradiation

In future information-based warfare, the widespread use of electronic information equipment and electromagnetic weapons will lead to increasingly complex and harsh electromagnetic environments on the battlefield [23, 24]. The electromagnetic protection performance of equipment will determine the advantages and disadvantages of the warring parties, and scientific methods are needed to verify the electromagnetic protection performance of equipment [25]. Traditional electromagnetic radiation sensitivity test methods have problems in assessing electromagnetic compatibility and protection performance. Wei Guanghui *et al.* proposed a method of combining injection and irradiation for the electromagnetic radiation safety margin test of interconnected systems, using the signal monitoring and injection functions of the electromagnetic injection-assisted test device. Taking the consistent response voltage at the equipment input port as the equivalence criterion, they deeply explored the equivalence of injection and irradiation methods. By adopting the design idea of cascading antisymmetric directional couplers, they determined the S-parameters of the six-port coupling module of the auxiliary

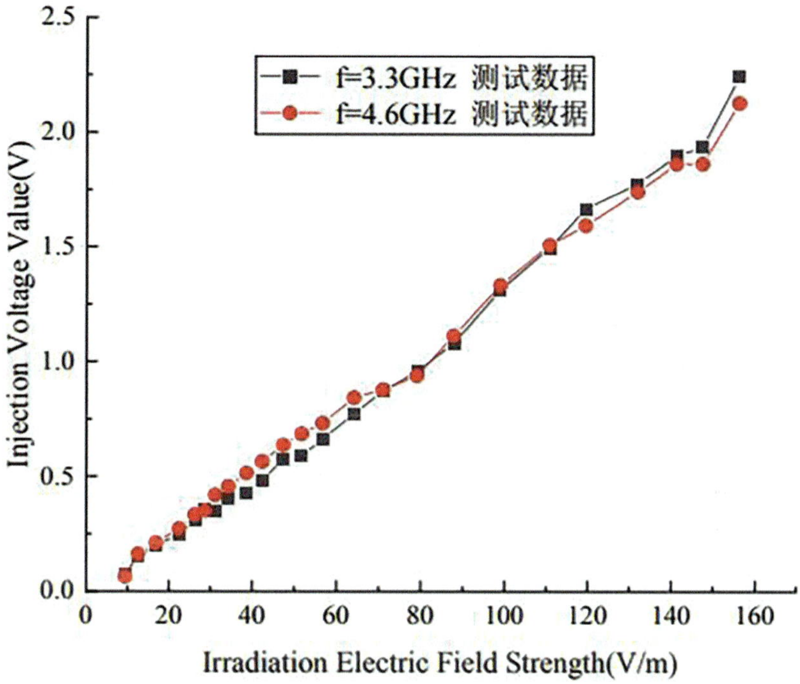

Figure 11.6 The relationship curve between irradiation field strength and equivalent injected voltage.

test equipment and proposed a new method of injection-equivalent-irradiation-effect test based on this coupling module. Experiments on the typical antenna-receiving-interconnection system showed that the irradiation electric field strength and the equivalent injection voltage have a linear relationship, as shown in Figure 11.6 confirming the effectiveness of the combined injection and irradiation method for electromagnetic radiation safety margin testing [26].

11.5 The Current Development Status of Electromagnetic Safety in Key Industries

11.5.1 The current development status of electromagnetic safety in intelligent connected vehicles

Intelligent connected vehicles (ICVs) are a strategic emerging industry that integrates a multitude of new technologies, including 5G, artificial intelligence, communications, electronics, mechanics, and new materials. While ICVs offer users convenient operation and superior driving experiences, the risks of electromagnetic interference (EMI), electromagnetic data leakage, and electromagnetic attacks are also on the rise. The safety accidents caused by these risks not only pose a severe threat to users' personal and property safety but may also endanger national and social security. Therefore, it is of utmost significance to carry out electromagnetic safety protection work for ICVs to ensure the functional safety of vehicle operation, the security of wireless networks, and the safety of electromagnetic data.

The electromagnetic safety of ICVs focuses on the typical testing scenarios of electromagnetic compatibility (EMC) for ICVs and the specific requirements and testing methods for evaluating the EMC performance of ICVs in these scenarios. The core objective is to ensure that the relevant functions of ICVs will not experience performance degradation or failure under complex and variable electromagnetic interference from both inside and outside the vehicle, thereby guaranteeing the stable operation of safety-critical functions such as vehicle control, warning alarms, data recording, and data transmission.

Countries around the world attach great importance to the key role of electromagnetic safety standards in leading the field of automotive electronics. The China Automotive Standardization Committee has specifically established the Automotive Electronics and Electromagnetic Compatibility (SC29) and Intelligent Connected Vehicles (SC34) subcommittees, which are responsible for conducting research and revision of relevant standards, effectively promoting the rapid development of automotive EMC technology. Consolidate the foundation of general standards: steadily advance the formulation and revision of EMC basic method standards to ensure the advancement of standards and consistency with international standards. Deepen the research of mandatory standards: taking mandatory standards such as GB34660 and GB/T18387 as the starting point, carry out research on implementation plans to promote the consistency of EMC testing for whole vehicles and components. Improve the electromagnetic safety system: orderly conduct research and standard formulation and revision in aspects such as testing scenarios related to automotive intelligence and networking, development and design planning, human protection, evaluation system, and electromagnetic environment adaptability. Expand new testing and evaluation technologies: conduct in-depth research on automotive EMC theory to provide a more solid theoretical basis for EMC design and development.

The development focus of electromagnetic safety for ICV manufacturers is as follows. China FAW Group Corporation places great emphasis on safety and health in the business of intelligent connected vehicles. Take the Hongqi EH7 as an example. This model has not only completed EMC tests, such as electromagnetic radiation and lightning strike, but also achieved the mass production launch of 12 key technologies, including active suppression of interference sources and high-performance shielding materials, with the maximum radiation level being only 2% of the national standard limit. In addition, it has invested 2.69 billion yuan to build an intelligent connected innovation test base, which can test items such as whole vehicle radiation immunity, electrostatic discharge immunity, and "radio frequency interference-radiation interference" of on-board receivers, and realize complex immunity and human electromagnetic protection verification tests. Changan Automobile, in terms of EMC performance development, not only meets regulatory requirements but also focuses on the needs of drivers and passengers for the safety, comfort, and reliability of vehicles. In the early stage of whole vehicle design, Changan Automobile analyzes and optimizes the layout of key components and the grounding arrangement of electrical systems based on the whole vehicle EMC design specifications and simulation technology. In terms of key components, it has applied the 10-layer hairpin flat wire motor technology to solve complex electromagnetic performance problems. BAIC new energy has established the capability for positive development of electromagnetic design, solving electromagnetic safety problems related to the integration of high-voltage, high-current, high-speed, and high-torque modules, and has built a 10-meter anechoic chamber for electromagnetic compatibility, covering a variety of special vehicle use scenarios and interference sources, which can fully verify the electromagnetic safety reliability of vehicles. At the same time, BAIC new energy has developed technologies such as electromagnetic interference suppression and interference filtering devices to improve the safety and reliability of electric vehicles. BYD has a whole vehicle EMC test laboratory, which has the capability to conduct EMC tests on whole vehicles, systems, and components. After multiple tests, the EMC-related tests took more than 900 hours. Under the condition of 120 km/h, the maximum electromagnetic radiation value in the vehicle is about 0.8 V/m, which is lower than the electromagnetic radiation value of a common household incandescent lamp, and the electromagnetic immunity to the external environment reaches 100 V/m. Geely Automobile has built an industry-leading EMC laboratory on its own, deeply studied the impact of electromagnetic radiation on human stem cells, formed a cell-level antiradiation safety design standard, and decomposed electromagnetic safety design to the system level, developing the Shield Electromagnetic Safety System. Effective radiation reduction measures have been adopted for high-voltage battery packs, high-voltage cables, batteries, and electric drives, achieving a mother–baby level of electromagnetic protection.

The development focus of electromagnetic safety for the ICV Innovation Service Platform is as follows. This platform is jointly established by the China Society of Automotive Engineers, the China Association of Automobile Manufacturers, and the China Intelligent Connected Vehicle Industry Innovation Alliance. Currently, the platform has built a whole vehicle wireless communication laboratory, an information security attack and defense laboratory, and a V2X security testing laboratory. Among them, the whole vehicle wireless communication laboratory is committed to solving many challenges of in-vehicle wireless communication technology in real deployment and has built a comprehensive integrated solution, including antenna system testing, SISO communication system verification, MIMO communication system performance evaluation, whole vehicle self-interference analysis, high-precision positioning system testing, and C-V2X consistency and interoperability verification.

China Automotive Technology and Research Center Co., Ltd. has the world's leading and China's authoritative third-party testing and certification platform in the automotive industry, with its electromagnetic compatibility service covering the entire automotive industry chain. The testing capabilities include EMC testing of standard driving, conductive charging conditions, steering conditions, braking conditions, and intelligent driving network communication conditions for automobiles. In addition, it has built an electromagnetic compatibility testing platform for whole vehicles, new energy key components, automotive-grade chips, and high-voltage components [27].

11.5.2 The current electromagnetic safety status of high-speed railway systems

The construction and operation of high-speed railways have not only fundamentally alleviated the tension in railway transportation and significantly enhanced the transportation capacity and service quality, but also effectively reduced the overall social transportation costs. Today, high-speed railways have become a preferred mode of transportation that combines efficiency, safety, and environmental protection. Behind the widespread popularity of high-speed railways, transportation safety has always been the core criterion of its technological development. Among them, the electromagnetic environment status and electromagnetic compatibility (EMC) performance of the high-speed railway system are key core technical elements related to transportation safety.

The high-speed railway system is a complex, giant system that integrates high-power traction electrical equipment and low-power train control equipment. Its electromagnetic environment comprises intentional and unintentional electromagnetic emissions from electrical and frequency-using devices such as traction power supply and train operation control systems. There are a large number of electromagnetic interference sources and sensitive equipment within this system, and the transmission and coupling paths of electromagnetic interference are complex and intertwined. In the early stages of high-speed rail development, electromagnetic interference-induced failures occurred frequently, posing challenges to the stable and reliable operation of high-speed train sets. At present, with the continuous innovation of high-speed rail technology and more than a decade of in-depth research and practice in the field of electromagnetic compatibility of high-speed rail systems, the characteristics of electromagnetic interference sources within the system, the transmission and coupling laws of electromagnetic interference, and the interference response mechanisms of sensitive equipment have been mastered. By implementing targeted anti-interference measures at the system level, the anti-interference capabilities of high-speed rail core technologies and key equipment have been significantly improved, and the related interference failure rates have shown a year-on-year downward trend.

Arc discharge transient interference and traction harmonic currents form the most important electromagnetic interference sources in China's high-speed rail system. China's high-speed train sets use a single-phase AC power supply and obtain 25 kV single-phase AC power from the catenary through the pantograph while traveling. To balance the load of the power supply system, the train needs to regularly "change phase" and go through the "over-electric phase separation" process. During this process, the contact condition between the pantograph and the catenary changes, forming an arc discharge phenomenon related to the train's acceleration, track conditions, and pantograph-catenary material. The energy of arc discharge is transmitted and coupled to on-board sensitive equipment in the form of radiation and conduction, becoming an important electromagnetic interference source within the high-speed rail system. In addition, high-speed train sets use a "AC–DC–AC" traction transmission system, which includes multiple traction converter stages. When the train is traveling normally and braking, the direction of current transformation and transmission is different. The traction rectifier and inverter use nonlinear devices to complete high-power current transformation, generating a large number of harmonic currents. When filtering is not sufficient, harmonic currents can cause overvoltage in the car body, destroy the overall grounding performance of the vehicle, and may also generate unbalanced currents on the rails, interfering with the trackside signaling system. Therefore, traction harmonic currents are also an important source of electromagnetic interference in the high-speed rail system.

China has proposed the following anti-interference technologies for the unique electromagnetic environment of high-speed rail and the electromagnetic compatibility characteristics of the high-speed rail system, and has achieved good results. First, research on high-speed rail transient pulse interference was carried out, and a multistatistical parameter measurement and analysis method was developed, which can comprehensively analyze transient pulse interference. A comprehensive technical solution was also proposed, covering key links such as high-speed data acquisition, large-capacity real-time storage, real-time data analysis, and multiparameter measurement, realizing the real-time synchronous accurate measurement of multiple statistical parameters in the time domain of high-speed rail transient pulse interference. This effectively solved the problem of being unable to capture and measure relevant electromagnetic interference in real-time when electromagnetic interference faults occur in high-speed train sets. In addition, a real-time monitoring system for electromagnetic interference of the onboard signaling system of high-speed rail has been successfully developed. This system can monitor and warn of the electromagnetic environment of the operating line in real-time, identify potential electromagnetic interference risks in advance, and thus prevent the signaling system from working abnormally due to electromagnetic interference, avoiding train operation accidents caused by it. Secondly, focusing on the safe operation of high-speed rail, the anti-interference performance of the signaling system was studied, and the "Electromagnetic Compatibility Technology and Laboratory Simulation Testing Platform for High-Speed Rail Signaling Systems" was built. Based on the test data of electromagnetic interference fault reproduction, starting from the traction power supply system, high-speed train set system, and integrated grounding system of high-speed rail, a multilevel electromagnetic interference protection technology for the signaling system facing the whole high-speed train set was proposed. This technology is low-cost and easy to implement, accurately solving the electromagnetic interference fault problems faced by the signaling system on the operating line. In practical applications, it not only reduces the failure rate of the online on-board signaling system but also saves maintenance costs. While ensuring the safe and stable operation of high-speed rail, it has created considerable economic and social benefits. Finally, the antitransient impact of current technology for track circuits was proposed, and an impedance matching device suitable for both high-speed and heavy-haul railways was developed. By applying this technology and device, the anti-interference capability of track circuits has been significantly improved, effectively solving the problem of interference to track circuits caused by unbalanced transient currents on the trackside and providing a strong guarantee for the stable operation of the railway signaling system [28].

11.6 The Development Trends of Electromagnetic Information Security Technology

11.6.1 The integration of acoustics, optics, and electromagnetics

Western countries have been continuously increasing their investment in technological research and development. In terms of espionage methods, they have abandoned the reliance on single technological pathways and instead adopted electromagnetic attacks as the core. They systematically integrate multidimensional information carriers such as acoustics and optics to advance various espionage plans and gradually establish a fundamental, comprehensive espionage capability system. Focusing on critical and sensitive isolated information facilities, the US government and military have jointly issued a series of regulatory standards, imposing strict requirements on the technical indicators of acoustic, optical, and electromagnetic protection. This indicates that the international community's research on attack and defense in the fields of acoustics, optics, and electromagnetics has transcended the traditional isolated mode and is moving toward the direction of the integration of acoustics, optics, and electromagnetics.

11.6.2 The systematization of electromagnetic risks

Initially, research on electromagnetic information security primarily concentrated on the risks of information leakage and protective measures caused by the electromagnetic emissions of information devices. Today, numerous information devices exist in the form of systems. In complex systems, it is easy for electromagnetic mutual interference to occur, and even cross-modulation, which can amplify the risks of individual devices. When conducting research, it is necessary to take into account both the risks of individual devices and the overall system risks. Meanwhile, the existence of electromagnetic Trojans also extends the electromagnetic risks of a single device to the entire system.

11.6.3 The proactiveness of electromagnetic attacks

In order to obtain intelligence data more conveniently and efficiently, electromagnetic attacks are evolving toward a more proactive direction. Attackers exploit internal personnel, vulnerabilities in information exchange, and the implantation of malicious software and hardware to make proactive electromagnetic attacks more targeted and efficient, thereby extending the range of electromagnetic attacks and enhancing the accuracy of information. Among the latest attack methods, illegally implanted electromagnetic Trojan programs can control the operation of computer hardware and transmit confidential information in the form of electromagnetic emissions. The electromagnetic Trojan exploits the electromagnetic leakage characteristics of information devices during operation, constructs special emission features for the encoding and transmission of sensitive information, and steals data. It possesses the characteristics of traditional Trojans, but in the information output stage, it employs a covert electromagnetic leakage emission method that is difficult to detect with conventional Trojan detection techniques. Another attack method is wireless injection technology, which typically uses high-power transmission devices to amplify specially encoded data and then inject it into the external cables of the target computer via antennas or coupling means. When the injected signal meets certain conditions, the computer will regard it as valid data for reception, even without a wireless receiver. If the injected signal is a computer virus, it can cause the computer to unknowingly receive viral data and potentially infect the entire network. According to disclosures by US intelligence officials, the US Department of Defense has developed a new device capable of remotely deploying computer viruses into enemy tactical systems, thereby deceiving their electronic computers at critical moments. The exposure of the US "Operation Shady Rat" in 2012, which aimed to conduct cyberattacks and obtain network information through the injection of wireless electromagnetic signals, has sounded a warning for future security. The development of wireless electromagnetic attack technology targeting physically isolated networks highlights the urgent need to enhance security measures to counter such sophisticated and covert threats [29].

11.6.4 The automation of electromagnetic detection

Electromagnetic emissions from computers can pose risks to information security, necessitating the testing and evaluation of these risks. Traditional testing methods, however, are fraught with numerous drawbacks, such as cumbersome testing procedures, low efficiency, insufficient scalability, and incomplete test results. To overcome these challenges, continuous research into the automation of electromagnetic detection is essential. On one hand, by leveraging general-purpose electromagnetic testing instruments to collect front-end electromagnetic data, and subsequently processing, analyzing, comparing, and generating reports on the data in the signal processing backend based on built-in standards and procedures, the automation of the electromagnetic testing process and data handling can be achieved. This transformation abandons the previous manual operation of instruments and the manual acquisition and processing of data, effectively reducing the interference of human factors and enhancing the objectivity and accuracy of test results. On the other hand, for specific application scenarios in electromagnetic detection, the development of dedicated electromagnetic detection equipment enables the integrated operation of data acquisition, analysis, and display. This not only lowers the requirements for the professional competence of operators but also improves work efficiency and makes the detection results more intuitive and comprehensible.

11.6.5 The normalization of electromagnetic monitoring

Traditional electromagnetic detection methods primarily target the unintentional electromagnetic leakage of information devices. However, due to limitations in the temporal dimension, they often fail to effectively address intentional electromagnetic attacks such as electromagnetic wake-up attacks, irregular timing attacks, and novel covert electromagnetic information transmission. In light of this, to guard against intentional electromagnetic attacks, detection methods are gradually shifting from short-term detection to long-term monitoring in order to further mitigate the risks of active attacks posed by abnormal electromagnetic signals. At present, countries such as the United States and the United Kingdom have initiated research and development of long-term monitoring technologies and equipment. For instance, CRFS, a UK-based company, has already launched corresponding devices capable of conducting long-term monitoring of the electromagnetic environment in specific locations.

11.7 Challenges and Prospects

The complexity of electronic devices and systems is continuously increasing. New types of electromagnetic attack methods, such as high-power microwave weapons and electromagnetic pulse weapons, have diversified electromagnetic security threats. How to protect electronic devices from damage caused by strong electromagnetic pulses under complex conditions is currently a key focus of electromagnetic protection technology. In the era of the digital economy, digital transformation is in full swing, and the connotation and extension of electromagnetic information security are also continuously expanding. Unmanned platform systems, represented by drones and intelligent robots, are on the verge of a period of rapid development. These information-driven integrated unmanned platforms will soon face severe challenges in areas such as control system security, communication security, software security, and electromagnetic interference attacks. Electromagnetic security protection technology is evolving toward a more integrated and systematic direction. It is necessary to establish new information security models and assurance modes and to integrate multiple technologies such as information processing, automated control, information security, and electromagnetic protection. This integration aims to achieve high-density interconnection of system links, enhance antijamming and antidestruction capabilities, and construct a multilayered and comprehensive electromagnetic security protection system.

References

[1] Su, D., Chen, G., Hu, R., Dai, F., Wu, Q., & Li, Y. (2021). Strategic thinking on enhancing China's electromagnetic safety capabilities. Safety and Electromagnetic Compatibility, (5), 9-11. https://doi.org/CNKI:SUN:AQDC.0.2021-05-001

[2] World Health Organization. (2018, December 4). What is the International EMF Project? [EB/OL]. Retrieved April 3, 2019, from https://www.who.int/peh-emf/project/EMF_Project/en/

[3] Bolte, J. F. B., Baliatsas, C., Eikelboom, T., et al. (2015). Everyday exposure to power frequency magnetic fields and associations with non-specific physical symptoms. Environmental Pollution, 196, 224-229.

[4] Gómez-Perretta, C., Navarro, E. A., Segura, J., et al. (2013). Subjective symptoms related to GSM radiation from mobile phone base stations: a cross-sectional study. Journal of Environmental Research, 3(12), e003836.

[5] Baliatsas, C., Van Kamp, I., Lebret, E., et al. (2012). Idiopathic environmental intolerance attributed to electromagnetic fields (IEI-EMF): A systematic review of identifying criteria. BMC Public Health, 12(1), 643.

[6] Wang, Y. (2003). Harm and Protection of Electromagnetic Radiation to Human Health. Arid Environment Monitoring, (01), 22-24. https://doi.org/CNKI:SUN:GHJC.0.2003-01-008

[7] Peng, R., Zhao, L., Zhang, J., Xu, X., Hao, Y., & Yu, C. (2019). Health hazards and protection from electromagnetic radiation. In Proceedings of the 9th National Toxicology Conference of the Chinese Society of Toxicology (p. 273).

[8] Zhang, X., Zhu, N., Li, C., Peng, H., & Dai, H. (2023). Assessment index system for the intelligence level of cognitive electronic warfare systems based on the OODA loop. Firepower and Command Control, 12, 85-93+99. https://doi.org/CNKI:SUN:HLYZ.0.2023-12-013

[9] Sun, Y. L. (2017). Networked design of the Gansu radio monitoring network. (Master's thesis, Lanzhou Jiaotong University). Retrieved from https://kns.cnki.net/KCMS/detail/detail.aspx?dbname=CMFD201801&filename=1017234162.nh

[10] Liu, T., & Zhang, J. Y. (2025). Design of electromagnetic safety protection system for the core area based on the "OODA loop". Radio Engineering, (02), 393-397.

[11] Wang, C. (2018). *Research on the electromagnetic radiation environment safety situation and protection technology in Fushun City*. Heilongjiang Environmental Bulletin, (02), 82-84. https://doi.org/CNKI:SUN:HLJO.0.2018-02-024

[12] Wang, B. G., Han, C. Z., & Zhang, Z. L. (2021). Analysis of the impact of single-sided shielding protection on electromagnetic information security. Safety and Electromagnetic Compatibility, (03), 47-51+79. https://doi.org/CNKI:SUN:AQDC.0.2021-03-013

[13] Liu, P. G., Liu, C. X., Tan, J. F., Dong, Y. F., & Yi, B. (2015). *Research progress on electromagnetic protection technology*. Journal of Ship Research in China, (02), 2–6.

[14] Liu, P. G., & Hu, N. (2024). *Theory and application of energy-selective electromagnetic protection method*. Chinese Journal of Radio Science, 39(3), 385–394+431.

[15] Kong, D. Q., Yang, B. P., & Li, F. (2022). Research on a prototype system for electromagnetic spectrum management and control based on GIS. In Proceedings of the 8th Annual International Conference on Network and Information Systems for Computers (pp.). Hangzhou, China. https://doi.org/10.1109/ICNISC57059.2022.00156

[16] Shi, J., Li, A. T., Li, Z., Xiao, S. G., & Wei, Q. (2024). Cooperative electromagnetic suppression methods for electromagnetic security management during major events. Journal of Electronics and Information Technology, (05), 1908-1919.

[17] Jiang, H. Y. (2011). *Electromagnetic leakage protection technology—TEMPEST technology*. Software, (05), 123–124.

[18] Cheng, W. L., Tang, S. P., & Lu, D. S. (2011). Safety margin assessment technology for electromagnetic compatibility of ships based on a data model. Ship Science and Technology, (02), 94-97. https://doi.org/CNKI:SUN:JCKX.0.2011-02-024

[19] Lei, J. M. (2019). New challenges in electromagnetic compatibility testing of connected and automated vehicles. Safety and Electromagnetic Compatibility, (05), 9-12. https://doi.org/CNKI:SUN:AQDC.0.2019-05-001

[20] Lv, G., Zhang, C. J., Sun, X., Du, X., & Zhu, M. (2017). Research on electromagnetic radiation immunity test methods for ADAS in intelligent vehicles. Safety and Electromagnetic Compatibility, (03), 34-37. https://doi.org/CNKI:SUN:AQDC.0.2017-03-012

[21] He, J. N., Wang, X. Y., Li, W., Dong, X. F., & Wu, H. (2022). Research on the impact of severe weather on the driving safety of autonomous vehicles. Automotive Times, (16), 179-182. https://doi.org/CNKI:SUN:SDQE.0.2022-16-058

[22] Zhang, G. J., Yang, S., Fan, S., & Yang, W. J. (2025). Verification method of electromagnetic safety for level 4 autonomous driving vehicles. Safety and Electromagnetic Compatibility, (01), 67-69+73. https://doi.org/CNKI:SUN:AQDC.0.2025-01-007

[23] Sun, G. Z., Liu, S. H., Chen, J. P., & He, Q. Y. (2006). Impact of battlefield electromagnetic environment on information warfare. Military Operations Research and Systems Engineering, (03), 43-47. https://doi.org/CNKI:SUN:JSYC.0.2006-03-009

[24] Miller, C. R. (2005). Electromagnetic pulse threats in 2010 (Report No.). USA: Center for Strategy and Technology, Air War College, Air University.

[25] Chai, Y. J., Meng, D., Li, J. H., & Li, Z. (2011). Research on high-intensity electromagnetic pulse effects in complex electronic systems. Radio Engineering, (01), 38-40. https://doi.org/CNKI:SUN:WXDG.0.2011-01-012

[26] Wei, G. H., Pan, X. D., & Lu, X. F. (2012). Electromagnetic radiation safety margin test method combining injection and irradiation. High Voltage Engineering, (09), 2213-2220. https://doi.org/CNKI:SUN:GDYJ.0.2012-09-011

[27] Ma, C., Hua, T. F., Bian, Y. L., Zhang, Q. H., & Han, Q. (2024). A Brief Discussion on the Development Status of the Electromagnetic Safety Industry for Intelligent Connected Vehicles. China Information World, (05), 76-78.

[28] Wen, Y. H. (2018). The Current Status and Prospects of Electromagnetic Compatibility and Electromagnetic Safety in High-Speed Railway Systems. Safety and Electromagnetic Compatibility, (06), 9-10.

[29] Miao, C. W. (2019). The Current Status and Development Trends of Electromagnetic Information Security Technology. Science and Technology of Confidentiality, (02), 5-11.

Index

About the Editor

Wai Yie Leong is a Senior Professor at INTI International University. She specializes in Industry 4.0 (IR4.0), wireless sensor networks, ultra-wideband, wireless communications, and brain signal processing for signal conditioning and classification. She is the Vice President of the Institution of Engineers Malaysia and Immediate Chairman of the Women Engineers' Section, Malaysia, on the Board of Directors of the International Network of Women Engineers and Scientists, Honorary Secretary of Women Engineers, The ASEAN Federation of Engineering Organisations (WEAFEO), Chairman of The Institution of Engineering and Technology (Malaysia Local Network) and Committee Member of World Federation of Engineering Organisation (Women in Engineering Committee). She holds a Ph.D. degree in electrical engineering from The University of Queensland (UQ), Brisbane, Australia.

For Product Safety Concerns and Information please contact our
EU representative GPSR@taylorandfrancis.com Taylor & Francis
Verlag GmbH, Kaufingerstraße 24, 80331 München, Germany